PRINCIPLES OF COLOR PROOFING

PRINCIPLES OF COLOR PROOFING

A MANUAL ON THE MEASUREMENT AND CONTROL OF TONE AND COLOR REPRODUCTION

MICHAEL H. BRUNO

GAMA COMMUNICATIONS
Salem, New Hampshire

Published by GAMA Communications, P.O. Box 170,
Salem, NH 03079, (603) 898-2822

Printed and bound in the United States of America.

FOREWORD

PRINCIPLES OF COLOR PROOFING — A Manual on the Measurement and Control of Tone and Color Reproduction is a very timely publication because of the increase in color printing, the need for color proofing, and the lack of objective literature on the subject. Its author, Michael H. (Mike) Bruno is a multi-talented individual, possessed not only of a kindly, loving, and gentle personality but also of a super-inquisitive and retentive mind. In his over forty-six years of research and service to the printing industry he has accumulated an abundance of knowledge of graphic arts principles and technology that has earned him a status in our industry which even a Plato would envy. Yet, at the same time, he is a man always on the prowl, gathering more and more valuable information. He is a walking encyclopedia — a source of knowledge that can relate today's electronic wizardry to yesterday's crude beginnings of color reproduction and with equal accuracy predict tomorrow.

His book, therefore, is a formidable one, a fascinating history of the progress from the press-proof to the off-press proof and an awesome recitation of all that can happen to change the appearance of the press print and the proof. Reading the volume, I was struck by its thoroughness, by the way Bruno correlates all the factors that can affect the appearance of the image in printing and proofing, and by his insight into new techniques and processes for producing, measuring and controlling color proofs and press prints. He has a unique ability to put useful information, new discoveries, complex mathematical and electronic functions into simple understandable language, telling us of new and better ways to do things.

This process of experimentation and discovery began even before Bruno worked out practical production procedures for protecting zinc offset plates from corroding during World War II, especially in the tropics. This was when he headed research at the Army Map Service. Mike was already an experienced research chemist in printing in 1941, having improved the photogelatin process, and photo-offset lithography,

I

both considered and used for printing maps by the Army Map Service. As head of research, Mike put into practice his printing knowledge and experience and adapted them to improving the stability of photo-lithographic plates, bringing order out of chaos and producing a result that filled a dire wartime need. His abilities and his results made not only the Army but later the lithographic industry sit up and take notice.

The farsighted group of lithographers who pooled their financial resources to reorganize the faltering Lithographic Technical Foundation at Glessner House in Chicago in 1945 after the war picked Mike Bruno to head the research department of the LTF (now GATF) and develop a team of research stars. He had the help of: Robert F. Reed, who headed research at LTF in Cincinnati for 20 years and remained as a consultant; and he assembled the great giants of graphic arts research including Frank Preucil, one of the best informed experts on color reproduction; Dr. Paul J. Hartsuch, who explored the chemistry of lithography and improved the reliability of the process; George W. Jorgensen, who developed many of the controls and targets used to measure and control the printing process; and Edward J. Martin, a craftsman with remarkable skills and extensive experience.

The purpose of the LTF, as Mike Bruno so aptly put it, was to do away with the little black book of sorcery, to develop and gather new usable and understandable information, and to disseminate that knowledge to the entire lithographic industry. No one was more aware than Mike Bruno of the need for standardizing and openly sharing knowledge.

My first exposure to Mike came during my attendance at the 1950 annual technical session sponsored by the Litho Clubs of America on Saturday morning following the NAPL convention. Mike was a prominent panel participant each year. His messages, his knowledge, and his demonstrations were unequaled. He always presented useful lithographic procedures, spoken in understandable language and abounding with practical, gutsy information and advice. Many of the sessions I attended had standing room only and the attending lithographers were so eager for Bruno's technical information that they often over-stayed their time. After several encounters with Mike during those sessions, sessions in which I prodded him with requests for more detailed information, we became close friends.

When Bruno left GATF in 1967 after twenty-two years of dedicated service he went to the International Paper Company to head up graphic arts research in its new research center in Sterling Forest, New York. As one of his duties he took over as editor of the well-known, often-used booklet *Pocket Pal*, a compact introduction to printing which explains in brief layman's language the many printing processes and procedures. It has become an authoritative treatise for artists, designers, advertisers, buyers of printing and students. It is the best publication of its type, without question, and has become very popular for the useful information Mike put into it.

After nine years with International Paper, Bruno retired, and was offered a professorship at the University of Missouri where he stayed for one year and then returned to industry in his own consulting business. During his more than forty-five years in the graphic arts, Mike has authored over two hundred articles for trade journals; he is consulting editor for three magazines, three encyclopedias and a dictionary; he was an annual contributor to the prestigious *Penrose Annual*, published in London before it stopped publication; and he writes, edits and publishes *What's New(s) in Graphic Communications,* a popular condensed newsletter internationally distributed. He has written several books other than this one, which is, I believe, his best; the culmination of his years and years of experience.

During those years, Bruno has traveled widely throughout North America, Europe, Australia, and the Orient, where his services are in constant demand where he can keep abreast of all developments in our rapidly changing and expanding industry. At his side throughout his travels, helping him organize his hectic schedule and fulfill his obligations to the industry is his wife Gilda, a gyro that stabilizes the dynamo, a true helpmate.

Mike absorbs and organizes knowledge about new developments with one noble purpose in mind — to make order. After his many encounters with the elite and the lowly in printing, he arranges his discoveries in an orderly, logical way and presents them in language which is clear and understandable to most readers.

Our industry has recognized the value of Bruno's achievements by presenting him, over the years, with awards enough to cover a large wall. The most cherished of these include the Gold Medal of the Institute of Printing in England, awarded to only a deserving few in graphic arts research and presented to Mike Bruno in London on June 23, 1983, and the Robert F. Reed Technology Medal of the Society of Fellows of the GATF, of which he was the first recipient in 1974.

Our industry will, perhaps, have to invent yet another prestigious medal to reward Mike for his achievement in this present volume *PRINCIPLES OF COLOR PROOFING — A Manual on the Measurement and Control of Tone and Color Reproduction.* This history, treatise and textbook fulfills Mike's quest for knowledge and his burning desire to pass that knowledge on, to inform and to share it with his fellows. Here Mike transforms an arcane subject into simple, understandable, interesting, and helpful reading. Here he presents a legacy to the industry and to us all.

J. Tom Morgan, Jr. ■ ■ ■

This book is dedicated to

Manfred R. Kuehnle who suggested the book
and encouraged me to write it.

and

My wife, Gilda, whose confidence, patience,
and understanding made it possible.

Contents

PREFACE

Color proofs are an integral part of the color reproduction process. They are made by many different processes for many different uses. They are used to predict the appearance of the final reproduction and to monitor and control the many steps of the reproduction process. For a color proof to be acceptable to a customer it must be a reasonable facsimile representation of the printed job incorporating all of the distinguishing visual characteristics of the printing process by which the job will be printed. And to be acceptable to the printer it must be capable of being produced consistently, reproducibly and predictably.

The proof for customer approval must look and preferably feel like the printed job. For this reason most proofs in the past have been made on printing presses (special proof presses and production presses) with the same paper and inks to be used on the printed job. Because such press proofs are very expensive, take a long time to make, and do not always reproduce the printing and visual characteristics of the production press, many efforts have been made to substitute photomechanical pre-press, or **off-press proofs**, as they are referred to in this book, for press proofs for customer approval. These efforts have met with considerable success in the United States and Canada, and it is spreading to Europe and Japan.

In addition to customer approval, proofs are needed and used in many stages of the color reproduction process for checking compatibility of a number of subjects to be printed on the same plate or job; and for internal quality checking and control. The closer these proofs come to matching the printing and visual characteristics of the printing process used for reproduction, the sooner they will be acceptable as guides for the pressroom and proofs for the customer. New developments and improvements in photomechanical proofing systems during the past ten years are bringing off-press color proofs very close to achieving these goals.

In order for a proof to reproduce or simulate printing characteristics, the proofing operator or supervisor must be thoroughly familiar with both the proofing process and the printing process and their ideosyncrasies. He must know what effects variations in printing conditions have on the appearance of the printed result and the ability to match the proof and the press print. The conditions which can vary in the printing process include the processing of the films that can affect dot structure; exposures in photography and platemaking that can affect dot sizes; ink tack, ink film thickness, temperature and pigment strength that can affect dot spread or gain, ink trapping, and ink gloss; temperature, pH and amount of dampening solution (in lithography) that can affect dot shape, size, and sharpness; effect of paper gloss, ink absorption, and ink gloss on the appearance of the print; and a host of other less obvious but equally important factors.

A thorough knowledge of the causes of variations in and the means for measuring and controlling printing characteristics and/or defects are important to consistency in printing. Once consistency is achieved, the ink strength, dot spread or gain, tone range, print contrast and other measurable image properties become characteristic features of the printing system used and are the characteristics that must be simulated in the proofing process to achieve a reasonable match with the press print.

Outline of the Book

The main purpose of this book is to describe how color proofs are made, how they can be measured, what they show and how to use them most effectively. Since proofs must duplicate what the printing processes produce the book describes each of the major printing processes and their characteristics; discusses the basic principles on which the processes are founded; depicts typical variations in printing materials and conditions and how they affect the printing processes and their characteristics; describes the color proofing processes in present use, their consistency and ability to duplicate variations in printing characteristics; and provides information on how to compare, measure, and evaluate proofs and press prints.

The book actually has two subjects and could be divided into two books. One is the "Principles of Color Proofing" which is a comprehensive description of the color proofing processes in current use. The other is "A Manual on the Measurement and Control of Tone and Color Reproduction" which is a detailed description and discussion of the proofing and printing processes and all the factors in their execution and use that affect the appearance of the color proofs and the press prints, their consistency, evaluation and comparison.

The information on the color proofing processes is tentative as the processes or the techniques for their execution can change or the processes can be discontinued as has happened with the Polychrome Chrome Guide and Spectra processes. On the other hand, the information on the measurement and control of tone and color reproduction which represents 60% of the text in the book will be valid as long as the printing and proofing processes remain in use. The book will be revised periodically to keep it up-to-date with current practices and new information derived from new studies.

The book is divided into ten chapters and four appendices which are organized as follows:

Chapter I — Introduction: A brief account of the uses for off-press color proofing systems and a history of their development.

Chapter II — The Color Reproduction Process: Brief descriptions of the major printing processes, letterpress, gravure and lithography and their distinguishing characteristics.

Chapter III — Color Process Characteristics and Variables Affecting Them: Discussions of the factors that affect tone reproduction in each of the printing processes, their causes and effects and how they can be controlled.

Chapter IV — Press Proofing: Descriptions of the state of the art in press proofing, its advantages and limitations.

Chapter V — Off-Press Color Proofing Systems — Overlay: Descriptions of the overlay off-press color proofing systems; 3M COLOR KEY, ENCO NAPS and PAPS, and DuPont CROMACHECK.

Chapter VI — Integral (Single-Sheet) Color Proofing Systems: Descriptions of the integral, single sheet, off-press color proofing systems; Direct Reproduction WATERCOTE and KWIK-PROOF, American Photo-Graphics FINAL PROOF, 3M TRANSFER-KEY and MATCH-PRINT, Agfa-Gevaert GEVAPROOF, DuPont CROMALIN, Keuffel and Esser SPECTRA and Kodak EKTAFLEX PCT.

Chapter VII — KC-Color Proof System: Description of the new KC-Technology and the KC-COLOR PROOF System by Manfred R. Kuehnle, former President, Coulter Systems Corporation.

Chapter VIII — Special Color Proofing Systems for Gravure: Descriptions of special modifications of off-press color proofing systems for halftone gravure conversion processes and special color proofing systems for existing gravure processes; DuPont CROMALIN, K&E SPECTRA, KC-COLOR PROOF, Ciba-Geigy CIBACHROME, and Kodak EKTACHROME RC-14 and EKTAFLEX PCT.

Chapter IX — Electronic Color Proofing Systems: Descriptions of digital color proofing systems; color previewer soft proofing systems by Hazeltine and TOPPAN, and digital hard proofing systems by Hell, Crosfield, Polaroid, and Coulter Systems Corporation.

Chapter X — How to Compare Color Proofs and Press Prints: Information on how to analyze and standardize printing and proofing so that proofs and press prints can be matched with reasonable consistency, reproducibility and predictability.

UPDATE: The text for this book was completed almost a year before the illustrations were finished. Typesetting was started almost immediately, but unavoidable delays in the completion of the illustrations caused a time gap during which some significant changes occurred in the proofing process markets, including definitions of requirements for proofing systems, development of new processes, and changes in existing systems. Rather than disturb the written and typeset text it was decided to prepare a separate section — the **UPDATE** — in which all the changes are described and discussed in the order in which they would appear in the text.

Appendix A — Elementary Principles of Color Theory for Color Reproduction: Properties of color and light, discussion of the three-color theory, color diagrams and the analysis and plotting of colors and color functions in graphic arts.

Appendix B — The Specification and Measurement of Color: Descriptions of color measurement systems and viewing standards.

Appendix C — Measurement and Control of Dot Gain: Results of experimental studies of dot gain by Franz Sigg, PIRA and Felix Brunner, and the measurement of dot size.

Appendix D — Miscellaneous Information: Miscellaneous information and conversion tables that do not logically fit in any other sections of the book.

References, Directory and Collateral Reading: List of references to literature in the text by author names, full names and addresses of manufacturers, suppliers, associations and institutes mentioned in the text; and suggested general collateral reading for more information on related subjects.

ACKNOWLEDGEMENTS

Many people deserve credit for helping to produce this book which took almost five years. I am particularly indebted to Coulter Systems Corporation, and Manfred R. Kuehnle for the opportunity to write this book and his writing of Chapter VII; for the help of Mike Liberacki who prepared some of the illustrations; and for the word processing by Janet Key and Tricia Traxler who typed most of the text. I want to thank RIT and Scott Regan, and Ken Jones of Salem High School for their work on the illustrations; Polaroid Corporation for completing and coordinating the illustrations; and EIKONIX Corporation and Scitex America for providing the facilities and personnel of their demonstration labs to produce electronic color separations of some of the color pages. The quality of the color reproductions should not be interpreted as representative of the systems used as most of the slides from which the reproductions were made were in poor condition and over 20 years old. In fact, without these systems some of them could not have been reproduced at all. I also want to thank Richard Gandelman and City Printing Company, where incidentally I learned lithography in the late 1930's, for printing all the color illustrations in the book.

The cover was designed by Jess Forest and the illustration was drawn from a 70X photomicrograph of a color proof. The original photomicrograph was made by Richard S. Ploss, scientist and photomicrographer at Coulter Systems Corporation.

I want to thank Sheila Ward for completing the typing and making the final corrections in the manuscript; also, all my professional associates and peers, in particular, Frank Preucil, Jean Chevalier, Robert P. Mason, Roy Hensel and Warren L. Rhodes, who took the time to review the text and offer many suggestions and constructive comments which were implemented to assure the currency and authenticity of the book's contents. In addition, I want to acknowledge the cooperation and encouragement of the manufacturers of the systems described and their help in supplying information about the systems, checking my descriptions of them and furnishing copy and materials for illustrations.

My special thanks are extended to Tom Morgan — one of the world's finest color lithographers, who has himself developed a halftone photographic off-press color proofing process mentioned in the text and described in the UPDATE and who has also written a book, his autobiography, "Kiss Impressions — My Love Affair with Lithography" — for his encouragement throughout this project and his kind words in the Foreword.

The publishing and production of this book were specialized functions that overwhelmed me. I have been involved in the production of many books but never had to publish one myself. I am, therefore, grateful to Fred Kleeberg for his generous help and invaluable advice in initiating me in the mysteries of book publishing. I am especially indebted to Frank Romano (GAMA) for arranging to have Bolger Publishing Corp. set most of the type and for his publishing of the book; and to Doug Seed for pasting it up. I want to express my sincere appreciation to Edd Shipley for his professional design of the book; and to his wife, Shirley, whose skilled and fastidious editing and proofreading are responsible for the book's grammatical accuracy, consistency and readability.

Many others have helped to make this book possible. I regret that there is not enough space to name them all. I sincerely hope they understand and that everyone who reads this book will appreciate the dedicated efforts and amounts of tender loving care so many have contributed to its preparation and production. Your comments will be appreciated.

Michael H. Bruno

Chapter I

Introduction

Proofing is vital to practically all printing. It shows the printer and customer what the job will look like after printing, so changes can be made, if necessary, before the job goes to press where it can waste expensive press time, paper, and ink if it is not right. Color proofing is a very important and critical step in the process of color reproduction as color proofs are made at different stages and for many diverse uses in the process. There are proofs for customer approval, compatibility proofs, proofs for quality control, and proofs for other uses.

Proofs for Customer Approval

The color proof, which is usually made before the production run for customer approval, is expected to be a reasonable representation of the printed job so the customer can determine what modifications, if any, are needed before printing. When approved it becomes the guide for pressmen to use during makeready to derive the OK sheet that is used for checking the printing during the run. If the proof does not reproduce the printing characteristics of the process there is the risk of difficulty in getting the printed job to match the proof, which can result in long, tedious, expensive corrections on the press, plate remakes, a dissatisfied customer and possibly job rejection.

Compatibility Proofs

Magazine and other periodical printers have another very important requirement for proofs. They receive advertisements from many different sources including advertising agencies and advertising departments of manufacturers. These advertisements contain subjects prepared by many different photographers and commercial artists and can consist of color transparencies of different sizes and types, color photographic prints or dye transfers and even artwork on board, paper or canvas in oils, water colors, or other media. Many of them are finished ads that have been used in other publications and films are supplied for reproduction that have been color separated, corrected and proofed by various trade shops, or engravers, using different colors, inks and papers for making the proofs.

The printer is usually faced with the task of combining a number of these subjects prepared by different sources and with different materials on the same plate. Proofs of the supplied films in the printer's colors and materials are absolutely necessary in these cases to make sure that all the subjects are compatible as they must all print from the same plate on the same press and with the same paper and inks.

This is what is called *compatible proofing* in this book. If some of the subjects do not look right, it is less expensive and more satisfactory to correct or remake them before they go to press, than to have to stop the press, remake the plates and struggle to reach a compromise in printing that often unbalances the other subjects and results not only in missed deadlines and higher costs but dissatisfied clients. Efforts to avoid such disappointments have been made by establishing standards like the *SWOP* colors for proofing web offset publication subjects and the *GTA Group I* and *Group V* standards so that all subjects made from supplied films should be compatible when printed together on any press.

Proofs for Quality Control

The printer also uses color proofs at many stages in the preparation of the materials for printing to evaluate the efficiency of his manufacturing processes and how the subjects will reproduce so he can avoid surprises at the press and be sure the product he produces meets the customer's requirements and expectations. Following is a partial breakdown of how and where color proofs are used in the hierarchy of operations involved in the reproduction process:

- *Camera and/or Scanner:* Proofs are needed and used to determine color balance, overall color correction, overall quality, size, screen angles and register.
- *Dot etching:* Check effects of local corrections.
- *Image Assembly (Stripping):* Check sizing, cropping, color breaks, crossovers, reversals, "fats" and "skinnies" (overlaps), screen angles, overprints and register.
- *Platemaking:* Check dot quality (gain or sharpening), position, register, color and other specifications of all elements on the plate or signature.
- *Press:* Pressman uses customer approved proof as a guide for print quality, ink strengths, color balance, register and progressive color guides if job is on a single or two-color press. The customer

approved proof(s) replaces the original(s) for producing the OK sheet for the press run.
- *Bindery:* Uses proof to check for layout, size, trimming, folding, imprinting, bleeds, margins, crossovers, etc.

Other Uses for Proofs

Color trade shops and *engravers* use color proofs as above and supply them to customers as guides for printing. *Publishers* use them for checking editorial and advertising color and supply them to printers as guides. *Advertising agencies* use them sometimes in large quantities for distribution to customers and publication printers; *newspapers* use them for checking advertising for Sunday and special editions; *commercial printers* use them for checking advertising folders, fake color process printing, color breaks on line color jobs, forms, books, labels, memos, posters, programs, etc. *Packaging printers* use color proofs to check designs, layouts and pre-press corrections as well as for making mock-ups of packages and displays. *Inplant printers* use them for internal presentations and sales promotion pieces, charts, visual aids and salesmen's samples. *Circuit board* manufacturers use them for checking registration and color breaks.

Such a large variety of uses for color proofs places a wide range of demands on color proofing systems. The ideal system would be one that satisfies the needs of all uses; but it may be overkill for some, too slow for others, and too expensive for many. This is the main reason why there are so many color proofing systems in use and still some in development. There seems to be ideal uses for all. Not all color proofing systems require facsimile color reproduction on the same substrate with the same inks or the same feel as the press print but to be useful they must all be consistent so that results can be dependable and predictable.

Press Proofs

For many years the only way to make proofs was to print them on a press. This involved making plates, mounting them on the press, making ready to run, and then running a few prints. Proofs of this type are very expensive because they involve labor intensive operations and the use of expensive materials (plates) and cost intensive equipment (press). Special proof presses have been built to eliminate the high costs of using production presses, but manpower costs are still high, as it takes a long time to make press proofs.

Press proofs have three important advantages: (1) they are printed on a press using printing pressure and the actual inks and paper to be used for the job; (2) multiple proofs can be produced at reasonable cost; and (3) progressive proofs* and proof books can be easily made. Press proofs are used extensively by advertising agencies requiring quantities of proofs for distribution to a number of customer representatives and printers. Progressive proofs are useful when four-color jobs are to be printed on single or two-color presses.

Many buyers of printing have the mistaken notion that a press proof will look exactly like the printed job regardless of how or where it is printed. This unfortunately is far from the truth. All presses are different, not only in design, but in performance. Even presses of the same design differ in ink transfer due to numerous variables including pressmen, paper, ink, roller and blanket composition and conditions, ink-water balance (in lithography), and roller and cylinder pressures. In fact, it is usually not possible to put a set of plates that have been printed on a press back on the same press, print them with the same inks and paper, and get the same result.

A press proof, therefore, is no guarantee that the printed job will look like the proof, even if it is printed on the same press with the same materials and pressman. Compensations must usually be made to relate the proof to the printed result. The situation is somewhat different in gravure. Practically all gravure printing is proofed on a press. In most instances, the actual printing cylinders are proofed, usually on production type presses. The introduction of halftone gravure could cause some changes in this practice.

Press proofing is described and discussed in Chapter IV.

Off-Press Proofs

Because of the limited correlation between press proofs and press prints and the time and expense to make them, there have been many attempts to develop and use less expensive and faster alternatives to press proofs especially for processes other than gravure. These are usually made by photochemical or photomechanical means and are referred to as *pre-press*, or *off-press color proofs*. Single color proofing papers using slow print-out silver nitrate emulsions like brownprint or Van Dyck paper (and now a polymer, DuPont DYLUX®*) have been used extensively in the industry to check layouts, completeness and accuracy of information, and sometimes register by making multiple exposures of the separate color flats at different exposure levels to print images at corresponding density levels.

Photomechanical color proofing was first introduced during World

---

Progressive proofs are single, 2-color, 3-color and 4-color proofs of the color separations or plates showing the appearance of the reproduction as colors are added in printing.

*DYLUX, DuPont registered trademark

War II at the U.S. Army Map Service as a means of prechecking drafted maps in less time, by eliminating the necessity to make negatives and plates and printing them. These were line images which were not as critical as halftone and continuous tone images. One method used was to make multiple exposures through appropriate filters on Ansco Printon color photographic print material, which was a newly developed product by Ansco (GAF) on a white opaque acetate base that could be processed in a single color developer. This method has been tried many times for making color proofs for gravure and offset, but is only now being considered for commercial application. Another method developed by Mr. Sam Sachs and used by the U.S. Coast and Geodetic Survey was to produce superposed bichromated albumin images on opaque white plastic of the separate negatives each of which was inked up in its appropriate color. This eventually developed into the WATERCOTE process which is still marketed in modified form by Direct Reproduction Corporation and others. The new FINAL PROOF process by American Photo-Graphics Co. is similar to this older process.

Overlay Systems

The success of photomechanical color proofing processes in mapping encouraged the development of a number of other systems for color proofing for commercial printing which, unlike mapping that used line images and special colors, used halftone images and process colors. The first successful products were the OZACHROME overlay films produced by Ozalid Corporation (GAF). These consisted of diazo coatings on individual films which when exposed and processed by ammonia vapor produced dyed images in colors similar to process inks. For a four-color proof a photographic print on paper was made of the black separation while the other three colors were on films (sometimes called *foils*) which were mounted in register on the black print.

The main advantage of the system was the ability to review the individual images and use them to assemble progressive proofs. The disadvantages, or limitations were: (1) only one set of process colors were available, and they were not good matches for the great variety of yellow, magenta and cyan process inks in use; (2) the plastic films used were not completely clear and colorless so the white paper and highlight areas of the proofs were dirtied and darkened; (3) while they were useful for checking loose fit and whether copy elements were in the right color or missing, the films were not dimensionally stable so register was not certain and proofs were not good matches for the printed job. They were seldom, if ever, accepted by the customer in place of a press proof. They were useful mainly for internal checking and quality control in the plant.

Considerable effort was devoted by the industry to improving the overlay system. DIAZACHROME by Tecnifax (later Scott Graphics and now James River Graphics) was the second system to be introduced but while it had a wider range of colors and clearer films, it suffered from the same limitations as OZACHROME.

3M COLOR KEY was the first overlay system to be introduced that was on a stable base and replaced the dyes with pigments. This system used polyester film and diazo sensitizers covered with pigmented coatings similar to subtractive type lithographic plates so that on development a pigmented image is produced. At first these systems suffered from the same limitation as the diazo films, i.e., grayed whites and highlights. Gradual improvements in color and clarity of the film have minimized this problem, although whites are still grayer than desired. Enco Printing Products, American Hoechst Corporation has developed a similar overlay system for positives and negatives, but using dyes instead of pigments, called ENCO NAPS (negative) and ENCO PAPS (positive), and DuPont has introduced CROMACHECK®* for negatives. These systems are described and discussed in detail in Chapter V. CHROME-GUIDE by Polychrome was an overlay process similar to Enco NAPS and PAPS but its manufacture and sale was discontinued in July 1984.

Overlay systems are used extensively by the industry, even though they are not normally considered good matches for the press print and are not generally accepted by many customers in place of the press proof. The problems have been grayed highlights and whites and the difficulty in handling and registering the four films. In addition, the advantage of the ease of preparing progressive proofs for the pressman to use in printing has practically disappeared with the almost exclusive use of four-color presses for process color printing. Overlay systems, on the other hand, are less expensive and easier to make than most integral systems and are used extensively for most internal quality control operations which represent over 60% of the uses for off-press color proofs.

Integral (Single Sheet) Systems

A number of attempts have been made to develop proofing systems with integral images on a single sheet or base to overcome the limitations and problems encountered with the overlay systems. As already mentioned, the first color proofing system introduced after the end of World War II was the single sheet, integral system by Direct Reproduction Corporation, called WATERCOTE. While the proofs were useful for internal quality control checking of layout, register, color breaks, trims, folds and bleeds, the colors varied and did not match those on the printed sheets. Lith-Kemco introduced PROOF-KOTE and B.

---

*CROMACHEK, DuPont registered trademark

Teitelbaum Sons had a KOLOR-KOTE process which were similar to WATERCOTE but both suffered from similar deficiencies. All these processes were developed before the general introduction of diazo plate processes. They used bichromated coatings which when exposed and inked contaminated the colors of the inks. American Photo-Graphics' FINAL PROOF has eliminated this problem with the use of colorless photopolymers and the Direct Reproduction Corporation's new process *dr Color Proof* may also be more stable. These systems are described in Chapter VI.

Several other color proofing systems were developed using other color printing techniques. The Potter/Cushing/Pitman process used a dye transfer system and Marcann International used a pigmented gum process but neither process has survived.

In the early 1960's several attempts were made to develop electrophotographic proofing processes based on the electrofax principle using paper coated with zinc oxide in a resistive binder as a photoconductor and toners consisting of ink pigments dispersed in liquid Isopar. The electrofax principle was introduced in the United States by RCA, and the use of liquid toners was developed in Australia by Ralph Metcalf and Robert Wright of the Australian government. It was not unusual then that the first electrostatic color proofing process, REMAK, was developed by Research Laboratories of Australia (RLA). Other groups worked on similar processes, but none ever got on the market.

REMAK produced some excellent integral proofs with all four images superimposed, but it had several vexing problems: (1) the zinc oxide was affected by variations in temperature and relative humidity so that expensive air conditioning systems with very tight control of these two variables were required; and (2) unexplainable variations in the photoconductors and toners from lot to lot affected reproductibility. The process was popular for a while, but most users have changed to other systems with the exception of a few installations in Europe and Australia.

In 1969, Staley/Graphics introduced a new color proofing process, the Colex 520 Pre-plate Color Proof System, developed at Batelle Memorial Institute, which produced an integral color proof based on the use of photosensitive adhesive polymers and dry powder toners composed essentially of ink pigments. This was the forerunner of other integral color proofing systems based on the use of dry toners and adhesive polymers including DuPont CROMALIN®* introduced in 1971 and the Keuffel and Esser SPECTRA proof first shown at PRINT 80.

The Staley Colex 520 and DuPont Cromalin systems both depend on a change in tackiness of the special polymers used due to exposure to light. This can cause problems with variations in the amount of toners

---

*CROMALIN, DuPont registered trademark

accepted resulting in fluctuations in color strength and scum or toning of the nonprinting area. Staley Colex 520 was discontinued mainly because of these problems. DuPont CROMALIN has survived them by introducing many innovations like controlled exposure and the use of automatic toning devices. The K&E SPECTRA proof has avoided the problems by the use of a non-photosensitive adhesive polymer which is independent of exposure and has a constant pick-up of toner while the image is produced by a conventional diazo sensitizer coated over the adhesive polymer layer. These systems are described in Chapter VI.

Kodak introduced the POLYTRANS Color Proof System also in 1969. It used pigmented photosensitive films which were combined to make the color proof using heat and pressure on a specially modified Vandercook Proof Press. While the process produced very reproducible proofs, it was discontinued about 1975 due to limited choice of colors, high cost of energy and proof press ($12,000) and competitive pressures from CROMALIN.

Other integral (single sheet) off-press color proofing processes were also developed during the late 1960's and the 1970's. Actually the first of the modern integral color proofing systems is TRANSFER KEY which 3M introduced in 1968. It is a modification of its COLOR KEY in which the individual coatings are successively transferred, exposed, and developed on a pigmented white plastic base and laminated together to produce an integral print on a single base. The latest development by 3M is MATCHPRINT in which a spacer layer is used between the laminated TRANSFER KEY coatings and the printing paper on which they are mounted to simulate dot spread in the proof and thereby obtain a closer match between the proof and the press-printed result.

Agfa-Gevaert GEVAPROOF is similar to 3M TRANSFER KEY in that it consists of four pigmented transparent photosensitive coatings on a carrier film. It uses a special base stock of polyester film coated on both sides with a white opaque layer. Like TRANSFER KEY, in making a GEVAPROOF each coating is transferred successively to the base sheet in a special laminator (using an alcohol/water solution) and then exposed and developed to remove the non-printing areas before applying the next coating. TRANSFER KEY and GEVAPROOF are negative systems. MATCHPRINT has both negative and positive processes. These systems are described in Chapter VI. Also in this chapter is a brief description of off-press color proofing systems using photographic color print materials, particularly Kodak EKTAFLEX PCT.

Proofing Studies

A number of studies on color proofing processes have been made by individuals like Franz Sigg and Felix Brunner and by research institutes.

These are discussed in Appendix C. One of these was an extensive study of photomechanical proofing systems made by A. J. Johnson of PIRA (the British Graphic Arts Research Association) and published in June 1980 as PIRA Report PR5 (R)/1980 entitled "A Study of the Correlation between Pre-press (or Photomechanical) Proofs and Lithographic Prints" (PR147a, available to members of PIRA). A summary of the properties (flexibility) of pre-press or off-press proofing systems included in this study are tabulated in Table I.

TABLE I-I

SUMMARY OF THE FLEXIBILITY OF
PRE-PRESS PROOFING SYSTEMS

(from PIRA Study PR147a — 1980)

Proofing System	Property				
	Ability to vary color of primaries	Ability to vary density of colorants	Ability to* produce proof on any stock	Ability to** vary dot gain	Ability to** vary dot loss
Overlay systems					
(negative)	No	No	No	No	No
(positive)	No	No	No	No	Yes
Cromalin					
(positive)	Yes	Yes	No	No	Yes
(negative)	Yes	Yes	No	Yes	No
Gevaproof					
(negative)	No***	No	No	Yes	No
Transfer Key					
(negative)	No***	No	Yes	Yes	No
(positive)	No***	No	Yes	No	Yes
REMAK					
(positive)	No	Yes (but limited)	Yes	No	Yes

*The fact that a proof can be produced on any substrate does not guarantee that it will appear the same on the proof as on the printed job. The production method could alter the appearance of the substrate so this property should be treated with some reservation.

**It is assumed that dot gain or loss is achieved by variation in exposure or by introducing a diffusing medium between separation and proof during exposure. Obviously it is then only possible to achieve gain with a negative system and loss with a positive system. Dot gain can also be duplicated by using spacers between image layers.

***Agfa-Gevaert produces two magentas for their Gevaproof system and 3M has added some new colors for use with the Transfer Key system.

This table indicates that there are a number of limitations in existing off-press systems that need to be corrected or eliminated before these systems will be accepted without prejudice by printers and customers alike in place of press proofs. Existing off-press color proofing systems are continually being improved and new systems are in development with the objective of achieving closer correlation between the proof and the printed product.

Other Proofing Systems

The KC-COLOR PROOF is a new color proofing system designed to overcome the deficiencies, or limitations, of existing systems. It has all the advantages of the REMAK system without its disadvantages. It is a crystalline, wholly inorganic system using cadmium sulfide as the photoconductor which is not affected by any but extreme variations in temperature and relative humidity. It has a wide range of stable toners, and most proofs can be made on the actual printing paper or substrate. The system has the added advantages of moderate material costs and short processing times. Complete four-color proofs can be made in times as short as 12 minutes, and the photoconductor can be reused immediately.

KC-Color Proofing Systems have been developed for lithography and gravure. In addition, the KC surface can be exposed by lasers so that *hard copy* color proofs can be made digitally from information in computer storage of electronic color page make-up systems like the KC-DIGITAL SYSTEM, also in development. The KC-Color Proofing Systems are described in detail in Chapter VII by Manfred R. Kuehnle, inventor of the KC-Technology.

Other digital color proofing systems are in development. A serious deficiency of electronic pre-press systems like Crosfield Studio 800, Hell Chromacom, Scitex Response 300 and 350 and Dainippon Screen Sigmagraph 2000 is the absence of systems to produce *hard proofs* (permanent records) from the images on the video screens *(soft proofs)*. Hell has developed a system called CPR 403 Color Proof Recorder which uses the digital data in the Chromacom system to produce a color proof on color photographic paper using two lasers for exposure. Crosfield has a Magnaproof system using the LogE/Dunn electronic color camera to photograph the image on the video screen and output it on color photographic paper. These and other proposed digital color proofing systems are described and discussed in Chapter IX. Also in this chapter is a review of the use of color previewers like the Hazeltine SP 1620 and the TOPPAN CP525 as color pre-proofing systems. In Chapter VIII are descriptions of off-press color proofing systems for gravure including modifications of the DuPont CROMALIN, SPECTRA, 3M

MATCHPRINT proofing systems and photographic color print processes like Ciba-Geigy CIBACHROME, Kodak EKTACHROME RC-14 and EKTAFLEX PCT.

Chapter X is the raison d'être for the book. It brings all the information together and shows how to use it. It suggests methods for analyzing and controlling the printing and proofing processes, how to set and use standards and how to match color proofs with press prints and vice versa. The four appendices A, B, C, and D contain general information related to the subject matter of the book but separated from it for ease of reading and maintaining continuity.

Besides the index, there are four additional sections of reference materials:

Illustration Codes, Credits and References
Glossary and References
Directory
Collateral Reading

Chapter II

The Color Reproduction Process

Indispensable to every color reproduction is a color proof that is a reasonable sample of what the printed job will look like if it was made with the same films or information data to make the proof. There are many places in the conventional color reproduction process where color proofs are needed as described in Chapter I. Why they are needed and how they are used is valuable information for the color proofer. To obtain this information the proofer should have a thorough understanding of the color reproduction process and its many stages, what the purpose of each stage is, how it affects the succeeding stages, how they combine to produce the final result, and how proofs are used to predict results, speed up the process, and make it more cost-effective.

THE PRINTING PROCESS

There are a number of processes besides photography which can reproduce quantities of a color original. These are the printing processes which are divided into two types: (1) plate and (2) plateless processes. The plate processes produce a print with ink on paper from an intermediate plate or image carrier on a mechanical device, or press, which has provisions for feeding paper in sheets or rolls into pressure contact with the image carrier; a means of inking the image carrier; and delivering the sheet or roll to which the inked images have been transferred, to supplementary or finishing operations. The common plate printing processes are: (1) letterpress, or relief printing; (2) lithography, or planographic printing; (3) gravure, or intaglio printing; and (4) screen, or stencil printing. There are a number of other processes which print from an intermediate plate such as flexography, steel die engraving and collotype, but these are variations of letterpress, gravure, and lithography which are the more commonly used processes for color reproduction.

The plateless processes use imaging techniques based on electrostatic, electrophotographic, photoconductive, thermal imaging and ink jet technology. With the exception of thermal imaging and ink jet printing, the image in these processes is created by electronic charging, light exposure, and toning with a dry or liquid toner; and the operations are repeated each time an image is to be produced. Examples of these processes are electrostatic copiers like Xerox, Ricoh, Cannon; electronic printing systems like Xerox 8700 and 9700, and IBM 3800 and 6700. Ink jet printing uses charged droplets of liquid inks controlled by computer activated signals to produce an image. Examples of this type of printing are AB Dick Videojet and Mead Dijit (now Kodak Diconix).

The major difference between plate and plateless printing, besides the type of equipment used, is that in the plate processes the image is produced once on the plate, and this is inked and transferred or printed on a press for the number of impressions or prints required. In the plateless processes a new image must be produced each time it is printed for the total quantity desired. The chances of producing 100 to 100,000 or more prints that look alike are much greater with a plate process than with a plateless process, in which the image must be created each time it is printed.

At the present time and for the foreseeable future, the color reproduction in quantity of color originals for commercial use will be done entirely by plate processes. No plateless system is yet capable of producing process color reproductions of commercially acceptable quality in quantity. This book, therefore, will be concerned only with the plate printing processes and concentrate mainly on those most generally used — letterpress, lithography, and gravure.

Letterpress

The oldest and most versatile method of printing is letterpress. Johann Gutenberg is credited with its invention using movable cast metal type about 1440 A.D. in Mainz, Germany. Actually similar processes were in use on the Greek island of Crete as early as 1500 B.C. using clay discs and in China and Korea during the 11th Century A.D. using bronze cast type.

Letterpress uses the relief method of printing (Figure II-1). It is the only process that can print directly from cast metal type. Most letterpress printing is done from chemically etched photomechanical metal plates, molded metal or plastic plates, or photopolymer plates on which the image, printing, or inked areas are raised, or in relief, and contact ink rollers during printing; and the non-image, non-printing, or uninked areas are depressed and are not contacted by the ink rollers. When a flexible (rubber or polymer) plate is used the process is called *flexography*. In most letterpress printing the image is transferred directly on flatbed or

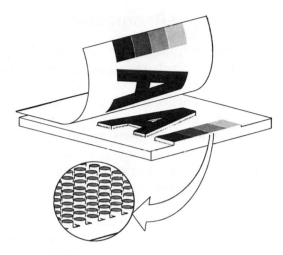

Figure II-1. Letterpress printing is produced from relief image elements such as cast metal type, etched metal plates, relief photopolymer plates, or duplicate plates from molds like stereotypes, electrotypes and rubber or plastic plates.

cylinder presses from the inked plate to the paper backed by a tympan covered steel impression cylinder or platen. The inks are viscous dispersions of pigments in oil-based resins and solvents. Flexography is printed like letterpress, except the inks are solvent-based and very fluid.

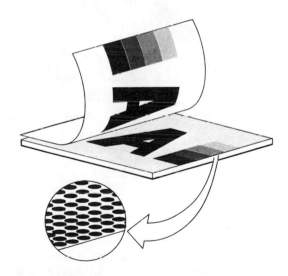

Figure II-2. Lithographic printing is produced from planographic plates with ink receptive image areas and water receptive non-image areas on the same plane.

Lithography

Lithography is a planographic process invented by Aloys Senefelder about 1800 in Bavaria, in which the image and non-image areas are essentially on the same plane, and the distinction between them is maintained by the physico-chemical principle that grease and water do not mix (Figure II-2). The image areas are ink, or grease receptive and water repellent, and the non-image areas are water receptive and ink, or grease repellent. The other distinguishing feature of lithography is that practically all of it is printed by the offset principle, i.e., the image is transferred first to an intermediate cylinder covered with a rubber blanket and from there to the printing surface or substrate, usually paper (Figure II-3). So much lithography is printed by the *offset* principle that the term offset is used synonymously with lithography. Letterpress and gravure can also be printed by the offset principle using an intermediate rubber blanket covered cylinder. When letterpress is printed this way it is known as *dry offset, indirect letterpress,* or *letterset.* Indirect gravure is referred to as *offset gravure.* Lithography is an economical process for text and picture reproduction and is the dominant process for most printing jobs.

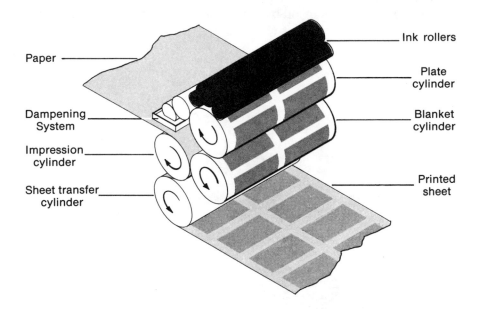

Figure II-3. Most lithographic printing is done by the offset process in which the inked image is transferred from the plate on the plate cylinder to an intermediate cylinder covered with a resilient rubber blanket and then to the paper feeding over the impression cylinder. (IP)

Gravure

Gravure is an intaglio process, the invention of which is usually credited to Karl Klic, or Klietsch, about 1880 in Germany. The image is engraved or depressed in a plane or cylindrical surface. The image areas consist of cells or wells etched into a copper cylinder or plate, and the surface plane of the cylinder or plate represents the non-image areas (Figure II-4). During printing the plate cylinder is rotated in a bath of very fluid ink, and the excess is wiped off the surface by a flexible steel scraper or *doctor blade,* leaving the ink in the thousands of recessed wells to form the image by direct transfer to the paper or other substrate as it passes between the plate and impression cylinder under very high pressure. Most gravure is printed on rolls of paper using cylinders instead of plates and is called *rotogravure.* Gravure is an excellent process for picture reproduction but its high investment and preparatory costs limit its use to long runs.

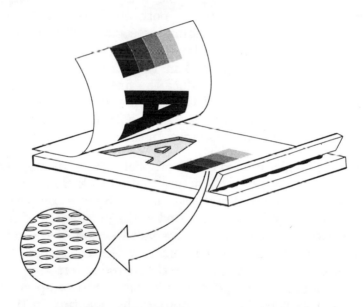

Figure II-4. Gravure printing is an intaglio process in which the image consists of wells in the surface of a cylinder which dips in a tray of ink, or is sprayed with ink, and the excess ink is wiped off with a doctor blade before it contacts the paper feeding between the plate and the impression cylinder.

Three types of images are used for gravure printing: (1) *conventional,* which consists of wells, all of the same size and shape, but varying in depth so that the tone range is achieved by different amounts of ink; (2)

variable area/variable depth, in which the wells vary in area, shape, and depth, resulting in a tone range not as long as conventional gravure but more controllable; and (3) *direct transfer*, or *variable area* in which all the wells vary in area but have essentially the same depth, resulting in images with controllable but short range.

THE PHOTOMECHANICAL PROCESS

In all these methods of printing the conventional reproduction process usually involves photomechanical methods including photographing the original and using the photographic record to prepare the printing surfaces. In the newer processes using electronic methods and computer programs electronic scanning, laser imaging, and electromechanical engraving are gradually replacing photography and photomechanics for preparing the plates or cylinders for printing.

Color reproduction in the graphic arts is founded on the same principles as color photography: i.e., both are based on the three-color theory of light in which the original is separated into three records corresponding to the additive primaries, blue, green, and red, and the three separate records are printed in the three subtractive primaries, yellow, magenta, and cyan to produce the final print (see Appendix A). Yule, in his book, "Principles of Color Reproduction," points out some important differences between color photography and the photomechanical or printing processes. In the photomechanical processes:

- An existing picture and not an original scene is usually reproduced.
- Numerous copies of each picture that all look alike are required.
- The photomechanical processes are much more complex.
- The photographic steps involved in the production of the printing plate often account for only a small fraction of the total cost so considerable handwork, mechanical or electronic correction, can be afforded to adjust the colors in the reproduction.
- The pigments in the printing inks have inferior spectral qualities to the dyes used in color photographs resulting in the necessity for the corrections mentioned above.
- The need for the use of variable size halftone dots to produce the tone values affect the purity of the colors produced (except in conventional gravure.)
- A fourth color ink, black, is usually needed to extend the tone scale and produce neutral shadows and make a four-color instead of a three-color reproduction which often results in objectionable screen patterns called moiré, when two, three, or four screened color images are combined.

The differences pertaining to the number of copies, complexity of the process, and cost are related to each other. The number of copies printed run from a few hundred for uses such as reports with limited circulation to millions for magazines and mail order catalogs. When large quantities or long runs are made, the complex processes involved in the preparation of the printing plates represent a small part of the cost of the entire process, and these preparatory stages can be profitable, even when made more complex, if they result in higher quality or greater economy in the printing operation. For example, preparing a set of color separation negatives or positives suitable for use with cheaper inks of inferior color quality is time-consuming and expensive, but for long runs the overall cost of the job using cheaper inks will be lower in spite of the higher preparatory costs. Where the runs are short the cost of the inks is small, and the preparatory operations necessary for making the plates account for a large proportion of the total cost, so they must be simplified as much as possible. For very short runs, it is sometimes cheaper to make photographic color prints than printed reproductions. The crossover point is of the order of 100 copies but varies widely depending on the materials and methods used and the quality level desired.

Types of Originals

For daily newspaper and weekly news magazine printing, current news pictures are often made directly from the original scene by means of color positive or negative transparencies or diffusion transfer prints like Polaroid. In almost every other use reproductions are made from a positive color transparency, a color photograph, or dye-transfer print of the transparency of the original, or a painting or other original art. In the early days of four-color process printing the great majority of originals to be reproduced were paintings, dye-transfer or carbro prints photographed by rapid succession of exposures or in a one-shot camera. This has changed markedly with the growth of color photography, so that about 90% of the originals (or copy) for reproductions are now color transparencies, and about 80% of these are of the 35mm to 2¼ × 2¼ inch (5.75 mm square) size. Paintings and color photographs are still used for various types of reflection copy (called "flat art," or "copy").

The types of originals for reproduction are classified or identified according to their tone ranges and contrasts. There are *high key* subjects like bridal scenes with much of the tone scale and detail in the highlight and middletone areas; *low key* subjects with low contrast and much of the tone scale and detail in the middletone and shadow areas; *portraits* with many delicate skin tones; *landscapes* with wide ranges in colors and contrast; *food* subjects with wide ranges in colors and color saturation;

and *commercial* subjects with product displays requiring accurate color or facsimile reproduction.

Outline of Color Printing

The process of printing simple black and white illustrations by letterpress or lithography is illustrated in Figure II-5. The process consists of three steps: (1) making a halftone negative from the original, usually in a process camera, by exposing a high-contrast photographic film through a halftone screeen; (2) using this negative to produce a printing plate by exposing it in contact with a sensitized metal plate; and (3) printing the plate on a printing press to produce black and white reproductions. The halftone dot structure is needed in the illustration because letterpress and lithography are binary printing processes (Figure II-6). They can print only one density of ink at a time so the intermediate tones, or the lighter and darker parts of the picture must be created by an optical illusion provided by the variations in the dot sizes in the halftone. As long as screen rulings of 133 lines/inch and finer are used, the normal eye cannot see the individual dots and interprets combinations of them as tone values according to the dot sizes.

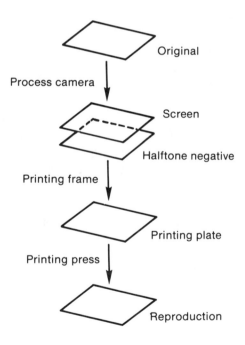

Figure II-5. Steps in printing a simple single-color reproduction. (Wiley)

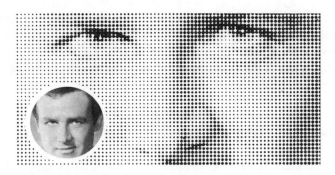

Figure II-6. The principle of halftone printing in which tones are reproduced by dots that are all the same density, are equally spaced, vary in area and are small enough so that in most printing (except newspapers) they cannot be resolved by the normal eye (screens finer than 125 lines per inch or 50 lines per cm). (IP)

To make a simple color reproduction this process is repeated three times (Figure II-7) using different filters in the camera lens, corresponding to the additive primaries blue, green, and red, and printing each plate with a color ink complementary to the color of the filter used to make the negative from which the plate was made. The plate made from the blue filter negative is printed with yellow ink, the plate made from the green

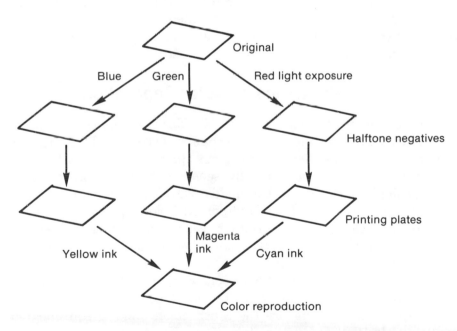

Figure II-7. Steps in printing a simple three-color reproduction. (Wiley)

filter negative is printed with magenta ink, and the plate made from the red filter negative is printed with cyan ink. The combination of printing from these three plates does not usually produce an acceptable reproduction. In practice a number of extra steps are needed to produce a satisfactory reproduction.

- Intermediate color transparencies are usually made from the original, and these are used in place of the original to make the separations.
- A fourth color (black) is printed to extend the tone scale and make the shadows neutral as the over-print of most combinations of yellow, magenta, and cyan lack blackness contrast.
- Color correction is needed for accurate color reproduction to compensate for the color errors in the inks, and this necessitates additional photographic steps (masking) or hand retouching and color proofs.
- Before making the printing plates an off-press color proof is made to determine if the corrections are adequate. This proof may be shown to the customer, or a press proof may be made for the customer to approve or indicate further adjustments.

The printing process for gravure is different, but the photographic processes are similar except that in conventional gravure there is no need for halftone images because conventional gravure is capable of printing different amounts of ink to produce different tone values. The only purpose of the screen in this type of gravure is to provide boundaries for the image wells for the doctor blade to ride over.

Principles of Color Separation

Most common light sources emit significant amounts of light of all wavelengths. The average or normal human eye has a large number of receptors over its sensitive area. There are three broad classes of receptors which perceive color: one generally sensitive to the short wavelength region of light (blue); one in the middle wavelength region (green); and one in the long wavelength region (red). All color reproduction methods, photography, television and printing use at least three light-sensitive receptors which simulate the receptors in the human eye.

There are a large number of *additive primaries* which stimulate one of the three receptors by using light sources rich in wavelengths to which one class of receptors is sensitive. The most common ones selected for photography and printing are the broad colors blue, green and red as represented by the Kodak Wratten Filters No. 47 (blue), No. 58 (green) and No. 25 (red).

Subtractive primaries subtract from the common broad band light source those wavelengths which stimulate one class of receptor. *Cyan* absorbs the long wavelength band (red); *Magenta* absorbs the medium wavelength band (green); and *yellow* absorbs the short wavelength band (blue). TV and some old photographic processes like Agfa starchgrain, Finlay and Dufaycolor are additive systems. Most modern photographic and all printing processes are subtractive.

In the process of color separation the original is divided into three separate records by photographing through each of three filters, each coresponding in color and light transmission to one of the additive primaries. When a red filter is placed on the camera lens and an exposure is made with white light, the negative produced is a record of all the red light reflected or transmitted from the subject. When a positive print is made from this negative, the developed silver in the film will correspond to the areas that absorbed red light which would be blue, green and black. In effect, the negative subtracted the red light from the subject, and the positive becomes a record of the color that absorbs red light which is *cyan*. The positive is known as the *cyan printer*. The negative is referred to as the red separation or the cyan negative (Figure II-8, page C1).

When the green filter is used the negative is a record of the green in the subject. The positive made from the negative is a record of the color that absorbs green which is *magenta*. The positive is the *magenta printer*, and the negative is the green separation or magenta negative (Figure II-9, page C1).

The blue filter produces a negative record of the blue in the subject. The positive is a record of color that absorbs blue which is *yellow*. This positive is the *yellow printer*, and the negative is the blue separation or the yellow negative (Figure II-10, page C1).

The three colors, yellow, magenta, and cyan, are the colors of the inks for process color reproduction. They are the *subtractive primaries*, because each color represents two additive primaries which are left after one primary has been subtracted, or absorbed, from white light. Each subtractive primary modulates the absorption of an additive primary· cyan modulates red absorption; magenta modulates green absorption; and yellow modulates blue absorption.

Color Correction

When the three positive images are on plates and printed on a press with available process inks, the results are far from being a reasonable reproduction of the original from which the separations were made. All the colors, except yellow and red, are dirty and lack saturation. Too much of the colors are absorbed by the inks and not enough light is reflected back to the observer. This is the cause of poor color reproduction such as pink skies, orange apples, and brownish grass. The eye can be fooled into accepting colors in reproductions of objects it is not familiar with but it cannot be fooled by the *psychological reference colors*, sometimes called *memory colors*. It knows that grass is green, skies are blue, apples are red and recognizes the flesh colors of skin tones. Deviations in these colors are not a fault of the theory but are due to deficiencies in the color of the pigments used in the inks (see Appendix A). Corrections or modifications must be made in the color separation films to compensate for the errors in the colors of the ink pigments. These corrections are made manually by dot-etching, photomechanically by masking, or electronically in scanning.

Masking: Masking is the means of tone* and color correction using low density images of the originals made through color filters as masks over the original to compress the tone range of the original transparency to that of the printing process and to correct for the color deficiencies in the pigments used in the process color inks (see Appendix A). The color deficiencies of the inks are shown in TABLE A-II in Appendix A and repeated here in part.

TABLE II-I

DENSITOMETER READINGS OF TYPICAL
COLOR PRINTING INKS

| | | Filters | |
Printing Inks	Red (25)	Green (58)	Blue (47)
Yellow	0.01	0.06	0.95
Magenta	0.10	1.15	0.46
Cyan	1.20	0.50	0.20

An ideal cyan ink should have a high density reading to the red filter and 0 readings to the green and blue filters. The cyan ink in Table II-1 absorbs some green and blue light so wherever it prints it appears too blue (green absorption) and desaturated (blue absorption). The main color deficiency (excess blueness) in the cyan ink is corrected by using a mask over the original during color separation that reduces the amount of magenta wherever the cyan prints.

An ideal magenta ink should have a high density to the green filter

---

*Tone correction or reproduction involves the comparison of the tone gradations between high-lights, middletones and shadows in the reproduction with those in the original.

and 0 readings to the red and blue filters. The magenta ink in Table II-1 absorbs some blue light and red light so wherever it prints it appears too red (blue absorption) with a slight loss in saturation (red absorption). The excess redness in the magenta ink is corrected during color separation by using a mask over the original that reduces the amount of yellow wherever the magenta prints.

The mask for the magenta is also used in making the cyan separation to increase its saturation and special masks are used to replace some color inks by black which is known as *undercolor removal* or *UCR*.

With some inks which contain pigments with poor spectral characteristics because of low cost, light fastness characteristics, or the desire to use trademark colors as process colors, a single mask will not correct for the excessive color errors in the pigments. These inks usually have additivity failure (see Appendix A) and in these cases *two-stage masking* is used in which the *principal mask* is made from the combination of a positive premask of the separation to be corrected and a negative of the separation used for the color correction.

Black Printer: Even after the corrections are made, the printed result is not satisfactory as the grays and deep shadows lack contrast. A fourth printer, *black*, is added to overcome this deficiency, increase maximum density, and provide better shadow detail, making color reproduction printing with inks a four-color process as compared with the three-color dye process of photography. The black printer can be made from the other separations.

Two types of black printers are used — *skeleton* and *full* (Figure II-11).

A   **B**

Figure II-11. Examples of (A) **skeleton** black and (B) **full** black. (HCM)

Most lithography has been done with skeleton blacks; and letterpress, especially in high speed magazine printing and gravure, has used full blacks. The trend is now toward the use of full blacks in all color reproduction processes to reduce the total cost of inks, as color inks are more expensive than black inks. When full blacks are used the other inks are reduced proportionately. This not only saves on the cost of color inks, but improves ink transfer or trapping on multicolor presses. As already mentioned, the method of reducing colors and printing a full black is called *undercolor removal* or *UCR*.

Achromatic Color Reduction: Processes are being developed in which no color is produced with more than two colors and black, called *achromatic color reduction*. It is now called Gray Component Replacement (GCR). The reproduction is still printed in four colors, but in most of the reproduction there are very few areas with more than two colors and black. Advantages claimed for these systems are: lower ink costs, elimination of moiré between colors, less trapping problems, and higher saturation of colors, especially on poorer grades of paper.

Color Separation Processes

There are two processes in general use for the color separation of originals: photographic and electronic scanning. The photographic process uses cameras, enlargers, or vacuum frames for making continuous tone and direct screen color separations. Cameras are used mainly for making continuous tone separations from large, rigid subjects like paintings, using camera-back-masking. Cameras can also be used to make direct screen separations. Enlargers are used extensively for direct screening of small (35 mm) color transparencies. Vacuum frames are used for making contact, continuous tone, or direct screen separations from original or duplicate transparencies at full size. Electronic scanners are used to make continuous tone and direct screen (contact screen and laser) separations from positive transparencies or color prints or originals on flexible substrates that can be wrapped around the drum of the scanner.

Photographic Color Separation: Color photography using continuous tone images in three dyes usually produces color reproductions of high quality with minimum manipulation and effort. Printing processes, on the other hand, which have to depend on halftone patterns, color pigments in inks, and the mechanical transfer of the ink to produce color images on a variety of substrates have great difficulty in achieving consistently good quality. As the need to improve quality and consistency increases, the preparatory operations involved in the production of the materials for making the printing plates are modified to compensate for process deficiencies and, therefore, become more elaborate, complicated, and expensive. The simple procedure for color reproduction previously outlined becomes a very complex process with numerous additional steps.

The simplest photographic color separation and correction process for the lithographic reproduction of a color transparency is the direct screening method which consists of the following steps (Figure II-12):

- Two photographic masks are made from the transparency by

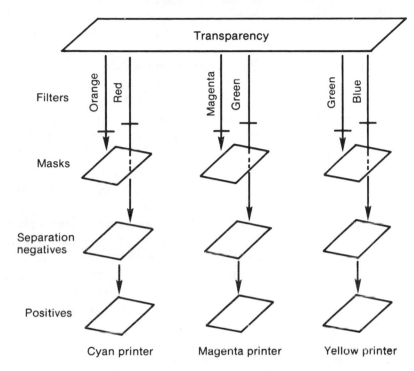

Figure II-12. Principles of negative masking method for direct screen reproductions of color transparencies (without the black printer). (Wiley)

exposing it in contact with a continuous tone panchromatic film: one mask is made with a Wratten No. 33 (magenta) filter and the other with a Wratten No. 58 (green) filter. A diffusion filter is used in making each mask and both masks are exposed and processed so they have a density range of about 45% of the density range of the transparency.

- The cyan printer (halftone separation) is made using the No. 33 filter mask in contact with the transparency, a gray contact screen, and a combination of a Wratten No. 23A (orange-red) and 0.6 ND (neutral density) filters.
- The magenta printer (halftone separation) also uses the No. 33 filter mask on the transparency with the gray contact screen and a Wratten No. 58 filter.
- The yellow printer (halftone separation) is made using the No. 58 filter mask over the transparency with the gray contact screen

and a Wratten No. 47B (blue) filter.

- The black printer (halftone separation) is made using the No. 33 filter mask over the transparency with the gray contact screen and a Wratten No. 85B (amber) filter.
- All separations are controlled by use of a step wedge on which the density of the highlight (A) middle-tone (M) and shadow (B) steps are kept within narrow tolerances.
- A color proof is made from the halftone separations and evaluated. It may show that one or more of the negatives needs to be remade. If only minor corrections are necessary, they can be done manually by a dot etcher. If the proof is close it may be shown to the customer or his representative who will specify what local or overall color changes may be required. When these adjustments have been completed a second proof is made for examination or customer approval. This operation is repeated until the customer is satisfied.
- The halftone negatives are assembled into page layouts along with the text and other copy, and the pages are imposed into the final layout or *flat* for platemaking. A color proof can be made at this stage for final checking and approval, or a brownprint or DYLUX proof is made for checking fit, folding imposition and register, and making sure that the copy is in the right position and on the right plates.
- Printing plates are made from the imposed flats.
- The plate is mounted on the press and the desired number of copies are printed. The pressman's job is to match the color proofs of the individual subjects, pages, or imposed layouts to produce the OK sheet for the job. There are many color measurement systems for the press which help the pressman in his judgment of color. In lithography, especially, there are many factors besides the paper and ink that can affect color reproduction, and the pressman's knowledge and recognition of them determine his proficiency, skill, and ability to match the proofs and continue to print reproductions of consistent tone and color quality. It is the color proofer's responsibility to produce proofs that a pressman with normal skill can match on the press in reasonable time and maintain quality and consistency without undue difficulty or interruption in printing.

The direct screen method of color separation is used primarily for lithography. It is the simplest method of color separation and correction, as it produces color corrected halftone separations directly. Direct screening is done photographically and on electronic scanners. Photographic direct screening uses enlargers for small transparencies, process cameras for reflection copy and large transparencies, and vacuum frames for transparencies of the correct size. In contact printing and transparency projection the masks are registered to the transparency. Masks can be custom made for reflection copy, and they are placed over the gray contact screen in the back of the camera — thus the term *camera-back-masking*.

The photographic color separation and correction procedures are the same for letterpress and gravure as for lithography except continuous tone positives are used for conventional gravure. Variable area/variable depth gravure also uses a continuous tone positive along with a halftone positive of the same image.

For these printing processes and for difficult subjects requiring special inks and two-stage masking, the indirect method of color separation and correction is preferred. In this method masks are used on the original as in direct screening but continuous tone negatives are made from which continuous tone or halftone positives are made in a camera. This method uses more film, takes longer, and requires more skill but it has more latitude and is capable of better correction.

Another method used to prepare the copy for color reproduction is to make duplicate transparencies of all the originals (transparencies and reflection copy) at the required size. The duplicates are assembled in the proper position or layout for a complete page, two-page, or four-page layout. The masks and screened separations are then made by contact. Variations in density range and color balance of the originals can be eliminated by adjusting the duplicating step so that all the duplicate transparencies can be treated in the same way. The efficiency of this method makes up for the cost of duplicating and the slight loss in quality in putting the reproduction another generation away from the original. Duplicate color prints using diffusion transfer material like Kodak EKTAFLEX PCT can be used in the same manner as duplicate transparencies. They have the advantage of looking more like the printed reproduction than the transparency.

Color Separation and Correction by Electronic Scanning: Electronic scanning is gradually becoming the preferred process for color separation and correction. It combines the ease of operation and economy of direct screening, the accuracy, and latitude of indirect separation and the high speed and precision of electronics. In 1983 there were more than 6,000 scanners in use worldwide with over 1,700 in the United States and Canada. It is estimated that 70-75% of the color reproductions made in the United States are separated on scanners.

The first electronic color scanner which eventually became the TIME, Inc. – PDI Scanner was invented by Murray and Morse of Kodak in the late 1930's. The basic principles of this scanner which are similar to most present day scanners are illustrated in Figure II-13. Figure II-14 is a picture of a typical commercial scanner. Light from a special scanning lamp is focused on a small spot on the original transparency which is mounted on a rotating drum. The light from the small spot is split into three beams and passed through red, green, and blue filters simultane-

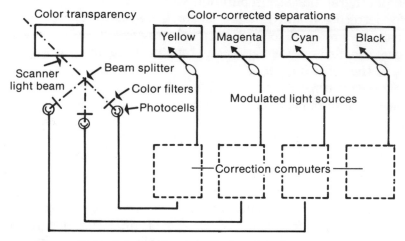

Figure II-13. Schematic of an electronic color scanner that produces 4 color corrected color separations simultaneously. (IP)

ously before being picked up by three photocells. The responses from the three photocells are transmitted to an analog computer which computes the color from the amounts of red, green, and blue light in it; computes the black printer and UCR; determines the amounts of cyan, magenta, yellow, and black inks required to reproduce the color with the inks and paper to be used; and controls the intensity of four special glow lamps which expose corresponding small spots on each of four photographic films — all in a matter of a few millionths of a second or before the

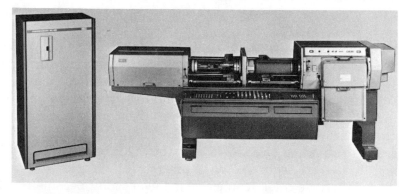

Figure II-14. Typical electronic color scanner. (HCM)

scanning motion has moved the spot appreciably. This operation is repeated for each spot on the original until the whole picture has been scanned and four color-corrected separations are produced on film. Some scanners make only one or two separations at a time.

As in photographic color separation methods the production of the printer separations (yellow, magenta, and cyan) depends primarily on the complementary light signals (blue, green, and red, respectively) from the original. The other two light signals (red and green for yellow, blue and red for magenta, and blue and green for cyan) also modify the output in a way corresponding roughly to the effect of two-stage photographic color-correcting masks. Scanning eliminates the necessity for making photographic masks.

The black printer can be computed by selecting the weakest of the three color signals from each spot. The amount of undercolor removal (UCR) is calculated by subtracting a proportion of the black signal from each of the other three signals, thus substituting black ink for part of the yellow, magenta, and cyan inks in the parts of the picture in which all three colors are present.

The analog computer also adjusts the gradation of each of the four signals to provide proper tone reproduction and color balance to the reproduction. At this stage fine detail can be enhanced either by a method similar to unsharp masking, using an additional large-spot photocell, or by electronic peaking to identify edges at which density changes. The signals resulting from all these operations control the intensity of the glow lamps which expose the film to produce the four color-corrected separation negatives or positives simultaneously or one at a time.

The images produced by these signals are continuous tone. Scanning is done at 500 to 1,000 lines per inch (200 to 400 lines per cm) so the scan lines are essentially invisible. Direct screen images are produced on scanners by using contact screens in contact with the films during exposure of the scanner signals, thereby converting light signals to halftone dots corresponding to the amount of exposure. Since the system is electronic it can produce either positives or negative continuous tone or halftone films.

In 1971, PDI developed a system for producing halftones by electronic dot generation. The system used a digital computer to convert and store an image with as many as 256 gray levels and transmit the information to lasers to produce halftone dots of the desired size and shape on film at conventional screen (0°, 15°, 45°, 75°) or other angles. Dr. Ing Rudoph Hell introduced a system for electronic dot generation using lasers for the Hell DC 300 scanner at DRUPA '72. At first the scanner was limited to fixed angles of 0, 45°, 18.4°, and 71.6°, but the newer Hell scanners, DC 350, CP 340, CP 341 and DC 399 are able to produce halftone images with conventional screen angles. The Crosfield Magnascan 520, Series

640 and Studio 800 scanners have systems for electronic laser screening which produce images with conventional screen angles. The Dainippon SG-801, SG-708 and Sigmagraph 2000 also produce electronic laser screened images with conventional screen angles. The Scitex systems produce electronic dot generated images with conventional angles. The KC-Digital System will also have laser imaging and electronic dot generation at any screen angle.

The images produced in the early scanners were the same size as the original. Mechanical systems were developed for enlargement and reduction by PDI in the early 1960's but the real breakthrough came when Crosfield developed an electronic system for continuously variable magnification in 1970. This was accomplished by converting the picture information to digital data using an analog-to-digital converter, storing the information briefly for a single scanning revolution, and releasing it onto the film immediately afterwards at a rate depending on the desired magnifications.

One problem with scanners using analog computers is that while the computers can make very complex calculations so that color corrections can be more accurate than is possible with photographic masking, they depend on highly skilled operators to make the proper settings on up to 100 control knobs on the scanner. Because of errors or miscalculations in knob settings, the expected or improved color correction is not always obtained, and this could account for the high makeover rate (up to 50%) of scans. An answer to this problem is the development of scanners with digital computers. The first of these was developed by Dr. N.I. Korman and J.A.C. Yule at Ventures Research and Development Corporation. This eliminated most of the control knobs by the use of look-up tables produced by scanning color charts printed by the process to be used for reproduction and using a digital computer to compute the transfer function needed to give accurate reproduction with the process. This scanner never reached commercial use.

The first commercial scanner using a digital computer for color and tone corrections was the Crosfield Magnascan 550. The first completely digital scanner in which all image processing is done digitally is the EIKONIX Designmaster 8000. All the color page composition systems like Crosfield Studio 800, Hell Chromacom, Sci-Tex Response 300 and Response 350, Dainippon Screen Sigmagraph 2000, and KC-Digital System use digital computers to accomplish sizing, positioning, color correction, and electronic dot generation of the halftone images for printing.

Tone Reproduction, Gray Balance, and Color Balance

Regardless of what method is used for color reproduction, tone reproduction, gray balance, and color balance are of utmost importance in matching a reproduction to the original and a proof to the reproduction. These all depend on the shape of the tone reproduction curves of the individual separation printers, and there are too many places in the printing process where the curves can be changed with damaging effects on the gray balance or color balance of the final reproduction. To help control the shape of the tone reproduction curves for each of the color separations, a gray scale or step tablet is usually mounted beside the original in addition to register marks.

Since it is not practical in production work to plot complete tone reproduction curves, especially on small transparencies, a three-step gray scale is used in which the steps are referred to as A (highlight), M (middletone), and B (shadow). In a negative or positive the density difference between A and B indicates the contrast, and the difference between A and M and M and B density ranges indicates the tone reproduction curve shape. Usually with these three steps under control, the rest of the tone scale is reasonably satisfactory. In any case conventional photographic procedures do not usually permit independent adjustment of more than three steps in the tone scale. This is, however, possible on most scanners, but there is too much room for error with all the control knobs available. The new digital scanners will improve this control. Independent control of shadow contrast in four-color printing is possible by adjusting the characteristics of the black printer.

Image Assembly - Stripping

After all the films (color separations, text, single, or two-color, line or halftone illustrations) have been produced and checked by proofing, they are assembled into page layouts according to the mechanical (layout) for the job, and the page layouts are then assembled or imposed into the form, flat, or signature for platemaking and printing according to the folding or cutting plan for the job. The operations of *image assembly*, or *stripping*, as they are better known, have been traditionally performed manually, but they are tedious and time-consuming. Not only are they expensive, but they are the most serious bottleneck in the whole preparatory process. Mechanical and electronic systems have been developed to eliminate the bottleneck.

Register

Despite the importance of tone reproduction, gray and color balance, the most critical attribute of color reproduction is register. For color reproduction four separate page layouts and plate-flats must be produced in which the images register as perfectly as possible. Ideally the tolerances should be less than ±0.001 inch as there are many factors in printing that can affect image size as pointed out in Chapter III. Manual registration is a tedious lengthy process which should not be attempted without a collimated magnifier as parallax in viewing can introduce serious errors in placement. Parallax is illustrated in Figure II-15.

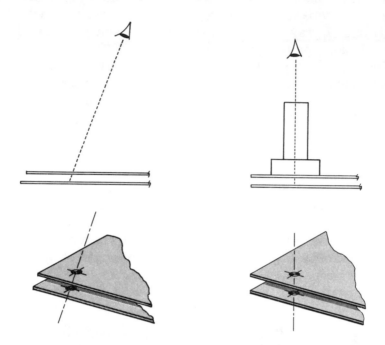

Figure II-15. Correcting parallax with a collimator. The eye can make errors in lining up register marks on multiple films (A). Sighting tube or collimating lens assures proper line up of multiple images (B).

Pin register systems are now commonly used to control placement and position of images (Figure II-16). They consist of punching holes or slots in films and copy and placing pins that fit in the holes or slots so the copy or several pieces of film can be held accurately during the positioning or exposure of images. Pin bars in which pins are spaced at the same distance as the holes in the film are used for positioning multiple images or making multiple exposures on films or plates. Pin register devices are indispensable to color reproduction, and systems have been developed starting with the copy and carried through all the preparatory operations to mounting the plates on the press.

Electronic systems for locating images in proper position and accurate register have also been developed. The color page makeup systems like Crosfield Studio 800, Hell Chromacom, SciTex Response 300 and 350,

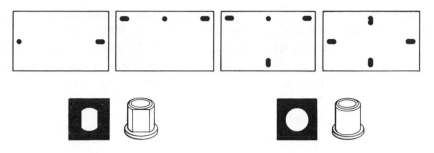

Figure II-16. Types of pin register and pins showing four different hole configurations and two types of pins to assure proper fit and distribution of errors when stretch or shrinkage in materials occurs. (GAM)

Dainippon Screen Sigmagraph 2000, and KC-Digital System have already been mentioned. These systems accomplish the complete preparatory operations from original copy to final film for press plate or the press plate directly and are often referred to as pre-press systems. Part of this system is the assembly of the images into page layouts and page impositions.

The pre-press systems are more sophisticated and expensive than many printers need or can afford so electronic systems have been developed to produce films which contain blank blocks that indicate the position of the individual image elements (Figure II-17). These systems are based on the techniques developed for computer aided design or

Figure II-17. Output of electronic page layout system to simplify and speed up image assembly and improve its accuracy.

drafting and computer aided makeup or machining (CAD/CAM) systems. Commercial examples are the Gerber Autoprep 5000, Shukosha CAD/ ACE automated layout system, and TOPPAN ARTCON Automated Drafting System. In addition, there are electronic image positioning systems by MISOMEX and OPTI-COPY. These speed up the operations of image assembly and have helped to eliminate this serious bottleneck in the preparatory process.

Platemaking

The preparatory operations for the three major printing processes, letterpress, lithography, and gravure are very similar. The differences between the processes become evident in platemaking. Each process uses different basic types of image carriers (plate or cylinder) which determine the characteristics of the image produced, the type of ink and press to be used, the number of impressions, and the speed with which they can be printed.

Practically all printing plates are made by photomechanical means using light-sensitive coatings on which images are produced photographically by light exposure of photographic negatives or positives in contact with the light-sensitive coating. The image produced can be the printing image as in most lithographic plates or serve as a template or resist for producing the printing image as in letterpress and gravure.

Letterpress

Plates for letterpress have images in relief and have been traditionally photoengravings on zinc, magnesium, or copper. They are always produced from negatives. In the United States halftone engravings in 120 line and finer are usually made on copper; in Europe they are made on zinc or magnesium. Most photoengravings are made by the *powderless etching* method and use full range negatives like lithography. The are not generally used for direct printing but for making molds for duplicate plates which include stereotypes, electrotypes, plastic and rubber plates. Stereotypes were used extensively for newspaper printing until they were replaced by photopolymer and lithographic plates. Electrotypes are used for magazine and commercial printing; plastic and rubber plates are used for packaging, specialties, and flexography. Photopolymer plates which use special photopolymer coatings that produce relief images after exposure and processing, are becoming the preferred plates for commercial and publication letterpress and flexographic printing.

Lithography

Plates for lithographic printing are planographic with the image and non-image areas essentially on the same plane and most use aluminum as the base. They are of many types, including surface, deep-etch, bimetal, photographic, electrostatic, diffusion-transfer, and laser.

Surface plates are plates in which the light-sensitive coating becomes the ink-receptive image area. Most are made from negatives, although there are a few positive surface plate processes. There are two types of surface plates, *additive* and *subtractive*. The ink receptive lacquer is added to the additive plate during processing. On the subtractive plate it is part of the precoating which is removed from the non-image areas during processing. Both diazo and photopolymer light-sensitive coatings are used to make surface plates, and there are presensitized and wipe-on plates of both types. Photopolymer plates are generally longer running plates than diazo, and these plates, when baked in special ovens after processing, are capable of runs above a million.

Deep-etch plates are always made from positives. On these plates the exposed coating serves as a stencil for the printing image from which the coating is removed during processing, and the areas are chemically coppered, lacquered, and inked to make them ink-receptive. Deep-etch plates are capable of runs in excess of 250,000 on sheet-fed presses. Because of the lengthy processing and the possibility of pollution of municipal sewer wastes due to the use of bichromated coatings, deep-etch plates are being phased out and replaced by positive photopolymer systems which are also capable of long runs.

Bimetal plates are used for very long runs in excess of one million mainly for long-run magazine publication printing and packaging. They are similar to deep-etch plates in that the coating serves as a stencil for the image areas which are developed out in processing and consist of copper or brass. The non-printing areas consist of aluminum, chromium, or stainless steel. There are two types of bimetal plates: (1) copper-plated on stainless steel or aluminum which are usually made from negatives, and (2) chromium-plated on copper or brass which are always made from positives. (The copper is usually plated on a third metal like aluminum or steel.) These are the most rugged and most expensive of lithographic plates and are used only for very long runs or jobs requiring frequent reruns. For magazine printing they are being phased out like deep-etch plates and replaced by long run oven-baked photopolymer plates.

Photographic plates are used almost entirely for duplicating printing and are never used for color reproduction. Their advantage is high exposure speed so the plates can be made directly from paste-ups of copy in a special camera equipped with a processor to produce a press-ready plate.

Electrostatic plates are another means of obtaining higher exposure speed. A number of electrostatic plates are in use mostly for laser imaging of newspaper plates. Another electrostatic plate in development is the KC-Crystalplate which uses a cadmium sulfide photoconductor that has higher speed and resolution (quality) than the other electrostatic plate systems.

Diffusion-transfer plates use the principle of Polaroid film. A negative of the image is produced on an intermediate silver halide coating, and the final positive image is transferred by diffusion to a specially-coated receiver material. Agfa-Gevaert and Kodak are leaders in this technology. The materials are used to produce screened prints, direct screen color separations, and printing plates for low-cost publications. Some quality is sacrificed in the transfer, and some plates have been capable of runs up to 50,000.

Laser Imaging: Several platemaking systems have been developed in which helium-neon (He/Ne) lasers are used to scan (read) a paste-up, and the information is processed digitally and used to operate Argon-ion lasers to expose (write) printing plates. Because digital signals are used, the read and write functions can be separated, and these systems are used to make plates in newspaper satellite plants. Also the write laser can be controlled by digital signals from computer memory, and compter-to-plate systems have also been developed. An obstacle to growth of these sytems is the slow speed of conventional lithographic plates. High speed photopolymer plates by 3M and Kodak, the electrostatic plates, and the KC-Crystalplate are examples of efforts to overcome this obstacle.

Gravure

As already mentioned, gravure is an intaglio process in which the image consists of discreet cells etched below the surface, and the non-image areas are kept clean by a doctor blade wiping over the surface of the plate or cylinder. Positives are used for making the image carriers for gravure. Since over 99% of the gravure printed in the United States is by rotogravure, practically all gravure image carriers are copper-plated steel cylinders. Very little sheet-fed gravure is printed in the United States, and copper plates are used for some of it. More sheet-fed gravure is printed in Europe, but most gravure is printed from cylinders. As already stated, there are three types of gravure, *conventional*, *variable area/variable depth*, and *variable area* (direct transfer) (Figure II-18).

In *conventional* gravure, the image which is on a continuous tone positive film, is exposed on a sensitized gelatin transfer medium known as *carbon tissue*, which has been previously exposed to an overall gravure screen pattern. (The screen consists of clear lines and opaque squares with the lines about one-third the width of the squares. Its main purpose in conventional gravure is to provide partitions to the image cells, or wells, to contain the ink and provide a surface of uniform height for the doctor blade to ride over.) After exposure, the tissue is transferred to the cleaned copper and developed with hot water to remove unexposed sensitizer. After transferring and processing, the carbon tissue consists of areas of exposed pigmented bichromated gelatin of varying hardness (permeability) corresponding to the amounts of exposure they receive.

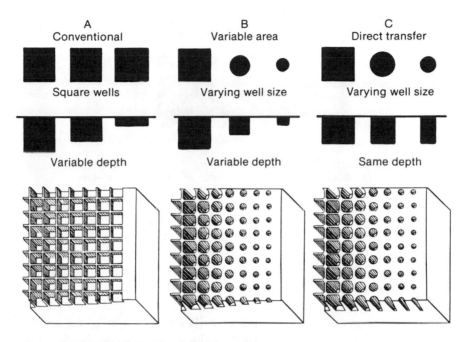

Figure II-18. Three types of gravure images: (A) conventional — variable depth; (B) variable area/variable depth; (C) direct transfer — variable area. (GTA)

The copper cylinder is etched with solutions of ferric chloride at varying densities. The water in the etch solutions swells the gelatin in the tissue in inverse proportion to the amount of exposure received. The highlights which received a lot of light are hard, swell slightly, and resist penetration of etch resulting in cells of shadow depth. The shadows have little exposure so the gelatin is soft in these areas, swell considerably, allowing the etch to penetrate to an appreciable depth. The cells representing tonal areas in between the highlights and shadows swell proportionately and have correspondingly varying depths.

The range of depths is from a few micrometers in the highlights to about 40 micrometers in the shadows. A magnified section of a conventional gravure image on a cylinder is illustrated in Figure II-19. This process produces prints comparable with continuous tone photographs since it prints with varying amounts and densities of ink. Therefore, it is used for high quality black and white and color reproductions like photographic catalogs and annuals, but the runs are necessarily short because of doctor blade wear of the very shallow highlight wells.

Figure II-19. Magnified view of image on conventional gravure cylinder — note variable depth of cells of same size.

The *variable area/variable depth* process, which is used for long run publications in the United States minimizes the problem of doctor blade wear of the highlights by varying the size of the cells as well as their depth. This process uses both a continuous tone and a special halftone positive of the subject and essentially the same materials and processing as conventional gravure. The smaller cells in the highlights are etched deeper to produce the same tone values so doctor blade wear is appreciably reduced. The cylinders are chromium-plated for long runs which also reduces wear effects on the highlights.

The *variable area* or *direct transfer* method is used primarily for packaging and textile printing. It uses only a screened positive for the image. The copper cylinder is coated with an acid resistant, light-sensitive coating; the screened positive is wrapped around the cylinder and exposed directly to it by a strong light through a narrow slit as the cylinder rotates slowly. The cylinder is developed, removing the unexposed coating, and etched, producing image cells which vary in area but with essentially the same depth. A magnified cylinder image made by this process is shown in Figure II-20. The range of tones is limited but satisfactory for most packaging and textile printing applications where run length, reruns, and consistency are the main requisites.

Figure II-20. Magnified view of image on direct transfer cylinder — note variable area elements with almost constant depth.

Controlled Engraving Methods: A major problem in the production of gravure plates and cylinders has been the unpredictability of tone values due to variations in the etching process. This variability of tones has discouraged and delayed the application of off-press color proofing to gravure. A number of processes have been developed to eliminate or minimize this deficiency. Controlled etching processes like Acigraf, Crosfield, and Gravomaster have been introduced using principles similar to the powderless etching processes of photoengraving. Crosfield has developed *Lasergravure,* an electronic system for laser engraving plastic coated cylinders producing wells in helical grooves of variable depth.

Electromechanical Engraving: The most widely used of the new systems is electromechanical engraving like the Hell Helioklischograph which is used almost exclusively for gravure magazine printing. In this process positive or negative continuous tone images on a special opaque white plastic called *bromides* are scanned photoelectrically as the cylinder is simultaneously engraved electromechanically by special diamond styli producing diamond-shaped pyramidal cells of varying area and depth (Figure II-21). Lasergravure and the Helioklischograph being electronic processes can be connected directly to scanners, pre-press color composition systems, or computers to allow production of cylinders directly from original copy or computer memories without any intermediate films.

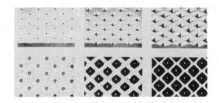

Figure II-21. Magnified view of image on Helioklischograph cylinder — note diamond shaped elements with variable areas and variable depths.

Halftone Gravure Conversion: The latest development in gravure is the use of halftone positives to produce printing cylinders on electromechanical engraving machines. Halftone positives make possible the use of off-press proofing systems in place of press proofing and the making of corrections on the films instead of the cylinders. This results in shorter lead times and economical use of gravure for runs as short as 150,000.

PRINTING

Each of the printing processes, letterpress, lithography, and gravure are capable of reproducing the same original with equally satisfactory results. There are still some distinguishing characteristics between the processes, but they are not significant except in unusual cases. Letterpress is distinguished by sharp, crisp printing, but usually with grainy or mealy images and sharp breaks or steps in gradient tints and vignettes.

Lithography is characterized by soft, smooth gradations of tones as in vignettes and color transitions as in skin tones, but usually with some variability in color balance throughout the run.

Gravure, especially conventional and to some extent variable area/variable depth, is ideal for the reproduction of pictures, as it has a long tone scale and strong, saturated colors even on poorer papers or with poorer ink pigments. Gravure, however, has poorer typographic resolution than letterpress and lithography.

In most cases the selection of the printing process for reproduction depends more on factors such as economics or cost, run length, availability of equipment, and delivery schedule than on the quality or appearance attributes of the reproductions.

Letterpress

There are four types of letterpress presses: platen, flatbed cylinder, rotary, and belt. Most color reproduction by letterpress is printed on rotary presses; sheet-fed, and web. All flexographic presses are rotary. Plates for rotary presses must be curved so duplicate plates made from engravings or wraparound photopolymer plates are used for printing. The press consists of as many printing units as there are colors to print. Each printing unit consists of an inking system, a plate, and impression cylinder between which the paper is fed (Figure II-22). The printing units can be in-line or arranged around a common impression cylinder as is done on many magazine printing presses. Many of these presses have *perfecting* features, i.e., the ability to print both sides of the sheet in one pass through the press.

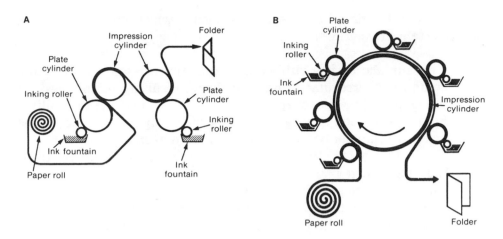

Figure II-22. Diagram of rotary letterpress presses printing (A) on both sides of the paper (perfecting) and (B) with six units around a common impression cylinder. (GAM)

Inks for letterpress printing are fairly viscous, and their rheology is important for proper trapping* of inks on multicolor presses. In general the ink printed on the first unit should have the highest viscosity or tack, and the other inks are printed in the order of decreasing tack. For best results, papers should have very smooth surfaces and preferably some compressibility to compensate for slight variations in makeready.

One of letterpress' most serious problems is the variable pressure exerted by different size image elements during printing. The same amount of *squeeze,* or overall pressure between two cylinders, or a cylinder and a flat surface, exerts greater pressure per unit area on small highlight dots than on the larger shadow dots. Extensive and expensive *makeready,* or adjustments of pressure locally, is needed to even out the printing impression so that highlights print without puncturing the paper and shadows print with a continuous, unbroken layer of ink. Precision electrotypes, wraparound plates, and pre-makeready systems help reduce makeready time and cost but it is still appreciable. Makeready in flexography is not very critical because the rubber and polymer plates used compress, distort, and conform to the paper surface, but the distortion limits the quality of the screened image (especially in the highlight areas) and register in printing.

Lithography

Lithography can be printed on sheet-fed and web presses. Practically

---

*For *proper trapping* of inks the same amount of ink should transfer to previous printed ink as transfers to unprinted paper (see Appendix A).

all lithography is printed by the offset principle which is responsible for four important advantages:

- The surface of the rubber blanket compresses slightly and conforms to irregular printing surfaces, resulting in the need for lower printing pressure or squeeze, improved print quality, halftones of good quality on rough surface papers, and the almost complete elimination of the necessity for makeready.
- The plate is not contacted by the paper or other printing substrate, thus increasing plate life by reducing abrasive wear from loose particles on the substrate surface.
- The image on the plate is straight reading instead of reverse reading, making checking of the plate simpler and faster.
- Less ink is required for equal coverage, thus speeding up drying and reducing smudging and set off.

Each printing unit on an offset lithographic press consists of a dampening system as well as inking rollers and three cylinders, plate, blanket and impression, and the paper feeds between the blanket and impression cylinder (Figure II-23). In addition to in-line and common

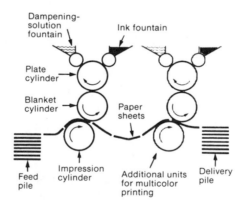

Figure II-23. Diagram of a unit-design offset lithographic sheet-fed press. (GAM)

impression cylinder designs as in letterpress, the offset process is the only one that can use presses with the blanket-to-blanket design in which the blanket of each printing unit serves as the impression cylinder for the printing unit opposing it and perfecting can be done in a single impression (Figure II-24). Other presses perfect by using means to turn the sheet or web over during the printing cycle.

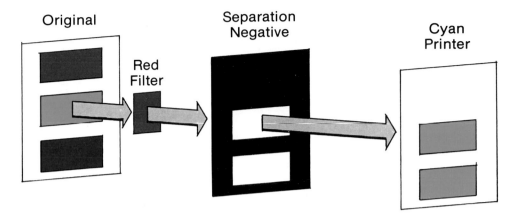

Figure II-8. **Cyan** printer is produced from color separation negative made with **red** filter.

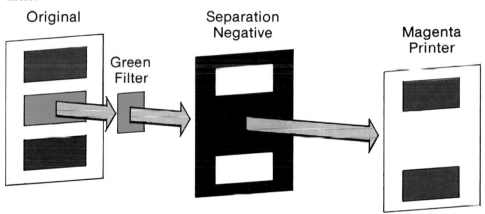

Figure II-9. **Magenta** printer is produced from color separation negative made with **green** filter.

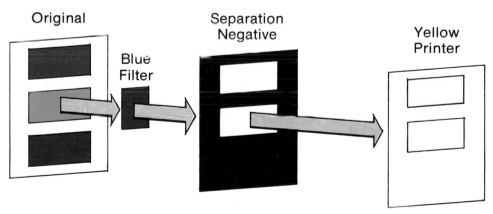

Figure II-10. **Yellow** printer is produced from color separation negative made with **blue** filter.

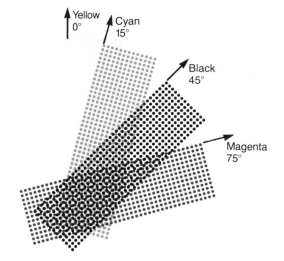

Yellow
0°

Cyan
15°

Black
45°

Magenta
75°

Figure III-5. Typical set of screen angles for 4-color reproduction.

Figure III-19. Typical appearance of under-trapping.

Figure III-8. Control panel of typical electronic color scanner with analog computer for color correction (Hell DC-300). (HCM)

Figure III-9. Control panel of electronic scanner with digital computer for color correction (Crosfield Magnascan 640). (Crosfield)

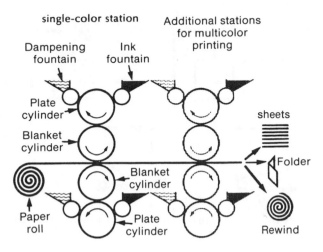

Figure II-24. Diagram of a blanket/blanket web offset lithographic press. (GAM)

For offset lithographic printing, inks are more viscous than letterpress inks; their rheology is very important for proper transfer but trapping is not as critical as in letterpress; they must resist emulsification by water; and they usually exhibit thixotropic properties, i.e., they have a false body and do not flow until worked on the rollers. Both smooth and rough surfaced papers can be used, but the papers must be reasonably pure and must not be affected by the combination of chemicals used in the dampening fluid. Problems with offset lithographic printing and their effects on tone and color reproduction are discussed in Chapter III.

Gravure

As already mentioned most gravure is printed on rotary web presses, and the process is called rotogravure. Like letterpress, a gravure printing unit consists of a printing cylinder, an impression cylinder, and an inking system (Figure II-25). Unlike letterpress and lithography, each printing unit is equipped with a hot-air dryer, and the printing cylinders are removable. Cylinders of different diameters or circumferences can be used so the press is capable of printing jobs of different sizes or print lengths.

Also unlike letterpress and lithography, the ink used in gravure is very fluid with very low viscosity, and trapping is not a serious problem as in letterpress and lithography because the inks are dried between impressions. The ink has a consistency similar to light cream and is applied to the printing cylinder by an ink roll or spray. The excess is removed by a flexible steel doctor blade and returned to the ink fountain. The impression cylinder is covered with a resilient rubber composition that presses the paper under high pressure or squeeze (about 150 pounds

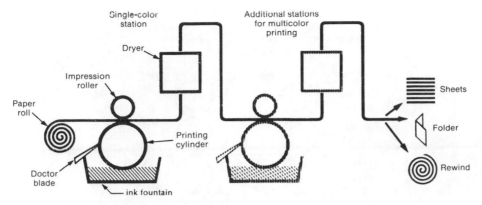

Figure II-25. Diagram of a rotogravure press — note the ink
hot-air dryers between printing stations. (GAM)

per lineal inch) into contact with the ink in the tiny cells in the printing surface. The paper must be very smooth and compressible to produce quality printing. Since the inks are very volatile, being mixtures of pigments, resin and solvents, they dry almost instantly with the help of the hot air dryers between the printing units of the press. The copper cylinders are chromium-plated for runs of a million or more. When the chromium begins to wear the cylinder is removed from the press, the chromium is stripped off, and the cylinder is rechromed and remounted in the press.

A quality problem in gravure printing is *dot skips* in the highlights (Figure II-26). These are caused by depressions in the surface of the paper

Figure II-26. Typical dot skips in highlights in gravure printing.

not contacting the image cells on the cylinder during printing despite the high pressure. Research at the Gravure Research Institute (GRI) has developed the Electrostatic Assist process which has minimized the problem in packaging and magazine printing.

BINDING AND FINISHING

Most printing is subjected to supplementary operations to convert it to finished products. The signatures in books and magazines must be collated, trimmed, and bound. Pamphlets and large advertising materials must be cut and folded. Labels are varnished and cut to size. Calendars are cut and stapled. Some greeting cards are die-cut, embossed, dusted with gold bronze, and folded. Letterheads, business cards, business forms, pads, etc., are cut to size and packaged with shrink wrapping or paper. Most package printing is scored and die-cut for shaping into packages. Printed metal is formed into cans, boxes, trays, and into odd shapes like toys, games, globes, etc. Other finishing operations are pasting, mounting, laminating, and collating, depending on the product. These are mostly mechanical operations and have no effect on the color reproduction itself, except as it affects the marketing of the product it represents.

QUALITY CONTROL

Most quality control is done during the printing operation and is actually statistical quality assessment to select products which are within acceptable tolerances for the job. The actual quality control should be done much earlier in the process, and if this is not done properly the rejection rate at the press is excessive. It should consist of (1) setting of specifications for the raw materials to be used and checking them to make sure they meet the specifications; (2) setting of reasonable standards and tolerances for the job; and (3) control of each step in the process to make sure the raw materials are used properly and the product of each step meets the standards and tolerances of the job. The most important function of quality control is the control of the process. How and why this is done is described in Chapter III.

Chapter III

Color Process Characteristics And Variables Affecting Them

The production of color proofs that properly represent or predict the appearance of printed reproductions depends on the ability to standardize the printing process and keep it under control. In color photography the color film and processing are standardized, and the tone rendering and color balance are usually built into the film so that the only means of adjustment is by varying the exposure. In the printing processes, however, there are innumerable points at which the shape of the tone reproduction curve and color balance can be varied. This is one of the main causes of poor reproductions, because, whether separations are produced photographically or by electronic scanning, there are so many adjustments to compensate for the variables in the printing processes that usually incorrect ones are used. Also each printing plant, each printing process, and each press in the plant has its own printing characteristics, and these are not easily analyzed, standardized, and controlled.

At the time John Yule wrote his book "Principles of Color Reproduction" in 1967 and the chapter "Color Reproduction in the Graphic Arts" in "Neblette's Handbook of Photography and Reprography" in 1977, there were three ways in which the problems of variations in color reproduction were handled. One was to adjust all steps in a process by trial and error until reasonably satisfactory results were obtained. This was the most popular method at the time with the limited knowledge and skills available. The second method was to standardize the photographic or electronic steps to fit average printing conditions and adjust printing conditions to conform. There were many attempts to accomplish this using instructions and targets produced by suppliers like Kodak, DuPont, Agfa-Gevaert and Fuji and institutes like the Graphic Arts Technical Foundation (GATF), Rochester Institute of Technology (RIT), PIRA (England), IGT (Holland), FOGRA (W. Germany) and UGRA (Switzerland) but none were entirely successful. The third method proposed was to determine the characteristics of the specific printing process and the materials used in it, and use sensitometric analysis to adjust the separation and correction steps to conform to the printing.

The industry has just become experienced and sophisticated enough to have some success with this last method. An attempt at making this method attainable has been made by Kodak in the development of its Customized Color Service in which a test target supplied by Kodak and printed by the plant under its normal conditions is sent back to Kodak for computerized sensitometric analysis on a spectrophotometer, and recommendations are sent to the printer regarding modifications to be made in the separation processes to fit the reproduction system. This method is described in Chapter X. The availability of computers and the development of appropriate software will help develop other systems to standardize and control color reproduction processes using test targets by GATF, RIT/T&EC, UGRA, FOGRA, Brunner and others. When the printing process has been standardized and can be controlled, the task of producing off-press color proofs that match the reproductions will be simplified.

Effect of Markets on Color Reproduction Practices

The printing industry is divided into two major market categories with each making different demands on the color reproduction process. The two major market divisions are (1) periodical publications like weekly and monthly magazines and (2) all other printing including commercial printing, packaging, labels, catalogs, books, greeting cards, art reproductions, etc.

One main dissimilarity divides these two categories which accounts for the differences in their demands on the color reproduction process. Periodical publications contain both editorial color, which the publisher can control, and considerable color for advertising by different manufacturers and advertising agencies which supply materials for reproduction from a number of sources. To save time and expense, many of the advertisers supply separations made by different engravers balanced for different inks, papers and even processes. Some are made for letterpress, some for web offset, and some for gravure and all are made for different printing conditions. A periodical printer who must combine all this copy from different sources onto one form or set of forms to be printed on one paper with one set of inks on one press is faced with a series of almost impossible compromises.

Color proofing is indispensable for this market as it indicates which subjects are compatible and which need corrections or remaking. Color proofing is the balance wheel without which periodical printing would be next to impossible. It is true that all web offset publications use SWOP standards for proofing and gravure magazines use GTA standards but even with these there are many variations and deviations from the standards. It is almost miraculous and a tribute to the experience and skill of color operators that color reproduction looks as well as it does in magazine publication printing.

For editorial color and for all other printing markets special copy is usually prepared for each job and all separations are prepared in-house or by trade shops or engravers over which the printer, customer or advertiser has control. For this type of printing, all separations and corrections can be made specially for the particular conditions of each job. Paper, inks and press are known and the characteristics of these can be used to optimize the correction process. Color proofing is used throughout the process to monitor it and make sure that all subjects are properly balanced. Printing for these markets lends itself to more rigid process controls so color reproduction results should be more consistent and of generally higher quality than for periodical printing which has little or no control of some of the preparatory processes used.

Evaluation of Color Prints and Proofs

The main difficulty with evaluating reproductions or color proofs is that exact reproductions are usually impossible because of (1) colors in the original which are outside the color gamut of the printing inks or proof colors; (2) differences in viewing conditions; (3) preferences for certain hues of *memory* colors like *skin*, *sky*, *grass* and *foliage* and (4) intentional color changes. The problem is especially difficult in the case of matching a color transparency, since it is impossible to reproduce the brilliance and tone range of a strongly illuminated transparency on a paper print. The usual solution is to surround the transparency with a brightly illuminated border which degrades its colors so they fall in a reproducible range, but most of the colors are too dark.

Making a quantitative analysis of the relationship between colors in the original and on the reproduction or proof is tedious and time-consuming, especially when compromises have to be made because of ink gamut limitations and wide differences in tone ranges. The usual practice, therefore, is to evaluate the reproduction or proof by comparing it visually with the original.

In setting up a new reproduction or color proofing process or in troubleshooting to find the causes of unsatisfactory color matches, the tone reproduction curve of the gray scale printed alongside the picture can be plotted and studied along with the reproduction of printed ink patches. These, however, may not exactly correspond to the reproduction of the picture because of metamerism, unevenness, and additivity and proportionality failures (see Appendix A). A number of other problems are encountered in reproduction, many of which are based on the fact that the color separation film does not usually "see" the colors in the same way the human eye does because of differences in spectral responses between the film and the CIE system (see Appendix B).

The reproduction process is based on complicated mathematical relationships like the Neugebauer equations, which even with simplifying assumptions have been impossible to solve except by trial and error methods. Now with the availability of computers and software, mathematical models are possible which are replacing the trial and error experiments of the past. The Neugebauer equations are based on the dot sizes of the halftone images used to make the reproduction. Therefore, anything that affects the dot sizes or effective tone values of the halftones has an effect on the final reproduction. The rest of this chapter is dedicated to descriptions and discussions of the factors in color reproduction by the major printing processes that can affect dot sizes, dot shapes, and/or tone values.

Factors Affecting Image Characteristics in The Printing Processes

Every step in the reproduction system has factors that can affect the characteristics of the individual image elements. The important steps in the processes as they affect color reproduction and are currently used are photography, halftone production, color separation and correction, image assembly, platemaking, and printing.

Pre-Plate Operations

The pre-plate operations of photography, contone and halftone production, color separation and correction and image assembly for all the major printing processes are very similar so they can be discussed together. Platemaking and printing factors for each process will be considered separately.

Photography

Photography has been the primary means for accomplishing color separation and correction for color reproduction for many years. With the advent of electronic scanners, especially those equipped with contact screens and electronic dot generation and electronic enlargement and reduction, scanning has gradually replaced photography. At the end of 1983 it was used to produce at least 70-75% of color separations made in the U.S. and Canada, 75-80% of those made in Europe and 90% of those made in Japan. The introduction of new all-digital scanners will continue to increase the use of electronic scanning and eventually will phase out much of the photographic color separation and correction, except for subjects that cannot be accommodated on scanners. Until these new scanners get firmly entrenched, photography will continue to be used and play an important role in color reproduction.

Evaluation of Color Transparencies: Since over 90% of the originals for color reproduction are color transparencies it is important that they are evaluated carefully so that at least all the subjects on the same printing form are in balance or some subjects may benefit at the expense of others, or vice versa, during printing. Factors to consider in evaluating transparencies for optimum color reproduction are exposure level; contrast or density range; color cast; color balance, particularly of memory colors; graininess; compatibility of dyes on retouched transparencies or prints; and manufacturer and type of color transparency film used. If transparencies are not in balance they can affect color separation and correction, color proofing and color printing. The differences between transparencies and how they affect reproduction are discussed concisely by Miles Southworth in his "Pocket Guide to Color Reproduction."

Photographic Defects: Most photographers are familiar with the functions of photography in color reproduction to produce sharp images of the correct size that register and have proper color and gray balance, but few are aware of the factors in photography that can affect these image properties. Supposedly well-corrected process lenses and filters have aberrations that can cause local distortions. Lenses have been found in use which can produce color separations that are the same size or fit overall but have local areas of misregister within the picture area. This has been noticed in processes where the black separation is made with split filter exposures. Filters with uneven thickness or wedging can also produce a similar defect.

A good test for lenses and filters to detect this is to photograph a grid with dimensions corresponding to the maximum coverage of the lens using split filter exposures with the sets of filters and lenses to be used. The test is also useful for checking for pin-cushion or barrel distortion, flatness of field, angle of coverage, and optimum aperture for a lens. These are all defects which can affect the appearance of the image and the ability to make a reproduction that looks like the original.

Processing including development and fixing, is an important step in the photographic process that can affect tone reproduction and color and gray balance. Automatic processing is used almost exclusively, but even with its extensive use operators still forget or neglect to use the devices or systems provided for its control, and development is often uneven, noticeable particularly on continuous tone films used for gravure.

Halftone Processes

The need for the use of halftone processes in printing was mentioned in Chapter II. Halftones consist of systems of dots all with the same spacing and density but varying in area and sometimes shape. They are optical illusions to create or simulate the visual impression of continuous tone images for picture reproduction.

Letterpress and lithography are binary processes which need halftones exclusively to reproduce pictures. Conventional gravure is not a halftone process, since it consists of cells of varying volumes which print different amounts, densities, or strengths of ink. The only reason for the screen, in which all the elements are the same size and shape, is to divide the image into cells, the walls of which contain the ink and maintain a constant height for the doctor blade to ride over. Variable area/variable depth gravure uses a combination halftone-continuous tone image. The screen pattern is used to reduce the effect of doctor blade wear on tone values especially in highlight areas. Variable area or direct transfer gravure is a halftone process with a short range in the shadows to maintain cells with discrete boundaries. The latest development in gravure is the conversion of the continuous tone images to halftones which are scanned on electromechanical engraving machines like the Hell Helioklischograph and Ohio Mechanical Engraver, and converted to variable area/variable depth gravure patterns on the cylinders.

There are three methods of producing halftone images: glass screen; contact screen; and electronic dot generation (usually by laser). The *glass screen* consists of two systems of parallel straight lines at right angles to each other. Each is etched into glass and inked with the widths of the inked lines approximately equal to the width of the spaces — 1:1 screen (Figure III-1A). (For conventional gravure the clear spaces are usually one-third the width of the inked lines — 1:3 screen). Glass screen photography requires special equipment and considerable skill and experience. It needs a special adjustable precision holder in the back of the camera, that can maintain short screen distances (1/8 inch – 1/4 inch) (3.2 – 6.3 mm) between the screen and the film. Lens aperture, aperture shape, and exposure are very critical factors that affect contrast and tone reproduction. Because most present day craftsmen do not possess the required skills and experience, glass screens are practically obsolete and have been replaced almost completely by contact screens.

Making halftones with *contact screens* is much simpler than with glass screens. Contact screens are on film bases and consist of vignetted dots with density gradients from edge to center (Figure III-B). There are gray contact screens used for direct screen color separation photography and dyed screens (usually magenta) for screening of black and white originals or separations. There are also square and elliptical dot screens for special tone reproduction effects, especially in the middletones; double and triple dot screens, particularly for improving highlight contrast; and special contact screens for gravure, to maintain cell boundaries in the shadows.

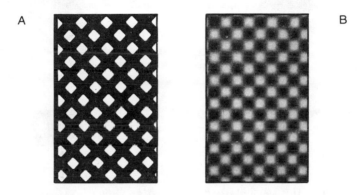

Figure III-1. (A) Enlarged view of glass cross-line screen for making glass screen halftones. (B) Enlarged view of film contact screen for making contact screen halftones. Elements are graded and can be black and white (silver) or dyed (usually magenta).

Contact screens are used in direct contact with the sensitized film on which the halftones are made. Contrast of reproduction can be varied within limits by *flash* and *bump*, or *no-screen* exposures. Flashing is used to reduce contrast especially in shadow areas, and bump exposures are used to increase contrast in the highlights. Contrast can also be increased by exposing through the back of the screen. With dyed screens additional contrast control can be achieved by the use of color filters during exposure.

The dot structures of halftones produced by glass and contact screens are different. Glass screens produced dots with very sharp regular shapes and long gradients or vignetting at the periphery of the dots so that considerable dot etching with chemical reducers was possible without sacrificing printing density (Figure III-2A). Contact screens, on the other hand, produce halftones with dots of slightly irregular shapes and fairly low gradients between edges and centers of the dots so that dot etching is limited before losing printing density (Figure III-2B). The slightly irregular dots produced by contact screens, however, generally conform to the shape of the detail in the original from which the halftones are made so they usually appear sharper and require much less correction by dot etching than glass screen halftones, unless local color changes are requested by the customer. Contact screens produce images with more detail and higher apparent sharpness than glass screen halftones, and this fact along with the simplicity of their use accounts for their popularity and preference over glass screens.

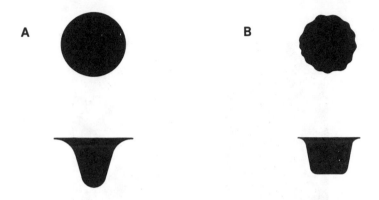

Figure III-2. (A) Enlarged cross-section view of glass screen halftone dot. Note long gradient and high density for latitude in changing dot size by dot etching. (B) Enlarged cross-section view of contact screen halftone dot. Note shorter gradient and lower density with less ability to change dot size by dot etching.

Electronic Dot Generation was described in Chapter II. Since the dot images are produced by high energy light sources like lasers on lith film and most films are processed in rapid access developers, they are of very high contrast, and the tone reproduction curves of the dots have high gradients with very short toes. Since the dot gradient curves have a toe, the dots can be etched 10–15% without loss of density. Some problems are encountered in etching dots produced on the Hell Chromagraph DC 300L, DC350, CP 340 and CP 341 scanners, as the dot images are produced by six fiber bundles exposing one-half of the dot and shifting to expose the other half. Each dot, therefore, consists of twelve separate fiber optic images which merge into a single image. This fractionally composed image element can change shape to conform to the detail represented. In etching, however, the boundaries of the separate fiber optic images can sometimes appear and the dot structure becomes broken or ragged.

Test for Printable Dots: Identifying dots that have excessive fringe or have been overetched and have lost density for printing is difficult. Dot fringe and density loss cannot be seen by normal illumination on a light table. The most effective way to identify them is viewing them with dark field illumination using light from a low angle. Dark field illuminators are available commercially but can be made simply by placing a black felt normal to the viewing angle about 6–8 inches below the top glass of a light table and using a lamp at about a distance of 10 inches and an angle of about 30° from the viewing angle (Figure III-3). The Enco Darkfield Viewer, a simple but effective cardboard box device for use with any ordinary light table is available free of charge from Enco Printing Products, American Hoechst Corporation.

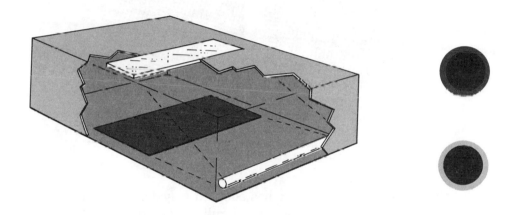

Figure III-3. Dark field illuminator for detecting fog or dot fringe around dots which is not visible by direct illumination but is penetrated by light during exposure.

Dot fringe can be readily identified in dark field illumination as a light grayish-white border around image elements. During contact printing or in platemaking all areas on the film with this appearance will be penetrated by light and will not produce an image. All films should be examined in this manner to make sure that all image elements visible with normal illumination are printable or to evaluate which visible image elements on the film are printable, and which are unprintable.

Some silver reducers or dot etching solutions like Farmer's Reducer (ferricyanide) leave yellow stains in the etched image areas. If these are not cleared they could prevent exposure and print as an image on plate coatings which are mainly UV and blue sensitive. Examining these areas with a blue filter can tell whether they will print or not on the plate.

Halftone Screen Patterns — Moiré: When two or more screen rulings are overprinted, objectionable interference or beat patterns result, called moiré (Figure III-4). If the screen rulings are at exactly the same angle no interference pattern or moiré will be seen. Printing at the same angle has not been recommended or practiced because a very slight shift in screen angle orientation such as can be caused by slight misregister in printing, or stretch or shrinkage of the paper due to absorption or desorption of moisture during printing, can result in noticeable color shifts and sometimes moiré. Even though four-color process inks should be transparent, the slightest opacity in any of the inks can cause color shifts between areas where the inks overlap in printing (subtractive mixture) and areas where they are adjacent (additive mixture).

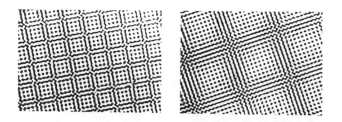

Figure III-4. Moire patterns caused by overlapping screen images. Note differences in patterns as screen angles change. Minimum patterns occur when screen angles are separated by 30 degrees. (IP)

For these reasons the industry has adopted a system of printing with a rosette pattern caused by the screen rulings being printed at fixed angles with relation to each other. It has been found that an angle of 30° between screen rulings produces a rosette pattern with the least noticeable and objectionable moiré. The angle is very critical. An error of as little as 0.1° can produce objectionable moiré when three or more colors are overprinting (Maurer). This small an error can be caused by misregister or displacement on the press.

A number of screen angle combinations are used (Figure III-5, page C-2). A common one is for the key or darkest color, to be printed at an angle of 45°. In most reproductions where a skeleton black is used, magenta is printed at 45°, cyan at 105°, yellow at 90° and black at 75°. In reproductions with a full black, two color and black, and Hell PCR, the black is printed at 45° and the magenta and cyan are printed at 15° and 75° depending on the angle of the yellow printer. What angle to use for the yellow has been a problem. Since the cross-line screen as used in halftone reproduction repeats patterns every 90°, only three colors can be spaced 30° apart in the 90° without repeating patterns (except with chain-dot or eliptical screens). The yellow, being the lightest color, is usually printed at 0° or 90°. This leaves an angle of 15° between yellow and cyan or magenta, and what angles the cyan and magenta are printed at depends on whether the subject has large even areas of red or green which can be affected by moiré. The closer the angles the more serious the moiré.

To minimize this moiré, yellow is sometimes printed with a different screen ruling than the other three colors. This was done frequently in letterpress magazine printing where the three colors were printed with 133 line (53 1/cm) screens and the yellow with 120 line (48 1/cm). This is done now on the Hell DC 300 laser imaged scans which have unconventional angles of 0°, 45°, 18.4°, and 71.6°. To minimize moiré each separation image is produced at slightly different screen rulings from 150 line (60 1/cm) to about 200 line (80 1/cm).

With improved tranparent inks and registering systems on presses, particularly web presses, trials have been run using all colors at the same screen angle. The system has been introduced for newspaper printing by Chemco, and RIT has run some trials for magazine printing. Results are surprising. Images are sharper with higher resolution. Moiré has not been a problem, but there have been serious color shifts causing a high rejection rate.

Color Separation

As described in Chapter II, there are three systems for separating an original into three color records and a black printer for four-color process printing. They are direct screening, indirect separation, and electronic scanning. The separation requirements for all printing processes are the same, but each separation system can produce slightly different image quality characteristics.

Indirect Separation is the oldest system of color separation in which four continuous tone negatives and two to four negative masks are made in a camera from the original through the appropriate filters, and then halftone positives are made from the negatives also in a camera (Figure III-6). In some cases where special inks are needed two-stage masking is used, in which a negative mask is placed in contact with a separation negative from which another mask is made that is used as the final mask for the separation negative from which the halftone positive is made. An *undercolor removal* (UCR) mask is also used especially for high speed web printing. The indirect process has a wide selection of correction options and is preferred by some craftsmen for high quality reproductions. Aside from being a time-consuming process, its main disadvantage is slightly diffused images due to errors in registering the many masks and dispersion of light in passing through the multiple layers of superposed films. Unsharp masks are used to hide this defect, but these often overemphasize edge contrast and result in image elements with shadowed borders or accentuated outlines.

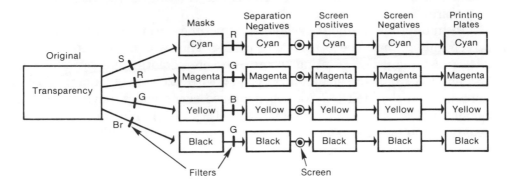

Figure III-6. Principles of indirect color reproduction process. (GAP)

Direct Screen separations are simple and fast to make as described in Chapter II. In the case of transparencies the color and tone correction masks are low density negatives made by contact of transparency and film using filtered light. They are placed in contact with the original, and halftone separations are made directly in a camera or enlarger using the appropriately filtered light and a gray contact screen (Figure III-7). In the case of flat art, like paintings, *camera-back masking* is used in which halftone separations are made by placing the mask and contact screen over the film in the back of the camera. If all the elements are at correct size, direct screen separations can be made by contact exposures with colored light of the sandwich of the original (or color duplicate to correct size), contact screen and mask.

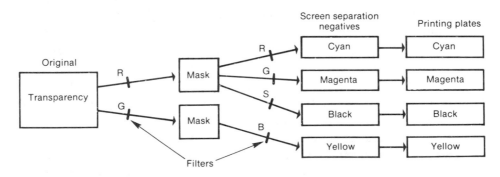

Figure III-7. Principles of direct screen color reproduction process. (GAP)

Direct screen separations are generally sharper and have higher resolution than indirect separations because usually fewer photographic operations and masks are used and there are less films to be registered and handled. Direct screen separations are used extensively for catalog illustrations of products with a lot of detail at reduced size like jewelry, watches, small parts, etc. The system does not, however, have the latitude and versatility of color and tonal correction of the indirect process and, therefore, is limited in quality and choice of inks, some of which would require two-stage masking for adequate color correction. The images may be sharper but the color correction may be poorer than the indirect process.

Electronic Scanning was described and illustrated in Chapter II. It performs all the functions of the direct screening processes electronically and accomplishes similar results without the restrictions or the limitations of these processes. Electronic scanners can duplicate the operations of single-stage negative, two-stage, and even three-stage masking, unsharp masking, edge and contrast enhancement without the problems of misregister and diffused images. They can output either negatives or positives, straight-reading or laterally reversed on the emulsion side, as continuous tone, contact screen, or electronically (laser) dot-generated images.

As described in Chapter II there are two types of computers used in electronic scanners; *analog* and *digital*. Most scanners in present use have analog computers which have wide — in fact too wide — latitude, and versatility in tone and color correction. These scanners have as many as 40-100 knobs for setting tone and color corrections and even with highly skilled operators, errors in setting account for up to 50% makeovers on analog scanners (Figure III-8, page C-2). Newer scanners with digital computers overcome this serious deficiency. The Crosfield Magnascan 550 was the first of these commercial scanners with digital computers for color and tone correction and adjustment of the separations to printing conditions. Newer models, like the Magnascan 640, are even more highly digitzed (Figure III-9, page C-2). Because of the elimination of the many knobs and ease of operation, productivity on these scanners is reported to be as high as three times that of scanners with analog computers.

New electronic scanners with all-digital separation and correction like the *EIKONIX* DesignMaster 8000 will eventually be preferred for producing color and tone corrected and process adjusted separations for optimum color separation and reproduction. This scanner records the three light values as digital data in computer memory in the CIELUV colorimetric space (Appendix B) which simplifies color correction appreciably and eliminates the necessity for rescanning.

Color Proofing is an integral part of the color separation and correction process, and this part of the reproduction process, especially electronic scanning, represents the most extensive use of off-press color proofing. Besides checking size, fit, and sharpness, color proofing is needed to validate the reproduction process; to determine how closely the colors in the reproduction match the colors in the original; if the range of tones from the highlights to the shadows corresponds reasonably to that of the original; and if the range of tones from the highlights to the middletones and the middletones to the shadows match the paper and printing conditions of the printing process.

It would be ideal if the proofing process could simulate the effect of the printing conditions on the highlight to middletone and middletone to shadow contrasts and produce the proof on the actual printing paper. As yet, no photomechanical proofing system can accomplish this completely, so compromises must be made to compensate for these deficiencies. Some are closer than others, but all those which use the actual printing paper also use protective films or overcoatings that affect the optical characteristics of the final proof. Expensive decisions such as makeover versus hand retouching are based on the compromises, so the process used must have reliability and consistency to strengthen the confidence of those faced with making the decisions. All the color proofing systems in current use and their characteristics are discussed in detail in the succeeding chapters.

Color page Make-up Systems are new sophisticated systems like Scitex Response 300 and 350, Hell Chromacom, Crosfield Studio 840 or 860, Dainippon Screen Sigmagraph 2000, and KC-Digital System, and the new generation of digital color scanners they will spawn, that may provide the answer to confidence in color proofing. At present they use soft proofing on high resolution color monitors. With the use of computer analysis of press conditions, ink and substrate characteristics, programs can be prepared for the systems to incorporate the effects of these on color reproduction into the soft displays for internal use. These eventually will be converted to hard proofs for customer approval and storage which will be output on equipment essentially similar to that used to make the printing films or plates.

Hell has developed such a system for its Chromacom, known as the Color Proof Recorder CPR 403, which uses Kodak RC-14, EKTAFLEX PCT or Fuji color photographic paper. Crosfield uses a LogE/Dunn color camera to produce proofs on color photographic paper. Polaroid is developing a system using a MacDonald Dettwiler Film Recorder and Coulter Systems Corporation is designing a hard color proofing output for its KC-Digital System. See Chapter IX for a discussion of these digital color proofing systems.

Color Stripping — Film Assembly

The major effects of the color stripping or film assembly operation on image quality can be register, moiré, and dot sharpening or dot spread or gain. The importance of register and the use of collimated light in mounting films has been mentioned in Chapter II. The effects of moiré and the importance of the accuracy of screen angles have been stressed in this chapter.

Dot sharpening and/or dot gain can be caused if films are mounted improperly so that the emulsion on the film is not in contact with the coating on the plate or proof material or the vacuum pressure is insufficient for intimate contact between the two surfaces. Dot sharpening generally occurs with positives and dot spread, or gain with negatives. In mounting halftone films on the assembly film, they should be placed so that the emulsion side is on the side that is placed in contact with the plate or proof material for exposure. If the emulsion is away from the exposure surface, the thickness of the film base or the thickness of the assembly film will cause light to spread during exposure resulting in sharpening of positive image elements and spreading of negative image elements. Figure III-10 illustrates right and wrong conditions for film mounting and exposure.

Figure III-10. Right and wrong conditions for film mounting for exposures (A) Emulsion to Emulsion — **Right**; (B) Emulsion to Back — **Wrong**.

The phenomenon of light spread is used in color proofing systems to simulate the dot gain that occurs in printing on the press, especially in lithography. In negative color proofing processes the use of a spacer during exposure can cause actual enlargement or spread of the dot images on the proofs which is reasonably controllable (Figure III-11). In positive systems the best that can be achieved by exposure is the same dot size on the proof as on the positive. In order to simulate the dot spread or gain that occurs on the press, spacers are used between the separate image layers on the proof as in overlay proofing (Chapter V). In these cases the light used for viewing casts shadows of the dots through the separating layers which create the illusion of enlarged or spread dots on the proof (Figure III-12). DuPont CROMALIN, Agfa-Gevaert GEVAPROOF, 3M TRANSFER KEY and MATCHPRINT create dot

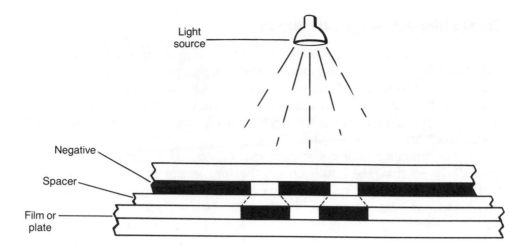

Figure III-11. Principle of physical dot gain with negatives using a spacer during exposure.

spread simulation by successively laminating the coating of each individual film on which the color images are formed on the substrate so that each color image is separated from the other images by the thickness of the coating. In addition, in CROMALIN, toner fog between the dots accentuates the apparent dot spread. The 3M MATCHPRINT system uses a separating layer between the sandwich of the TRANSFER KEY images and the substrate on which the combined images are mounted to simulate dot gain on the press.

The final color proof for predicting what the reproduction will look like should always be made from the same films which are used to make the printing plates. Color proofs are usually made to check the final color corrections before assembling the films for platemaking. In the color stripping and film assembly operations a number of films are used to

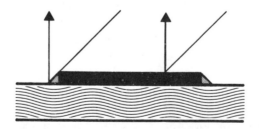

Figure III-12. Principle of optical dot gain with positives. Shadow of dots cast through separating layers in proofs simulate physical dot gain on press. (DuPont)

compose the final layout or page. Contact positives or negatives or duplicate films are usually made of partially assembled units for combining into a final layout from which a single contact film is made. Because of dot spread or sharpening due to light spread with insufficient vacuum or flopped films during exposure, the tone values or dot sizes on the combination films are not always the same as on the films from which the combinations were made.

Besides checking to see if all elements on the job are in place and in the proper color (color-breaks), the main reason for making proofs of the final flat prior to platemaking is to make sure that no serious errors in register, tone or color balance have been introduced in the image assembly operations.

Platemaking and Printing

The plate, or cylinder, is the hub of every plate printing process; letterpress, flexography, lithography, and gravure. It is the image carrier that translates the information developed in the preparatory operations into a form for recording on the printing press. The press cannot print anything that is not on the plate. Sometimes the press will print images sharper than the plate, i.e., image elements or dots will print smaller than they are on the plate and some small highlight dots can disappear or not print at all. At other times the press will print images fuller than the plate, i.e., image elements or dots will be spread or print larger than they are on the plate and tints as open as 75–80% on the plate can print solid.

These effects are caused not only by the printing process and press but also by the paper and ink. A print made from the same plate printed on the same press with the same ink on coated paper will be sharper and stronger in color than one printed on uncoated book paper, and this will appear sharper than one printed on newsprint. In letterpress and lithography a print made from the same plate, printed on the same press and paper, with reasonably viscous ink will appear sharper than one printed with soft ink.

If the printing process and press characteristics are consistent and predictable and the materials are the same, their effects on the final print can be compensated for in the making of the negatives or positives used to make the plates. If a job is to be printed on coated stock, the tone reproduction curve of the halftone (or variable depth conventional and variable area/variable depth gravure) images on the plate should have higher contrast in the region from the highlights to the middletones and lower contrast in the region from the middletones to the shadows than if it were to print on uncoated book paper; and the differences should be larger if it were to print on newsprint. These tone reproduction curves are illustrated in Figure III-13.

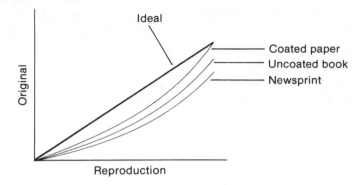

Figure III-13. Typical tone reproduction curves of halftone films for subjects printing on coated, uncoated and newsprint papers. These compensate for the effects of dot gain in printing on these papers.

Letterpress — Flexography

Appearance Characteristics

According to the method of printing, each printing process has unique distinguishing characteristics which affect the appearance of the image and the size and shape of the individual image elements. Letterpress is distinguished by a crisp, sharp appearance. When the relief elements of the letterpress image come in contact with the ink rollers on a press, they are inked all over, and some of the ink spills over the edges. During the impression between the plate and the paper, the ink is further squeezed over the edges so that the image elements reproduce with light ink in the center, uninked ridges around the periphery of each element, and a border of ink that spilled over the edges (Figure III-14A, page C-4). Type and halftone dots under magnification have characteristic rings of ink around them. Halftone dots printed by letterpress are "doughnut-like" in appearance under magnification. The sharp inked borders create the illusion of crispness and sharpness. Flexography can be differentiated from letterpress as the ink fringes and rings are sometimes blurred (Figure III-14B, page C-4).

Letterpress printing has another distinguishing characteristic — *embossing*. The sharp edges of the relief type and halftone dots are pressed into the paper during the impression so that the image of the type or dot is embossed or indented into the paper. It can sometimes be detected by feel or by low angle illumination on the back of the print (Figure III-15). The degree of embossing is a measure of the effectiveness of the *makeready* on the form. This embossing is the main reason for makeready (see Chapter II). Sometimes it is so serious that on lightweight papers small highlight dots actually puncture the paper.

A 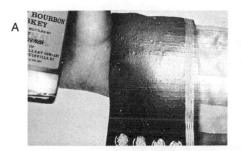 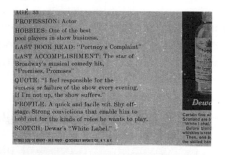 B

Figure III-15. Typical embossing in letterpress printing with average (magazine) makeready. (A) Embossing; (B) Type image on back of sheet causing embossing.

Another appearance characteristic of letterpress is *mottling* or *galvanizing* in shadow areas (Figure III-16). It can be caused by poor formation in the paper, resulting in uneven ink absorption; by uneven hardness of the tympan sheet covering the impression cylinder; or by uneven makeready under the tympan sheet, resulting in variable pressure over the shadow areas during the impression.

Figure III-16. Characteristic mottling or galvanizing in letterpress shadow areas.

Platemaking

The printing plate consists of information in a form that can be reproduced on the press. In letterpress, flexography, and lithography the images consist of dots with variable areas. In gravure it consists of dots with the same area and varying depths, dots with varying areas and depths, and dots with varying areas, depending on the process used. Dot size changes in letterpress, flexography, and lithography are characteristic of some of the platemaking processes used, and these need to be controlled in order to assure consistency of the printed product. It is preferable to make all the tone corrections in the films from which the plate is made so that platemaking can be standardized and will not require subjective judgments based on years of experience of highly skilled craftsmen. The newer platemaking processes with standardized procedures that allow automation in exposure and processing are preferred, mainly for this reason.

The conventional process of photoengraving for making letterpress and flexographic plates, which used four-way powdering and multiple etches or *bites* and is obsolete now, is a classic example of creating tone values in platemaking. As the acid in the etch removed metal to create relief in the images for printing, the sides of the dots were also etched reducing the sizes of the dots. The powdering was done with an acid resistant asphalt, called *Dragon's Blood*, which was baked on the sidewalls of the image elements. Multiple bites were used to minimize lateral etching, but even with these precautions negatives used for photoengravings had at least 25% dots in the highlights with all the other tone values compressed into the short scale remaining. So the tone reproduction and contrast of the reproduction was actually created by the *photoengraver/fine etcher* who skillfully extended the tone scale by etching the highlight dots down to the desired 5% or finer and adjusting the dot sizes in the rest of the image to conform to the contrast needed to suit the image, printing conditions, paper, and ink.

This long, tedious and skill intensive process has been replaced by the *powderless etching* process which uses a special chemical banking age that deposits a gelatinous acid resistant coating on the sidewalls of the dots and allows the acid to etch vertically with minimal lateral spread (Figure III-17). This process allows the use of negatives with the proper dot sizes for the tone reproduction desired in the printed reproduction and requires minimal fine etching, thus reducing platemaking time and cost by eliminating much of the need for the exceptional skills of the fine etcher.

Photopolymer plates have gone one step further in standardizing the process by automating exposure and processing and in some cases even the coating operation. These are now the preferred plates for direct

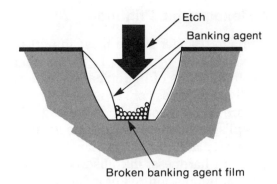

Etch
Banking agent

Broken banking agent film

Figure III-17. Principle of powderless etching. One application of etch is used which builds up banking agent on sides of etched areas to protect them from undercutting. (GAM)

letterpress and flexographic printing, but there have been some problems with ink receptivity, ink transfer, and solvent resistance on the press. For long run magazine printing *electrotype* duplicate plates are still used and these are made from powderless-etched engravings usually on copper.

The need for *duplicate* plates requires the use of molds from which duplicate plates are made. In order for molds to release properly from the original plate, the dots and other image elements like text characters must have slanted sides called shoulders. This is another important characteristic of the relief dot structure. Satisfactory molds cannot be made from plates with mushroomed crowns or vertical shoulders (See Figure III-18), and plates with such dot characteristics are unsatisfactory for direct printing. Mushroom-topped dots can break in printing. Laser engraved flexographic cylinders, with straight or vertical sidewalls, have restricted image resolution and detail.

Figure III-18. Letterpress dot with mushroom crown caused by undercutting of solution during etching. (GAM)

Letterpress and Flexographic Printing

Uniformity of image transfer is the most important requirement for letterpress and flexographic printing. Letterpress printing surfaces usually consist of combinations of individual plates locked up in position on the bed of a flatbed press or the cylinder of a rotary press. Flexographic plates are mounted on cylinders using sticky-back tape. The conditions for accomplishing uniform overall image transfer are: perfectly level image elements or plates all at the same height; an equally level, smooth, and uniform (in hardness, ink absorbency and thickness) paper or substrate surface; an impression roll or cylinder which is parallel to the plate surface; and an inking system with even ink distribution and rollers parallel to the plate surface. An extremely important factor in obtaining plate levelness and maintaining it during printing is *makeready*, mentioned and described in Chapter II. Variations in levelness of the plates or smoothness of the paper, worn type or plates, or the presence of pits or craters in the plates or paper surfaces cause variations in ink transfer and missing or broken halftone dots, lines or type characters, and/or embossing.

A major advantage of *flexography* is that the soft and resilient plates conform to the impression cylinder and substrate surfaces so that levelness of the plate and substrate surfaces and uniformity of the impression pressure are relatively easy to achieve. The soft rubber or resilient polymer plates flow and distort under pressure, overcoming the pressure differentials of uneven image element height and area so that makeready is much less critical. The distortion, however, limits the fineness of the screen and the register tolerance that can be maintained, especially on unit and stack type presses. Central impression cylinder presses are much more stable, and quality four-color jobs with screen rulings as fine as 150-line have been printed on these presses using precision polymer plates, reverse-angle doctor blades, and ceramic anilox rollers.

Ink Trapping: A serious problem affecting the appearance of letterpress prints is undertrapping of inks on multicolor presses resulting in weak overprinted colors with noticeable mottle (Figure III-19, page C-2). As defined in Chapter II and discussed in Appendix A, "for proper trapping of inks the same amount of ink should transfer to previously printed ink as transfers to unprinted paper during printing." Undertrapping is the condition that exists when less ink is transferred to previously printed ink than to unprinted paper. This condition is common on multicolor letterpress and lithographic presses, on which the ink on a printing sheet is still wet from one impression when it enters the next impression. The *viscosity* or *tack* of the ink and its *film thickness*, the *ink absorptivity* of the paper, and the *time interval* between printings are the major factors affecting ink trapping on the press.

A general rule in multicolor printing is to use inks in decreasing order of tack: i.e., *the first ink printed should have the highest tack and each succeeding ink should have a lower tack than the previous one*. This rule has many exceptions. The important factor in ink trapping is for the *previously printed ink to have a higher tack than the overprinting ink at the instant of transfer*. The tack of an ink at the instant of transfer is a function of the *intrinsic tack* of ink (as measured on an inkometer); the *ink film thickness* (thin films have higher effective tack than thick films); the *ink absorptivity* of the paper (the more absorptive the paper is, the more vehicle is drained from the ink and the portion left on the surface is stiffer and tackier); and the *time interval between transfers* (the longer the time interval the more ink vehicle is absorbed into the paper and the tackier the ink becomes). The tack of the first ink down is limited by the strength of the paper. If the surface strength of the paper is too low for the tack of the ink used, the paper will pick or split during printing.

Ink trapping can also be a problem and affect the appearance of multicolor prints when they are printed by successive impressions on single-color or two-color presses. It is often claimed that proper or correct trapping of inks is obtained when printing is done on single color presses. In many cases the wet ink will not transfer or trap on the dried ink. This is sometimes called *crystallization* and is caused by ink containing non-drying oils, waxes, or paste driers containing cobalt, and the presence of excessive spray powder. If a job requires more than one printing, the first-down ink should have no grease, wax, or excess drier, and little or no spray powder should be used.

As pointed out in Appendix A the *overprint colors* are more significant in color reproduction than the actual colors used for printing since most of the picture consists of mixtures or overprints of the colors rather than the pure colors by themselves. Therefore, ink trapping is a very important characteristic of color reproduction. For optimum quality, ink trapping should be within 85-90% of proper trapping and it should be consistent. For an off-press color proof to match the press print it must not only match the ink colors, but also their trapping. How to measure ink trapping is described in Appendix A.

Ink trapping is not an important factor in flexography. Flexographic inks are very fluid, consisting of volatile solvents and vehicles with little or no tack. When printed on absorbent substrates the inks are readily absorbed so that they are almost dry before the next impression. When non-absorbant substrates are used, presses are equipped with hot-air dryers between printing units so the volatile solvents are evaporated and the ink is relatively dry by the time it reaches the next impression.

Mottling: As already mentioned another characteristic defect of letter-press is mottling in solids and deep shadows. It is a spotty appearance due to either variations in ink density or finish resulting in variations in gloss or bronzing, often referred to as "galvanizing." It can be caused by variations in ink absorptivity or formation in paper, ink characteristics, or excessive printing pressure and is a difficult appearance characteristic to reproduce on an off-press proof.

Still other defects in letterpress printing are *hickies* and *spots* which can be caused by dried ink skin; particles of ink rollers; poor housekeeping, such as dust or dirt from a ceiling or accumulated spray powder on parts of the press; and loose particles of paper dust or coating loosened by the cutter or trimmer. The particles become attached to the plates and print with a dark center and white perimeter, and if small enough become lodged between the dots of halftone engravings and print as unwanted dots until scrubbed out (Figure III-20). Hickies and spots are also serious printing defects in lithography.

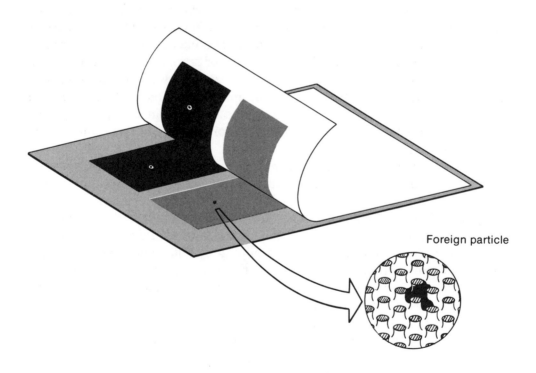

Figure III-20. Hickeys and spots in printing caused by for-eign particles attached to plates and interfering with ink transfer.

Lithography

Appearance Characteristics

Lithography has several distinguishing appearance characteristics. Image elements have fairly *uniform density* overall and reasonably smooth edges (Figure III-14C, page C-4). The same dot size in lithography will print a darker tone value than in letterpress because of the more even distribution of ink on lithographic printed dots.

Dot gain is another characteristic of lithography. The dots on the press print are larger than on the press plate because ink spreads slightly when it wets a surface. Because the lithographic plate and blanket are planographic and the image is transferred from the plate to the blanket and then to the paper, even with normal pressure, the elements or dots comprising the image are about 5% larger than the dots on the plate. Unfortunately the dot gain is not constant as it is affected by many factors to be discussed later in this section.

An occasional appearance characteristic of lithographic printing is a *mealiness,* or *salt and pepper,* appearance of solids or shadows (Figure III-21). This is caused by the ink-water balance and is due to water droplets which collect on inked areas and prevent ink transfer.

Figure III-21. Typical mealy appearance of lithographic shadows caused by disturbances in ink-water balance.

Platemaking

Lithographic platemaking is simple, requires less time and skill, and costs are lower than for the other processes. The ease and economy of making plates for lithography has been one of the main reasons for the advancement and popularity of the lithographic process. One of the problems of lithographic platemaking is the large number and variety of plates in use, each with essentially its own characteristic image properties. Both positives and negatives are used for platemaking.

There are additive and subtractive *surface plates*; wipe-on and presensitized positive and negative *diazo plates*; positive and negative presensitized and wipe-on *photopolymer plates; deep-etch plates*, in-plant and pre-coated; and positive and negative *bimetal* and poly or *multimetal plates*. In addition, there are *photographic plates; electrofax* (zinc oxide) and *organic photoconductor electrostatic plates* and *laser-exposed plates*. These plate types are described in Chapter II. Some of the image characteristics and factors affecting the tone reproduction of these plates are described in this section.

Platemaking Controls: The GATF Sensitivity Guide (Figure III-22) (sometimes identified as the Stouffer gray scale) is the most dependable means for controlling exposure and development of the light-sensitive coatings used in platemaking. It is a continuous tone gray scale with 21 numbered steps and a density difference of approximately 0.15 (square root of 2) between steps or 0.30 between every two steps; i.e., the light transmission from step 3 to 5 is cut in half, or doubled from step 5 to 3. (A density difference of 0.3 between films is equivalent to doubling the light trasmission or cutting it in half). When the sensitivity guide is exposed with a negative on a plate the low numbered steps are solid and the high numbered steps are clear. The last numbered step that develops solid is a measure of the amount of light exposure received by the coating.

On negative plates, steps 5 and 6 are generally considered satisfactory for dot size rendition and plate life. If step 4 is solid the plate is underexposed and the exposure on the next plate should be doubled to bring it to step 6. If step 7 is solid the plate is overexposed and the exposure on the next plate should be reduced 30% to produce a solid step 6.

Figure III-22. GATF Sensitivity Guide with numbered steps in gray scale with density differences of about 0.15 between steps.

On positive plates the low numbered steps are clear and the high numbered steps are solid. Most plate manufacturers recommend that exposure of positive plates be based on the last numbered step that develops *clear*. The clear step numbers recommended by various manufacturers range from 3 to 5. The exact step depends on the type of plate, processing, and press printing characteristics and should be determined by printing tests. Deviations from the standard are made when plates, processing, or press conditions are changed or when deliberate changes in dot sizes are desired.

While the GATF Sensitivity Guide is a reliable measure and control of plate exposure and potential plate resistance to wear, it is not a conclusive measure of dot size in platemaking. It can indicate dot spread and/or sharpening due to light spread during exposure but it does not record light spread and dot size changes caused by lack of vacuum contact between film and plate, the use of spacers in exposure and exposure through the back of the film (film emulsion away from plate emulsion). To measure these effects, the *GATF Star Target* and *GATF DOT GAIN SCALE* were developed.

The *GATF Star Target* is illustrated in Figure III-23. It consists of a 3/8" (9.5 mm) pinwheel with 36 spokes emanating from the center. A good target has 1600 lines/inch (63 lines/mm) at the center. A good plate can reproduce up to 1000 lines/inch (39.4 l/mm). A plate with excessive light spread or dot gain or loss will show a decrease in lines/inch (l/mm) in the Star Target. The target can be calibrated to indicate the degree of dot size change as it magnifies dot size changes 23 times.

Figure III-23. GATF Star Target for indicating dot gain, slur and doubling. (GATF)

The *GATF DOT GAIN SCALE* is illustrated in Figure III-24. It is based on the principle that fine screen tints are more sensitive to dot gain than coarse tints, so in situations causing dot spread or gain images with fine screens darken more rapidly than images with coarse screens. This is why coarse screen images are easier to print and require less control.

Figure III-24. GATF Dot Gain Scale and Slur Gauge. (GATF)

The Dot Gain Scale consists of a series of ten numbered steps 0 to 9 containing fine screen tints [200 l/in. 80 l/cm] in decreasing order of dot sizes as the numbers increase, in a block ¼ x 1⅜ inches (6.4 mm x 40 mm) containing about a 30% tint of a coarse screen [65 l/inc. 25 l/cm]. The scale is made so that the density of step 2 is about the same as the background so step 2 disappears on viewing the scale. This then is the right step for correct exposure and development on a plate. As dot spread increases the densities of the numbers also increase and higher numbers disappear, as shown in Figure III-25. The scale is designed so an increase in one step is approximately equivalent to 3-4% dot gain in the lower numbers and 4-5% gain in the higher numbers.

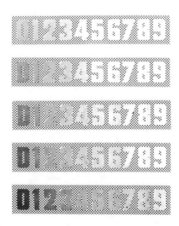

Figure III-25. Dot gain scales showing effects of dot gain or spread during printing on the press. (GATF)

The scale can be used to control exposure and development in contact printing of films and in platemaking and in indicating dot gain in printing. For printing a *Slur Gauge* was added to the target. The original Slur Gauge (Figure III-26) does not differentiate well between slur and

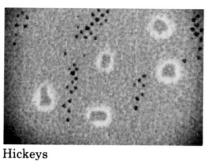
Hickeys

Wrinkling

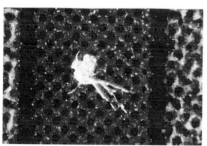
Picking

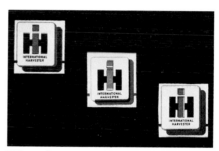
Misregister

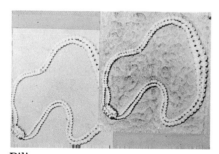
Piling

Curl (Tail-End Hook)

Figure III-28. Typical defects in lithography caused by disturbances in the ink-water balance during printing.

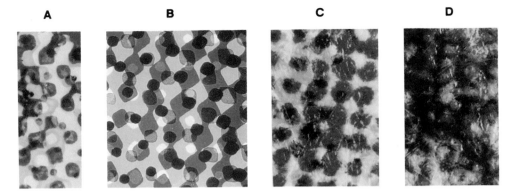

Figure III-14. (A) Enlargement of **letterpress** printing showing border effects of ink spilling over edges of relief image elements. (B) Enlargement of flexographic printing showing less border effects than letterpress. (C) Enlargement of lithographic printing showing full coverage of image with slightly ragged perimeter. (D) Enlargement of gravure printing in picture areas showing blurring of cell boundaries due to ink spread.

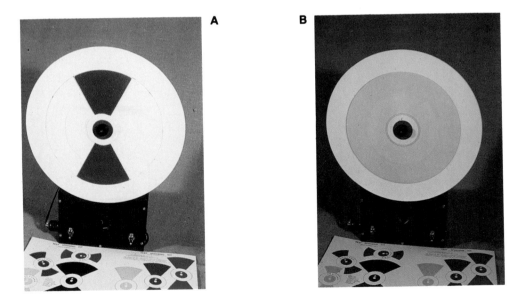

Figure III-32. Use of Maxwell discs and printed segments to check effects of paper color, brightness and fluorescence on printed colors. (A) Stationary; (B) Rotating. (GATF)

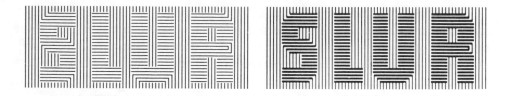

Figure III-26. Enlarged view of GATF Slur Gauge. (A) Old gauge which did not differentiate slur and doubling. (B) New gauge which does. (GATF)

doubling. The Star Target is better for this. *Slur* spreads the center of the target in an *oval* shape — *doubling* creates a *figure 8* design in the center of the Star Target. These are illustrated in Figure III-27.

| Normal | Dot gain | Double | Slur |

Figure III-27. Enlarged views of GATF Star Target showing simulated (A) symmetrical dot gain; (B) doubling; (C) slur. (GATF)

Surface Plates: The light-sensitive coating on surface plates, after exposure, becomes the ink-receptive image area. The way the image is produced on the plate can affect its structural, or dot size characteristics. Exposure is critical on surface plates since it governs the amount of physical change in the photosensitive coating, and this generally determines its *abrasion*, or *wear resistance*, and plate life on the press. Usually, the longer the exposure the greater the wear or abrasion resistance, but light spread during exposure can have a serious effect on dot size. A compromise must be reached between dot size change and plate life.

At least 25 inches (635 mm) of vacuum should be used in the vacuum frame during exposure and enough time should be allowed between turning it on and starting the exposure to ensure intimate contact between the film and the plate during exposure. Newton rings between the plate flat and the glass can be a good indicator of proper contact. Even with this close contact there can be light spread due to *halation* of light from the surface of the metal plate (usually aluminum) through relatively thick coatings of sensitizers and angular illumination, especially at the edges of the plate. If negatives are used for exposure the light spread results in dot gain and filling-in of shadow areas. If positives are used dots are sharpened and fine highlight dots can disappear.

There are two methods of producing the images on surface plates — *additive* and *subtractive*. On *additive* plates the developer consists of an emulsion of an ink-receptive lacquer and a desensitizing gum mixture. The balance between ink-receptive (oleophilic) and water-receptive (hydrophilic) components is critical. It requires considerable skill in manipulation to get the correct amount of developer on the plate. Enough must be used to dissolve and remove all the unexposed sensitizer or the non-printing areas will take ink and scum on the press. Also image elements, especially halftone dots will retain fringes of coating which print as spread dot elements, but this is usually uneven and streaky and is worn off during printing by fountain solution.

If too much developer is used and not rubbed down properly, a thick coating of lacquer is left on the image which results in good plate life but variable dot spread that also gradually decreases as the dampening solution on the press bathes the image and removes the excess lacquer fringes during printing. If the developer is rubbed down too vigorously, the thin coating of lacquer results in sharp dots with no additional spread or fringe but short plate life on the press. These effects are not generally seen on the GATF Sensitivity Guide.

On *subtractive* plates the ink-receptive lacquer is coated over the photosensitive coating in manufacture, and developing removes it along with the coating in the non-image areas. As long as development is complete dot size is much more consistent on subtractive plates and is affected only by exposure which can be monitored and controlled by the Sensitivity Guide.

Deep-Etch and Bi-Metal Plates: These plates are gradually becoming obsolete but as long as some are used, their characteristics should be known. In deep-etch platemaking the photosensitive coating is used only as a resist. The coating is bichromated gum arabic or polyvinyl alcohol which become insoluble in aqueous salt solutions on exposure to light. A *positive* is used for exposure, and *development* with concentrated salt solutions of calcium and zinc chlorides removes the unexposed coating from the metal in the image areas. The metal is *etched* slightly in these areas which are then *chemically copperized* and covered with *lacquer* and *ink*. The exposed coating is removed by *soaking* in *warm water*, after which the plate is *desensitized* with an *acidified gum etch* and *gummed*.

The developing and etching steps are critical for dot size changes. Overexposure sharpens the image as does underdevelopment. Overdevelopment causes dot spread. Overetching not only deepens the image cavity but also spreads it causing dot spread or gain. Again there is a delicate balance between exposure, development, and in this case, etching. The GATF Sensitivity Guide is very helpful in controlling tone reproduction and dot sizes on deep etch plates. Plates are usually developed to step 7 or 8, and the etching step advances the scale to step 6 or 7, whichever is desired.

Bimetal or *multimetal* plates of the copper/chromium or brass/chromium type are similar to deep-etch plates in that they are made from positives and are subject to the same type of dot size changes from exposure, development, and etching with the exception that the etching which involves removal of the chromium from the image areas is stronger. This causes more dot spread which must be compensated by overexposure. Normal development is usually used to remove the unexposed coating in the image area. The GATF Sensitivity Guide is an *absolute* necessity in *controlling exposure* and *etching* to achieve proper dot size on these plates. Slight variations in these can cause appreciable changes in dot sizes.

Exposure and *etching* are also critical on bimetal plates of the copper-plated aluminum or stainless steel type made from negatives. These plates have a tendency to produce sharpened images or images with dot loss, rather than dot gain. Exposure especially with separators between the negative film and the emulsion on the plate causes a spread image or dot gain on the plate. Etching to remove the copper from the non-image areas spreads laterally into the image causing the dots to sharpen. The *balance between overexposure and etching* is extremely critical and even when monitored by the GATF Sensitivity Guide requires extreme skill and experience.

Craftsmen like deep-etch and multimetal plates because of their *latitude in exposure, development, and etching* which produces a wide range of dot sizes to compensate for variations in paper and press conditions. In the hands of trained and experienced craftsmen this ability to vary dot sizes becomes an important advantage for these plates, but this variability of dot size reproduction can be disastrous with less skilled craftsmen with limited experience in this type of platemaking. Also, the need for manual and visual adjustments prevents the ability to automate processing which is so important to increased productivity and consistent operation. This is a main reason for the preferential use of photopolymer plates. Another strong reason is the *water pollution hazards* caused by the *bichromated* sensitizers used in most of the coatings and by the chemicals in the etches used for deep-etch and bimetal plates. As a result of these deficiencies and limitations deep-etch and bimetal plates are being phased out in favor of photopolymer plates.

Lithographic Printing

In contrast to the ease and economy of carrying out lithography's pre-press, preparatory, and platemaking operations and processes, printing on a press by the lithographic process is much more complex and difficult than printing on a press by any of the other major printing processes. Even with highly skilled craftsmen, printing on a lithographic press is subject to inconsistencies in the product and quality caused by many problems not encountered by the other processes. Lithographic presses *run slower, produce more waste,* and *require more manpower* than presses producing equivalent products by the other major printing processes.

Ink-Water Balance:　　Lithography's major problems are (a) the need for printing with two fluids — *ink and water* — and (b) the *delicate balance* which must be maintained between them. Most of the troubles encountered in lithographic printing are caused by variations in the ink-water balance. The basis of lithography is generally attributed to the concept that *oil (grease or ink) and water do not mix.* This concept is not entirely correct. For lithography to function the *ink and water must mix slightly!* Completely waterproof ink will not print on a lithographic press — the shadows will not stay open and the background will tone. If the ink absorbs too much water, it will waterlog, emulsify, become very short, and will not transfer from the ink rollers to the plate, plate to the blanket, or blanket to the paper. There is a very limited range of ink and water mixtures within which satisfactory lithographic printing can be accomplished, and this is known as the *ink-water balance.*

An appreciable part of the makeready time on a lithographic (offset) press is consumed in establishing an ink-water balance. Once this is achieved and the press continues to run, a dynamic equilibrium results and the printing is reasonably consistent; i.e., the ink densities on each sheet are relatively constant. *As soon as the press stops,* however, *the ink-water balance is destroyed, and it must be reestablished when the press is started up again.* In effect, the new start-up is similar to a new but shorter makeready. On a sheet-fed press it generally takes 10 to 15 sheets, and on a web press, 200 to 250 signatures before a new equilibrium is established. While this is within the limits of an acceptable ink-water balance, it is not always the same as the balance before the stop. This causes differences in ink densities and color balances in the lots printed between stops and accounts for the numerous variations in these throughout the run, which are characteristic of much lithographic printing. On sheet-fed presses waste sheets are used to reduce the waste, but on web presses the bad signatures must be discarded. In either case if the waste sheets or bad signatures are not removed they broaden the variability and can sometimes cause rejection of the job.

A number of printing defects are caused by the ink-water balance and the use of water in the lithographic process. *Mealiness* has already been mentioned as an appearance characteristic of lithographic printing. It is caused by water droplets on the surface of the ink on the image areas which, if excessive, can prevent transfer of ink to the image areas from the ink form rollers. In describing the lithographic principle the statement is usually made that because ink and water do not mix, water from the dampening rollers does not transfer to the ink on the image areas on the press and ink does not transfer to the water on the non-image areas. Actually, some water does transfer to the image area and because the ink is hydrophobic, the water breaks up into tiny droplets about 0.001 inch (0.03 mm) in diameter. Some of the drops coalesce and get large enough to interfere with the transfer of ink from the ink form rollers. Others mix into the ink creating a water-in-ink emulsion which transfers to the blanket and if enough water droplets are present can transfer to the paper when the ink splits on the blanket, causing the little white spots in the printing, sometimes called *snowflaking* or *snowflaky solids* (Figure III-22, page 74). Alcohol dampening solutions, quick-set, and emulsion inks have helped to reduce this defect.

Other printing defects caused by the ink-water balance and/or the use of water in lithographic printing include: *misregister; paper curling; buckling and wrinkling; ink piling; coating piling-image* and *non-image; tinting; picking, hickies and spots.* Most of these have both a direct and indirect effect on print quality: direct, because the appearance of the print is affected; indirect, because the defects like paper curling, buckling, or wrinkling affect the runability of paper on the press causing frequent stops, which, because of the changes in ink-water balance, result in increased variations and fluctuations in ink and color balance of the printed products. Some of these image defects are illustrated and described in Figure III-28, page C-3.

Many of these defects are caused by deviations in paper properties and variations in ink and dampening solution characteristics such as *amount of solution,* its *composition, pH,* and *temperature.* A number of means of minimizing these defects have been developed. New dampening systems like the Dahlgren have been introduced which use some alcohol in the dampening solution. These cause less changes in the print due to dampening, and establish ink-water balances after press stops in less time and with less waste. Refrigerated dampening solutions, mixers and recirculators are also used to stabilize dampening action on the press. New emulsion type inks with 15–30% emulsified water (depending on the pigment) increase dampening latitude, accelerate reestablishment of the ink-water balance, reduce waste and print sharper with less dot gain.

Trapping: While *trapping* is a problem in lithographic (offset) printing, it is not nearly as serious as in letterpress (direct) printing. There are several reasons for this. Lithographic inks are more viscous, tackier, and stronger (pigment strength) than letterpress inks so thinner ink films are used. In addition, the double ink split between plate and blanket and blanket and paper on an offset press results in thinner ink films which are tackier than the thicker films used on direct letterpress presses so they set faster and trap better.

There is a condition of *back-trapping* or transferring of inks on multi-color offset presses which does not exist on multi-color direct printing presses. Since the ink is still wet on the print as the sheet travels from one impression to the next, some of it transfers from the print to the succeeding blanket causing a build-up of all preceeding colors on the blankets. Besides causing doubling and aggravating dot gain, this condition can sometimes cause problems with ink and coating piling and/ or picking on the last or second to the last blanket because, as the ink on these blankets starts to dry, it gets tacky and creates an additional pull on the paper which can cause the types of defects mentioned if the paper is weak or has poor water resistance.

Color Sequence: In process color reproduction little regard is usually given to the color ink sequence in printing. In principle, as long as the color inks are transparent, it should be possible to print them in any order and obtain the same results. Unfortunately, this is not true for two main reasons: (1) the color inks are not completely *transparent* and (2) the *trappping* characteristics of the inks can cause color differences due to changes in ink sequence. This problem has been studied by the IARIGAI "Working Group on Standardization" and results of their study has been published in Publication No. 1 "Ink Sequence in Process Color Printing." This was also one of the factors covered in the study on SWOP Standards conducted by The Graphic Communications Association (GCA) in 1982 with 16 printers who printed test targets on the same form with advertising films and reported in the "Quality Control Scanner" Volume 3, Number 6.

There are 24 possible combinations of the three color process inks: *yellow, magenta,* and *cyan,* and *black.* The traditional sequence of the colors in printing has been yellow, magenta, cyan and black (Y-M-C-K). The main reason for this sequence was the fact that the yellow pigment used was a derivative of lead chromate which was opaque so it had to be printed first down; otherwise if printed over other colors it would hide them and not produce overprint colors. The introduction of transparent yellow pigments like benzidine yellow, created opportunities for changing the color sequence in printing. When this was done considerable improvements in color quality especially of overprints was noticed on many jobs.

Indiscriminate changing of color sequence, however, resulted in many changes in color and inability to match the colors on jobs printed with the same inks and paper but with different ink sequences. It was found that the color process inks were not completely transparent and in color printing the subject always had a slight cast of the last color printed. In the IARIGAI study it was noted that the lack of transparency of most commercial inks is small so the variations in color are barely noticeable in most instances but with other types of inks, such as heat-set inks used in web offset printing, the opacity can be sufficient to cause significant color variations when sequence changes.

As important as transparency, are the trapping characteristics of the inks. One of the reasons for changing the Y-M-C-K sequence is the fact that most subjects contain a lot of yellow. With yellow printing first most of the subject area on the paper is covered with ink which causes trapping problems right from the start as ink transfers better to blank paper than to wet ink. Printing yellow last improves trapping as more of the other inks print on the paper with less overprinting. When most printing was done with the Y-M-C-K sequence, process inks were graded in tack with yellow having the highest and black the lowest tack. This assures sufficient tack at transfer so that as much ink transfers to the wet ink as to the blank paper. With changing sequences most process ink sets are supplied with the same tack and depend on the ink "tacking up" between printings or units. The extent to which this occurs depends on the speed of the press and the distance between units. Tack at the instant of transfer, therefore, depends on speed and time between transfers. These become very critical on high speed and common impression cylinder (CIC) presses.

Interestingly, both studies reported that the most popular sequence of colors for process color printing are cyan, magenta and yellow (C-M-Y) with black printed before, after or between the colors. In the GCA study, which was limited to web offset printing, 14 of the 16 printers used this sequence; only one used the traditional Y-M-C-K sequence. The IARIGAI study covers all process color printing in Germany (FOGRA) and Switzerland (UGRA) and presses from single to four color. Their results are as follows:

IARIGAI COLOR SEQUENCE STUDIES
FOGRA and UGRA

Type of Press	Ink Sequence
4-color	K-C-M-Y
2-color	C-M-K-Y
Single Color and Proofing	C-M-Y-K

Other factors found in the IARIGAI study that are associated with color sequence and can affect the appearance of the final print are: *back-trapping* which is serious if black ink contaminates the colors; *dot gain* with the recommendation that the colors important to the reproduction, like yellow and magenta in fleshtints, be kept at the end of the sequence; *gray balance* which is affected mostly by magenta; *moiré patterns* especially in reds and greens caused by the 15° angle between yellow and magenta or cyan; and *register* problems with the recommendation to put the color with least visual contrast, yellow, on the unit causing the problem.

In the GCA study it was found that the C-M-Y printing order, despite poor trapping, had a self correcting effect on overprint colors. To the human eye both cyan and magenta appear to be contaminated: cyan by magenta, and magenta by yellow causing cyan and magenta overprints (blue) to appear too purple and yellow and magenta overprints (red) to appear too orange. Color correction during color separation should correct this but not completely. If magenta overprints yellow (Y-M) as in the Y-M-C order, even with 100% trapping the overprint would be too orange; but if yellow overprints magenta (M-Y) as in the C-M-Y order, the insufficient trapping of the yellow over the magenta produces a better red with less orange and more blue. A similar situation occurs with the blue overprint. With the M-C order the reduced cyan over the magenta produces a blue that is too purple: with the C-M order the blue has less red and is cleaner.

These studies have shown that there is no one correct or optimum color sequence for printing all process color. The preferred order appears to be cyan, magenta and yellow (C-M-Y) with the black before after or in between. If a sequence is adopted as standard, inks can be graded in tack so trapping can be more consistent and controllable. Also standardization of sequence can assure more consistent results when the subjects are printed on more than one press or in different locations especially in web offset where heat-set inks with less transparency are used. In any case color sequence should be an important factor to consider in making off-press proofs to match press prints.

Dot Gain: All the printing defects in lithography mentioned so far are the result of poor operating skills and/or the use of defective materials, improper techniques or controls. They are correctable or convertible to a constant or reproducible base by the use of reasonable skills, care, and proper materials, techniques and controls. On the other hand, *dot gain*, *dot spread* or *press gain*, as it is also called, is a characteristic defect of offset lithography (Figure III-29). It is a built-in integral part of the offset lithographic printing process, and even though it can vary on the same press and from press to press, it must be predicted and simulated when

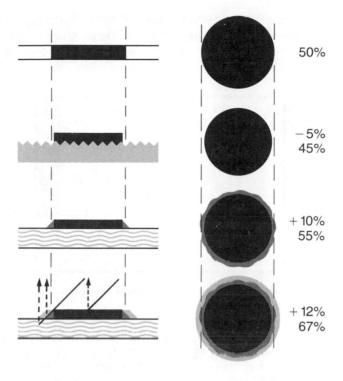

Figure III-29. Factors contributing to dot gain from the positive film to the press print. (DuPont)

making press or off-press proofs to match press prints. It is the most important characteristic of the press print that the proof must duplicate for it to be considered an acceptable representation of the press print.

There are two types of dot gain: *optical* and *physical*. Optical dot gain is present whenever ink or toner is transferred to paper. This occurs with all printing and proofing processes and is due to internal reflections and light refractiveness within the paper. This is described in the section on *Paper Types*. Physical dot gain is a mechanical enlargement of dot size which can occur in contacting negative and positive films in photography, in platemaking, and during printing on the press, particularly in lithography. Physical dot gain that occurs on the press (often called *press gain)* can be *symmetrical* or *circumferential* — i.e., even all around the dot; *directional* as in *slurring;* and/or *irregular* as in *doubling.*

Physical or mechanical dot gain is a printing phenomenon which is caused on an offset press by the spread of ink during the impression when the inked image is transferred from the plate to the blanket and the blanket to the paper or other printing substrate. A number of studies of the mechanism of both optical and physical dot gain have been made.

Notable among these have been the studies by RIT (Sigg, 1970), DuPont (Brunner, 1979) and PIRA (Johnson, 1980). These studies are summarized and evaluated in Appendix C - Measurement and Control of Dot Gain.

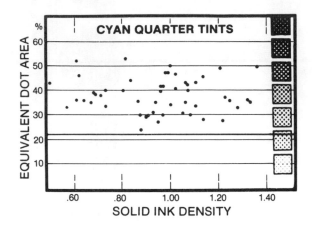

Figure III-30. Extent of dot gain found in LTF/GATF first Color Survey in 1958. 240 lithographic plants printed the same target and sent results to LTF/GATF for analysis. This shows variations in dot sizes from 23% cyan tint of over 30%. Plotting them against ink strengths shows no correlation. (GATF)

Dot gain or spread, if consistent, can be simulated in press and off-press color proofs in a number of ways as will be described in the sections on these color proofing processes. Unfortunately, dot gain is not consistent and this has imposed some very serious limitations on both the press and off-press color proofing systems. The extent of dot gain variations in printing is illustrated in Figure III-30. This is a plot of the results of one of the tests made in the first GATF Color Survey (1957). It shows the range of dot sizes printed from the 23% dot area of a standard film sent to 240 printers who cooperated in the survey. All the targets measured were from subjects printed on sheet-fed presses.

Table III–I (reprinted from the Quality Control Scanner, Graphic Arts Publishing Co., Livonia, NY, Vol. 2, No. 9) shows variations in dot gains of standard tints printed by 16 web offset printers in a study conducted in 1982 by the Print Properties Committee of the Graphic Communications Association (GCA) of the Printing Industries of America (PIA). The test target was the 40% tint on the GATF proofing bars negative.

The reason for the inconsistencies in dot gain or spread is the large number of factors that can affect dot gain such as *screen ruling, type of paper, paper color, press speed, ink film thickness, ink temperature, ink strength, impression pressure, cylinder diameters, types of blankets, slur, doubling, fill-in,* and *scumming.* Each of these factors will be discussed separately.

TABLE III-I

WEB OFFSET PRINTED DOT GAIN
(GCA — 1982)

40% tint on GATF Proofing Bars

Color	120 line screen			150 line screen		
	min.	*max.*	*ave.*	*min.*	*max.*	*ave.*
Cyan	52	74	60	57	82	64
Magenta	52	70	60	56	73	65
Yellow	53	65	63	56	84	67
Black	58	84	68	56	84	70

Screen Ruling: The effects of screen ruling on dot gain were studied by S. Rosen, graduate student at RIT and reported in The Quality Control Scanner, Vol. 2, No. 9, mentioned above. As the screen ruling increased from 65-line to 150-line dot gain increased in the middletones. The dot gain was independent of the paper and was only 2% for the 65-line screen, 15% for 120-line and 28% for the 150-line screen. The curves are illustrated in Figure III-31. Most control targets for lithography (such as the GATF Dot Gain Scale described in this chapter) use this relationship of dot gain to screen ruling by making the screen ruling in the target finer than the ruling in the printing. (Most targets have a range of screen rulings.) Any variation in printing conditions that can cause dot gain will show on the control target before it affects the printing so it can be corrected before any serious damage to the image is done.

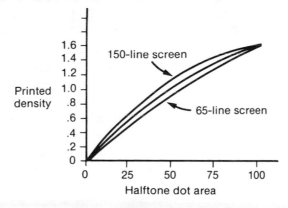

Figure III-31. Influence of screen ruling on dot gain — from Quality Control Scanner, Vol. 2, No. 9. (GAP)

Paper Types: There are three major categories of paper types: *uncoated*, which includes newsprint, roto news, some magazine papers, most book paper, bond and text grades, *coated*, which includes most magazine papers, high finish and glossy papers for covers, books advertising, and promotion; and *cast-coated*, which includes the very high finish papers like Kromekote and Lustercote. Each of the paper types has widely different properties mainly associated with *brightness, gloss, smoothness, ink absorptivity,* and *refractiveness,* or *light absorption within the paper.* Most of these factors affect actual or apparent (optical and/or mechanical) dot gain as well as hue and grayness of printed color, factors studied by Preucil (GATF, 1963) and Leekley (Institute of Paper Chemistry, 1978).

Uncoated papers are very ink absorptive, require thick films of ink, and print with considerable dot gain. In addition, uncoated papers have high refractiveness with considerable surface and internal reflections which lower the light refectance and darken the paper between halftone dots so that these areas exhibit considerable optical dot spread.

Uncoated papers also exhibit *two-sidedness* (except papers made on twin-wire machines). Paper made on a conventional Fourdrinier paper machine has two sides: a bottom or *wire* side which is in contact with the wire on the machine; and a top or *felt* side which contacts the felts in the drying section of the machine. The appearance and printing characteristics of the two sides are different. The wire side is rougher than the felt side as the fillers and fine fibers can drain out of the wire and often the wire pattern can actually be seen by low angle illumination. The felt side is preferred for printing as it is smoother and has more even absorption of ink. The wire side is stronger and is preferred when very tacky inks must be used and quality is not important.

The effects of two-sidedness are most noticeable on color jobs with *crossovers,* which are illustrations that cover parts of two adjoining pages. In many crossovers part of the illustration is on the felt side of the paper and the other part is on the wire side. Since both sides print differently, corrections must be made in the films for one side to match the other side. Crossovers are often on different signatures. Where different papers are used in the same publication, crossovers may involve paper of one type on one side of the illustration and another type on the other side. In the planning of color reproduction the color separator and proofer should be aware of crossovers, how they will lay out and print. Paper from twin-wire machines have less two-sidedness. Both sides print about the same — better than the conventional wire side and slightly poorer than the felt side.

Coated papers are not affected as much by two-sidedness and show less of the effects of uncoated papers. Cast-coated papers show the least.

Paper Color: The color, brightness and fluorescence of the paper can have selective effects on optical dot gain particularly in the highlights and lighter tints where the paper surface is partially exposed. The effect in the middletones and shadows is obscured by the ink unless the printing is on brightly colored or pigmented paper. A buff shade of an off-white paper will optically appear to increase the size of yellow and red dots and reduce the effect of cyan dots so that a tint of yellow, magenta and cyan dots that print a neutral gray on a neutral paper will appear pinkish on the buff paper. A blue tinted or fluorescent brightened paper with blue reflectance will optically increase the size of the cyan and magenta dots and reduce the effect of yellow dots resulting in the neutral tint appearing bluish. The effects of paper color, brightness and fluorescence on printed colors can be checked using a rotating motor jig and Maxwell type discs of printed ink segments and discs of paper samples (Figure III-32, page C-4). These color shifts reemphasize the need for using the same paper or substrate for proof and press print.

Press Speed: The faster the press runs the sharper is the printing and the lower and more consistent is the dot gain. Press speed is, therefore, another variable that can be controlled and factored into the proof equation.

Ink Film Thickness: The thicker the ink film the greater is the dot gain. In fact, *dot gain increases as the square of the ink film thickness* (see Appendix C — PIRA Study). This is a very important factor and is the main reason highly pigmented (strong) inks are used in lithography. With such inks satisfactory ink densities are printed with relatively thin films which produce minimum dot gain. There are, however, limits on pigment strength and thinness of ink films. Inks with high pigment loading print with lower gloss and less brilliance. As ink films reduce in thickness, separation or ink splitting forces increase until incomplete ink coverage is reached. As the separation forces increase so does the tack of the ink which can cause picking of the paper and even splitting or tearing. With thinner ink films stronger papers are required to resist the additional forces that cause picking. Also ink film thickness on the press, measured with a Gardner Ink Film Thickness Gauge, should not be less than 0.0002 inch (0.005 mm) or images on plates will wear due to insufficient lubrication of the ink during the impression. (See Chapter X.)

The trend in publication and advertising printing is toward the use of lighter weight papers to offset rising mailing costs. Thinner papers are weaker so a compromise must be made between the papers and the ink film thickness. This, therefore, is a variable that the pressman has to contend with and try to control. When picking occurs his first option is to soften the ink which reduces its tack and strength so he needs to run a thicker ink film to achieve the same ink density and this increases dot gain. If papers and inks are tested in advance on printability testers this variable can be minimized.

Ink Strength: It is a common misconception among printers that the stronger a color is run on the press, the wider the gamut of color, the brighter the colors and the higher the visual contrast it produces. In other words the color is more efficient. This would be true if the pigments used in the process color inks were ideal, had single color absorptions (yellow-blue, magenta-green, cyan-red) and had no unwanted absorptions or contamination by other colors (yellow in magentas and magenta and yellow in cyans). The problem of ink strength was studied and reported by M. Edelmann of C. H. Lorilleux, Paris, France, in 1958, and Frank Preucil, GATF, in 1965. Edelmann called his function *Vivacity* and Preucil called it *Visual Color Efficiency.*

These studies showed that the stronger a color was printed the brighter it became until it reached a maximum brightness and gamut beyond which it increased in grayness and became dirtier. Preucil found that optimum color strength is a function of the grayness of the ink (see Appendix A). The cleaner an ink is, i.e., the lower its grayness, the more efficiently it prints high densities. The higher the grayness the lower the maximum density at which optimum strength is reached and the ink becomes grayer or dirtier as its density increases. This relation of percent grayness to visual color efficiency is shown in the curves in Figure III-33. The effects of increasing ink strengths on tints is even more startling than on solids. There are actual color reversals in the tints. Instead of

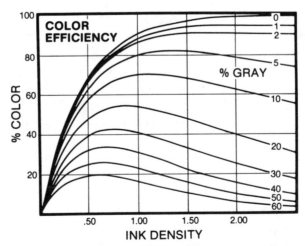

Figure III-33. Effects of percent grayness in inks on their visual color efficiency. The higher the percent grayness of an ink the grayer (dirtier) it becomes as its strength is increased. (GATF)

mixtures of yellow and cyan dots becoming greener as cyan ink strength is increased with constant yellow ink strength, they go through maximum green and then reverse and appear yellower.

This information stresses the importance of making a proof and press print at the same ink density or strength and using the same pigments in both. Otherwise the color reversal and graying effects will be different causing variations in the appearance of the reproductions that would be difficult to evaluate, analyze or interpret.

Ink Temperature: The temperature of the ink is an important factor in dot gain as it affects ink viscosity and rheology which in turn affect ink wetting and spreading. Most modern web offset presses have temperature controlled distributing rollers in the inking system on the press. Some systems have been designed for sheet-fed presses, especially for use in connection with the running of waterless plates.

Impression Pressure: The higher the impression pressure or squeeze between plate and blanket and blanket and paper, the more the ink will spread and the higher will be the dot gain. Good pressmen try to run with minimum pressures. There must be enough squeeze to maintain contact between the cylinders overall. Cylinders are ground to close tolerances of ±0.0005 inch (0.013 mm). Plates have tolerances of ±0.001 inch, (0.025 mm); blankets have tollerances of ± 0.001 inch, and packing sheets have tolerances of ±0.0005 inch. Therefore, in order to insure overall contact of the plate, blanket and impression cylinders, squeeze of at least 0.003 inch (0.076 mm) must be used. This is equivalent to an impression band of about 3/16 inch (4.8 mm) which amounts to an impression pressure of about 50 pounds per lineal inch (8.9 kg/cm) or about 200 pounds per square inch (.36 kg/cm²). As long as this pressure does not vary, the dot gain will be reasonably constant.

The pressure, however, can vary. If the packing sheets are soft they can mat under the plate and blanket and printing pressure is reduced. As the pressure decreases the image lightens or loses density and the pressman usually compensates for it by increasing the ink feed and ink film thickness which increases dot gain and eventually must be compensated by increasing the dampening feed. This chain of events disturbs the ink-water balance and ink and color balance are changed. Before the pressman realizes what has happened several thousand sheets or signatures can be wasted.

Impression pressure can also change by blankets swelling due to the action of incompatible solvents in the inks or the blanket washes. The higher pressure causes increased dot gain and higher ink densities. A reverse chain of events occurs and ink-water balance is again disturbed and more sheets and signatures are wasted. The test of a skilled craftsman is the pressman's ability to recognize these events when they occur and deal with them expeditiously so he can maintain a dynamic equilibrium and print continuously with minimum interruptions and waste. This is a variable that could be difficult to factor into a proof equation.

Cylinder Diameters: Plate and blanket cylinders should be packed so that they have the same effective diameters and therefore run at the same speed. Even though plate and blanket cylinders are packed so they have the same physical diameters, when impression squeeze is applied to the two cylinders as during printing, the effective diameters change. Since the rubber blanket on the blanket cylinder is elastic and deforms under impression, it collects or bulges in the entrance and exit sides of the nip and behaves as though it has a larger diameter (Figure III-34). In such a configuration the blanket cylinder is effectively driving the plate cylinder (and the impression cylinder which is also rigid) and this can vary dot gain and distort dot shapes.

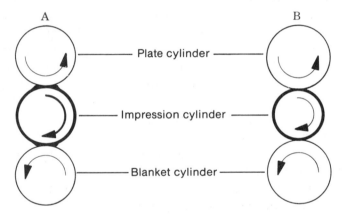

Figure III-34. **True Rolling Concept.** (A) If plate, blanket and impression cylinders are packed to equal diameters the blanket cylinder acts larger and drives the other two. (B) For all cylinders to travel at the same surface speed ("True rolling") blanket cylinder must be underpacked 0.0005 inch (0.01 mm) for each inch (25 mm) of cylinder diameter.

To compensate for the apparent differences in diameters and surface speeds, the plate cylinder is overpacked so it has a larger diameter than the blanket cylinder which is underpacked an equivalent amount and the squeeze pressure is split between the two cylinders. The amount of over and underpacking can be calculated mathematically but is approximately 0.0005 inch (0.013 mm) *for each inch (25 mm) of cylinder diameter;* i.e., with 8 inch (203 mm) diameter cylinders the plate cylinder is packed about 0.004 inch (0.11 mm) above bearers, and the blanket cylinder is packed about 0.001 inch (0.025 mm) below bearers, allowing 0.003 inch (0.076 mm) squeeze for impression pressure. The impression cylinder is the same diameter as the plate cylinder. This is known as "True Rolling,"a concept developed by Albert Kuehn and Ben Sites in the Research Department of Miehle Printing Press Company, now a division of Rockwell International.

If the plate blanket and impression cylinders are not all of the same effective diameter, there is a tendency for the blanket cylinder to drive the others, resulting in slippage which causes excessive plate wear and serious distortions in the printing elements such as directional dot spread or *slurring*. The use of compressible blankets alleviates this condition and minimizes the wear and distortion effects on the image. Presses in Europe do not ride on bearers and pressure compensations are made by using helical gears. Press cylinder packing is a pressman's responsibility and must be monitored constantly under optimum operating conditions.

Types of Blankets: In general, two types of blankets are in regular use: *conventional* and *compressible*. Most conventional blankets are composed of mixtures of natural and synthetic rubber composition layers over a special fabric base. Some are composed of special synthetic rubber composition with solvent resistance so they do not swell when used with high-solvent heat-set type inks. Compressible blankets are made with a thin rubber layer over a compressible cellular fibrous base as in the W.R. Grace Polyfibron blanket or with a plastic compressible layer between the rubber surface and the fabric back as in most of the other compressible blankets.

Natural rubber and synthetic rubber composition is soft and elastic so it can conform to surface irregularities like rough uncoated papers, but they are not compressible — they *distort* under pressure. When pressure is exerted in one area the displaced rubber causes a deformation in the neighboring area (Figure III-35). On conventional blankets the deformation, especially in the nip, can cause slippage of the blanket particularly on coated paper in dot areas from middletones to solids, resulting in directional distortion of the dot gain called *slurring*. The ink acts as a lubricant. In highlight and dot size areas approaching the middletones which are surrounded by non-printing open areas no slippage occurs and dots retain their conventional shape. In middletone areas and larger dot sizes up to solids, where the perimeters of the dots join neighboring dots, the lubricating action of the ink causes the blanket nip to slip through the impression resulting in the image distortion or defect known as slurring.

Compressible blankets, on the other hand, compress under impression and do not exhibit the accumulation of rubber in the nip even under moderately excessive impression pressure. Therefore, compressible blan-

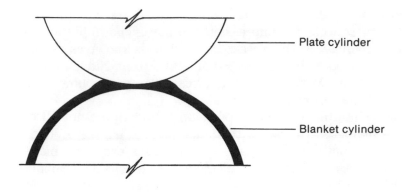

Figure III-35. Distortions in the nip between conventional blankets and the plate cylinder.

kets are more tolerant to pressure changes, do not distort image elements, and maintain more consistent dot gain, dot sizes, and dot shapes during printing. The use of compressible blankets improves the consistency of lithographic printing and simplifies the correlation of off-press color proofs to press prints as they help to stabilize the most elusive variable in lithographic printing — dot gain. Despite these obvious advantages appreciable lithography is still printed with conventional blankets.

Slur: Slur is a directional image element (dot) distortion occurring in middletone to solid areas mainly on coated paper (Figure III-36). The mechanism of slurring was described in the previous section. It is caused by slippage of the blanket in the nip and is aggravated by excessive back, or impression cylinder pressure and thick ink films which increase the lubricating action of the ink. It is corrected by reducing back cylinder pressure to a minimum, running as thin an ink film as possible without causing picking and plate wear problems, and using compressible blankets. Slur is a printing defect that cannot be incorporated in the off-press proof and should be corrected on the press.

Doubling: Doubling is a printing defect that can appear like slur in the shadows but is also in the highlights and usually varies from sheet to sheet. Doubling generally occurs in multicolor printing. The ink from the first color printed is picked up from the sheet by the second blanket and prints back on the next sheet. If the press is printing in exact register, the back printing causes no problem except a slight increase in dot size. If the press is not printing in exact register, a ghost or lighter dot prints between the original dots and increases the tone and color value (Figure III-37).

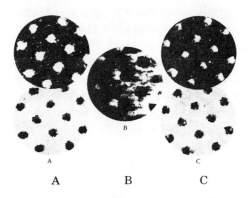

Figure III-36. Slur due to slippage of blanket in middle-tone to solid areas. A) normal print; B) unusually bad; C) slight slur. (GATF)

Figure III-37. Comparison of normal halftone and halftone with doubling. (GATF)

The misregister can be caused by end play in any of the press cylinders, backlash in cylinder gears, excessive wear in the gear train or bearings, and on sheet-fed presses by sheets slipping in the grippers. Doubling can also occur on a single-color press by wavy, tight-edged or buckled paper prematurely contacting the blanket before the impression and picking up ghost dots out of register with the actual printing. Like slur, doubling cannot be duplicated on an off-press proof and should be recognized and corrected on the press.

Fill-in: Fill-in is similar to slur but is usually symmetrical. It is a filling in of the deep shadow tones caused by thick films of soft ink and excessive pressure. It is actually extreme dot gain which can be reduced by using stronger inks and thinner ink films.

Scumming: Scumming is a printing condition in which the non-printing areas lose their desensitization or affinity for water, and take ink. Its effect is to darken the non-printing areas between the dots and create an effect similar to excessive optical dot gain. It can be caused by an *improperly made plate; too soft an ink; too much ink; too much acid, like oleic acid, in the ink; abrasive pigment in the ink; too much plate-to-blanket pressure; improper ink or dampening roller settings;* and *worn or dirty dampening rollers.* The scum is permanent and must be removed by washing the plate with a solvent and desensitizing the non-image areas on the plate with a plate etch, gumming, and drying. In most instances it is more economical to make a new plate.

Other Image Defects: Other printing defects such as *ink set-off, show through, strike through, tinting, ghosting, gloss ghosting,* and *chemical staining* can affect the appearance of images, but they are definitely printing problems that should be corrected by the pressman before press prints are considered acceptable. With all of the potential problems and factors that can affect image quality and consistency in lithography, it is almost a miracle that the process works so well and leads the other processes in use. Fortunately for lithography off-press color proofs are not expected to simulate all the image defects: they must be capable of being matched by the press OK sheets which are considered representative of the press run. Trying to match any other sheet in a lithographic run could be a risky gamble.

Other Planographic Processes

There are four other planographic processes that are related to lithography which are used to a small extent for color reproduction and provide limited markets for off-press color proofs. They are: *dry offset,* or *letterset; waterless lithography* or *driography; collotype;* and *screenless lithography.*

Letterset: Dry offset or letterset is not strictly a planographic process like lithography, but it uses an offset press. The plates are relief wraparound plates, but with much shallower relief than letterpress. The process marries most of the advantages of letterpress and offset lithography but inherits some of the limitations of lithography.

Advantages are:

- Makeready is even less than lithography as there is no ink-water balance.
- Ink trapping is improved over letterpress but not as good as lithography.
- Acceptable quality printing can be done on rough surface stocks.
- Color variations in printing are much less than lithography with printing consistency almost equivalent to letterpress.

- Waste is much less than lithography and almost equal to letterpress; letterpress papers and inks can be used for printing.

Limitations are:

- Inks must be softer and with less tack than lithographic inks to prevent picking and tearing of paper.
- Dot gain is between lithography and letterpress.
- Misregister and paper wrinkling can be due to wavy or tight edge paper.

The advantages far outweigh the limitations making letterset a reasonably controllable and predictable process susceptible to monitoring with off-press color proofing. It is used extensively in metal decorating and to some extent in packaging.

Waterless Lithography: *Driography,* as this process was called by 3M, was introduced in 1970 and withdrawn from the market in 1977. The process was planographic and eliminated the need for water in printing by using a silicone rubber in the non printing areas which did not wet with ink and therefore printed clean. The plate had an aluminum base coated with a diazo sensitizer and a layer of silicone rubber. After exposure to a negative and development, the image consisted of ink on metal and the non-image areas consisted of silicone rubber. The silicone rubber had a very low surface energy and had good resistance to wetting by ink, but it had a tendency to tone on the press after several thousand impressions due to increased ink temperature and continual contact by the inked rollers. Modifying the ink composition and using temperature controlled inking systems helped but not enough to make it a reliable process.

TORAY of Japan introduced a similar process in 1977 called *Waterless Lithography.* It differs from the 3M process in that the plate is made from positives and the silicone rubber in the non-image areas is cured by exposure making it more resistant to wear and toning on the press. In addition special inks have been developed for the process. The TORAY proces has been successful on runs as high as 85,000 in Japan and has produced similar results on tests in the United States. It has not been popular in the United States because not much lithographic printing is done from positives except some web offset magazine printing and label and packaging printing where new subjects are combined with old subjects which are already on positive films. A negative process has been developed. The process appears to be capable of quality printing with high color densities on coated stock and good uniformity of product with minimum waste. How it will print on other stocks remains to be learned.

The absence of water on the blanket could cause excessive debris and heating effects which can cause toning — the main reason for the withdrawal of the 3M process.

Collotype: Sometimes called photogelatin, collotype is a continuous tone process used mainly for short runs of art reproductions, posters, counter cards, etc., using bichromated gelatin and an ink-water principle of printing not like lithography. Glass plates were used originally on hand-fed flatbed presses, but metal plates are now used on old direct-printing poster presses. Continuous tone negatives are exposed on plates coated with bichromated gelatin. After exposure the plate is developed in water and dried, during which process the gelatin reticulates and forms a structure for retaining ink during printing. Before printing, the plates are soaked for about 30 minutes in a solution of essentially glycerin and water, during which the gelatin swells in inverse proportion to the amount of exposure it received. The highlights which received little exposure swell the most; the shadow areas which received a lot of exposure swell the least; and the areas that received intermediate exposures swell accordingly. The plate is mounted on the press and printed with a very viscous ink and a means for controlling the relative humidity of the atmosphere in the pressroom.

The printing is started with a reduced ink at fairly low humidity. As prints are made from the plate, the ink is stiffened and the relative humidity is gradually increased until it can no longer maintain image contrast, at which time the printing is stopped; the plate is resoaked in the glycerin and water solution, and the RH is reduced. After about 20 minutes of resoaking the cycle of varying ink and RH is resumed and printing proceeds for another 300–500 impressions. It is the most critical and demanding of the printing processes. Actually, because the tone reproduction of the print depends on the moisture content of gelatin and this varies with each print made, no two prints are exactly alike. Off-press color proofing can be useful as a guide to determine the adequacy of the original negatives to reproduce the original.

Screenless Printing: The screenless printing process has been around long enough for a patent on the process to expire. The patent issued to M. Ruderman was so restrictive that it discouraged use and development of the process. Now that the patent has expired, there is more activity in this area again.

Screenless lithography uses continuous tone positives and photopolymer lithographic plates which are printed on lithographic presses with conventional inks and dampening systems. A number of plate systems can be used; Howson Algraphy and Enco Printing Products have plates particularly suited for the process. As would be expected the tone reproduction of the press print depends on the tone reproduction of the positive and that of the plate. The tone reproduction of the plate depends on the roughness (or smoothness) of the plate surface and the thickness of the sensitive coating on the plate which are interdependent variables; i.e., the coating thickness varies with the roughness of the plate surface. Platemaking is a critical exposure-development process in which the tone reproduction curve varies with the exposure and development of the plate.

After the plate is made and mounted on the press, the handling on the press is no different than any other lithographic plate. In fact, it has been reported that the plate is much more tolerant to ink thickness variations. As ink-densities are increased, shadows do not fill in as in halftone printing. Effects similar to dot gain appear to be minimized. The printing on positive plates is from the depths of the grain, and it has a grainy appearance similar to the reticulation of collotype printing. Screenless printing is being used commercially and could find more applications as controls are developed for the process. One of the important controls it will need is an off-press color proofing system with continuous tone capability.

Gravure

Appearance Characteristics

Gravure printing can be detected readily in type and line matter as it has irregular serrated edges which are characteristic of gravure and are caused by the cells in all gravure image areas (Figure III–38). Some techniques have been developed for evening out the serrated edges in line images by the use of finer screens and multiple exposures but it is still evident under high magnification.

Laser

Figure III-38. Enlargement of gravure printing showing serrated edges of line printing due to image cell structure.

Gravure picture image elements have different appearances under magnification depending on the type of cylinder making process used. *Conventional* gravure has elements of the same size which vary in depth (see Figure II-19) that result in images with elements which vary in ink density or strength but not in size. Actually the very soft liquid ink that is used for printing spreads after transfer so that the final image is a mixture of small ink areas varying in density with practically indistinguishable individual cell elements or boundaries (Figure III—14D, page C-4). The visual effect of a color reproduction under magnification is a mish-mash, but without magnification is essentially continuous tone with highly saturated colors that are not dirtied by internal reflections or refractiveness in the paper because all of the surface of the paper in the image areas is covered with ink.

Variable area/variable depth gravure consists of image elements of variable shape and density. The ink spread during transfer makes some of the dot shapes irregular and fills in the shadows, but in the middletone and highlight areas the individual elements vary in size and density and are visible under magnification even though they are spread and distorted. Images produced from cylinders made on electromechanical engravers like the Hell Helioklischograph are of the variable area/variable depth type and have characteristic diamond shapes (see Figure II-21).

Variable area/direct transfer gravure consists of image elements of variable size (see Figure II-20). The soft ink spreads during transfer making the dots irregular in shape but still evident. The dots are all essentially of the same density.

The characteristic gravure appearance defect of *dot skips* in the highlights (see Figure II-26) was mentioned in Chapter II. This defect has been minimized by the use of electrostatic assist on the press during printing, but it occasionally recurs and should be recognized as a paper surface deficiency.

Like letterpress, gravure also has a characteristic *mottle* in the shadow areas. Unlike letterpress, it is an ink flow phenomenon and appears like fish scales, ink creeping or crawling (Figure III-39). It can usually be corrected by adjusting the viscosity and flow properties of the ink.

Figure III-39. Mottle in gravure printing due to ink creeping or crawling.

Gravure Cylinder Making

Gravure plate and cylinder making is the most difficult of the platemaking processes to carry out and control and consequently requires extensive training and exceptional skills. As already stated, gravure is a form of intaglio printing in which the image consists of wells, or cells, engraved in a copper-plated steel cylinder with the walls, or boundaries, of the cells at the same height as the cylinder surface. During printing the non-image areas are kept clean, or free of ink, by a doctor blade which removes the ink from these areas as it scrapes over the cylinder and the top surface of the cell walls. The tone reproduction and density range of the inked image depends on the *maximum* and *minimum depths of the cells;* the *range of depths;* the *relationship between them;* and all the *factors* in printing that *affect ink transfer,* including, but not limited to, *cell geometry; ink volume, viscosity,* and *surface tension* which affects *release from the cell; printing pressure;* and *paper or substrate characteristics like ink-wetting and elastic properties.*

One of the most complicating factors in gravure image reproduction is the fact that continuous tone, or variable density images are used. The conversion of the continuous tone values in the positives to correlated cell volumes in the plate cylinder is much more complicated and difficult to control than converting the same values to halftone dots for letterpress or lithographic platemaking. There is a mathematical relationship (Yule-Nielson Equation) between the dot areas on the halftones and the transmittance or reflectance of the original from which they are made so halftone processes are predictable and relatively easy to control (Appendix C). No such mathematical relationship exists between the tone values on a gravure positive and the corresponding cell depths or volumes on the gravure cylinder. The relationships are empirical and are affected by a number of dependent and independent variables. Halftone gravure conversion using electromechanical engraving will simplify this problem.

Conventional Gravure: As described in Chapter II, in conventional gravure the continuous tone positive and gravure screen are exposed in succession onto carbon tissue which is mounted on the copper-plated gravure cylinder and developed after which it serves as a resist for etching the cylinder. There are factors in each of these steps that affect the correlation between the tone values on the positive and the cell volumes in the printing cylinder.

The carbon tissue must first be sensitized in a solution of potassium bichromate, dried, and stored under refrigerated conditions. The *light sensitivity* of the carbon tissue and its rate of swelling which determines the exposure of the continuous tone positive and the screen depend on the *concentration of the bichromate solution;* its *pH;* the *bath tempera-*

ture; immersion time; drying and *storage conditions.* The *exposure* is further dependent on the *temperature; relative humidity; time between removal from storage and start of exposure;* and *time between end of exposure and development* (dark reaction) unless the tissue was returned to refrigerated storage (40°F) (5°C). Development is affected by the *temperature of the water* (90°–115°F)(32°–46°C), *complete removal of the unexposed bichromate,* and *uniform drying,* otherwise the etch penetrates unevenly. Amount and rate of etching is affected by *time;* the *swelling* of the gelatin; its *moisture content;* the *bath concentration;* its *temperature* and *pH;* the *relative humidity;* and the *composition of the electroplated copper.*

Keeping all these variables under control takes the skill of a master craftsman, and even with all his knowledge and experience, there are sufficient errors and deviations in the process to require considerable manual revisions and re-etching which are responsible for much of the high cost of gravure cylinders and the long time it takes to make them. The presence of these variables, their uncontrollability, and their unpredictability has been a main cause for the failure of off-press proofing and the reason proofing is done with the actual printing cylinder.

Variable Area/Variable Depth Gravure: Plate and cylinder making for variable area/variable depth gravure is plagued by all the same variables as conventional gravure plus others involved in the production of the halftone images and correlating the cell depths in the cylinders with the varying dot sizes in the halftones. The *halftones* have short tone reproduction scales, are produced by special gravure contact screens, and are affected by all the factors in making contact screen halftones such as: *type of film* and *developer; exposure time; color temperature of light source;* the *relation between flash, main and bump exposures; density range;* and *screen angles.* As with the other variables in carbon tissue sensitivity, exposure, development, and etching, any variations in the halftones can cause noticeable differences in the optical appearance of the print which are impossible to predict or duplicate in an off-press proof.

Direct Transfer Gravure: Because direct transfer gravure is strictly a halftone process which does not use carbon tissue or other type of resist, and the optical appearance of the print does not depend on variable depth of the cells, as all the cells are essentially the same depth, the process has less variables than the other gravure processes, and is more reproducible like lithography and letterpress. The use of the process, however, is limited to cereal, food, laundry packaging, and textiles where the short tone scale of the reproductions is secondary to consistency and long cylinder life.

Other Gravure Processes

Controlled Etching: Due to the large number of variables in conventional and variable area/variable depth gravure and the limited quality of direct transfer gravure, a number of other processes for making gravure cylinders that are more predictable and reproducible without sacrificing quality have been developed and introduced. Since etching has been the main source of variability, *controlled etching* processes like *Acigraf, Crosfield, and powderless etching,* as used in letterpress, have been introduced. While these processes have been responsible for improvements, they have not been entirely satisfactory, as the variables in halftone production and carbon tissue sensitivity, exposure, development, and swelling are serious enough to cause unpredictable and uncontrollable changes in reproduction.

Electromechanical Engraving: A more effective approach to cylinder reproducibility and control has been by the use of electronic processes. In these, the cylinders are produced by electronic scanning and electromechanical engraving of the images, which eliminates the two most serious causes of variations, the carbon tissue and the chemical etching. The first of these electronic scanners and electromechanical engravers was the Hell Helioklischograph first introduced in 1967, followed by the Ohio Electronic Engraver in 1978. Electromechanical engraving has been so successful in reducing variability and improving predictability and reproducibility of cylinders that it is now the preferred and accepted method of cylinder making for magazine and periodical printing which represents a large share of the gravure printing market.

As described in Chapter II the Helioklischograph scans positive or negative continuous tone prints on a white plastic base with a special photo-electric head which transmits the image information to a computer that in turn converts it to impulses relayed to a special engraving head that uses a diamond stylus to produce diamond-shaped pyramidal cells in the copper cylinder that vary in area and depth according to the tone values being reproduced (Figure III-40).

The system has sufficient reproducibility to encourage the use of off-press proofs. A number of these have been tried. DuPont has a Cromalin gravure proofing system. Rocap of Meredith-Burda has developed a system using Kodak RC-14 color paper. K&E has introduced the SPECTRA color proofing process for gravure. These systems are described in Chapter VIII. The KC-Gravure Proofing System developed by Coulter Systems Corporation is described in Chapter VII.

Since digital processing is used in the Helioklischograph, the input scanner can be replaced by an electronic color scanner or electronic color

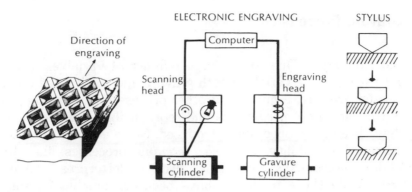

Figure III-40. Principle of the Hell Helioklischograph and mechanism of engraving. (GTA)

page make-up system, so that direct engraving can be done right from the original without the necessity for intermediate films and prints. Engraving can also be done off-line from digital data stored on a disc. In such systems there is no intermediate film from which off-press color proofs can be made. Soft proofing is done on CRT screens. Digital systems for making hard proofs were introduced at DRUPA 82 by Hell and Crosfield. Others, like Coulter Systems Corporation and Polaroid, are developing digital systems for making off-press color proofs. These digital color proofing systems are described in Chapter IX.

Even though electromechanical engraving eliminates carbon tissue and etching and their innumerable variables, it has some problems of its own. A major one is moirè which has been minimized by producing three shapes of cells — normal, elongated and compressed diamond shapes. These in effect change the frequency of the screen rulings which reduces moirè. A second problem is uneven development resulting in side to side variations in density on the continuous tone bromides. Another serious problem is uneven diamond wear in the engraving heads. As multiple engraving heads are used to cover the full width of the cylinder, the variation in density of the bromides and uneven diamond wear produce cells with uneven depths for the same tone values on the originals. Both these problems result in the need for expensive retouching or re-etching on the cylinders to even up the cell depths to produce even tone values.

Lasergravure: The Lasergravure system by Crosfield is another means introduced for producing gravure cylinders reproducibly. It is an electronic system in which cylinders coated with a special plastic are engraved with a laser to produce images consisting of cells with variable depths in helical grooves. A magnified view of a Lasergravure image is shown in Figure III-41. Since this is such an unusual image configuration not much is known about it; what its distinguishing characteristics are; and what affects them. The first system has been installed in England, and when more is learned about its printing characteristics and consistency, the feasibility of using off-press proofs to predict printability can be determined.

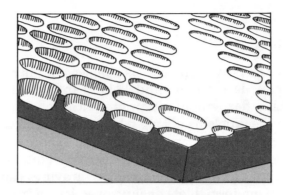

Figure III-41. Enlargement of Lasergravure image. (Crosfield)

Halftone-Gravure Conversion: A very promising approach to simplifying and reducing the cost of gravure cylinder production is the conversion of halftone positives made for lithographic printing to positives for gravure. Systems for accomplishing this have been known and used for a number of years but as long as the systems used carbon tissue and chemical etching they were subject to the numerous variables inherent in these steps and off-press color proofing was not satisfactory. At DRUPA 82 a number of new systems for halftone-gravure conversions were introduced using special reading heads on electromechanical engravers to convert halftone positives to engraved images on the cylinders. These processes show promise of reproducibility and control and, along with these, the economies of using off-press color proofing and making corrections on the halftone films instead of the printing cylinders.

The main reason the gravure industry has been attracted to the concept of halftone-gravure conversions has been the ease and economy of the pre-press operations for halftone systems like lithography and the availability of acceptable off-press color proofing systems for lithography. With the development of controllable and reproducible methods for converting from the halftone positive to the gravure printing cylinder to produce prints that resemble the litho proofs, the concept of an off-press color proof for gravure becomes a reality.

These systems will become important factors in the future expansion of gravure and will make it attractive and cost competitive in shorter run packaging, specialties and magazine printing (150,000) as they will benefit from the economies of halftones and off-press proofs, corrections directly on the films, and the reliability of electronic scanning and electromechanical engraving. Eventually gravure will develop a halftone system consistent with gravure press-print tone reproduction and compatible with lithography and conventional halftone off-press color proofing systems.

Gravure Printing

Printing by the gravure process is simpler and more straightforward than printing by letterpress and lithography and about equal to flexography. Like flexography, it prints with solvent inks and is not concerned with the problems of long ink trains; ink rheology like ink tack, trapping, and piling; and paper picking and piling which plague both letterpress and lithography; and the numerous additional problems that besiege lithography. Unlike flexography, gravure can produce color reproductions of uniform high quality over longer runs and at higher speeds than the other printing processes. And all the pressman has to worry about beside paper tension and the folder is ink viscosity, temperature, doctor blades, register controls, electrostatic assist, and between-unit dryers.

Most of these functions have automatic controls and once set allow the presses, which are up to 106 inches (269 cm) wide, to run at speeds in excess of 2,500 feet (762 meters) per minute — almost double the speeds at which letterpress and lithography are run. Publication presses, in particular, are so wide that sway of rollers and cylinders can cause problems with uneven impression pressures and paper tension. Special gravure presses for printing specialties such as paper tissues, towels, napkins, etc., are made in sizes up to 212 inches (535 cm) wide and run at speeds up to 5,000 feet (1524 meters) per minute! Halftone gravure conversion is making the use of narrow-width 40 inch (1 meter) presses viable and cost effective for the shorter runs.

Advantages: Gravure printing has many advantages over the other printing processes. Most of the gravure in the USA is printed on rotary presses. Some sheet-fed gravure is printed in the United States and Europe. As already mentioned rotary gravure presses are larger than letterpress and lithographic presses; they require less manning, run faster, and are more productive. Running costs of gravure presses are, therefore, lower than the other processes.

Printing is done from *cylinders* and presses are designed to take different size cylinders. This is more of an advantage in packaging and specialty printing than in publication, periodical, and supplement printing where print sizes are more standardized. Cylinders also can print continuous patterns like giftwraps, wall coverings, textiles, woodgrains, etc.

Solvent inks are used which eliminate many of the problems associated with ink rheology that can have such a detrimental effect on letterpress and lithographic printing such as trapping, picking, piling, etc. Associated with solvent inks is the advantage of drying the inked images between printings. Gravure presses are equipped with hot air drying units between each printing station so the ink on the freshly printed image is dried, or at least set, before reaching the next printing station. Thus ink trapping is always done on a dry or very tacky (set) ink surface which results in complete transfer that often appears like overtrapping because the ink transferred to a previous ink layer dries with a higher gloss and looks stronger than the same ink which transfers to previously unprinted paper and is absorbed into the surface of the paper.

The most significant advantage of gravure, particularly conventional and variable area/variable depth gravure is that, unlike the regular variable area halftone processes used in lithography, letterpress, flexography and, to some extent, variable area gravure, the gravure image is composed of areas with varying amounts of ink corresponding to the tones represented in the image. The image has essentially a *continuous tone* structure due to the variable densities of the ink covering most of the area of the paper. This is definitely true of conventional gravure where all the image elements are the same size and shape and vary in density and is true to a large extent in variable area/variable depth gravure because of the lateral spreading of the solvent ink during impression.

Contone Printing: The fact that most of the area of the image on the paper is covered with ink results in another unique advantage of gravure. As mentioned in the section on *Lithographic Printing* and discussed in Appendix C the light reflected from the paper is the difference between the surface and internal reflections (refractiveness). In halftone processes the white area of paper between the dots reflects less light than the unprinted paper. This causes a darkening of the tones in black and white printing equivalent to a dot gain and a graying or dirtying effect in color printing. It is most serious on uncoated papers, less on coated papers, and least on cast-coated papers. Since this effect is absent or minimized on conventional and variable area/variable depth gravure, the same pigments as used in lithographic, letterpress, and flexographic inks print with greater purity and saturation in gravure.

This, combined with the overtrapping of inks due to drying between colors, gives gravure the advantage of producing prints with higher brilliance and purity of color than prints by the other processes printed with the same pigments on the same paper grades. Gravure, therefore, can print with poorer and cheaper pigments and still achieve the quality of reproduction of the other processes on the same paper. This factor also accounts for the fact that gravure can produce good quality reproductions on poorer grades of paper like newsprint. Some of these advantages will be eroded with the trend to halftone gravure, necessitating the use of better pigments as in European gravure printing.

Limitations: A serious one is the use of solvent inks which cause *fire* and *explosion hazards* that require explosion-proof fittings on the press and high investment costs for presses and installation. Another is *air pollution* caused by solvent emissions. All publication printers have solved this by the installation of expensive solvent recovery systems. Packaging and specialty printers use mixed solvent due to the many different substrates used and resort mostly to incineration of the emitted solvents to eliminate air pollution.

In addition to problems related to paper feed, tension, register, folder and/or rewind which are typical of all web presses, the pressman has to adjust and control *ink viscosities,* which determine the character of the ink lay — whether it is *screening* (like undertrapping) or *crawling* (mottle) (see Figure III-39); *dryer temperatures* which also affect these characteristics plus *tacky prints, set-off, picking* or *blocking* in the rewind; and *doctor blade length* and settings which affect the wiping of the cylinder and the cleanliness of the nonprinting areas.

The print quality problem of *dot skips* in the highlights (see Figure III-26) has been successfully eliminated or minimized by the Electrostatic Assist process, developed by the Gravure Research Institute as mentioned in Chapter II. The skips are caused by depressions in the surface of the paper not contacting the image cells during printing. In the Electrostatic Assist process a charge is induced in a special electroconductive rubber composition that is used to cover the impression cylinder. The charge penetrates the printing paper or board and changes the shape of the meniscus of the ink in the image cells so that it contacts the irregular substrate surface. The mechanisms of formation of the "dot skips" and the Electrostatic Assist process are shown in Figures III-42 and III-43. The process not only alleviates the problem of "dot skips" but also reduces the impression pressure required for printing and allows good quality printing on lower grades of paper and board.

The most serious limitation, or disadvantage, of gravure so far has been the necessity for press proofing. Because of the nature of the process, the variables described in the section on cylinder making, and the need for corrections made directly on the cylinder, gravure printing cylinders have to be proofed to make sure the proper corrections have been made. When more automation, predictability, and reliability are introduced into the process, as with the use of halftones in place of the continuous tone positives, off-press color proofing will become a viable process. In the meantime, a good off-press color proofing process that can simulate the visual appearance of gravure prints can be a valuable assist in checking the photographic images used to make the cylinders to make sure they have the desired image characteristics to produce cylinders that require less or hopefully no re-etching.

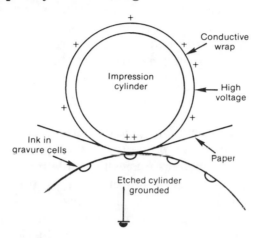

Figure III-42. Mechanism of Electrostatic Assist (ESA) process for gravure. (GRI)

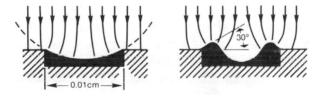

Figure III-43. Principles of electrostatic assist — how it improves ink transfer in gravure. (GRI)

Future

Gravure is the first of the printing processes to go from the original copy directly to the printing cylinder commercially. The new electronic page make-up systems will accelerate this trend. At the 1983 meeting of the Gravure Technical Association (GTA), Hell announced it is continuing research and development on electron beam etching of gravure cylinders which will eliminate the deficiencies of electromechanical engraving such as uneven diamond wear. GRI announced it is working on laser assisted engraving of cylinders.

Eventually digital systems will be developed that will not only display soft proofs of the images on CRT screens, but will digitally calculate the distortions required in the stored data to produce a hard proof that simulates the gravure print. An attempt at accomplishing this was introduced by Hell at DRUPA '82. This, and other systems for making hard proofs are described in Chapter X. Halftone-gravure conversion will simplify many of gravure's pre-press operations, reduce the time to execute them and their costs and make gravure a cost effective process competitive with web offset in runs down to 150,000.

Control of Color Printing

Letterpress, flexography and gravure are printing processes with relatively consistent printing properties as they involve interrelations between paper and ink which are basically stable materials and the press which is a machine with controllable and predictable mechanical functions. In letterpress, once the plates are mounted on the press, makeready is completed, inks with graded tack and papers with smooth compressible surfaces are used, consistent reproductions of good quality can be produced in runs over a million (if the plates are chromium-plated). As long as the inks and paper don't change and the plates are kept clean, scrubbed occasionally to remove coating and debris that collects in the halftones, and watched for wear they will run essentially trouble free until the job is complete.

In flexography, after the plates have been mounted and registered, the doctor blades in the inking systems adjusted, nip pressures set and the paper, or other substrate, started feeding, about the only factor the pressman needs to control is the viscosity of the ink and this can be done automatically.

In gravure, after the cylinders are mounted in the press, the ink fountains filled, the doctor blades adusted and the impression pressures and ink viscosity controls set, the press will run at speeds of up to 2500 feet (762 meters) per minute with little attention to the printing cylinder except periodic checking for doctor blade wear.

Lithography is entirely different. As already stated, printing by the lithographic process is much more involved and complicated requiring much higher skills than letterpress, flexography or gravure. Lithographic printing is subject to so many aberrations and defects that even with highly skilled craftsmen there are inconsistencies in the printing, press productivity is lower and waste is higher than in other processes. There are printing defects such as mealy solids; misregister; paper curling, buckling and wrinkling; ink piling; coating piling on the image and non-image areas; tinting; picking — hickeys and spots — few of which affect the other processes and all caused by the need for water and an ink-water balance in printing.

Because the image is on a planographic surface (image and non-image are esentially on the same plane) and the image is transferred to an intermediate blanket, which is also plane, the ink on the image has a tendency to spread causing the defect, dot gain. And as already described, dot gain can be affected by a number of factors including screen ruling, paper type, paper color, press speed, ink film thickness, ink temperature, ink strength, impression pressure, cylinder diameters, types of blankets, slur, doubling, fill-in and scumming. The control of all these factors in printing is a pressman's nightmare. The fact that pressmen do as well as they do is a tribute to their skill, tenacity and the numerous control targets and methods developed to help them identify defects, measure them and keep them under control.

Control Strips and Targets: The philosophy of control strips and targets is to make them as small as possible and still complete enough to detect variations and defects that can destabilize printing, affect its consistency and degrade its quality. Also targets must be more sensitive to printing variables and defects than the halftone images being printed so the changes in the target images serve as warnings to pressmen before the variables cause serious defects in the actual printing. There are targets to detect changes in the four colors in *tone reproduction, register, fanout, fan-in, moiré, solid densities, dot gain, slur, doubling, fill-in, blinding, mealiness, trapping, resolution* and *gray balance*. Altogether these targets are useful for controlling separations, color correction, contact printing, platemaking, color proofing and printing. Some have already been described like the GATF Sensitivity Guide, Star Target, Dot Gain Scale and Slur Gauge. It is helpful to use targets for warnings and control but targets use up valuable space on the paper which can be expensive. Also it must be remembered that what is important is what is happening to the image — not the target. Sometimes defects occur in the image, like hickeys and spots, that do not show on the targets, and vice versa. Targets are indicators of impending problems. To be sure, the pressman still has to examine the whole printed sheet periodically. The targets will tell him what to look for. The printed images on the sheet will confirm or deny it, or they may show other defects and trends not indicated on the targets. Color control strips and targets are illustrated and discussed in Chapter X.

Densitometers have been used for measuring the targets and comparing them with the targets on the proof or the OK sheet. Densitometers suffer from two serious limitations — poor agreement between instruments and slow speed. The problem of poor agreement between instruments has been solved in part by the use of printed color charts or references to calibrate the densitometer such as the GTA (Gravure Technical Association) Gravure Ink Standard Color Charts; the Revised Specifications for Web Offset Publication printing (SWOP) published by the American Association of Advertising Agencies (AAAA or 4A's) and the Magazine Publishers Association (MPA); the IPA (International Pre-Press Association) Standard Offset Color Reference, the GATF Munsell/Foss Color Chart and others. The slow speed of making readings is being solved by the use of high speed microprocessor controlled density measuring heads and processing systems, on-press and off-press.

Press Color Measurement and Control Systems: The first high speed off-press color measurement systems were introduced by MAN-Roland and Heidelberg at DRUPA '77 (Figures III–44 and III–45 and X–2 and X–3). These were specific systems for their presses using special color control targets. Microprocessors and video displays were used to compare readings on printed sheets with comparable ones in memory for proofs or OK sheets. In 1978 Tobias introduced the SCR Scanning Densitometer which is a low cost, high speed off-press color density measurement system that can be used with any press. It is capable of making 54 color measurements in four colors across a 40 inch (1016 mm) sheet in 8 seconds. At DRUPA '82 Gretag introduced a new off-press high speed scanning densitometer, D-732 — similar to the Tobias SCR Scanning Densitometer — which can make 200 color measurements recording 3840 pieces of color data, in six colors, across a 40 inch (1016 mm) sheet in 6 seconds! These are described in more detail in Chapter X.

Also at DRUPA '82 MAN-Roland and Heidelberg both introduced advanced press color control systems and new systems incorporating similar principles for measuring images on plates and using the information to pre-set the ink fountains on the press so makeready times could be reduced. Each press manufacturer and others produced similar systems called plate scanners. Typical systems are described and illustrated in Chapter X. Three new on-press densitometer systems were also introduced at DRUPA '82 which help to shorten the time between reading the instrument and taking the necessary action to make the adjustments because the readings are made directly on the press avoiding the delay in removing sheets from the delivery of the press and measuring them. These, too, are described and illustrated in Chapter X.

It is interesting to note that all of the instruments developed for color measurement and control, except one, depend on the pressman to make the final decision for correction. The information regarding defects or other quality affecting factors is displayed on a visual display screen (VDT) or printed out on a printer and the pressman decides what correction is needed — whether ink should be increased, decreased,

Figure III-44. Off-press MAN-Roland color measurement and control system. (Rockwell)

Figure III-45. Heidelberg color measurement and control system — CPC-2. (H-E)

changed in tack or washed up, or whether the problem is caused by a disturbance in the ink-water balance. The exception is the MAN-Roland CCI system which is a closed loop system that automatically adjusts the ink feed as the readings of the off-press densitometer indicate. It has a manual override so the pressman can make the ink-water balance corrections.

Press Automation: These new on-press and off-press high speed densitometer systems for measuring and controlling color densities, along with controls of ink-water balance and ink roller temperatures by independent laboratories like Grapho-Metronics (Munich, West Germany) and automatic blanket washers by manufacturers like Baldwin-Gegenheimer (Stamford, CT) can lead to almost completely automated operation of lithographic presses. Not only will these accessories help presses have faster press speeds with higher productivity, more consistent quality, less waste, and lower cost; they will make possible better predictions of press production prints and matching of off-press color proofs to them. How they can be used to improve the correlation between press prints and color proofs is described in Chapter X.

Chapter IV

Press Color Proofing

There are many reasons for making color proofs in printing, most of which have already been mentioned. It may be redundant to state that the most important reason is to see what the printed job will look like. This, of course, is what the customer is interested in. What is of equal importance to the printer is the ability to catch errors in register, color layout, omission, or duplication, etc., before they reach the printing press and become expensive to correct.

Most printing jobs are custom made. They consist generally of numerous pieces of heterogeneous copy supplied at different times by different sources and they are generally under extreme time and cost pressure. In addition, relatively insignificant deviations from standards such as slight misregister of color images, misfit of image components, or misalignment of screen angles can cause visual imperfections in the printed image which if not detected by some means of proofing are serious enough to require expensive down-time on the press to make corrections, wait for new plates, and in extreme cases cause rejection of the job.

Photomechanical proofs have been used very effectively in the preparatory operations in lithography and to some extent in letterpress, flexography, and gravure to check the progress and accuracy of the color separation, color correction and assembly of the many film components of most color jobs. But because of the great risks of introducing errors in the composition and imposition of complex color elements on a job and the high costs of correcting them on the press, final color proofs for letterpress, flexography, lithography, and gravure have traditionally been produced on proof presses. Such proofs have the advantages of being produced on the actual printing paper, with the same printing inks to be used on the job, and once makeready has been accomplished, a number of prints and progressive proofs can be produced.

It is true that these proofs have many of the characteristic defects of the printing process used such as dot gain, trapping, mottling, snowflakiness, etc. (in lithography), but while they are reasonable representations of the printed job, they are not exact facsimiles because of the great number of variables in the printing processes in addition to paper and ink.

The appearance of the final prints made on the press are affected by a number of other factors such as the number of ink rollers in and the design of the ink train on the press; the settings of the rollers; the ink viscosities; the printing order of the inks; their temperatures; the relative humidity of the paper; the diameters of the plate, impression and blanket (in lithography) cylinders and their settings; the ink-water balance (in lithography); and numerous less obvious variables.

In addition, press proofs take a much longer time to produce than off-press photomechanical proofs, and because they use printing plates and presses, they require highly skilled craftsmen, all of which make the press proof much more expensive than off-press proofs. For these reasons, a number of attempts have been make to substitute off-press proofs for final press proofs with some success in lithography in the United States and Canada; very limited success in letterpress and flexography where powderless etched and photopolymer plates are used; and so far, no success in gravure, which situation could change with the development of new color proofing systems like the KC-Color Proofer for Gravure, described in Chapter VII and the introduction of halftone gravure conversion processes described in Chapters III and VIII.

This chapter contains information on typical press proofing systems used for making final color proofs for letterpress, flexography, lithography and gravure, their intrinsic and distinguishing characteristics, and how well they compare with production press printing.

Press Color Proofing for Letterpress

The proof press has been an indispensable part of the letterpress process. A simple press called a "galley proof press" is used for pulling galley proofs which are checked for errors in text composition and imperfections in the cast type. For making reproduction proofs from cast metal type for use as text copy for photoengravings, gravure and lithographic art work, there are precision proof or test presses which are also used to proof single-color engravings and four-color engravings, one color at a time. In 1937 Vandercook introduced the first completely powered two-color proof press, and in 1946 it followed with the popular high speed four-color test press with four sequential printing stations that could approximate the wet-on-wet printing of high speed production web letterpress presses by making a complete four-color proof in four seconds.

These are flatbed presses which can be used to proof original plates and flat stereotypes or electrotypes before curving. Curved stereotypes are not usually proofed. Special proof presses are made for proofing curved electrotypes. The cylinders must correspond to the diameters of the printing cylinders for which the electrotypes are made, so a special press is needed for each size cylinder. The Flower Multi-Diameter Proof Press, introduced in 1962, can be used to proof electrotypes with different curvatures as the press will accommodate cylinders of different diameters. These presses also have flat beds on which the paper is mounted. In addition, these presses are single color only so wet-on-wet proofing of curved electros is not possible.

Four-color engraver's proofs are not usually made from the actual printing plates but from the original plates from which the molds and duplicate plates for printing are made. Any changes in dot element sizes due to making the mold and casting or electroplating the duplicate plates can cause variations in the tone and color reproduction of the final production press prints. Also even though wet-on-wet printing is done on the four-color proof presses, their speed is at least one order of magnitude slower than production press speeds which can cause serious deviations in ink transfer and trapping.

Even though the press proof is made on the same paper and with the same inks as the production press, the print does not necessarily match the production press print because it is made from different plates, with different makeready, different impression pressures, and run at different speeds. With the advancements being made in off-press proofing systems, it would be reasonable to predict that press proofing for letterpress could be successfuly replaced by one of the new systems, but it may never happen because the volume of letterpress printing is declining and the usual incentives for process improvements are missing.

Press Color Proofing for Flexography

Three and four-color process printing by flexography is less than two decades old. It has only been practical since the introduction of central impression cylinder presses, reverse angle doctor blade ink distribution systems, and photosensitive direct plates like the Corning Photosensitive Glass plate and photopolymer plates.

To reduce set-up and makeready time on flexographic presses, special presses known as Mounters-Proofers, have been introduced (Figure IV-1). These are used for mounting plates on the actual printing cylinders in correct position for printing, and proofs are pulled in a special paste ink

Figure IV-1. Mosstype Mounter-Proofer proof press for flexography.

to make sure the plates are in register for printing. The checking is not done image-to-image but to a layout. Precision measuring devices are used. At DRUPA '82 a special press for mounting four-color process plates was introduced by BIEFFEBI, called "Preprint," in which the precision of mounting is monitored with a microprocessor.

The actual color proofing for flexography has been done on the production press or on special presses introduced during the past few years. The two types of color proof presses used in the United States are manufactured by George Moulton Successors, Ltd. (GMS) and by D. Timmins & Sons, Ltd., both in England and both of whom are also manufacturers of color proofing presses for gravure. In fact, both the GMS and Timmins proof presses are available so that flexographic and gravure cylinders can be proofed interchangeably.

Since color process printing is still in emerging stages in flexography, standard operating procedures for proofing and printing have not yet evolved. Some converters make color proofs on color proof presses and try to match the proof with the prints on the production press. Others use DuPont CROMALIN or other proofing systems to determine the characteristics of the films the printing plates are made from; print the plates on a production press to determine their tone and color reproduction characteristics; and use this data to establish a correlation between off-press proofs, proof press proofs, and production press prints. In this way they can use the proof press to predict the appearance of the production print without having to make expensive modifications on the press. With sufficient experience and proper controls in platemaking and on the press it is expected that off-press proofing will become consistent and reliable enough to replace color press proofing in flexography.

Press Color Proofing for Lithography

Final color proofs for lithography have been made traditionally on special proof or production printing presses, but they are gradually being replaced by photomechanical off-press proofs as these become more reliable and consistent and come closer to matching the ink and substrate characteristics of the press print. As a matter of fact in the United States and Canada, photomechanical, or off-press proofing for lithography has advanced to the point where more proofs are produced by photomechanical means than by presses (actually over 60%). This is not the case in Europe or Japan where off-press proofing is used for internal quality control but most final proofing is still done with ink on paper on proof presses. The introduction of CROMALIN Eurostandard Color Proofs controlled by Brunner color targets is increasing confidence in off-press color proofing by lithographers in Europe.

Flatbed Proof Presses

Three types of presses are used for color proofing: flatbed, rotary, and production presses. In the flatbed proof press the plate and paper are mounted on separate stationary platens on the flatbed, and the blanket is mounted on a cylinder which rides on two gear tracks, one on each side of the stationary platens (Figure IV-2). To make a proof the plate is dampened and inked and as the blanket cylinder is rolled over the two platens it picks up the inked image from the plate on the first platen and transfers it to the paper on the second platen. The plate is changed and the next color is pulled in the same manner repeating the process for as many colors as are needed to complete the proof.

There are three types of flatbed proof presses for lithography: (1) *hand-operated,* on which the dampening and inking of the plate are done by hand, and the blanket is rolled manually over the plate and paper platens; (2) *power-driven,* on which the dampening and inking are done manually, and the blanket cylinder is motor-driven as it rides back and forth over the plate and paper platens; and (3) *automatic,* on which the dampening and inking are done automatically as on a production press, and the blanket cylinder is motor-driven over the plate and paper platens. What flatbed presses are in use are mostly of the automatic type which produce more uniform proofs, in less time, and at lower cost than the manual and power-driven presses.

Figure IV-2. Consolidated International Automatic flat-bed offset proof press for lithography.

Figure IV-3. F.L.A.G. Offset Press 104 — Flat-bed offset proof press for lithography. (Bobst)

All flatbed presses are single-color. In addition, most suffer from register problems, slur, gear streaks, long wash-up times (especially for a color change from black to yellow), ink drying before reaching the stock, and almost impossible water balance control. Automatic inking and dampening have eliminated most of these problems. At DRUPA '77, F.A.G., a subsidiary of Bobst SA (Switzerland) introduced a new automatic flatbed proof press which has simplified proofing on flatbed proof presses (Figure IV-3). Known as the *F.L.A.G. Offset Press 104,* the press eliminates the ink wash-up problem by the use of interchangeable roll-in inking units, which can be washed and inked with the next color while another unit is running on the press. Dampening control is improved by the combination of a dampening unit and refrigerated plate platen which helps to establish and maintain an ink-water balance quickly. Plate and paper mountings are precision machined and can be set to an accuracy of ± 0.01mm (0.0004"). The drive is from a two-speed brake motor with gearbox and helical rack and pinion gear to eliminate gear marks and streaks.

Rotary Proof Presses

Multicolor production presses have been used for years to proof critical jobs, but the first rotary press designed specifically for proofing in lithography was the *Vandercook R04* introduced by Vandercook & Sons (now a division of Illinois Tool Works, Chicago, IL) in 1968. It is a compact, four-color proof press of unique design using three cylinders (Figure IV-4). Image size is 22 x 28 inches (559 x 711 mm), and plate size is 25 1/4 x 31 inches (641 x 787 mm). All four plates are mounted in tandem on the plate cylinder with each plate having is own inking and dampening system; four blankets are mounted on the blanket cylinder which is the same size as the plate cylinder; the impression cylinder is large enough to take a 23 x 29 inch (584 x 737 mm) sheet. The impression cylinder makes four revolutions to each revolution of the plate and blanket cylinders, and in each revolution of the impression cylinder the next color is transferred to the sheet so that a four-color proof is produced in each revolution of the plate and blanket cylinders. Production of the press was terminated in 1978 at which time 60 units were in use worldwide. Service and spare parts are handled by Charles Germain Company (19 West 24th Street, New York, NY 10010).

At the 1982 TAGA annual conference Bobst Champlain announced a new rotary four-color proof press with common impression cylinder design. The press is 28 x 41 inches (711 x 1041 mm) in size and has four independent plate and blanket couples positioned around a large central impression cylinder around which the sheet is carried as it receives

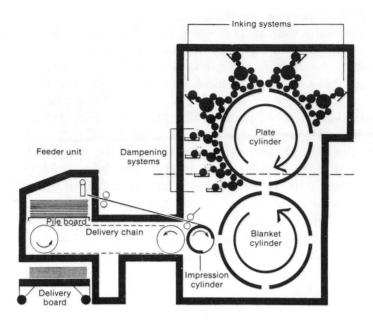

Figure IV-4. Schematic drawing of Vandercook RO4 rotary offset proof press for lithography.

transfers of each of the four-color images in tandem (Figure IV-5). The press, known as the F.L.A.G. Speedproof 4C, was shown as a prototype at DRUPA '82.

Production/Proof Press: As previously stated, multicolor production presses have been used for proofing critical process color jobs for years. With the almost exclusive use of four to six-color presses for color reproduction printing, production presses have been used more extensively for proofing, but because of their high hourly cost and low productivity when proofing, special smaller four-color presses have been used and dedicated specifically for proofing. One of the first of these special production/proof presses was the OMCSA Aurelia press with electronic drive which allowed independent makereadies including plate and blanket changes on each unit without interference with the other units.

As press proofing for lithography is the standard operating procedure in Europe, there were a number of special production/proof presses at DRUPA '82. Typical among these was the new Hell Colormetal CHRO-MAPRINT 4074 ICCCS (for "Integrated Continuous Color Control System") press which had an on-line densitometer and manual or closed loop control of inking. It had a number of other desirable features but it was withdrawn in 1983.

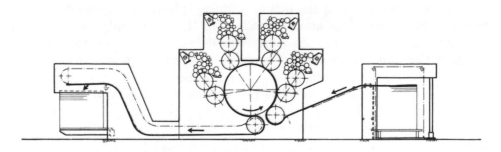

Figure IV-5. F.L.A.G. Speed Proof 4C rotary offset proof press for lithography. (Bobst)

Also announced at DRUPA was an on-press densitometer for sheet-fed offset presses developed by IGT, the Dutch graphic arts research institute in Holland. It was demonstrated on a Miller-Johanisberg sheet-fed offset press. This instrument reads out densitometer values on the sheets as they are being printed and compares them with pre-set or OK values, but the adjustments to the ink fountain, if necessary, must be made manually. Grapho-Metronics (Munich, West Germany) demonstrated a plate dampening measurement and control instrument on a Roland Press and showed an ink temperature control device for the ink rollers of a press in its booth at DRUPA '82. Accurate control of proofing and printing on a press may require the use of all these instruments and possibly others to control the variables that cause the deviations in printing that prevent press proofs from matching press prints.

How Good Are Press Proofs?

In lithographic printing the most critical variable is dot gain. The types of dot gain and their causes are described in Chapter III-*Lithographic Printing* and some of the studies made to determine the factors that affect dot gain and its control are summarized and evaluated in Appendix C. Briefly these studies showed that (1) optical gain in an off-press proof can simulate the total dot gain, including optical and mechanical gain of a press print (Felix Brunner/DuPont); (2) mechanical press gain varies with the paper, screen type and ruling, press speed, blanket type, ink viscosity, and the square of the ink film thickness (A. Johnson/PIRA); and (3) dot gain varies with the shape of the dots and reaches a maximum at about 45% dot area for square and about 60% for round dots (F. Sigg/RIT).

The results of these tests should help to dispel the myth that press proofing is the only sure method for making color proofs that match press prints in lithography. The main advantages of press proofs are that they are usually made on the actual printing substrate, and a quantity of proofs and progressives can be made at little additional cost. The fact that printing ink is used on a press does not mean that the ink will produce the same result on the substrate on the proof press as it does on the production press. Because of dot gain and differences in speed and impression pressures between the proof press and the production press, the amount and rheology of the ink must be changed to get some correspondence between the results from both presses. Changing the amount and rheology of the ink changes its transfer characteristics so the fact that an acceptable result can be obtained on the proof press does not mean it can be duplicated and printed on the production press where the printing conditions are different. In addition different plates are generally used, and often the plates used for proofing have different exposures and use spacers during exposure to spread the dots to simulate dot gain on the production press. The plates for the production press are usually made with sharper dots.

In most proofing situations there is hardly time to makeready the plates and establish an ink-water balance for a stable running equilibrium. This can take as long as it takes to print 1,000 to 5,000 sheets on a production press. Therefore, most proofs made on a proof press are intermediate prints which would correspond to prints made on a production press during makeready or before a stable equilibrium is reached. There is no assurance that the production press can obtain the same results and maintain a stable equilibrium for optimum productivity and minimum variation. The print may be at one or the other end of an extreme range that is difficult to maintain under running conditions. Usually the production press is required to match the press proof which has been signed by the customer rather than the other way around.

Since a compromise must be made in the printing, similar compromises made with off-press proofs could lead to equally acceptable results. Off-press proofs are less expensive to make and, what is often more important, take less time to make so there is no holdup in going to press especially on jobs with short lead times. Also, the advances made in off-press color proofing systems have brought them much closer to producing consistent proofs that are acceptable matches to press prints. This accounts for the increased use of off-press proofing for lithography in the United States and Canada and is attracting attention in Europe, with the introduction of Eurostandard CROMALIN.

Press Color Proofing for Gravure

The situation with proofing for gravure is quite different from lithography and letterpress. As a matter of fact, as recently as 1956 when

Cartwright and MacKay published their comprehensive book on "Rotogravure" the question of whether to proof or not was still being debated, and many jobs went to press without proofing.

Gravure is used extensively in three broad market sectors: (1) *Publication and Advertising* including newspaper supplements and preprints, long-run magazines, mail order catalogs and advertising printing such as calendars, coupons, seals, stamps, and art reproductions; (2) *Packaging* including folding cartons, flexible (film) packaging, gift and package wraps, and labels; and (3) *Specialties* including floor and wall coverings, textiles, heat-transfer printing, decorative laminates like Formica, security, social, and commercial engravings (intaglio), toilet and facial tissues, napkins, towels, cigarette filter tips, plastic containers, pills, ceramics, siding, wallboard, wood paneling, etc.

Gravure has traditionally been a long-run process (one million and more) and, with such long runs, preparatory costs are a small percentage of total costs which are dominated by paper, ink, and press operating costs. In addition, long-run gravure printing for publications, packaging, and specialties usually have long lead times which allow time for cylinder proofing, re-etching, and reproofing. With increases in regional editions in publications, shorter deadlines and lead times and smaller inventories in packaging, there has been a trend in gravure toward shorter runs (300,000 or less) which have made gravure printers more conscious of preparatory costs that in turn have made web offset more competitive with gravure.

In short- and medium-run gravure, cylinder and other preparatory costs become a much larger percentage of the total cost of a job. According to studies made by GRI, typical man-hours to make a large publication gravure cylinder are about 20 hours, most of which are for proofing, re-etching, and finishing. Another limitation of gravure is the necessity for retouching continuous tone positives and the traditional page-making operations which cost about twice as much as for web offset with halftone films. In addition, web offset has the advantage of the ease, speed, and low cost of off-press pre-proofing. Proofing, therefore, is a subject of major concern to gravure printers.

Because gravure is an intaglio process in which the reproduction of tone values depends on the volume of ink in the cells in the printing plate or cylinder and how it is transferred to the substrate, the only way at present to predict how a set of separations will look when printed is to make a printing plate or cylinder from them and print it on a press with the same paper, inks, and print controls to be used on the production press run. The deviations from the original are analyzed to determine if the positives need correcting and a new plate or cylinder should be made, or if the corrections can be made on the plate or cylinder used for the first proofing and then reproofed. In either case what corrections are made in the printing medium must be repeated in the photographic films from which the plate or cylinder was made, unless the medium being proofed is the actual printing cylinder and no other use is expected to be made of the films.

Operating procedures for gravure proofing differ between the various market sectors and between the United States, Europe and Japan. In Europe and Japan most gravure printers prefer to make their own engravings from copy supplied directly by publishers and advertising agencies. In the United States there are a number of trade service companies that supply positives, proofs, and progressives to advertising agencies and printing cylinders to printers. Most publication printers in the United States are large enough to perform all the preparatory or prepress operations but use supplied positives, proofs, and progressives from advertising agencies of some advertising pages which are made by trade shops. Some packaging and specialty printers produce such a diversity of subjects that they depend on trade shops to supply all or most of their preparatory materials including printing cylinders.

Even though all the subjects on a printing form have been preproofed and corrected individually after they are all assembled on the form and the printing cylinder is made, it is proofed on a full-size press to make sure all the elements print satisfactorily with the same ink and paper to be used on the press run. Because chemical etching is so unreliable, uncontrollable, and unpredictable (as shown in Chapter II) and electromechanical engraving can be affected by unbalanced bromides on the scanning drum and uneven diamond wear in the engraving heads, chances are risky that images made on small presses can match those made from corrected films on full-size printing cylinders printed on large proof or production presses.

The practice of having to proof, re-etch, and reproof final printing cylinders and individual subjects, which are made in trade shops, is a major reason for the high cost of cylinders and the need for long lead times in gravure and accounts for the economics that favor gravure for long runs and web offset for shorter runs. In addition, on films accompanying proofs from trade shops the corrections made on the plates or cylinders used to make the proofs are often not transferred to the films. Off-press proofing systems are used to check the color separations from the scanners and the corrected bromides (for electromechanical engravers like the Hell Helioklischograph and Ohio Electronic Engraver) for color accuracy before the printing cylinders are made; but so far, these proofs do not have the desired tone reproduction qualities needed to replace the press proof. This may come with the new off-press proofing systems like the KC-Color Proofer for Gravure (Chapter VII) and the use of halftone gravure conversions (Chapters II, III and VIII) which are growing in popularity and use.

Gravure Proof Presses

Three types of gravure proof presses are in use: (1) drum-type; (2) sheet-fed; and (3) roll-fed. The drum-type proof press is used primarily for proofing subjects for the packaging and specialty markets. Sheet-fed and small roll-fed proof presses are used to produce page-size proofs and progressives for advertising agencies of subjects to be printed in a number of publications. Full size roll-fed proof presses are used by publication printers to proof the actual printing cylinders before and after re-etching.

Drum-Type Proof Press: The drum-type gravure proof press is a single-color press which can proof practically all sizes of gravure cylinders for packaging (Figure IV-6). The drum which serves as the impression cylinder is usually about six feet (183 cm) long with circumference of five to six feet (152 cm-183 cm) and is covered with cured rubber or a rubber blanket.

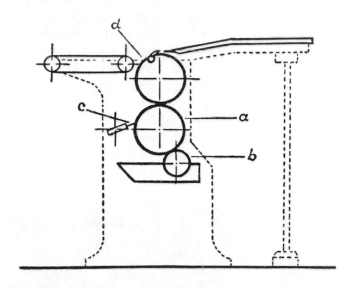

Figure IV-6. Drum type proof press for gravure. (GTA)

In operation, the substrate is attached to the impression cylinder. The engraved cylinder to be proofed is inserted in the press and registered by means of a register scope which is aligned with a register mark on the cylinder. The impression roll is contacted with the engraved cylinder; the doctor blade is set in position on the engraving; ink is poured in the trough created by the blade and the engraving; and the impression pressure is set. As the drum is turned by the operator, the inked image is transferred to the substrate, after which the impression is backed off, the engraved cylinder is washed up and taken out of the press. The procedure is repeated for each subsequent color. When the composite proof is completed, the substrate is removed from the drum and evaluated.

To achieve representative and reproducible proofs very rigid controls of impression pressures, doctor blade angles, ink formulations, and ink viscosities are necessary. The inks used in proofing have the same pigments as the inks used on the production press, but ink strengths and viscosities are adjusted to correlate with production press conditions. Because ink viscosity is so important some presses use central ink systems with automatic viscosity controls.

The main advantages of the drum-type proof press for packaging are ease of ink changes and the ability to proof any substrate from 1 1/2 mil (0.04 mm) polyethylene to heavy paper board. Its major disadvantage is the time required to make duplicate proofs and progressives.

Sheet-fed Proof Press : There are a number of sheet-fed proof presses used mainly by trade shops to proof individual advertising pages for publications. They vary in design from hand-fed converted laydown-type machines, like the L&M Engraver's proof press which proofs from engraved cylinders to the more sophisticated machine-fed type, like the Palatia press which uses engraved wraparound plates (Figure IV-7). The main difference between these presses and the drum-type is that the substrate is fed into the press instead of being attached to the impression drum. This makes register more critical and limits the type of substrates that can be used, but makes it possible to produce a quantity of proofs and progressives with little additional time and cost.

Figure IV-7. Palatia sheet fed press for printing proofs for gravure. (GTA)

In operation, the cylinder or plate to be proofed is mounted in the press; a pan or fountain of ink is raised so that the printing or plate cylinder rotates in the ink; and the doctor blade is positioned on the printing cylinder. The press is turned on; the printing cylinder rotates in the ink bath; the doctor blade wipes the excess ink off the non-printing areas; sheets of the substrate are fed through the press, guided and positioned by a series of grippers and side guides; and the substrate is delivered in a pile after printing. The second color cylinder or plate is mounted in the press; the ink is changed; the doctor blade is set; and the sheets printed with the first color and blank sheets for progressives are fed through the press. This operation is repeated as many times as there are colors. Standard inks are required to make the process cost-effective and ink characteristics and printing conditions must be correlated to the production press.

Roll-Fed Proof Press: As with sheet-fed proof presses, there are a number of roll-fed proof presses which are used primarily for publication proofing. Most are full-size with designs similar to production presses. Some are roll-to-roll and others feed into a sheeter. The important feature is that they proof all four colors in one pass through the press. Printing proofs is almost exactly like running a production press except that the presses run slower and usually without electrostatic assist. The inks must be adjusted by extending them with solvent to produce the color or strengthening them by addition of pigment to correlate the ink strengths with the prints produced at production speeds. While the matches between proofs produced on these presses and production prints are generally creditable, there are enough uncertainties and misses that even this expensive and time-consuming method of proofing is not the optimum answer to color proofing for gravure. This answer may come from the trend to halftone gravure and its ability to use off-press proofs.

Correlation of Press Proof with Press Print in Gravure

All printing processes are systems for information transfer. The efficiency of the printing process to transfer information depends on the weakest link in the process. In halftone processes like letterpress and lithography information loss occurs primarily at the halftone stage. According to Dr. Werner Kunz (Research Director at Burda GmbH, Offenburg, West Germany) in his paper on "Ink Transfer in Gravure Process" in the 1975 TAGA Proceedings, the largest information loss in gravure printing occurs in the transfer of the ink from the printing cylinder to the paper. Because of the sensitivity of the image in gravure to ink transfer and the difficulty of correlating this between the proof and production presses, the assurance with which a press proof can match a press print in gravure will always be subject to question.

In his paper Kunz discusses four factors that influence ink transfer; two *active* ones; the press and printing cylinder; and two *passive* ones; the ink and the paper. He lists three parameters under each factor that define its effects on ink transfer. These are listed in Table IV-I.

Table IV-I

FACTORS AFFECTING INK TRANSFER IN GRAVURE

1. Press
   a. Speed
   b. Doctor blade
   c. Impression roller

2. Printing Cylinder
   a. Cell Geometry
   b. Shape of ink meniscus in filled cell
   c. Ability of ink transfer

3. Printing Ink
   a. Viscosity
   b. Interfacial-physical properties
   c. Temperature

4. Printing Paper
   a. Smoothness
   b. Elastic properties
   c. Interfacial-physical properties

He illustrates and discusses each of these factors in detail. Important conclusions from his paper relating to factors affecting ink transfer and consequently the correlation between press proof and press print are:

- Differences in speed are a main cause for the differences between proof and print.
- The doctor blade is one of the most sensitive instruments in gravure that can affect the appearance of a print.
- Impression roller diameter is critical and should be larger as printing speeds are increased.
- Geometry of the cell is very important to ink transfer. Cells produced by electron beam etching appear to have ideal shape and hardness for good ink release in transfer.
- Difference of shape of ink meniscus in ink-filled cells was studied by interference microphotographs which led to conclusion that doctor blade wiping is more efficient on round cells.
- Ability of ink transfer from chrome is much higher than for copper.

- Ink viscosity is a critical factor in ink transfer and accounts for prints being better at high printing speeds.
- Temperature is important because of its effect on viscosity. Constant temperature would be preferred.
- Elasticity is equally important to smoothness in paper for good printing quality.
- The wetability of the paper surface for ink and the interfacial-physical properties of the ink are important to proper ink transfer.

Trying to keep all these factors under control and adjust them so they correlate the printing condition of a proof press with those of a production press requires the talents of highly skilled and experienced craftsmen and even with all these skills it is not usually possible to duplicate exactly in a proof the printing results on a production press. According to Cartwright and MacKay in "Rotogravure" there are a number of differences between press proofs and production press prints due to the way the two are made.

- Print quality is generally better on the production press as the work has a chance to "settle down," which seldom happens on a proof press. Sometimes proofs have a smoother appearance than press prints because of better dot printing from the combination of slow press speed and slow drying ink.
- Proofs are generally made from bare copper cylinders which tend to print fuller than chromed images especially in the lighter tones.
- The need to reduce color strength on the proof press by the addition of extenders tends to lighten the shadow tones more than the light tones.
- Reducing ink viscosity with thinner on the proof press is very critical, as shadow tones begin to show a "wormy" effect. This is the limit for viscosity reduction, and yet the work should not print so dry as to prevent good trapping of succeeding colors, such as blue or black printed over fairly full yellow and magenta (red).
- The hardness of impression rollers is important for printing. A fairly hard roller (about 95 Shore durometer is required for printing on smooth machine-finished papers, while a softer roller is better for rough paper surfaces. Normal pressure is about 100 lbs. per linear inch — with a 6" diameter impression roller. This gives a "flat" (line of contact) of about 1/2 inch.

According to the superintendent of proofing in a large publication gravure printer with six divisions manufacturing cylinders and old proof presses with speeds of 125 feet per minute, the most serious problem in gravure press proofing is to simulate the ink transfer of production presses. A number of factors contribute to this problem including ink viscosity variations, use of reclaimed solvents, and variations in ink strengths due to reductions in cell volumes from decreases in cell depths from about 50μ to 40μ due to the trend over the past five years from chemically-etched to electromechanically engraved cylinders. He felt that better proof press speeds would be about 250 feet per minute but even with these, correlation between press proofs and production press prints would be uncertain and unpredictable.

These difficulties in correlating press proofs with press prints can account for the tremendous interest in halftone gravure which started with the conversion of halftone positives for offset lithography to positives for gravure cylinders. Aside from the ease of making halftone positives which reduces the time and cost of preparing the films for gravure, resulting in shorter lead times, the main advantages of using halftones for gravure is the ability to use off-press proofing systems that are so effective in offset and enable the making of corrections in the films rather than on the cylinders. These operations not only speed up the process but reduce cylinder costs so much that gravure can become competitive with web offset in runs down to 150,000.

Chapter V

Off-Press Color Proofing Systems — Overlay

Photomechanical off-press color proofing systems for *internal quality control* applications have been in use for over 40 years. Photomechanical and electronic off-press color proofing systems for *simulating press prints* and replacing press proofs have been in active development for over 20 years. They are coming into more prominence and extended use because of (1) improvements in their quality and consistency; (2) the high cost of press proofs, the time it takes to make them and their limited reliability; and (3) customer education. Off-press color proofs can be made in less than one-fourth the time and one-fifth to one-tenth the cost of press proofs. The slowest of the systems can produce proofs in less than one hour and most of them have no more variability than press proofs.

Three types of off-press color proofs are in use: (1) *Overlay*, in which each color is on a separate film and these are combined in register and backed with a reflective surface to produce a composite color proof that can also be used as progressive proofs; (2) *Integral*, or *single sheet*, in which all the color images are superposed by multiple exposures, lamination, or transfer to a single base which can be viewed only as an integral proof; and (3) *Electronic*, or *digital*, in which the individual color separation images are digitized and (a) combined to produce a composite three-color *soft proof* on a color monitor, cathode ray tube, or video display terminal (VDT), or (b) converted to a *hard proof* on a color proofing medium.

The off-press color proofing systems discussed in this book are:

(1) *Overlay systems* in general use which are 3M *COLOR KEY*, ENCO *NAPS* and *PAPS*, and DuPont *CROMACHECK* (Chapter V).

(2) *Integral*, or *single sheet*, systems which include the oldest in continuous use, Direct-Reproduction Corp. *WATERCOTE*, and its

modifications, and a new one using similar technology by American Photo-Graphics Corp. called *FINAL PROOF;* Agfa-Gevaert *GEVAPROOF;* 3M *TRANSFER KEY;* 3M *MATCHPRINT;* DuPont *CROMALIN;* Keuffel and Esser (K&E) *SPECTRA* Proof; and Kodak *EKTAFLEX* PCT (Chapter VI).

(3) New *electrophotographic* system by Coulter Systems Corp., *KC-COLOR PROOF* (Chapter VII).

(4) Color Proofing Systems for *gravure:* CROMALIN, SPECTRA, 3M MATCHPRINT, KC-COLOR PROOF and the color photographic print systems; CIBACHROME, KODAK RC-14 EKTACHROME AND EKTAFLEX PCT (Chapter VIII).

(5) *Soft proofing* on *Electronic previewers* in use which are the *Hazeltine SP1620 Separation Previewer* and the *TOPPAN CPC 525, Video Color Proofing System* (Chapter IX).

(6) *Digital color proofing* including the *Hell CPR 403 Color Proof Recorder, Crosfield Magna Proof,* using the LogE/Dunn Versa Color Camera, *Polaroid/MacDonald Dettwiler Film Recorder,* and *KC-Laser Printer LP610* (Chapter IX).

There is another way by which off-press color proofs are differentiated: color proofs made from halftone positives or negatives for halftone printing processes, mainly lithography; and color proofs made from continuous tone films for gravure and other processes like collotype and screenless lithography. Off-press color proofing systems will be discussed separately for (1) halftone printing processes and (2) contone/halftone. Since most of the color proofing systems have been developed and used mainly for halftone printing processes, these will be discussed first along with their applications to halftone printing. In the cases where color proofing systems are used for both halftone printing and gravure, like DuPont CROMALIN, K&E SPECTRA, KC-COLOR PROOF and photographic color proofs, they will be discussed in both Chapter VI and Chapter VIII.

This chapter consists of descriptions of the overlay off-press color proofing systems in common use, their intrinsic characteristics and the similarities and differences between them.

OVERLAY OFF-PRESS COLOR PROOFING SYSTEMS

As described in Chapter I photomechanical off-press color proofing was first used during World War II for pre-proofing maps which were composed of a number of separate line images. After the war many attempts were made to develop similar systems for color proofing 4-color process reproductions which consisted of halftone images. Among the products showing considerable promise were overlay systems using diazo dye images that were produced by exposure and development of individual films.

The first of these systems was *Ozachrome,* introduced by Ozalid Corp. (GAF) in the early 1950's. It used a limited choice of colors and relatively clear films. While the proofs could be used internally for initial checking of layout, register and fit, and whether copy was in the correct color, they could not be used for final checking or shown to customers for color approval as misregister was a problem. They had severely grayed whites and highlight tints and the colors were poor matches to the printing ink colors. The next development was *Diazochrome* by Tecnifax (later Scott Graphics, and now James River Graphics) which offered a wider choice of dye colors and slightly clearer films but they still suffered from the same limitations of grayed whites and highlights.

It was not until 1960 when 3M introduced COLOR KEY which used color pigments and clearer dimensionally stable polyester films that the overlay system began to replace press proofs for internal quality control uses. While they are not generally accepted by customers for color approval, they are used extensively internally as they are easier to make and less expensive than all but a few of the other systems. It is estimated that 60% of the off-press color proofs used are made by the overlay method.

COLOR KEY Proofs

COLOR KEY Contact Imaging Material is manufactured by 3M. It is available only for making color proofs from negatives. A COLOR KEY Proof consists of a composite of four separate polyester films, 0.002 inch (0.05 mm) thick, each coated with a diazo light sensitive coating which is covered with a pigmented lacquer containing the pigment color to be represented by the film. There are nearly 40 Color Key hues, including 26 Pantone Matching System (PMS) colors, and a wide selection of process colors to match most process color ink combinations used in the industry. COLOR KEY has a dot retention range from 3–97%, 18-month shelf life and is available in sizes from 10×12 inches (254 mm $\times$ 308 mm) to 25 $\times$ 38 inches (635 mm $\times$ 965 mm). The films should be stored in their original light-tight container when not in use unless yellow safelights are used. Their light sensitivity is low enough to allow handling and processing under normal room light.

Procedure for Making COLOR KEY Proofs

In use, the Color Key film is placed in the vacuum frame with the pre-sensitized ink pigmented coating facing away from the light source (emulsion notches in upper left hand corner of film (Figure V-1A). The negative separation film to be exposed is placed with its emulsion side in contact with the back of the Color Key film. Exposure is made to a high intensity ultra-violet (UV-rich) light source like carbon arc, mercury vapor, pulsed xenon or metal halide lamp. Exposure time should be sufficient to produce a solid 4–5 (clear 6) step on the GATF Sensitivity Guide (see Chapter III),

A   B

Figure V-1. Notches in color proof films — (A) upper left for Emulsion/Back exposure. (B) upper right for Emulsion/Emulsion exposure.

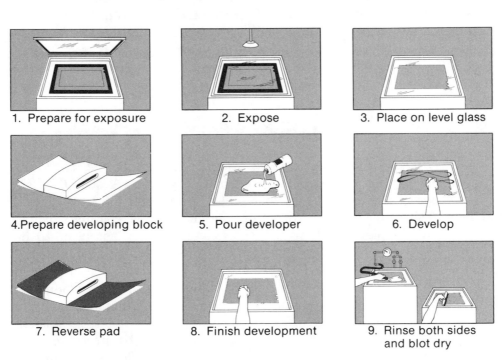

1. Prepare for exposure   2. Expose   3. Place on level glass

4. Prepare developing block 5. Pour developer   6. Develop

7. Reverse pad   8. Finish development 9. Rinse both sides
                                                      and blot dry

Figure V-2. Steps for making 3M COLOR KEY proofs. (3M)

Processing can be done manually on a flat glass surface at 70° to 80°F (21° to 27°C) using a Webril proof pad with a figure 8 motion and light to moderate pressure until all the coating in the non-image areas is loosened. (Temperatures above 80°F (27°C) result in tender images; temperatures below 70°F (21°C) cause slower, more difficult development.) The film is rinsed thoroughly on both sides to remove all loosened coating, squeegeed firmly on the uncoated side with a soft rubber squeegee and dried with newsprint or other absorbent paper. The steps are illustrated in Figure V-2.

Alternatively, exposed Color Key film can be processed in the 3M MR-424 Color Key processor which automatically develops, rinses and dries 3M COLOR KEY, TRANSFER KEY or negative MATCHPRINT in sheets up to 26 inches (660 mm) wide at the rate of 18 inches (457 mm) per minute. The sheet of exposed film is guided onto the entrance rollers where transport rollers carry it to a presoak station and then a belt holds the film against the rotating developing brush which also meters developer solution to the film. After development the sheet is dried and delivered onto the unit's collection tray. The processor employs a flammable mixture so it should be used in a well ventilated area and kept away from heat and open flames; and personnel should avoid prolonged breathing of vapors which should be vented to the outside through a 300 cfm (8.5 cubic meters per minute) exhaust hood.*

After processing, each Color Key film is inspected to insure proper dot size which is related to exposure. Dot loss indicates underexposure (low Sensitivity Guide numbers) and screen plugging or halation indicates overexposure (high Sensitivity Guide numbers) or lack of vacuum contact (use GATF Star Target or GATF Dot Gain Scale or other similar scales for control). Exposing through the back of the film makes exposure conditions very critical. To produce the final proof, the Color Key films are mounted in register with the emulsion side down or facing a white fluorescent cover stock as a reflective backing sheet for the proof, such as Beckett "Hi-White," Simpson-Lee "Vicksburg Starwhite," or Mead "Meadbrite." The preferred order of laydown of the colored films is *yellow, magenta, cyan* and *black — Y M C K* (Figure V-3).

3M Color Key is a relatively inexpensive, simple and rapid overlay color proofing system designed primarily for internal plant use. They have the additional advantage of all overlay systems that each color can be checked individually or in combination with other colors as with progressive proofs. Like all overlay systems they have the disadvantage of grayed whites and highlight tints due to light absorption in the polyester films and internal reflection of light between the film surfaces in the composite assembly of all the films in the proof. Graying of the

---

* 3M Instruction Sheet MR-424-F (722) VP.

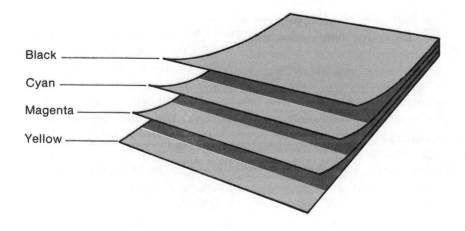

Figure V-3. Cross-section of 3M COLOR KEY proof showing order of laydown — YMCK. (3M)

middletones due to light spread, refraction and diffusion between the film layers is equivalent to optical dot gain (as described in Chapter III and Appendix C) which could simulate that obtained with offset printing on uncoated papers and newsprint. In any case, the darkening of the highlights is excessive and does not correspond with any of the dot gain curves found by Franz Sigg, Felix Brunner, and others in their studies (Appendix C).

NAPS/PAPS Proofs

NAPS and *PAPS* are overlay proofing systems manufactured and marketed by Enco Printing Products, American Hoechst Corporation. NAPS is the acronym for *Negative Acting Proofing System*; PAPS is the acronym for *Positive Acting Proofing System*. The systems have the following common features:

- Both can be processed either separately or together in the same developer by hand or machine. The developer is an aqueous solution without any organic solvents which can process all colors, except white, in widths up to 25 inches (635 mm) at a speed of 26 inches (660 mm) per minute. Both are available in sizes 10 × 12 inches (254 mm × 308 mm) to 25 × 38 inches (635 mm × 965 mm) (special sizes available on request); shelf life of both is 12 months.
- Substrate is 0.003 inch (0.076 mm) thick which improves handling without compromising resolution.
- Emulsion-to-emulsion exposure is used making the system less

sensitive to exposure variations and thus capable of optimum dot reproduction.

- Dyed sensitized coatings are used instead of two coatings of sensitizer and pigments as used on 3M Color Key. Colors of the dyes are more transparent than pigments so individual films can be assembled in any sequence.

PAPS is supplied only in the process colors yellow, magenta, cyan and black and its use requires a post-exposure of each film to stabilize the colors. NAPS is supplied in the same process colors and, in addition, an alternate cyan and magenta, and supplementary colors red, green, blue, orange, brown and white. The standard NAPS magenta is close in hue to *rhodamine Y* and the alternate magenta matches *lithol rubine*. The alternate cyan is stronger than the standard cyan. NAPS colors do not require post-exposure. The *opaque white* NAPS film is different from the other colors and requires special handling in exposure and processing.

Procedure for Making NAPS/PAPS Proofs

In use, the magenta NAPS or PAPS film is placed emulsion side up in the vacuum frame (notches in upper right hand corner of sheet) (Figure V-1B); the separation film to be proofed is positioned emulsion side down, on the NAPS or PAPS film so there is emulsion-to-emulsion contact between the two films; and full vacuum is drawn before starting exposure (appearance of "Newton rings" indicate good contact). The magenta NAPS film is exposed to produce a solid 5 – 6 (clear 7) on the GATF Sensitivity Guide. This exposure is used for all the other NAPS films. To determine the correct exposure for PAPS film, the magenta PAPS film is exposed to produce a clear step 3, ghost 4 on the GATF Sensitivity Guide and this will be the correct exposure for all the other films in the set. Any high intensity UV-rich light source can be used for exposure, preferably of the metal halide or high pressure mercury vapor type.

The steps for manual processing are shown in Figure V-4. The exposed NAPS or PAPS film is placed on a slightly tilted flat surface. Best visibility is provided by a white plastic sheet. Developer is poured on a pad of non-woven cotton wrapped around a developing block and, using a light sweeping motion, the developer is spread completely over the surface of the film. It is allowed to stand about 20 seconds and for the next 40 seconds, or so, the same light sweeping motion is used to remove softened coating, adding developer as necessary, to keep the film flooded so pad glides across it. Both sides of the film are rinsed with tap water [about 70°F (20°C)] for about 20 seconds to stop development

Place exposed film
on flat surface

Pour developer on
cotton wrapped block

Remove softened coating
from unexposed areas

Rinse both sides of
film with water

Blot film with
clean newsprint

Figure V-4. Steps for making NAPS and PAPS proofs.
(ENCO)

action. The amount of water used to rinse the film and flush the sink should be about six times the amount of developer used. The film is blotted with clean newsprint until all water droplets are absorbed.

PAPS film must be exposed again after developing for the same length of time as the first exposure in order to stabilize the colors. This is the post-exposure referred to earlier.

For automatic processing of the films, a special NAPS/PAPS processor is available which uses the same developer as for manual processing and, in one continuous operation, automatically develops and dries films up to 25 inches (635 mm) wide at a speed of over two feet (610 mm) per minute. A schematic of the processor is shown in Figure V-5. In use, a sheet of exposed NAPS or PAPS film is fed through the feed rollers of the processor onto a transport belt which carries the film through the water-base developer and under the oscillating applicator. Developer is sprayed through the base of the oscillating applicator as it gently wipes the softened coating from the non-image areas of the film. As the film leaves the developing section it moves through rollers which squeegee off the developer and travels to the rinse section from which it goes to the drying section and then into the receiving tray — all at the rate of 26 inches (660 mm) per minute.

To complete the composite proof the films are mounted in register on a white fluorescent paper or cover stock. ENCO recommends mounting the films with emulsion side up as already mentioned, any color sequence can be used because the dyes are very tyransparent. Sequences of *magenta, yellow, cyan* and *black — M Y C K;* and *cyan, yellow, magenta* and *black — C Y M K* are suggested. For improved reproducibility the

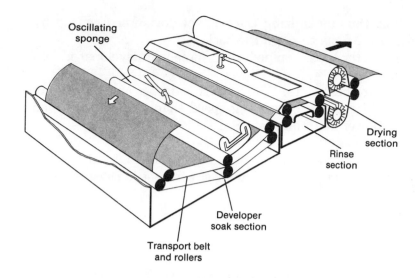

Figure V-5. Schematic of NAPS/PAPS Processor. (ENCO)

same base stock and color sequence should always be used. A finished hand processed proof can be made in 14 minutes and in 7 minutes with machine processing.

Advantages claimed by the manufacturer for the NAPS/PAPS proofs over 3M COLOR KEY proofs are:

• Generally better dot reproduction than COLOR KEY as the NAPS/PAPS films are exposed emulsion-to-emulsion with the separation

TABLE V-I

COMPARISON OF AUTOMATIC PROCESSORS
FOR OVERLAY SYSTEMS

	3M	Enco-Hoechst
	MR-424	CF-251
Proof Process	Color Key	NAPS/PAPS
Chemistry	Solvent Base	Water Base
Ventilation	Warning: Vent Required	None
Speed	18″/min. (457 mm)	26″/min. (660 mm)
Electrical	120 V-AC	120 V-AC
Cost*	$11,800** (12/82)	$10,600 (2/84)

*List prices not including discounts.
**Includes freight and handling charges.

films, thus minimizing the risks of dot spread caused by exposing negative films through the back.
- One water base, non-polluting, fume-free developer is used for both films.
- Superior flesh tints; NAPS black is deeper and richer in color.
- One-third faster processing speed than COLOR KEY and 15% to 20% lower material cost. (See Table V-I.)

Limitations of the system are similar to 3M COLOR KEY; i.e., grayed whites and highlights indicating lower contrast in these areas than on the press print.

CROMACHECK Proofs

CROMACHECK is a totally dry overlay negative color proofing system manufactured by DuPont that produces images by exposure only and requires no processing. It is a peel-apart system in which each color film consists of a negative-working UV-sensitive photopolymer precoated with the appropriate process color pigment and protected on the top and bottom by thin polyester films. The top film is 0.002 inch (0.05 mm) thick and is shiny; the bottom film is 0.005 inch (0.13 mm) thick and is frosty. Color films are available in sizes 11 × 14 inches (279 mm × 356 mm), 16 × 20 inches (406 mm × 508 mm), 20 × 24 inches (508 mm × 610 mm), and 25 × 38 inches (635 mm × 965 mm). Exposure changes the adhesive characteristics of the photopolymer so that the exposed parts corresponding to the clear areas of the negative adhere to the top film and the unexposed areas adhere to the bottom film. Processing or separation of the image and non-image areas of the subject is accomplished by peeling the two films apart. The positive image remains on the top film and becomes one of the four films in the overlay proof, and the bottom film is discarded.

Besides the film which is labeled Cromacheck Overlay Color Proofing Film (C4/CO), the system consists of a vacuum easel which is commercially available from M.P. Goodkin, Inc., or Bychrome Co.; a vacuum frame; a UV-rich light source like metal halide (preferably diazo type or photopolymer type with Kokomo filter) or pulsed xenon; and a bright-white (fluorescent) base stock similar to those used in the other overlay systems. The Cromacheck films should be stored in the plastic pouches and boxes supplied until ready for use. Ideal storage conditions are: temperature — 68°-72°F (20°-22°C) and relative humidity — 40 – 50%.

Procedure for Making CROMACHECK Proofs

After punching the Cromacheck film for register it is placed in a vacuum frame with the shiny side in contact with the emulsion side of the separation negative (edges around film should be masked, otherwise "kinks" result when films are peeled apart); a high vacuum is pulled to insure good contact, and the exposure is made. Exposures are of the order of 15 to 30 seconds depending on the power of the light source and its distance from the frame.

Correct exposure is determined by placing a sheet of magenta or cyan Cromacheck Overlay Film in a vacuum frame shiny side up; a DuPont Exposure Control Target (negative) is positioned emulsion side down about one inch (25 mm) from any corner; a high vacuum is applied and a series of test exposures are made by using a cardboard mask above the vacuum frame glass. After exposure the vacuum is released, the Cromacheck film is peeled apart and the results are evaluated. *Optimum* exposure is represented by sharp highlight dots without plugging the shadows (95% dots); *Overexposure* or *poor vacuum drawdown* shows dot spread with plugging of halftones from middletones to shadows; *underexposure* shows dot sharpening with loss of highlight dots. Once optimum exposure is determined it is used for all the films in the set of separations. If the vacuum frame is large and the subject is of moderate size all four images can be exposed at the same time, or if the image is too large, two can be exposed at a time thus shortening proof making time.

CROMACHECK does not require development or wet processing. The image is produced immediately by the exposure in the top layer and becomes available for use by peeling it apart from the bottom layer which is then discarded. To simplify the peel-apart procedure a vacuum easel is used to hold down the film while the top layer is removed. The polymer is adhesive and a steady pull is needed to prevent defects in the image. Reasonably priced vacuum easels are available from two manufacturers. As of September, 1983 M.P. Goodkin Co. offered a 25 × 38 inch (635 mm × 965 mm) easel complete with vacuum pump for $310. Bychrome Corp. had four sizes of easels complete with pumps; 11 × 14 inch (279 mm × 356 mm) at $225; 16 × 20 inch (406 mm × 508 mm) at $261; 20 × 24 inch (508 mm × 610 mm) at $311; 24 × 28 inch (610 mm × 711 mm) at $371; and a 30 × 40 inch (762 mm × 1016 mm) easel was promised for mid-1984.

The vacuum easel, which has four heavy duty suction cups, is mounted securely on a 30″ high flat table with smooth top. Double faced tape is applied to the left and top edges of the easel as shown in Figure V-6. The exposed film (shiny side up) is placed on the easel with the

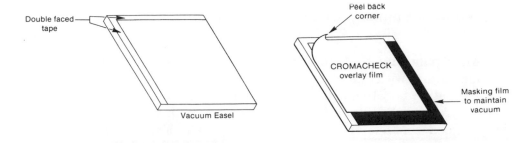

Figure V-6. Procedure for separating CROMACHECK proof. (DuPont)

"peel" corner in the top left corner of the easel; the vacuum is turned on until the film has a pebbly appearance (uncovered area of the easel should be masked with film to assure maximum vacuum drawdown and prevention of film being pulled off during the peeling process); masking tape is used on the peel corner to separate the top layer which is carefully pulled back about one inch (25 mm); the top layer is then completely removed by firmly grasping the corner and pulling the film with a rapid motion without hesitation until the entire layer is removed. After all films have been pulled apart they are registered on the bright-white base stock with the shiny sides up. Recommended sequence is *yellow, magenta, cyan* and *black — Y–M-C-K.*

COMPARISON AND USES OF OVERLAY SYSTEMS

A comparison of the salient features of the four overlay color proofing systems by three manufacturers described in this chapter is shown on Table V-II. As can be seen from the table there are many similarities and a few differences between the processes. Most of the products look very similar with a few distinguishing differences. They all have the advantages of reasonable speed and relatively low cost but suffer from the limitation of grayed whites and highlight tints due to internal reflections between the separate films.

This limitation of grayed whites can be eliminated by establishing optical contact between the films with the use of colorless liquids between the film layers. This technique brightens the whites and light tints but is very messy and unwieldy so it has never been incorporated in any of the systems.

Despite this limitation these systems have become well established in the industry. Many printing plants, trade shops and engravers use overlay, integral and press proofing to satisfy the broad spectrum of their customer's requirements. Overlay proofs have found a large number of applications, enough to make them the most widely used off-press proofing medium representing over 60% of the off-press color proofing market. Among these applications are:

- Evaluation of color separation quality before originals are removed from the camera, enlarger, vacuum frame, or scanner.
- Guide for color correction by dot etchers.
- Checking the accuracy of composition, color breaks, overlaps, registration, etc., on final flats before platemaking.
- Initial and/or final proof for customer approval in cases where there are good communications and mutual trust and confidence between printer, engraver, and customer.
- Progressive proofs as a press guide.
- Visual aids for Viewgraphs or slides.
- Design applications

TABLE V-II

COMPARISONS OF OVERLAY COLOR PROOFING SYSTEMS

Colorants	3M Color Key COLOR KEY	Enco-Hoechst NAPS PAPS	DuPont CROMACHECK
	Pigments	Dyes	Pigments
Number of Colors	40	12 4	4 (1983)
Film Thickness	0.002"	0.003"	0.002"
Shelf Life	18 mos.	12 mos.	—
Exposure	E/B	E/E	E/B
Chemistry	Solvent	WB	None
Auto Processor	MR-424	CF-251	None
Proof	E-down	E-up	E-down
Color Order	YMCK	any	YMCK
Material Costs*	(1/82)	(2/84)	(9/83)
Films/sq. ft. (929 sq. cm.)/color**	$ 1.31	$ 1.44	$1.30
Developer/Gal.	$20.05	$16.25	Vacuum Easel $300.00

CODE
  E = Emulsion   B = Back   Y = Yellow   M = Magenta   C = Cyan
  K = Black   WB = Waterbase

*Basic costs: list prices as of September 1983 not including quantity or size discounts.
**Based on prices for 20"x24" (508 mm x 610 mm) film in quantities of 50 to 100 per box.

Overlay off-press color proofs appeal to the preparatory (pre-press) departments as they are easy to make and usually produce substantial time savings. Salesmen like them because they get faster customer response and better customer reaction and satisfaction especially if the overlay proof is used for color approval as the production press print is usually brighter and cleaner, particularly in the highlights, than the proof. To management, the overlay off-press proof can often mean higher productivity and lower costs in the highly labor intensive pre-press departments.

Chapter VI

Integral (Single Sheet) Color Proofing Systems

The first off-press color proofing system used in the industry was an integral system in which all the colors were combined on a single sheet or base. The process was *WATERCOTE* by Sam Sachs of Direct Reproduction Corp. which was a variation of the process Sachs had developed and used for pre-proofing maps at the US Coast and Geodetic Survey (Washington, D.C.) during World War II (see Chapter I). Overlay proofing systems came later.

As mentioned in Chapter V, the integral (single sheet) color proofing systems in general use are *WATERCOTE* and its modification, *KWIK-PROOF;* American Photo-Graphics Corp., *FINAL PROOF;* Agfa-Gevaert *GEVAPROOF;* 3M *TRANSFERKEY* and *MATCHPRINT;* DuPont *CROMALIN;* Keuffel and Esser *SPECTRA;* and Kodak *EKTAFLEX PCT.* These processes will be discussed in groups: WATERCOTE, KWIK-PROOF, and FINAL PROOF use superposed coatings of sensitized inks on plastic bases; GEVAPROOF, TRANSFERKEY and MATCHPRINT use pigmented sensitized coatings transferred to a single base; CROM-ALIN and SPECTRA use adhesive polymers; EKTAFLEX PCT consists of photographic dye layers. Another integral proofing system has been introduced which uses electrophotographic principles. It is the KC-COLOR PROOF which is described and discussed in Chapter VII. A number of other systems have been introduced, used for a short time and discarded in favor of the listed processes. Some of them were mentioned historically in Chapter I.

The integral off-press color proof comes the closest to having the capability of simulating a press print as it consists of a combination, or composite, of all the colors in the reproduction on a single base. The reason there are so many processes and more are being developed, is that no single off-press color proofing process completely satisfies the scenario of an ideal proof with ink images on paper. All the processes differ from press prints in that the final image does not consist of individual ink layers on paper (the most common print substrate) but it is composed of ink layers on a dimensionally stable base like polyester film (WATERCOTE, KWIK-PROOF, FINAL PROOF, TRANSFER KEY, MATCHPRINT, and GEVAPROOF) or individual toner images on thin polymer layers laminated together on the printing substrate or a special paper base (CROMALIN). SPECTRA and EKTAFLEX PCT are different. SPECTRA consists of toner layers transferred to the actual printing substrate covered by either an adhesive and film layer or a layer of photopolymerized adhesive polymer. It comes closer to simulating a press print in structure than the other processes because it has fewer layers covering the toners and is on the actual printing substrate. EKTAFLEX PCT is a color print material on a paper base consisting of three dye layers in gelatin.

SUPERPOSED SENSITIZED INK COLOR PROOFING SYSTEMS

There are three color proofing systems that use four superposed sensitized inks coated and processed in sequence on a single base — WATERCOTE, KWIK-PROOF and FINAL PROOF.

WATERCOTE and KWIK-PROOF Proofing Systems

WATERCOTE and KWIK-PROOF are off-press color proofing processes manufactured by Direct Reproduction Corp. They employ dispersions of printing inks in photosensitive coatings which are coated on a dimensionally stable plastic base. After coating and drying the base is exposed to the separation negative for that color, developed in water and dried. The base is then recoated with the next color ink, dried and exposed to the appropriate separation negative, developed and dried, after which the process is repeated for the other two colors resulting in a composite proof consisting of four ink pigment images on a plastic base. KWIK-PROOF is similar except that it has shortened processing procedures depending on the uses for proofs.

Other differences between WATERCOTE and KWIK-PROOF are:
• In the WATERCOTE process the photosensitive inks are coated on the base in a plate whirler and in the KWIK-PROOF process a

wipe-on technique is used to apply the light sensitive inks to the matte base.

- WATERCOTE can use bases with glossy or matte finishes to simulate coated or uncoated paper, while KWIK-PROOF uses only a matte finished base.

Plastic sheets for both processes are available in sizes up to 54 × 76 inches (1372 mm × 1930 mm) in thicknesses of 0.003 inch (0.08 mm), 0.005 inch (0.13 mm) and 0.010 inch (0.25 mm). Forty colors including process colors and a clear reducer are available, all of which can be mixed to make hundreds of colors. Sensitized colors forWATERCOTE have a 12-month shelf life; KWIK-PROOF sensitized colors are 10% higher in cost and have a 9-month shelf life.

WATERCOTE and KWIK-PROOF have base sheets that can be coated on both sides so that two-sided proofs can be made that represent a complete 16-page signature on a 25 x 38 inch (635 mm x 965 mm) sheet, 32-page signature on a 38 x 50 inch (965 mm x 1270 mm) sheet, or 64-page signature on a 50 x 76 inch (1270 mm x 1930 mm) sheet. These can be checked for register, layout, folding, trims, crossovers and other complicated design features.

Procedure for Making WATERCOTE Proofs

The steps for making WATERCOTE proofs are shown in Figure VI-1. The base sheet, glossy or matte, depending on whether the final print will be on coated or uncoated paper, is punched for pin register and mounted on the bed of a plate whirler; the sheet is wet with water (glossy sheets must be pretreated with a Watercote primer). The proper sensitized color ink is poured on the base while whirling and allowed to whirl until dry.

The coated base sheet is placed in a vacuum frame; the separation negative corresponding to the color of the ink is placed on the base with the emulsion side of the film in contact with the coated surface of the base; a high vacuum is pulled (about 25 inches [635 mm] of mercury) to

Coat in whirler

Expose to negative

Develop with water spray

Figure VI-1. Steps for making WATERCOTE proofs. (DR)

insure intimate contact of the two surfaces; and exposure is made using a high intensity, UV-rich light source like metal halide, mercury vapor, pulsed xenon or carbon arc. Correct exposure is that needed to produce a solid step 4 on the GATF Sensitivity Guide. The exposure is different between colors but their ratios are constant. After exposure the base is removed from the vacuum frame, placed in a sink with a flat platform and developed with a fine water spray.

After drying the base sheet is mounted on the bed of the whirler again and coated with the sensitized ink of the next color. When dry, it is placed in the vacuum frame, registered with the appropriate separation negative, exposed, developed and dried. The operation is repeated with the other two color inks and separation negatives.

The result is a 4-color proof in printing ink pigments on a plastic base that can be used for many checking functions and comes close to simulating a press proof. A disadvantage of the process is the length of time required to make a proof — 30 – 45 minutes.

Procedure for Making KWIK-PROOFS

The steps for making KWIK-PROOFS are shown in Figure VI-2. The KWIK-PROOF process differs from WATERCOTE in several ways. It is much simpler and faster. Slightly more viscous inks are used which can be applied to the matte plastic base by a wipe-on technique. A small amount of the light-sensitive color ink is poured on the base, spread with a KWIK-PROOF block and buffed until dry. The coated base is placed in a vacuum frame; the appropriate negative is registered on pins with the emulsion side facing the coated base; and the base is exposed to a high intensity UV-rich light source. The exposed base can be developed in

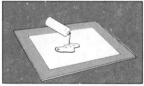
Pour color on sheet

Spread and wipe dry

Expose

Wash with water

Figure VI-2. Steps for making KWIK-PROOFS. (DR)

water like WATERCOTE, recoated with the next color, exposed, washed and repeated for the next two colors.

To shorten proof-making time for proofs to be used for checking register, color breaks, etc., the following procedure can be used. Without developing after exposure, the base is immediately coated with the next color ink, registered with the appropriate separation negative and exposed. (Each new color ink develops the preceding one.) There is color contamination in the proofs which is not objectionable for some uses. This procedure is followed for the other two colors. Upon completion of the final exposure the base is placed in the sink and washed thoroughly with water. Total time for making a KWIK-PROOF is about 20 minutes. A variation of this procedure is to process cyan and black without developing in between and exposing and developing yellow and magenta in sequence. There is less dirtying of colors with this procedure. These proofs are not intended for color approval.

dr COLOR PROOFS

Since the introduction of precoated and presensitized plates for lithography the use of the whirler for in-plant coating of plates has diminished so that now the method and the whirler are almost obsolete. Most modern day plate rooms do not have whirlers. Because of this and the length of time required for making WATERCOTE proofs considerable research has been done on the development of a new coating method for WATERCOTE. A new color proofing system has been developed called *dr COLOR* which uses a new unique coating method which consists of a drum around which the plastic base is wrapped and coating is done by placing a bead of sensitized ink in the nip between a polished steel rod and the base and slowly rotating the drum. The system is automated and will not only make more consistent coatings with controllable ink densities but will speed up the process considerably and could replace both WATERCOTE and KWIK-PROOF.

FINAL PROOF Proofing System

Like WATERCOTE and KWIK-PROOF, *FINAL PROOF* is a negative off-press color proofing system which uses light-sensitive (photopolymer) inks with the same pigments as color process printing inks. The system was introduced at PRINT 80 by American Photo-Graphics Corp. and is in limited use in the U.S. and other countries. It is a simple process consisting of a coater, and a developing machine in which water is the only chemical used. The major difference between FINAL PROOF and WATERCOTE is in the method of coating.

FINAL PROOF uses a polyester coated proofing base or sealed printing substrate and calibrated precision wire wound Meyer rods for controlling the sensitized ink film thickness in the coating which in turn determines the solid ink density of that color on the proof. Seven different coating rods are used with numbers from 8 to 14. The density differences between consecutively numbered rods is about 0.05 density units. A #11 rod produces coating film thicknesses, with the light-sensitive inks, that result in ink densities on the proof corresponding approximately to the SWOP Standards: Yellow 0.95; Cyan 1.25; Magenta 1.35; and Black 1.45.

The coating unit with built-in drying system and paper roller (for clean up) coats substrates up to 20 × 25 inches (508 mm × 635 mm) manually with a Meyer rod. The developer unit is semi-automatic in operation, can develop a proof up to 20 × 30 inches (508 mm × 762 mm) in size, and uses only water for development. The recommended light source for exposure is mercury vapor; metal halide and pulsed xenon lamps can be used but they require Kokomo filters. Other materials needed for making proofs are polyester proofing base; sealer and sealer solvent for coating substrates other than the polyester proofing base to make them water resistant; pigmented photopolymer inks in tubes; and a special mat used as a backing in coating

Procedure for Making FINAL PROOFS

To make a FINAL PROOF the substrate is punched with a pin register system so it can be registered with the separation films and held in the coater. The Meyer coating rod is positioned across the substrate in the coater; a bead of the first sensitized ink is placed between the leading edge of the rod and the substrate; and the rod is drawn manually with a smooth motion across the surface of the substrate. The Meyer rod meters the proper amount of the ink on the substrate to produce the correct ink density of that color on the proof. The ink is dried in seconds by moving the drying unit over the coated surface.

The separation negatives corresponding to the ink color and coated substrate are placed, emulsion-to-emulsion, in register in a vacuum frame; the vacuum is drawn; and the exposure is made with a high intensity mercury vapor lamp. Correct exposure can be determined with a GATF Sensitivity Guide. After exposure the substrate is developed in the FINAL PROOF developer unit with plain water, and dried. Coating, exposing and developing are repeated for each of the other colors. The order or sequence of colors can be varied to correspond to the order of printing on the press. If the wrong sensitized ink is applied or there are defects in the coating, it can be washed off with water and the correct color reapplied.

Benefits claimed for the FINAL PROOF process are:

- Accurate dot-for-dot reproduction from film to proofing base.
- Dot gain can be simulated by overexposure or the use of a spacer during exposure.
- Repeatability
- Proofing on both sides of the base.
- Ability to proof on a variety of bases by use of the sealer.
- Ability to change image density by use of different coating rods.
- Simple procedure for making proofs with minimum training.
- Full 4-color 20 × 24 inch (508 mm × 610 mm) proofs can be made in 20 to 25 minutes.
- Lower cost than most of the other color proofing systems offering similar simulations of press prints

Installations of the process use the proof both for internal checking and customer approval.

DIRECT TRANSFER COLOR PROOFING SYSTEMS

There are three off-press color proofing systems in which four precoated pigmented sensitized layers are transferred and processed in sequence on a single base — GEVAPROOF, TRANSFER KEY and MATCHPRINT.

GEVAPROOF PROOFING SYSTEM

GEVAPROOF, manufactured by Agfa-Gevaert is also a negative off-press color proofing system that uses pigmented light-sensitive coatings, but, unlike WATERCOTE, KWIK-PROOF and FINAL PROOF, the pigmented coatings, which consist of photochemically insolubilized gelatin layers on separate films, the coatings are transferred from the films to the substrate and the protective films are removed before exposure and processing. The final proof, thus, consists of four pigment images in register on the plastic base.

The GEVAPROOF system consists of the following materials and equipment:

- Gevaproof S base — dimensionally stable 0.007 inch (0.18 mm) polyester film coated on both sides with a smooth white opaque layer that can receive images on both sides.
- Six separate pigmented light-sensitive films: Gevaproof J-yellow, Gevaproof C2-cyan, Gevaproof M2-magenta, Gevaproof MBS-magenta "British Standards," Gevaproof Mg-magenta (cold), and Gevaproof B2-black. Each pigmented light-sensitive emulsion, consisting of gelatin, a light sensitizer and a process color pigment, is coated on a temporary thin cellulose triacetate base which is stripped off and discarded after the emulsion has been transferred to the Gevaproof S base.
- Two solutions: an *alcohol/water* solution to effect transfer of the pigmented sensitized coatings to the base, and an *activator* solution (supplied as two packets in water soluble powder form — Gevaproof G650P) which hardens the gelatin in the image areas between exposure and processing.
- Four simple machines for carrying out the process: *Gevaproof 100* — a tray with built in timer and indicator to check alcohol/water balance; *Gevaproof 200* transfer unit; *Gevaproof 300* drying unit; and *Gevaproof 400* unit for activation and washing. Gevaproof units 200 and 300 can be stacked to conserve space.
- *Gevaproof L* — lacquer supplied in a spray can to produce high gloss proofs to simulate coated paper if necessary.

Procedure for Making GEVAPROOFS: The steps for making GEVAPROOFS are shown in Figure VI-3. The sheet of Gevaproof S is

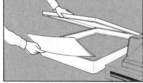

1. Immerse base sheet in alcohol solution

2. Place moist base sheet in transfer unit

3. Transfer color sheet to base sheet

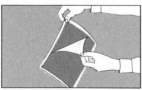

4. Remove temporary base of color sheet

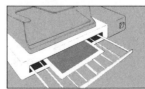

5. Place sheet in drying unit

6. Expose to separation negative

Figure VI-3. Steps for making GEVAPROOFS. Steps are explained in text. (AG)

immersed for at least 90 seconds in the alcohol/water solution at cool room temperature (65° – 68°F — 18° – 20°C) in the Gevaproof 100 tray. The mixture should consist of 2 parts of ethyl alcohol and one part water and should have a specific gravity of 0.870. The ratio of alcohol to water in the mixture is critical as the mixture is used to moisten the gelatin in the color layer when it is brought in contact with the base. If the ratio is correct, the gelatin swells and adheres to the base. If there is too much alcohol in the mixture, the gelatin does not swell much and has less adhesion. If ethyl alcohol is not available, isopropyl alcohol can be used with the same ratio of alcohol to water. When isopropyl alcohol is used the Gevaproof S is wet with plain water (no alcohol) for one minute before the first color is transferred. The alcohol/water mixture is used for the succeeding colors.

The moistened Gevaproof base sheet is placed in the Gevaproof 200 transfer unit and aligned with a color sheet like Gevaproof C-2 (cyan) with the matte, or emulsion, side in contact with the base. The foot switch is turned on and the color sheet is transferred to the Gevaproof S. After about 30 seconds the temporary base or backing film of the color sheet is stripped off and only the color layer remains on the Gevaproof S. The sheet is placed in the Gevaproof 300 drying unit which takes about one minute to dry the combination of Gevaproof S and color layer (Gevaproof C-2).

All the separation negatives and the color layers should be punched on a pin register system to insure proper register of the images on the proof. The dry Gevaproof S with Gevaproof C-2 color layer is registered with the cyan separation negative and exposed to a high intensity UV-rich light source like mercury vapor or pulsed xenon. Proper exposure is usually the time required to produce a solid step 6 on the GATF Sensitivity Guide (density of about 1.0). All colors use about the same exposure except the Gevaproof B (black) which requires about three times the exposure. The exposed sheet is immersed in the Gevaproof G650 activator solution at cool room temperature (65°F – 18°C) for at least 30 seconds. After the sheet is removed from the activator solution the coating is washed from the unexposed areas in a washing tank using lukewarm water (95 – 105°F — 35 – 41°C).

After washing, the sheet of Gevaproof S with the cyan image is immersed again in the alcohol/water mixture for at least 90 seconds. The next color is transferred to the moistened Gevaproof S as already described and all the succeeding steps are performed. This procedure is repeated for the other two colors. Color sequence can be matched to the color order of the inks on the press. After all four color images have been transferred to the Gevaproof S and washed, it is again immersed in the alcohol/water mixture. With image side up, the proof is run through the rollers of the Gevaproof 200 transfer unit to remove all excess water and prevent the possible formation of drying marks in the Gevaproof 300 drying unit.

While the procedure appears complicated, GEVAPROOFS are consistent in density, reasonably independent of corrections due to human error or changes in techniques and are relatively simple to make. No special climatic conditions are required — it handles well at relative humidities between 30% and 75% and room temperature of 68 - 75°F — 20 - 24°C). If the air is too dry, stripping of the film base from the color sheet may be difficult. In such cases up to 10% water can be added to the alcohol/water solution. The activator solution must be protected from strong light, must be prepared fresh daily and be used at temperatures below 68°F (20°C). Wash water should be between 95° and 105° F (35 - 41°C) and filtered to prevent local blistering from water impurities when transferring succeeding color sheets. Softened water should be avoided as it can interfere with proper transfer of succeeding colors. Distilled or demineralized water is recommended for washing.

TRANSFER KEY and MATCHPRINT Proofing Systems

TRANSFER KEY and MATCH PRINT are similar off-press color proofing systems, manufactured by 3M, that use four pigmented sensitized layers transferred to a single base. Both use the same materials and equipment except that:

- TRANSFER KEY is a composite 4-color proof laminated to a transfer base: MATCHPRINT is a similar 4-color proof laminated to the actual printing substrate but with a spacer between the proof and the substrate.
- MATCHPRINT is capable of simulating higher press dot gain such as experienced on web offset presses.
- TRANSFER KEY is available only as a negative process; MATCHPRINT has a negative and a positive process.
- Negative MATCHPRINT has a special yellow color sheet which is the first color down on the proof and has a spacer and adhesive layer for lamination of the final proof to the printing substrate. The materials needed for each process are base sheet; pigmented photosensitive films corresponding in color to the process colors; a laminator and an automatic processor. Negative TRANSFER KEY has 10 color sheets, 5 *magentas*, 2 *cyans*, 2 *yellows*, and a *black*, including the SWOP colors; 3M MR-530 TRANSFER KEY Laminator; and 3M MR-424 COLOR KEY/TRANSFER KEY Processor. Positive MATCHPRINT has 4 color sheets — the SWOP

colors magenta M51, cyan C25, standard yellow and black; uses 3M MR-527 Positive Proofing Laminator and 3M MR-427 Positive Proofing Processor.

Procedure for Making TRANSFER KEY Proofs

The TRANSFER KEY sheet of the first-down color, usually yellow, is positioned on the carrier belt of the 3M MR-530 TRANSFER KEY Laminator and the foot switch is turned on. The sheet goes through the machine cycle once during which the protective polyester backing film adheres to the blanket on the rotating drum (a close-up of the TRANSFER KEY color sheet is shown in Figure VI-4). The protective paper liner is removed and the transfer base is positioned on the carrier blanket. The foot switch is depressed and as the machine goes through a laminating cycle the color layer is stripped from the polyester film and laminated to the transfer base. The lamination process takes 90 seconds per color for sheets up to 25 × 38 inches (635 mm × 965 mm).

The base is removed from the laminator and placed in the vacuum frame where it is exposed emulsion-to-emulsion to the appropriate color separation negative with a UV-rich high intensity light source. (Calibration procedure for the exposures is similar to COLOR KEY [see Chapter V]) After exposure, the base is processed in the 3M MR-424 COLOR KEY/TRANSFER KEY Processor where it is developed at the rate of 18 inches (457 mm) per minute. The TRANSFER KEY sheet for the next color is mounted onto the laminator along with the transfer base with the first color image, and the procedure for the first color is repeated for the remaining three colors. The result is a composite 4-color proof

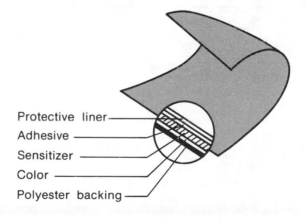

Figure VI-4. Cross-section of Transfer Key color sheet. (3M)

with good color fidelity, dot-for-dot reproduction and dot gain of about 8 – 10% which is equivalent to average good offset sheet-fed printing.

Procedure for Making Negative MATCHPRINT Proofs

As already mentioned the negative *MATCHPRINT* yellow is different from the *TRANSFER KEY* yellow. A close-up of the negative MATCHPRINT yellow is shown in Figure VI-5. The negative MATCHPRINT yellow color sheet is placed in the vacuum frame with the color coating in contact with the emulsion of the yellow separation negative. A high vacuum is pulled and the film is exposed. Exposure calibration is the same as with negative COLOR KEY with the same type of UV-rich light source. The yellow color sheet is processed in the 3M MR-424 COLOR KEY/TRANSFER KEY Processor and exits dry. The TRANSFER KEY color sheet corresponding to the next color is placed on the 3M MR-530 TRANSFER KEY Laminator and rotated for one cycle as in making a TRANSFER KEY proof. Instead of the TRANSFER KEY base, the imaged and processed yellow color sheet is placed on the carrier belt of the laminator and the pigmented sensitized layer of the next color sheet is transferred to the surface of the yellow color sheet.

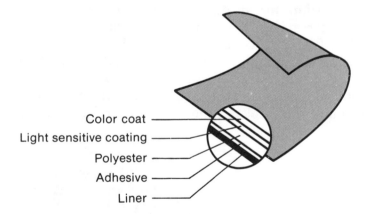

Color coat
Light sensitive coating
Polyester
Adhesive
Liner

Figure VI-5. Cross-section of negative Matchprint yellow color sheet. (3M)

This combination is placed in the vacuum frame with color layer up and the separation negative corresponding to the color layer is placed in emulsion contact with the color layer. After a high vacuum is pulled and the image is exposed the combination is processed in the automatic processor. The same procedure is followed with the other two colors. The composite 4-color proof is mounted on the laminator with the top against the blanket on the drum. The actual press substrate is fed in on the carrier belt. The liner on the proof is removed and the 4-color composite proof is laminated to the press substrate. The polyester base (0.002 inch or 0.005 mm thick) acts as a spacer between the proof and the substrate which produces optical dot gain of about 20 – 24% in the middletones. This optical dot gain is equivalent to the mechanical dot gain experienced in average magazine printing on publication stocks which are usually groundwood coated papers on publication web offset presses (Chapter III and Appendix C).

Procedure for Making Positive MATCHPRINT Proofs

A special 3M positive MATCHPRINT base is used for positive MATCHPRINT proofs. It is a high quality white paper 0.009 inch (0.23 mm) thick, designed for use in the 3M MR-527 heat and pressure lamination process without shrinkage or registration problems. The Matchprint Contact Imaging Material with the color coat consists of a varnish pigment and sensitized coating sandwiched between functional layers to facilitate transfer. A close-up showing the construction of the sheet is illustrated in Figure VI-6. The MATCHPRINT base is laid on the entrance tray of the 3M MR-527 Positive Proofing Laminator and aligned with the index mark. The color sheet is aligned emulsion side down on the color coat entrance tray, and the laminating arm is activated which automatically laminates the color coat to the MATCHPRINT base using heat and pressure. The laminator operates at 32 inches (813 mm) per minute and has a built-in vacuum precleaning unit which removes any foreign material from the proof sheet before lamination. The entire lamination process takes only 40 seconds for a 20 x 24 inch (508 mm x 635 mm) separation.

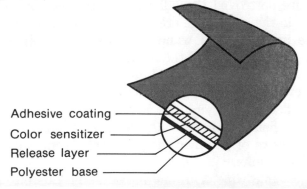

Adhesive coating
Color sensitizer
Release layer
Polyester base

Figure VI-6. Cross-section of Matchprint Contact Imaging Material. (3M)

The polyester carrier film is removed, the combination of base and color coat is placed in the vacuum frame where it is exposed color coat-to-emulsion of the appropriate separation positive using the same type of high intensity UV-rich light source as used for the negative MATCHPRINT. Both photopolymer and diazo bulbs can be utilized. Exposure is calibrated using the 21-step GATF or 10 step 3M Sensitivity Guide with correct exposure showing a clear step 3 with a slight "ghost" in step 4. The exposed combination is automatically developed and dried in the 3M MR-427 Positive Proofing Processor. After processing, the combination is ready for immediate lamination of the next color in the sequence, followed by exposure and processing. The same procedure is repeated for the remaining two colors.

The entire lamination, registration, exposure and processing sequence takes approximately 5 minutes per color or about 20 minutes for the full 4-color proof. The result is a positive single sheet proof comparable in quality and uses to the negative MATCHPRINT Proof.

ADHESIVE POLYMER – DRY POWDER COLOR PROOFING SYSTEMS

The first color proofing system applying the principle of producing images on photosensitive adhesive polymers using dry pigments was Colex 520 Pre-plate Color Proof System developed at Batelle Memorial Institute and introduced by Staley/Graphics, a division of A.E. Staley Co., in 1969 (Chapter I). In this process a coating of fast drying light-sensitive adhesive polymer was applied to a special proofing paper. The coating was exposed to a color separation positive and developed by application of a special color developing powder with an applicator pad. (Light exposure destroyed the adhesive properties, or tackiness, of the photopolymer in the non-image areas.) Excess powder was removed with an air nozzle and a special wand was used to apply warm moisture saturated air which intensified the image to its proper hue and strength. If exposure was correct the non-image areas did not accept the colored developing powder. A clearing solution was applied to clear the non-printing areas and after drying the procedure was repeated for the other three colors. A finished proof consisted of the base covered with the image in four layers of polymer with four color toners corresponding to the 4-color process inks.

About the same time, DuPont introduced "Custom Toning Film" which was being used for graphic or package design, type proofs, decals and comprehensive proofs and modified it as a color proofing medium.

The Custom Toning Film consisted of an adhesive photopolymer coated on a base film and protected with a thin sheet of polyester (MYLAR®)* film. Exposure was made with a positive color separation; the MYLAR film was removed and the image (non-exposed area) was toned with a dry pigment toner. A transfer device was used to transfer the pigmented images to a wide variety of "receptors," using heat and pressure to produce a color proof. From this technology came the evolution of the CROMALIN off-press color proofing process — used all over the world.

The major problem with these processes was difficulty in controlling exposures so that the non-image areas retained some adhesiveness, or tackiness, and they toned. Colex 520 was discontinued mainly for this reason. Cromalin was completely reformulated and continually improved until it has become a controllable, reproducible process that enjoys an appreciable share of the *customer approval* and *compatible proof* off-press color proof markets.

Keuffel and Esser in its development of the SPECTRA Color Proof process avoided this difficulty by the use of a non-photosensitive adhesive polymer which is independent of exposure and has constant pick-up of toner. The image corresponding to the areas where toner is picked up is *created* by a diazo sensitizer over the adhesive layer and only toner is transferred to the proof base which can be the actual printing substrate. CROMALIN and SPECTRA are the processes that will be described and discussed in this section.

CROMALIN Proofing Systems

Two CROMALIN color proofing systems, positive and negative, are produced by DuPont. The processes are relatively simple, consisting of Cromalin film, dry pigmented toners, a laminator, and toning equipment. A color proof is prepared by laminating Cromalin film (positive or negative) to a selected substrate, exposing it in contact with a positive or negative (depending on the type of Cromalin film used), removing the cover sheet and toning the tacky image with the appropriate color toner corresponding to a printing ink. Repeating the procedure for each process color separation produces a 4-color CROMALIN proof. The materials and equipment used in these two processes are:

Cromalin Film: Positive Cromalin film consists of a tacky or adhesive photopolymer layer sandwiched between a protective polypropylene sheet and a MYLAR polyester film base (Figure VI-7). When the photopolymer is exposed through a film positive, the exposed areas which represent the non-image areas harden and lose their tackiness so they do not accept toner during the toning step. The unexposed areas, on the other hand,

*MYLAR, DuPont registered trademark.

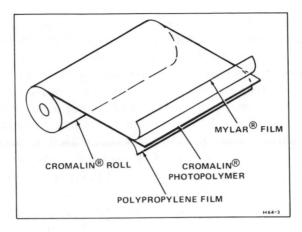

Figure VI-7. Cross-section of positive Cromalin film. (Du-Pont)

which represent the image areas remain tacky and accept the toner.

Negative Cromalin film has a construction similar to the positive Cromalin film except the photopolymer used has a reverse reaction. It is hard and non-tacky until exposure when the exposed areas soften and become tacky and the unexposed areas remain hard and non-tacky. When a negative is exposed to the negative Cromalin film layer the image areas are exposed rendering these areas on the photopolymer layer tacky so they receive toner and the non-image areas are not exposed leaving them hard and non-tacky and non-receptive to the toner.

Toners: The toners are dry colorants (dyes or pigments) which are designed to adhere to the adhesive (tacky) photopolymer. In positive CROMALIN this is the unexposed area; in negative CROMALIN it is the exposed area. Process color toners are available to match most color process inks. In addition, special process colors are available that address industry specifications such as SWOP, GTA Group I and Group V, and Euroscale inks. Other toners are available which can be blended to simulate most ink hue and strength requirements. When hand toning, the same process toners can be used for both positive and negative working CROMALIN, metallic and fluorescent toners are for positive film only. For machine toning, special toners have been developed to optimize mechanical toning characteristics.

Receptors: The recommended base for positive CROMALIN is 12 point Kromekote or DuPont's stable base, Stablecote™ SPR-15; for negative CROMALIN it is DuPont's PRS-12 or stable base, Stablecote™ SNR-15.

Laminator: The CROMALIN Laminator (Model PN 2700, or Model 50) is used to laminate the Cromalin film to the proofing receptor under precise conditions of temperature and pressure. As the Cromalin film unwinds from a feed roll the polypropylene film is stripped from the Cromalin film and wound onto a takeup roll. The remaining film of adhesive photopolymer layer on the MYLAR base feeds through two rolls where it is laminated with heat and pressure to the proof receptor.

Toning: There are two methods for toning CROMALIN proofs. Toning has been a source of variability in CROMALIN proofing so it has had considerable attention from development engineers which has resulted in a number of improvements.

I. *Automated Toning:*
- *ATM 2900* and *ATM II:* The most efficient, fastest, productive and reproducible toning of CROMALIN proofs is done with the Automatic Toning Machine — ATM 2900 and the smaller, more compact and less expensive ATM II. The ATM 2900 especially is responsible for the enviable reputation CROMALIN proofs enjoy in the off-press customer approval and compatible proof markets worldwide.

II. *Hand Toning:*
- *Toning console:* In the regular Toning Console the exposed film is toned manually using an applicator pad, drawing the excess toner off with vacuum and removing the remaining toner with a Las-Stik® cloth.
- *Autotoner System:* The Autotoner System consists of four toner applicators with four detachable cleaning pads and an extra of each. They are designed to use a vacuum cleaning station which facilitates reproducible, clean and fast toning of both positive and negative images with greater operator-to-operator and proof-to-proof consistency and repeatability.

Cromalin Press Finish System: Among the other factors contributing to CROMALIN's success is the CROMALIN Press Finish System which provides for simulation of the color and finish of the substrate used for optimum process color control and press printing guide.

Eurostandard CROMALIN: Another factor is the system of color scales, controls and targets developed by Felix Brunner of System Brunner (Switzerland) for measuring and controlling dot gain on positive

Eurostandard CROMALIN color proofing for the European market (Chapters III, X and Appendix C). Brunner has developed similar targets and controls for North American production of CROMALIN proofs. This system is known as CROMALIN Offset Com Guides/System Brunner (in both positive and negative CROMALIN).

Procedure for Making Positive CROMALIN proofs:

There are only three steps involved in producing each color of a positive CROMALIN proof and these steps are used four times to make a 4-color proof: laminating, exposing and toning.

- *Laminating:* The Cromalin film must first be properly loaded on the feed roll and threaded through the laminator for operation which involves making sure that the film roll will unwind properly and it is firmly gripped in the machine. The thread-up diagram is shown in Figure VI-8. After the laminator is properly threaded up, the *heater*

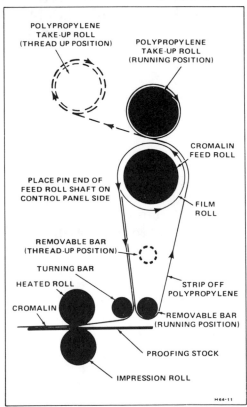

Figure VI-8. Diagram of laminator thread-up for mounting Cromalin film to base sheet. (DuPont)

switch is turned on and a light goes on when the heat roll temperature is correct for lamination (220-250°F, 104-122°C). The receptor being wider than the Cromalin film is inserted firmly into the nip of the heated roll and the impression roll. The drive motor is turned on and the film is held taut as it feeds through the rolls. The leading edge of the film is trimmed off the proof as it clears the laminator. After the trailing edge of the paper clears the rollers by 1 to 2 inches (25mm-51mm) the drive motor is switched off and the film is cut at the receptor's tail edge. The proof should be exposed within 5 minutes of lamination.

- *Exposing:* The laminated sheet, either prepunched or after punching for press register, is placed in the vacuum frame using 12 point Kromekote as a backing sheet. The first color separation (usually yellow) is positioned in register with its emulsion side down along with color bars and strips for measuring and evaluating proofs. Proper exposure is predetermined from test exposures using the Cromalin Offset Com-Guide/System Brunner Control Strip. Toner should be applied to the proof within 5 minutes after exposure. Any one of three methods can be used for toning the proof.

- *ATM 2900:* The Automatic Toning machine, ATM 2900 consists of a cabinet with four drawers, each containing mechanisms and materials for automatically applying and cleaning toner or one color on a CROMALIN proof up to 27 x 40 inches (686 mm x 1015 mm) in size in less than one minute. The four separate toning stations are built as pull out drawers so that each functions independently permitting almost continuous operation of the ATM with different proofs and/or colors being toned in each drawer at the same time. Toner application is controlled automatically and excess toner is recovered for reuse, effecting savings in toner consumption of up to 50%.

- Operation of the ATM 2900 is very simple. After exposure and removal of the top protector sheet by peeling it off at a low angle from the trailing edge of the receptor sheet, the operator feeds the proof sheet into the appropriate toning station which automatically activates the toning and cleaning mechanisms in that station or drawer. Toner density is controlled externally by varying the transport speed. In less than 1 minute the toned and cleaned proof is delivered to the catch tray ready to be laminated and exposed for the next proofing color. Users report increased proofing productivity of 30-50% and improved proof consistency with the ATM 2900.

- *ATM II:* The ATM II is more compact, smaller and less expensive than the ATM 2900 and takes the same size proof and tones each color on a 27 × 40 inch (686 mm × 1015 mm) proof in less than one minute. Consistency, repeatability and toner economy are compatible with the ATM 2900 but productivity may be slightly lower during peak production periods since only one proof can be toned at a time. Toning cassettes are easily and quickly changed and interchanged. Extra cassettes may be kept on hand for special process colors, for switching from positive to negative operation, or applying press finish surface treatment. In addition it has easy access, a single control panel with microprocessor control, digital speed readout, infrared feed detectors, automatic toner recovery, programmable speed control and automatic drive shutdown.

- *Manual Toning:* The exposed Cromalin film is placed on the toning console and secured with magnets or tape. A corner of the MYLAR sheet is separated from the proof base and in one continuous motion is peeled off at a low angle starting from the trailing edge. The first color is applied using a fully loaded applicator pad. The loaded pad is patted over the entire proof (should be reloaded if proof is larger than 20 × 24 inches [508 mm x 610 mm]) and briskly and without pressure the pad is moved over the proof using the toning pattern shown in Figure VI-9. Toning is continued for 20 cycles. Excess toner is carefully wiped off the proof with a Las-Stik® cloth and pushed into the vacuum slot along the edge of the console.

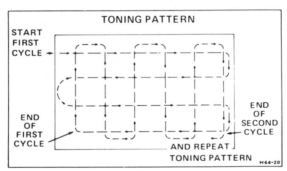

Figure VI-9. Toning pattern for manual toning of CRO-MALIN proofs. (DuPont)

- *Autotoner:* The Cromalin Autotoner system consists of five toner applicators, five cleaning pads, a foot switch and a vacuum station. Each hand held toner applicator has a molded toner housing frame, shaker bar, two snap-on toner pad assemblies, toner release handle and an oval plastic cap for use during refill. The cleaning pad is a plastic housing with cleaning material attached to the bottom. An applicator is used as a handle and the two are easily assembled/disassembled by means of magnetic latches. The vacuum station holds four toner applicator cleaning pad assemblies and is mounted on the Cromalin Toning Console (Figure VI-10). Toner is removed

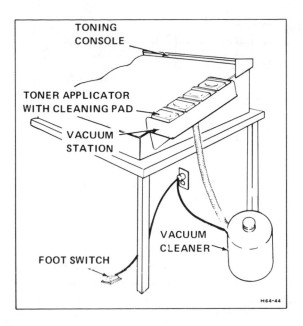

Figure VI-10. Autotoning station for toning CROMALIN proofs. (DuPont)

from the cleaning pads through vacuum slots in the forward edge of the vacuum station which is connected to a customer supplied shop vacuum. The foot switch provides convenient operator control of the vacuum cleaner.

- After the toner applicator assembly has been set up and properly conditioned and the proof mounted on the console with tape at two diagonal corners, the metal tab on one end of the toner applicator is pressed to release the magnets holding the unit to the cleaning pad. The toner pad is checked; excess toner is removed with the clean-up pad; and is placed on the upper corner of the proof. The handle is pressed to open the slot between toner pad assemblies and at the same time is shaken twice without lifting it from the proof. (Shaking is effective when the movement of the shaker bar inside the pad can be heard.)

- The autotoner pad is moved horizontally (sideways) with a slow sweeping motion and a 75% overlap on the return cycle as shown in Figure VI-11. (The first cycle is the most important and care must be taken to perform it correctly.) The first cycle is completed with a vertical pattern and 75% overlap. Toner should be dispersed regularly to make sure of complete coverage. Twenty more cycles (no pressure) should be completed with normal (slight) overlap. The pad is inserted in the cleaning pad, vacuumed to make sure it is clean and used on the proof to clean excess toner from the edges and

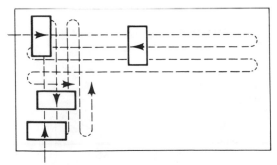

Figure VI-11. Toning pattern for automating positive CROM-ALIN proofs. (DuPont)

console. The pad is vacuumed and used to clean the proof horizontally after which it is vacuumed again and used to clean the proof vertically. Using a clean Las-Stik® cloth the edges of the proof are cleaned after which it is ready for the lamination of the next Cromalin film layer.

• *Finishing Positive CROMALIN Proof:* After toning, the lamination, exposing and toning steps are repeated for the remaining colors. The recommended sequence is *yellow, magenta, cyan,* and *black* — *Y-M-C-K.* An additional laminated and fully exposed layer of Cromalin film is recommended to protect the proof. The final exposure should be 10 times the normal image exposure. The cover sheet can be left on the proof until it is ready to be examined or used, at which time it is stripped off.

Procedure for Making Negative CROMALIN Proofs

Some of the differences between negative and positive Cromalin materials have been mentioned. The important one is the coating on the films. Differences in composition of materials cause differences in the procedures for making the proofs. The equipment is the same and general procedures are similar — how they are used can differ. This description of the procedure for making negative CROMALIN proofs will not repeat the instructions where procedures are the same but will describe the steps where procedures are different.

• *Laminating:* Procedures are the same as for positive CROMALIN except that negative film is laminated at a lower temperature 210 – 225°F (99 – 107°C) with a set point of 218°F ± 3°F (103°C ± 2°C) and laminators used with positive film must be adjusted by a DuPont representative for alignment and pressure of the laminating rolls. Laminating should not be started until the laminator is at the proper temperature. Temperature can be verified by the temperature gauge on the front of the laminator.

- *Exposing:* Procedures are the same. All non-image areas should be masked with UV opaque materials like goldenrod as any light-exposed areas will accept toner. Peeling of the coversheet is critical. Cover sheet tears can occur at register holes or at nicks accidentally caused by the trimming knife during lamination; and peeling too slowly can cause loss of highlight dots.
- *ATM 2900 and ATM II:* The procedures for the ATM 2900 and ATM II are exactly the same as for positive CROMALIN.
- *Manual Toning:* Procedures are the same as for positive CROMALIN except only 10 toning cycles are used.
- *Autotoner:* The procedure is the same as for positive CROMALIN except that the toning pattern is different. The pattern used is almost the same as the one used on positive CROMALIN with the manual toning console. This is illustrated in Figure VI-12. The only difference is that during the first cycle the operator may go over the same path again to make sure that the image is completely visible at the end of the first cycle. This repeat coverage technique is used only during the first cycle. At the end of the first cycle, the autotoner pad is turned 90° and the second cycle is started with no pressure with the standard up and down motion. This type of application is continued for eight more cycles.
- *Finishing:* Finishing is the same as for positive CROMALIN except that the MYLAR is not stripped from the proof as it is fragile without the cover sheet.

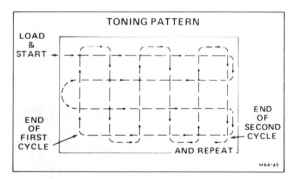

Figure VI-12. Toning pattern for autotoning negative CROM-ALIN proofs. (DuPont)

Cromalin Press Finish System: The Press Finish System is a means of converting CROMALIN proofs so they appear to have the visual appearance of the conventional paper stocks used in printing. In this way CROMALIN proofs can be made to produce a closer match to the appearance of press prints. The system consists of four delustering toners and a Press Finish Tint. The delustering toners simulate both the gloss and shade of the four common types of printing papers such as:

- *Press Finish Commercial Toner (PFC)* for commercial paper stock.
- *Press Finish Publication Positive Toner (PFP/P)* for web offset publication paper for proofs made with positive Cromalin film and *Press Finish Publication Negative Toner (PFP/N)* for proofs made with negative film.
- *Press Finish Supplement Toner (PFS)* for simulating newsprint and supplement paper.

The Press Finish Tint produces an overall random dot pattern for the acceptance of toner on the proof to be press finished and to avoid the possibility of moiré patterns.

The steps in applying Cromalin Press Finish to a proof are:

- A layer of positive Cromalin film is laminated to the last color layer (positive film is used for both positive and negative CROMALIN proofs).
- Under vacuum the completely color toned proof is exposed through the Press Finish Tint using a normal dot-for-dot exposure.
- The cover sheet is removed and the proof is toned with the Press Finish toner corresponding to the paper used in the press run.
- The proof is cleaned to remove excess toner and after cleaning, a positive CROMALIN proof is post exposed overall without vacuum for 10 times the normal exposure. Negative CROMALIN proofs do not require post exposure. Despite all the polymer layers on the CROMALIN proof its total thickness, not including the base, is about 0.001 inch or 0.025 mm which is about five times the thickness of the ink films on a press print. A cross-section of the finished proof is shown in Figure VI – 13.

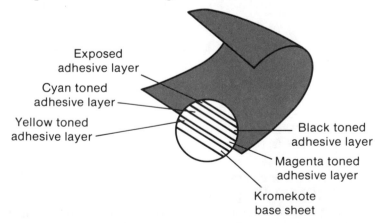

Figure VI-13. Cross-section of CROMALIN proof.

Eurostandard CROMALIN: An exhaustive study of the ability of CROMALIN to simulate dot gain was made by Felix Brunner of Switzerland in 1981. As a result of the study he developed special color scales and targets for measuring and controlling dot gain of positive CROMALIN proofs. The control system has been reasonably successful in helping CROMALIN compete with press proofing in Europe. These and other studies of dot gain are described in Chapters III, X and Appendix C. The use of the targets help make CROMALIN a more controllable, reproducible and predictable process. Brunner's work in Europe was with positive printing processes and with positive CROMALIN. He has studied printing processes using negatives in the U.S. and Europe, from which studies he has developed suitable controls for negative CROMALIN. The compact version of the system Brunner control strips designed for off-press proofing (CROMALIN Offset Com-Guides/System Brunner) are available directly from DuPont. The System Brunner print control bars, for use across the full width of the printing form, are available from System Brunner U.S.A.

SPECTRA Proofing System

As already mentioned, SPECTRA, manufactured by Keuffel and Esser, is also an adhesive polymer-dry toner color proofing system but the polymer used is not photosensitive so toning is not a critical operation. The image is formed by a diazo coating over the adhesive polymer. The tackiness of the polymer remains the same so the amount of toner transferred to the proof image is independent of the method or technique of application. Also the final proof does not have the build-up of polymer layers like CROMALIN. It consists of just toners and one thin polymer layer and film or two thin polymer layers transferred to the actual printing substrate so it comes closer to simulating the structure of the press print than most other color proofing systems. Other characteristics of the process are:

- It uses negatives so dot gain or dot sharpening can be simulated by variations in exposure and/or use of spacers during exposure.
- All colors are processed before transfer so they can be used as progressives like overlay proofs, checked for necessary changes before transfer, or remade, if necessary without discarding or affecting the other colors.
- Two-sided proofs can be made for checking layouts, side to side register, crossovers, trims, bleeds, folding, etc.

The equipment and materials needed for making SPECTRA proofs are:

- *SPECTRA film* which consists of a polyester base either .003 inch (0.076 mm) or .004 inch (0.10 mm) thick, coated with an adhesive polymer not affected by relative humidity changes, covered with a diazo-type photoresist and an overcoat to protect the film prior to development (Figure VI-14).

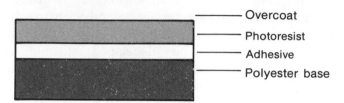

Figure VI-14. Cross-section of Spectra film. (H-E)

- *Automatic processor and chemistry* which is used to develop the exposed diazo type coating in the image areas, and after toning, to remove the coating from the non-image areas. The processor contains lights to expose the non-image areas after processing the image and a recirculating filter for collecting the toner removed from the non-inage areas during the second development.
- *Toning console* which is similar to the CROMALIN Toning Console but using a simple 3M developing pad for application of toner.
- *Toners* which are dry powders corresponding to printing ink pigments. There are 14 process colors in addition to the SWOP colors. Toners can be blended to reproduce most ink hues and strengths.
- *Receptor Sheets* which are intermediate sheets for transfer of images from SPECTRA films to the final substrate. There are two types of receptor sheets: Receptor Sheet R2 and Photorelease PRR. *Receptor Sheet R2* consists of a polyester base, which can be either glossy or matte, coated with an adhesive polymer and covered with a peel

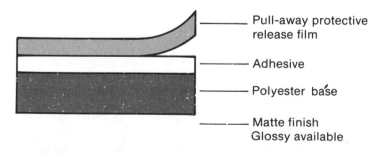

Figure VI-15. Cross-section of Receptor Sheet R2. (H-E)

away protective release film (Figure VI-15). *Photorelease PRR* is similar to Receptor R2 except that it consists of a photopolymerizable adhesive layer on a matte polyester base (Figure VI-16).

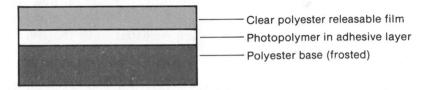

Figure VI-16. Cross-section of Photorelease Receptor Sheet PRR. (H-E)

Procedure for Making SPECTRA Color Proofs.

There are six steps in making SPECTRA color proofs; exposing, processing, toning, reprocessing, laminating, and mounting.

- *Exposing:* Four sheets of SPECTRA film are registered with the four color separation negatives in a color set, emulsion-to-emulsion, and exposed in a vacuum frame. If size permits all can be exposed at the same time, as the same exposure is used for all colors, unless some colors need to be sharpened or spread to simulate printing faults or defective press units. A high intensity UV-rich light is used for exposure. Correct exposure can be determined with the GATF Sensitivity Guide.
- *Processing:* The exposed films are fed into the special automatic SPECTRA Film Processor. During processing the diazo-type coating is dissolved and removed in the exposed (image) areas. (This is the reverse type of reaction as compared with conventional diazo coatings used in negative platemaking in which the non-image [unexposed] areas are removed.) After processing is complete and as the film exits the processor the non-image, undeveloped areas are exposed to special UV lights in the processor.
- *Toning:* The color toner corresponding to the separation negative is applied to the film with a simple pad like the 3M developing pad. No special application patterns, sequences and/or cycles are required as long as sufficient toner is applied. The images cannot be overtoned as the adhesive properties of the polymer are constant.
- *Reprocessing:* After toning, the film is rerun though the processor to remove the diazo-type coating left on the non-printing areas. The residual toner on these areas is collected in the recirculating filter.
- *Laminating:* Either Receptor Sheet R2 or Photorelease PRR (depending on the type of proof to be made) is mounted on the

receiver cylinder of the laminator, the release film is removed and the film representing the last color down in the printing sequence is mounted on the transfer cylinder. The cylinders are closed and rotated to transfer the toner image from the color film to the receptor sheet. The polyester carrier film is peeled off and the film representing the third color down is mounted on the transfer cylinder. The transfer operations are repeated until the color toner images from all the films have been transferred to the receptor sheet.

- *Mounting:* The difference between the use of Receptor Sheet R2 and Photorelease PRR is in the last operation in finishing the proof. The receptor sheet with the composite image of all the toner images for the SPECTRA films is fed into the laminator in contact with the printing substrate and the two are laminated together with the pressure of the laminator and the tackiness of the adhesive layer on the receptor sheet.

- If the Receptor Sheet R2 is used the color proof is complete consisting of the substrate, the ink toners, the adhesive layer and the polyester cover sheet (glossy or matte, as selected) (Figure VI-17).

- If the Photorelease PRR Receptor Sheet is used the proof must go through another operation. The composite proof is placed in the vacuum frame and exposed for 2 to 4 times the normal exposure (enough exposure to allow the base to be stripped from the proof). After removal from the frame the base film is stripped from the proof which then consists of the substrate, the ink toners, and the photopolymerized adhesive polymer layer that acts as a protective coating on the proof (Figure VI-17B). Total thickness of all the layers on the substrate is about 0.001 inch (0.025 mm) as in the CROMALIN proof.

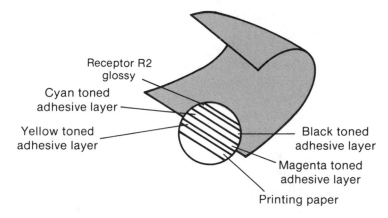

Figure VI-17A. Cross-section of SPECTRA proof with receptor sheet R2 (H-E).

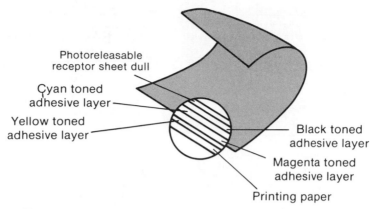

Figure VI-17B. Cross-section of SPECTRA proof with receptor sheet PRR (H-E).

The main differences between the SPECTRA proofs made with the two receptor sheets is that the one made with the Receptor Sheet R2 can simulate the appearance of gloss inks on coated paper if the glossy base is used. The SPECTRA proof made with the Photorelease PRR receptor sheet has a dull appearance and looks more like a print on uncoated paper.

PHOTOGRAPHIC COLOR PROOFING SYSTEMS

As mentioned in Chapter I, the first color proofing system developed for proofing drafted maps was based on the use of *ANSCO PRINTON* color paper, manufactured by Ansco Corporation (formerly Agfa-Ansco) which later became part of General Analine and Film Corporation (GAF). Ansco Printon color paper was an integral photographic color print paper consisting of three silver-halide emulsion layers containing different dye-couplers that after exposure to negatives through appropriate filters and development with a dye-forming developer each produced a dye image corresponding to one of the three subtractive primary (process) colors; yellow, magenta and cyan. After the silver image was fixed, bleached, and washed out, the result was a full-color composite print of the map the separation negatives represented.

The principles of color image formation using color dye couplers in the emulsion layers and one dye former in the developer is shown in Figure VI-18. This is the principle on which *Kodacolor, Ektacolor, Agfacolor, Fujicolor* and other color materials with the *-color* suffix are based. *Ektachrome, Anscochrome, Agfachrome, Fujichrome* and other color materials using the *-chrome* suffix are similar except they are positive/positive materials and require chemical or optical reversal during processing. Kodachrome is different. The dye couplers are not

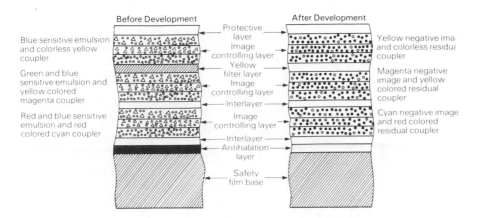

Figure VI-18. Principle of color formation in Fujicolor type color materials. (Fuji)

incorporated in the emulsions; dye coupling of the individual layers is done sequentially during processing using special dye-coupling developers for each layer.

While many attempts have been made to use color print papers for color proofing, none have been successful until recently and most of the recent applications have been for proofing positives for gravure. These processes are described in Chapter VIII. Some of the problems associated with the use of color photographic papers for color proofing have been:

- They are continuous tone processes which do not reproduce half-tones well.
- They are three color systems, without black, so the black separation must be exposed in each layer.
- The yellow dyes produced with the available dye couplers and formers are too orange in hue, containing too much magenta, so pure yellows and bright greens cannot be reproduced properly.
- The dyes are cleaner and have different hues than the ink pigments so to reproduce the hues of the pigments multiple exposures through several filters must be made and since exposures are short, to begin with, the mixtures of exposures are difficult to duplicate and control.

As mentioned in the Preface, J. Tom Morgan, Jr., has developed a halftone photographic color proofing system which eliminates most of the deficiencies of color photographic processes. It uses conventional color photographic paper like Ektachrome or Fujichrome so it is limited to three colors but can readily achieve a black. It produces proofs with much purer yellows and greens. It matches ink hues by exposure combinations like other color photographic systems but, by the use of special processing, it is capable of modifying the hues of the dyes to make proofs with much better color matches to press prints. It can match the purer yellow hues that match conventional yellow printing ink pigments. These pigment hues cannot be matched by the orange-yellow hues of the dyes in color photographic papers. It can also change the hues of the magenta and cyan dyes to match the SWOP colors.

One of the systems covered in Chapter VIII, Kodak EKTAFLEX PCT, has worked around some of the problems of color photographic systems and has found application in, and been promoted for, color proofing for processes other than gravure.

EKTAFLEX PCT Color Proofs

Because Kodak EKTAFLEX PCT is a diffusion-transfer process, color proofs can be made much more simply and faster than with conventional materials. Diffusion transfer is a one-step photographic process, like Polaroid, based on the transfer of a soluble silver complex and reduction of the transferred silver to form a positive image on a receiver sheet. Processing is done automatically with a premixed, single-batch chemical without any need for temperature control, fixing, washing or even running water.

To make an EKTAFLEX PCT color proof, four exposures are made with a special computerized light source on a negative EKTAFLEX PCT film which is processed in emulsion/emulsion contact with a sheet of EKTAFLEX PCT paper in a special processor. The film-paper sandwich is left for 10 minutes after it leaves the processor when it is peeled apart. The proof is on the paper and the film is discarded.

The equipment and materials needed for making EKTAFLEX PCT proofs are:

- *EKTAFLEX PCT Negative Film* which is negative-working color film coated on an opaque polyester base — the emulsion side is yellow-green and the base side is black.
- *EKTAFLEX PCT Paper* which is a resin coated receiver sheet about 0.004 inch (0.1 mm) thick with an opaque carbon layer — available in both glossy and matte surfaces.
- *EKTAFLEX PCT Activator* which is the processing chemical and is noncontaminating so it can be flushed down any drain.
- Conventional *open-face vacuum frame, cutting board, light table* and a *pin register system.*
- *Log E Multiflex 9100 Programmable Light Source System,* developed by combined research of Kodak and Log E which consists of a double filter wheel with twin disk filter holders mounted under a contact light source (Figure VI-19). Both exposure and appropriate

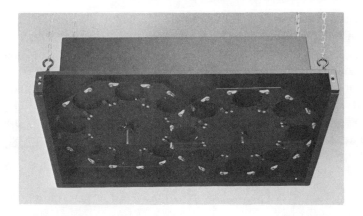

Figure VI-19. LogE Programmable Light Source system showing dual filter wheels (with housing removed) for exposure control. (LogE)

neutral density (ND)/color filter combinations are programmed and controlled by the system which uses a microprocessor to control both filter positioning and exposure timing. Light distance is at least 6 feet from the film. Exposure sequence, filters and toning can be pre-programmed from calibrations derived from the press-sheet. Exposures are fast, semiautomatic and are claimed to be very repeatable.

- *Log E Multiflex 9100 Processor* which is a 16 inch (406 mm) tabletop processor designed for quick processing of exposed EKTAFLEX PCT negative film with EKTAFLEX PCT activator. It is a single-soak, double-path processor; the exposed film takes one path through the activator soak and the receiver paper takes a "dry" path through the processor and is laminated to the wet film as it emerges from the activator. Wider processors are in development.

- *EKTAFLEX PCT Exposure Guide* which consists of four separation guides, or masks (one for each color) to be attached to the separation negative and used as a means to measure and control proof density and hue error.

Procedure for Making an EKTAFLEX PCT Color Proof

There are 13 separate steps in making an EKTAFLEX PCT color proof. Four of the steps are done in room light and the other nine in a darkroom.

The following steps are done under ordinary room illumination:

- The exposure guide is mounted, in register, on one edge of each separation.
- The separations are placed in order next to the vacuum frame. The exposure order is cyan, magenta, yellow and black.
- The edge guide of the register punch is set for the size of the EKTAFLEX PCT film to be used and a sheet of EKTAFLEX PCT paper is placed emulsion (white) side down on a surface convenient to the processor.
- The appropriate "run" sequence is selected for the Log E Exposure Programmer.

The following steps are carried out in a darkroom under a Kodak Safelight Filter No. 13 (amber) using a 15 watt bulb at 8 feet from the film surface.

- A sheet of EKTAFLEX PCT film is punched, with emulsion side up and placed on the vacuum frame with emulsion up.
- The cyan halftone separation negative is placed over the EKTAFLEX PCT film in the vacuum frame, emulsion side up, or away from the film, so that the image appears reversed or wrong reading as viewed on the vacuum frame.
- The vacuum is applied and when drawdown is complete the ADVANCE key on the exposure programmer is pressed. Two exposures are made automatically: one to red light and the other to green light.
- The cyan separation is removed and the magenta separation negative is placed over the film; the vacuum is applied; the exposure program ADVANCE key is pressed; and two exposures are made — one to green light and the other to blue light. The same procedure is followed with the yellow (one exposure to blue light) and black (three exposures to red, green and blue light) separation negatives.
- After exposures are complete the film is placed, emulsion side up on the feed tray of the processor against the left side guide and is fed manually into the nip of the rollers *under* the separator fin in the center of the feed tray. The job (foot) switch is touched to advance the film a short way into the feed rolls.
- The EKTAFLEX PCT paper is placed emulsion side down on top of the film against the left side guide and manually fed into the nip of the rollers *over* the separation fin of the feed tray. The DRIVE switch is pressed and both the film and paper are pulled into the processor, each following a different path — the film into the activator for 20 seconds and the paper over a "dry" path to meet the film as it leaves the activator bath where both are laminated together.

• The film-paper sandwich emerges into the exit tray of the processor and is left there for 10 minutes ±0.5 minute after which the transfer is complete and the film is peeled from the paper and discarded.

The EKTAFLEX PCT color proof on the paper is a quality alternative to overlay proofing and can be used as an economical quality control tool to check the separation film for registration, color breaks, and correction while the original is still on the scanner. Because the yellow dye in the EKTAFLEX PCT color proof is too orange, it does not make a good proof for customer acceptance. EKTAFLEX PCT could find some use for compatibility proofing to check films from different sources for ability to print from the same plate with the same inks and paper. The major use for EKTAFLEX PCT Color proofs is for gravure proofing and as the output for digital color proofing systems such as Hell CPR 403 Color Proof and the Log E/Dunn Color Camera System described in Chapter IX.

CHAPTER VII

Electrostatic Proofing — KC-COLOR PROOFING SYSTEM

By: Manfred R. Kuehnle, formerly *President*
Coulter Systems Corporation

Electrostatic color proofing systems are based on electrophotographic principles and therefore require the following components and means for using them:

- A photoconductor, means for charging it electrostatically and exposing it optically.
- Proofing inks or toners and means for applying them to the photoconductor.
- A substrate, preferably the actual press paper or other substrate, and means to transfer the ink or toner image to it.

Electrophotography is well-suited for color proofing because it offers a reusable light-sensitive medium with wide exposure latitude; the controlled application of a wide variety of proofing colors with essentially total transfer to almost any kind of receptor paper; and a high degree of control over each process step. These features influence the type of proof produced and assure the accurate production of halftone screen dots with controlled dot gain for lithography and halftone gravure. In both cases the proof should be prepared on the customer's press paper with the same pigments as used in his standard printing inks. Proofs can be made for magazines, newspapers, commercial printing, packaging, or other specialty printing tasks. Not all electrophotographic processes have these characteristics which make them suitable for this application, so in this section we will discuss KC-Proofing Technology and its predecessor "REMAK" and explore the specific attributes of KC-Technology that qualify it as an exceptional pre-press proofing process.

REMAK COLOR Proofing System

The first color proofing system to use electrophotographic principles was REMAK which was mentioned and briefly described in Chapter I. REMAK was developed in Australia and introduced about 1960 by the Research Laboratories of Australia. It was based on the electrofax system of xerography which used a zinc oxide photoconductor in a highly resistive organic binder, like silicone, coated on paper and toned with a liquid toner. The electrofax process was developed by Young and Greig at RCA in 1954 and the liquid toner technology was originated by Metcalf and Wright of the Australian government where the process was being investigated as a means of proofing maps.

The state-of-the-art in electrostatic imaging systems at the time when electofax and liquid toning were introduced was such that the image resolution achievable with the new process was a real breakthrough. An interesting application of the process was the development of a map printer for the U.S. Army by RCA and Harris Corp. that was truck mounted and capable of printing 2,000 maps per hour from five positive 70 mm color pulls (line separations) of the original map.

The REMAK process was the first to exploit the resolution capability of the electrofax/liquid toner system for color proofing. It consisted of a charger-printer in which the zinc oxide coated paper was charged and exposed, trays for colored toners dispersed in the organic liquid, Isopar, and an overspray to apply a protective coating on the final proof.

A negative charge of about 300 volts was applied to the zinc oxide coated paper; a color separation positive (black or cyan) was registered with the charged paper and exposed for several seconds to an incandescent point light source which neutralized the charge in the exposed (non-image) areas.

The image areas which retained the charge were developed by immersing the sheet in a tray containing the liquid toner corresponding to the color of the separation positive. After drying, the imaging cycle of charging, exposing, toning and drying was repeated for the other three colors with the yellow last. Cycle time for each color was about 8 minutes.

After all four colors were applied and dried the proof was treated with the overspray to protect it from damage in handling.

The process had several magenta and cyan toners which could be mixed to match a wide range of ink hues, and a density reducing agent to control ink color strengths. A process for transferring the individual toner images from the zinc oxide coated sheet to the actual printing substrate was also developed.

Because the charge acceptance of the zinc oxide/organic binder was very sensitive to the conductivity of the air in contact with the coating, the process demanded very stringent control of the relative humidity in the working area which required a dedicated space for the proofer with elaborate and expensive air conditioning. Also, due to the high surface voltage (300 volts) on the photoconductor surface, exposure did not completely discharge the non-image areas and left a variable residual charge on them resulting in inconsistent random toning on the proofs. In addition, any variations in the electrical properties of the photoconductor or toners between lots caused variations in the processing that affected the consistency and reproducibility of the proofs. For these reasons and the improvements in quality of the newer processes like CROMALIN and TRANSFER KEY the process was discontinued by most users except for a few in Europe and Australia. Other electrostatic proofing processes were developed but none reached the marketplace until the development and announcement of the KC-Color Proofing System in 1982.

KC-Color Proofing System

The KC-Color Proofing system is based on a new technology which uses a low voltage, high charge density electrophotographic material with submicron resolution and high edge acutance that has created new applications for electrostatic processes in both analog and digital imaging systems. Along with the photoconductor, new liquid toners have been developed which discern small voltage differences as low as ¼ volt so a long scale of continuous tone reproduction can be rendered as well as binary halftone images.

With a new photoconductor and toners, and a new technology for their use, the KC-Color Proofing System has been able to eliminate all of REMAK's limitations while retaining all of its superior qualities and providing additional benefits. The KC-Color Proofer is an essentially automated system using a new unique completely inorganic, electrically anisotropic, crystalline photoconductor (cadmium sulfide) on a metal base: The "KC-Crystalplate." The electrical properties of the KC-Material, unlike zinc oxide, are relatively unaffected by variations in ambient temperatures from 10C to 40°C and relative humidities from 30% to 70%. In addition, the KC-Crystalplate accepts an exceptionally high coulombic charge density while maintaining a low charge voltage (35 volts) and discharges completely to 0 voltage at full exposure. These characteristics have placed formidable demands on the new toners, called proofing inks, which have met the challenge and are remarkably consistent and controllable in use.

Besides these improvements, the system is capable of producing 20 × 24 inch (508 mm × 610 mm) 4-color proofs in 10 minutes on the actual printing substrate with proofing inks that match the printing inks in spectral and optical characteristics. Proofs made with the KC-Proofing System for both lithography and halftone gravure come closer to matching the press print than proofs prepared with any of the other off-press color proofing systems, as there are no intermediate layers on the proof to affect its optical appearance and feel. Also, it is the most highly automated and most productive of the analog color proofing systems in use and is the only one with the capability of producing proofs in either a direct or indirect mode of transfer. In addition, it can generate double sided proofs which enables the production of sample signatures and their collection into a facsimile composite proof for the whole job.

The KC-Color Proofer consists of the following components shown from left to right on Figure VII-1, page C-5.

- *Control Panel* with start and stop, ink sequence, and all process parameter adjustment and monitoring.
- *Flip-over platen* on which the electrophotographic imaging member (KC-Crystalplate) is mounted.
- *A paper holding platen* which holds the paper and maintains registration.
- *Film mount* stationary transparent plate of quartz-coated Lucite with interchangeable register pins to which the positive or negative films are registered and attached.
- *Light source* (100 watt) featuring pinhole projection of collimated light which follows a folded path for exposing the positives on the KC-Crystalplate from beneath.
- *Corona charging station* for charging the KC-Crystalplate prior to exposure.
- *Electrometer* for measuring the apparent surface voltage on the plate to serve as reference for density control.
- Five *color inking stations* with independent elevating mechanisms for transferring the proper color proofing ink (special electrostatic toners) to the KC-Crystalplate.
- *A vacuum slit* which removes excess wetness from the inked image to create a "moist" residual image
- *Cleaning station* for cleaning the plate after the ink transfer.
- *Discharge means* for discharging the residual image on the plate after transfer.
- *Transfer station* with two modes of transfer — single or double —

with the paper platen holding the final receptor sheet for the double transfer mode and an intermediate offset sheet plus a special electrically conductive roller. During transfer the conductive roller presses against the underside of the offset sheet to transfer the image from the KC-Crystalplate onto the offset sheet and thereafter in a second step onto the final receptor paper. In the single transfer mode the offset sheet is the substrate for the final proof.

Procedure for Making KC-COLOR PROOF

The following steps are involved in the operation of the KC-Color proofer. These are illustrated in Figure VII-2:

| Load | Pump | Charge | Expose | Ink | Transfer | Erase | Clean | Reset |

Figure VII-2. Steps for making a KC-COLOR PROOF which are the automatic steps in the operation of the KC-Analog Color Proofer.

- The operator mounts the appropriate positive or negative transparency on the register pins on the copyboard.
- The platen on which the KC-Crystalplate is mounted is positioned above the positive to be exposed.
- When the operator presses the appropriate color select button on the control panel, the platen moves laterally, accepts a corona charge rendering the photoconductor light sensitive, and moves back to the start position. The voltage attained by charging is measured.
- Vacuum contact is made automatically between the positive and the plate, and the plate is exposed with the aid of a light integrator (typically 5 - 10 seconds).
- The platen again moves laterally, after breaking the vacuum contact, as the corresponding color ink tray rises to make a liquid junction contact with the KC-Coating on the plate.
- While the exposed image is being inked, the surface of the offset intermediate sheet is moistened with a dielectric liquid to effectuate the movement of the entire color image from the KC-Crystalplate to the offset sheet and thereafter to the final paper (ping-pong inks).
- Immediately after inking the wet image passes a *vacuum nozzle* which removes most of the liquid and leaves a moist image behind.

- The moist image then passes over a *wetting station* which adds a fine layer of dielectric liquid on top of it, like a thin foil, to aid the transfer to the intermediate offset sheet. This vital step makes the transfer insensitive to ambient conditions while adding a medium which enables electrophoretic mobility for the ink particles.
- Transfer to the intermediate offset sheet takes place via the traverse of a conductive roller which presses the offset sheet against the KC-Crystalplate surface.
- While the KC-platen returns, the transfer to the final receptor paper is accomplished if the double transfer mode is used.

The plate is now ready for the next image, and the cycle is repeated several times to produce a four- or five-color proof. The completed proof can be made in 10 minutes. In normal proof preparation, all operations on the proofer are automatic except the selection of color sequences and the placement of the positive films on the registration pins.

Principles of Operation

The KC-Color Proofer has exclusive properties due to the extraordinary characteristics of the crystalline photoconductor and the color proofing inks which comprise the KC-Electrophotographic System. This system consists of three subsystems, each of which has unique characteristics: (1) the imaging cycle with the steps of the charging and subsequent contact exposure of the film separation onto the KC-Crystalplate; (2) the ink application; and (3) the transfer process. These are described briefly to help explain the mechanism of electrostatic color proofing.

Imaging Cycle: The KC-Crystalplate which is the imaging member of the KC-Electrophotographic System consists of a stainless steel plate that is completely coated with a crystalline layer of photoconductive material. This layer is deposited and grown in large radio frequency sputtering machines. A typical coating is 3500 Angstroms thick (0.35 micrometer) with a uniformity tolerance over the surface of 2.5 percent. (Figure VII-3, page C-5.)

At the initiation of the imaging cycle the KC-photoconductor layer is electrostatically charged, typically on the order of 35 volts, after which it is returned to the start position, brought into vacuum contact with the color separation film and exposed. During exposure the charged layer is discharged in proportion to the amount of exposure and finally to zero when struck with approximately 40 ergs/cm^2 of energy (daylight spectrum) (Figure VII-4).

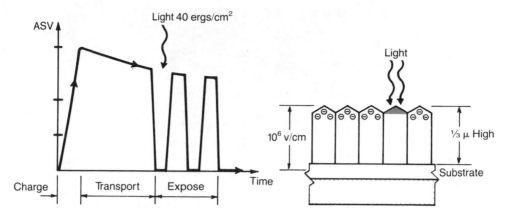

Figure VII-4. Mechanism of charging and exposing the KC-Photoconductor.

The charge density exceeds 5×10^{12} electrons/cm^2 and thereby generates an intense field within and outside the photoconductor. The field lines reach above the surface and attract, in a predictable manner, ink particles to the latent image during the inking process (Figure VII-5).

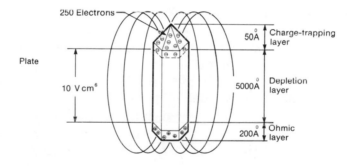

The Crystallite as discrete information storage element

Figure VII-5. Charge characteristics of the KC-Crystallite which make it a discrete information storage element.

The system has an inherent ultimate theoretical resolution capability of 10,000 line-pairs/mm. Practical resolutions of 1,000 line-pairs/mm have been readily achieved (Figure VII-6). This resolution capability far exceeds the requirements of existing printing and proofing processes and thus offers accurate renditions of the color imagery represented by a set of color separation films.

Figure VII-6. Enlargement of high resolution pattern formed with KC-Toner Ink showing resolution of 1000 lines pairs/mm.

For the system to function properly, it requires an accurate selection of the charge voltage V_0 and a precise amount of light energy to expose the image correctly in the contact frame. Thereafter the predictability of the process depends on the built-in rate of dark decay. For example, the system is set up so that the image arrives at the inking station 105 seconds after charging and V_{105} is 22 ± 1.25 volts. At this voltage the innate ink characteristics will produce the desired D-max. during the passage of the KC-Crystalplate.

The KC-Photoconductor differs from other phtoconductors in many ways, such as its anisotropic electrical properties, which enable it to maintain high resolution imagery without lateral charge migration, i.e., without resolution loss as long as a charge remains. Another important feature comes from the "discharge to zero" capability which eliminates the formation of fog during the inking process. Finally, the photoconductor — due to its structure — is predictable in its behavior in a broad range of ambient conditions, and thus will charge to the same voltage level and dark decay at the same rate as is required for this precise image forming process.

The system is calibrated from time to time and monitored electrically during each proof cycle. For this purpose an electrometer is installed adjacent to the charging station to provide a means for measuring the apparent surface voltage on the KC-plate after charging and to automatically adjust D-max densities to the desired level.

Ink Application: As the KC-Crystalplate, held by the platen, arrives at the inking station, any one of five inking trays is selectively waiting in an elevated position to "kiss" the photoconductor surface with a thin layer of electrostatic ink. To avoid precise mechanical tolerances, the inking station is spring-loaded and slides with its shoes against the photoconductor surface to establish an accurate gap between the KC-Crystalplate and the development electrode. As it moves along, the image is formed in accordance with the voltage prevailing at any given area, and it reaches the prescribed density level at an exact point in time. The platen moves back and forth to assure total area uniformity before it proceeds to the transfer station. Prior to arriving at the transfer station, the platen passes a vacuum nozzle which removes excess wetness and undesired migrant ink particles and, with the aid of a post wetting station, establishes an image of the correct "moistness."

The proofing inks were developed using the actual pigments of the printing inks and are made electrostatically responsive through the addition of special chemicals which respond to the presence of an electrostatic field when in solution. The typical particle size of these inks is less than 1 micron, which allows the accurate reproduction of just about any image whether projected or produced by contact. The particles exhibit the same degree of transparency, after fixation, as the printing ink and hence allow an accurate pre-press reproduction of the printed particle deposit which, at its maximum, reaches approximately 15 microns (wet). (Figure VII-7.)

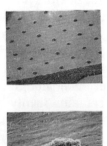

Figure VII-7. Enlargement of toner ink image on KC-Crystalplate. This is a 2% tint in a 150-line screen image. Note the size distribution of the sub-micron size toner ink particles.

The actual thickness of the ink on the development electrode is about .020 inch (0.05 mm), which leads to very rapid development of the image during the first few seconds of initial contact. The number of particles deposited on the surface respond to the charge voltage of the latent image and will develop the full dynamic range in a few seconds covering the highlights, the midtones, and deep, yet open, shadows which were recorded on the KC-Crystalplate at the exposure station.

On its way to the transfer station, as already stated, the platen with the photoconductor passes a floating vacuum slit which removes by suction any excess amount of liquid and leaves only a slightly moist image remaining on the surface. Said image then receives an overlay of dielectric fluid to provide mobility and shield the image from ambient conditions (humidity).

Image Transfer: When the inked image on the KC-Crystalplate arrives at the transfer station the particles are still electrically alive, and they will thus allow the transfer from the photoconductor to the offset sheet and from there to the final paper.

The offset sheet is firmly clamped and held under tension in a subframe which is registered by means of pins first to the KC-platen and then to the paper platen. The same registration technique is employed at the exposure station. Accurate registration is assured within 0.0015 inch (0.04 mm). Moisture problems in the offset sheet are suppressed through prewetting it to the saturation point with dielectric liquid, the same solvent as is used to dilute the ink (Isopar G). The prewetting technique enables the transfer roller to always find dependable electrical conditions during the transfer process regardless of ambient conditions. As a result, the system is capable of transferring images to newsprint, magazine paper, plastic coated paper, and flexible packaging materials.

In color proofing it is necessary to deposit several layers of ink on top of each other (Figure VII-8, page C-5), a function which is accomplished in this electrostatic proofing process by drying the transferred image immediately after it is deposited on the paper. Before the next transfer step, the sheet is again prewet even though it already has an image on it. The previous "dead" image remains firmly anchored on the press paper while the next layer of color is deposited on top of it.

Immediately after transfer the KC-platen moves back towards the exposure station and the image is ready for transfer to the paper platen. Progressives as well as final proofs can be produced in the same station. While the transfer is taking place the operator can load the next separation film onto the copyboard and so is ready for exposing the next color. Drying of the image after each step is accomplished with a warm air fan. The amounts of vapor generated in the drying process are well below the standards prescribed by OSHA and are barely detectable in the proofing room.

The concept of two transfer modes, single step or two-step offset, is exclusive with the KC-Color Proofer and makes it the most versatile of the off-press proofing systems, allowing emulsion-to-emulsion exposure of all the positives regardless of image orientation (lateral reversal). Other proofing systems must make contact films to change image orientation and maintain emulsion/emulsion contact during exposure which is the most reliable means to control dot size. The necessity to make contact films not only increases proofing time and costs but can also introduce image degradation and dot size changes. Proofs for direct printing processes like gravure, letterpress, Di-Litho, and flexography are made by single, or direct transfer; proofs for offset printing, primarily lithography, require double, or indirect, transfer.

Process Characteristics

The control of density levels, gradation characteristics, resolution, color chromaticity, and overall uniformity can best be understood by considering the innate elements which determine the quality of a KC-Proof. These elements are:

- The combination of tone and binary response of the proofing inks to the electrostatic field emanating from the latent image.
- The "discharge to zero" capability of the photoconductor which provides a repeatable anchor for the correct exposure point.
- The absence of edge effects — which plague other photoconductors — due to each crystallite forming a tiny electrostatic field domain. Solid areas are thus uniformly reproducible.
- The insensitivity of the proofing ink and photoconductor to a broad range of ambient moisture and temperature.
- The resolution capability innate in both ink and photoconductor.
- Ability of the proofing ink to be superimposed without trapping or bleeding problems.
- The *predictability* and *repeatability* of all functions essential to forming a good proof image: Charge — Expose — Ink application — Transfer — cleaning and reuse.

The "triple entente" of photoconductor, proofing ink, and method of imaging provide several degrees of freedom, which do not exist equally in other proofing systems. They account for the uniqueness of the KC-Color Proofing System and the fidelity of the proofs it produces.

Chapter VIII

Special Color Proofing Systems for Gravure

Three types of special color proofing systems for gravure are discussed in this chapter: (1) modifications of the off-press color proofing systems discussed in Chapters VI and VII for the new halftone gravure conversion processes; (2) modifications of DuPont CROMALIN and K&E SPECTRA color proofing systems for use with conventional gravure processes using continuous tone, gravure halftone and combinations of contone and halftone positives; and (3) photographic color proofing systems like Ciba-Geigy CIBACHROME, and Kodak EKTACHROME RC-14 and EKTAFLEX PCT.

As pointed out in Chapter IV, gravure's most severe limitations have been (1) its lack of suitable off-press color proofing systems; and (2) its complete dependence on expensive, time-consuming press proofing and cylinder corrections. The success of off-press color proofing in lithography for reducing production times, lead times and preparatory (pre-press) costs has stimulated the other printing processes, especially gravure, to work desperately on ways to derive the same benefits. Gravure's dependence on press proofing has kept it out of the lucrative medium-run publication, commercial and packaging markets because of the high preparatory costs and long lead times forced by the press proofing operation which is further aggravated by the high skill demands, lost production time and high cost of having to make manual color corrections directly on the printing cylinders.

Most of the off-press color proofing systems described in the previous chapters have been developed and are used primarily for lithography which is the most widely used process for publications, commercial and packaging printing. These fast, economical, off-press color proofing methods not only contribute to but account for many of the advantages lithography enjoys over the other processes, particularly gravure. These systems are also used by the other halftone processes like flexography and letterpress, but only to a very limited extent, with considerable modifications, by gravure. With the exception of KC-Color Proofing and EKTAFLEX PCT none of the processes already described is capable of proofing continuous tone (contone) subjects directly; so to use these processes for making proofs for conventional and variable area/variable depth gravure, special conversion contact screens must be used. Other photographic color proofing processes like Ciba-Geigy CIBACHROME and Kodak EKTACHROME RC-14, have contone capability but neither of these has the reliability, or confidence yet, to encourage gravure printers or customers to use them in place of press proofing. This is beginning to change with the introduction of *halftone gravure*, initially called *offset to gravure conversion O/G*, which can use conventional off-press color proofing systems with minor modifications for previewing press prints.

COLOR PROOFING FOR HALFTONE GRAVURE CONVERSIONS

Halftone Gravure has been responsible for an almost complete revamping of gravure pre-press operations especially for the preparation of electromechanically engraved cylinders for publication printing. Processes have been developed for converting conventional halftones, like those used for lithographic reproduction and which can be proofed by existing off-press color proofing systems, so that they can be scanned on electromechanical engraving machines like the Hell Helioklischograph and Ohio Electronic Engraver to make variable area/variable depth image cylinders for printing on gravure presses (see Chapter III). When the color proofing processes are balanced for gravure and the engraving machines are adjusted properly, the press prints made from the printing cylinders look enough like the off-press color proofs that the proofs are considered as acceptable guides for reproduction.

A most important feature of these systems is that if corrections are necessary they are made on the halftone film instead of the cylinders, as presently done. This is a momentous breakthrough for gravure that can change the whole course of its pre-press operations and reshape its future. The bait that is attracting gravure to halftone processes is the time and cost savings resulting from the use of halftone positives, off-press color proofs, and corrections on the films. These will shorten lead times and make gravure an attractive process for (1) shorter run publications (down to 150,000) which has been the exclusive domain of lithography; and (2) enable it to handle regional or demographic editions on larger circulation publications, which have also been exclusive features of letterpress and lithography.

Modifications Needed

For publication and catalog printing which uses electromechanical engraving almost exclusively and which represents the largest share of gravure printing, halftone gravure could well replace contone positives completely. Pre-press operations for these types of gravure will be essentially the same as for lithography. Some work has been done in Europe in which the same halftone positives were used for lithography and gravure. Magazines have been printed in France with crossovers in which one side was printed by lithography and the other side by gravure with little or no noticeable difference in color and tone quality. With the present state of the art this would not be possible in the U.S. mainly because of the big difference between the hues of gravure and lithographic inks. For ideal results, therefore, different inks and probably different screens and tone reproduction curves may be needed.

The present off-press color proofing systems such as those described in Chapters V, VI, and VII, will be used for both lithography and gravure with modifications. They will have to be adjusted to match the pigments in gravure inks. In addition their tone reproduction characteristics may have to be changed to match those of gravure. All of the processes are undergoing these changes. A report of 3M's work on modifying its MATCHPRINT color proofing system for gravure was presented by Dr.

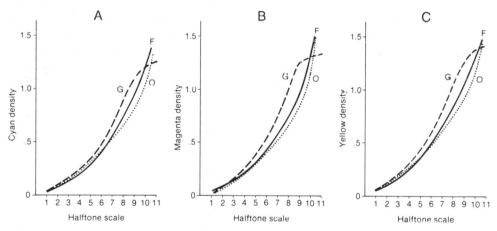

Figure VIII-1. Typical tone reproduction for halftone positive (F), gravure printing (G) and lithographic printing (O) for cyan (A), magenta (B) and yellow (C) according to studies at 3M. (GRI)

R. DeMaster at the GRI Annual Meeting November 9 – 12, 1983. Typical tone reproduction curves for halftones, lithography and gravure for all three colors derived in these studies are shown in Figure VIII-1.

To accomplish the ideal of using the same halftone positives and off-press color proofing system for both lithography and gravure will require some changes in the gravure process especially in the U.S. The spectral characteristics of gravure inks used for publication printing in the U.S. may need to be modified to compensate for the dirtying of tints typical of halftone printing (Chapter III). Cleaner pigments will be needed that will be closer in hue and grayness to those used in Europe which are similar to those used in lithographic inks. This could account for the remarkable success of halftone gravure in Europe and slower progress in the U.S. Another reason for the slower progress in the U.S. is the presence of moiré patterns when halftones made for offset lithography are used for making the gravure cylinders. The reason for this is the extensive use of 133 line (52.4 lines/cm) screens for printing magazines on web offset presses in the U.S. while halftone screens of 150 line (60 lines/cm) or finer are commonly used in Europe. The finer the screen ruling used in the halftones, the less chance there is of the occurence of moiré patterns on the reproductions.

COLOR PROOFING SYSTEMS FOR EXISTING GRAVURE PROCESSES

Despite the revolution in pre-press operations for publication and catalog gravure, the present gravure processes using contone or halftone positives and/or combinations of contone and halftone positives will continue to be used for art reproductions, calendars, photographic annuals, advertising printing, packaging and other specialties so they will still need a suitable off-press color proofing system specifically for gravure. This need will exist until halftone gravure and electromechanical engraving are refined and adapted for these uses.

Of the off-press color proofing systems described in Chapter VI that have application to gravure processes other than halftone gravure, CROMALIN and SPECTRA have been modified so they can be used to proof conventional and variable area/variable depth gravure. 3M introduced a color proofing system for gravure in the mid-70's but discontinued it and in 1983 introduced a modified MATCHPRINT Color Proofing System for the new halftone gravure processes.

The KC-Color Proofing System has continuous tone capability which would make it an ideal process for conventional and variable area/variable depth gravure, but in view of the increasing emphasis on halftone gravure, all development efforts have been concentrated in this direction and work on adapting the KC-Process to contone gravure systems has been suspended. The Kodak EKTAFLEX PCT proofing process is properly suited for gravure as it has both contone and halftone capability; but since it is a photographic process it will be discussed in the section on Photographic Color Proofing Systems for Gravure.

CROMALIN Gravure Color Proofing Systems

The original CROMALIN gravure color proofing process for conventional and variable area/variable depth gravure, introduced in the mid-1970's, used the continuous tone separation positives and a gravure screen for exposing the CROMALIN proof. Proofs produced by this procedure did not match the press prints consistently so the procedure was changed in the late 1970's to the use of intermediate halftone positives made by exposing the contone separation positives onto Cronar White Light Duplicating (CRW) Film using a set of special matched, pre-angled, gray contact screens. Alternative procedure is to a halftone negative camera film such as Command Halftone Film (CHF). This halftone negative is then contacted onto Bright Light Etching (BLE) Film for a hard dot contact used in preparation of the CROMALIN proofs.

The CROMALIN Gravure Color Proofing System consists of the following materials and equipment:

1) For making the *intermediate halftone positives:*
   Materials:
   • Cronar White Light Duplicating (CRW) Film, 0.004 or 0.007 inch (0.102 or 0.178 mm) thick. For the two step *screening* plus contact procedure use the fims mentioned above.
   • Set of four special Cromalin Gravure Screens (CGS) — matched, pre-angled, gray contact screens.
   • 3-step GTA Standard Color Scales.
   Equipment:
   • Standard vacuum frame with contact light source and exposure control device for making contact screen positives.
   • Transmission densitometer.
   • Automatic film processor.

2) For making the CROMALIN proofs:
   Materials:
   • CROMALIN film and toners.
   • Kromekote paper or similar receptor stock.

- GTA Gravure Ink Standard Color Charts.
- GTA Group I and Group V Paper Stock.

Equipment:
- CROMALIN laminator, toning console and applicators.
- Exposure unit with UV light source and light integrator and film.

Procedure for Making CROMALIN Gravure Color Proofs

The procedure for making CROMALIN Gravure Color Proofs involves first the making of intermediate halftones which are then used to make the proofs. The steps involved include:

For making the halftones:
- Selection of the calibration standard.
- Preparation of the screens.
- Calibration of the screen exposures.
- Exposure and processing of the halftones.

For making the proof:
- Preparation of the receptor stock.
- Calibration of the CROMALIN exposure.
- Making of the CROMALIN proofs.

These steps are described briefly in the following sections. Detailed instructions are provided in Section 12 of the *DuPont Operators Manual.*

Intermediate Halftones

- *Selection of Calibration Standard:* The GTA Gravure Standard Ink Color Charts for Group I and Group V inks and papers are used as the calibration standards. The GTA 3-patch target is used to calibrate the intermediate halftones and the final color proofs to the GTA Color Charts.
- *Preparation of Screens:* The screens are prepared by punching register holes in, or attaching register tabs to, the edge of each screen and identifying it by placing the proper CROMALIN color label on the back (shiny side) along the punched edge. The yellow label is attached to the 90° screen; magenta to the 75° screen; cyan to the 15° screen; and black to the 45° screen.
- *Screen Exposure Calibration:* The exposures are made emulsion/emulsion between the screen and the Cronar White Light Duplicating (CRW) Film. The object is to produce an integrated net dot density of 0.04 to 0.06 in the highlight step of the GTA target

with all four screens. After all screens are calibrated and development conditions are established, a set of four matched screened GTA 3-patch targets is made with the targets side by side on one CRW film (or CHF for two step procedure) and one set for each screen (Figure VIII-2). These are used for calibrating the correct exposures for making the CROMALIN proofs.

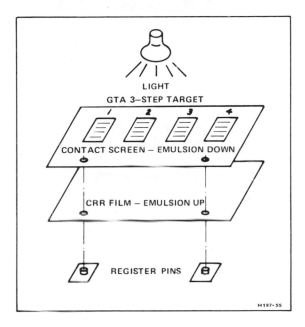

Figure VIII-2. Screen exposure calibration for making the intermediate halftones for CROMALIN gravure proofs. (DuPont)

• *Halftone Positives:* The intermediate halftone positives to be used for making the CROMALIN gravure proof are made from the continuous tone color separation positives used to make the image on the printing cylinder, or the bromide prints used on the electomechanical engraving machine. The halftones are made by putting each contone film in contact with the appropriate screen which is in emulsion/emulsion contact with the CRW film. GTA 3-patch targets attached to the positives are used to evaluate the dot values of the halftones. When all halftone positives have integrated densities of 0.04 to 0.06 in the highlight steps of the GTA targets they are considered satisfactory for making the proof.

CROMALIN Gravure Color Proof

• *Preparation of Receptor Stock;* Group I or Group V paper can be laminated to the usual Kromekote or similar receptor stock of regular CROMALIN proofs. The lamination is done by applying a Cromalin film to the Kromekote, removing the cover sheet, applying the Group I (newsprint) or Group V (magazine paper) stock to the tacky surface, covering it with another Cromalin film and hardening it with a ½ minute exposure in a Cromalin exposing unit.

- *Cromalin Exposing Calibration:* The screened GTA 3-patch targets, produced in the screen calibration step for making the halftones, are used as the controls in making the CROMALIN proof. Exposure is adjusted so that there is a good visual density match between the highlight and middletone patches on the proof and the corresponding steps on the GTA Gravure Standard Ink Color Charts. The toning cycles are varied so as to get a good density match between the midtone patch and the corresponding step on the color chart. These conditions are established for each color and should be checked when emulsion numbers of the Cromalin films change.

- *Making the CROMALIN Proofs:* The procedures for making CROMALIN gravure proofs are the same as for conventional CROMALIN proofs as long as all the calibration and evaluation procedures are satisfied. The order of color is also the same — Yellow, Magenta, Cyan and Black — Y-M-C-K.

- A DuPont 30-step wedge is available in place of the 3-step patch for calibration of gravure proofing for gravure processes not using the GTA Standard Ink Color Charts. A representative press sheet or color chart must be used and tones must be blended or modified to match the hues and strengths of the inks used.

CROMALIN Proofing for Hard Dot Gravure

Hard dot gravure is variously called *halftone, direct, direct transfer,* and *variable area gravure.* It differs from the new halftone gravure processes in that the halftones are used to expose the cylinder directly without any intermediate conversion and the etching process used spreads the dots producing an image in which all the dots have different areas but the same depth. The halftones must have a dot structure that produces an image with a wall around each dot to support the doctor blade and keep the ink from running out of the wells during printing.

The halftone positive appears as in Figure VIII-3(A) compared with a conventional (lithographic) halftone positive that would print the same tone values on the press print (Figure VIII-3[B]). The maximum allowable dot percentage in the shadow area is approximately 68% (0.50 integrated dot density). Because of ink spread during printing this size dot eventually prints as a deep shadow or solid on the press (97-100% dot). Where side etching is a factor, the largest dot size on the positive

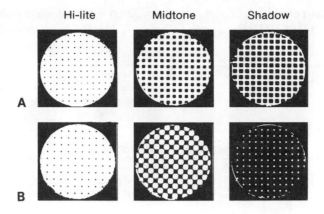

Figure VIII-3. Comparison of gravure screen positive for (A) Hard Dot Gravure and (B) Offset lithographic halftone. (DuPont)

(corresponding to a solid color on the printed page) may be as low as 50% (0.30 integrated dot density). A photomechanical proof made directly from these halftones would lack color density and saturation in the shadows and would appear weak and washed out. In order to produce a proof that looks like the print the halftone positives used to make the cylinder must be converted to a new set of positives for the proof in which the dot size range corresponds to the spread of the dots in etching and printing on the press. The halftone gravure CROMALIN proof process provides a means for producing the spread positives with which conventional CROMALIN proofs can be made using appropriate toners.

Materials and Equipment Needed:
- Bright Light Etchable Film — BLE-4.
- DuPont Cromalin Target — HARD DOT GRAVURE.
- DuPont CROMALIN Offset Com Guide Positive Target.
- Vacuum frame with suitable high UV exposure source.
- Rapid access or lith film processor.
- Transmission densitometer.
- Punch register system.

Procedure for making Hard Dot Gravure CROMALIN Proofs

Calibration: Before making the spread positives from which the proofs are made the system must be calibrated. A dot-for-dot negative is made from a gravure halftone positive, with a solid color or deep shadow area having an integrated dot density from 0.30 to 0.50, by exposing it with a HARD DOT GRAVURE target (Figure VIII-4), emulsion-to-emulsion,

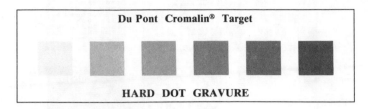

Figure VIII-4. Hard dot gravure target for calibrating the Hard Dot Gravure CROMALIN proof system. (DuPont)

on BLE-4 film. Using this negative the standard exposure is determined to make a dot-for-dot positive on BLE-4 film with the emulsion of the negative facing away from the emulsion side of the film. This standard exposure is used to calculate the amount of exposure needed to produce the spread positives for the proof from the nomagram shown in Figure VIII-5.

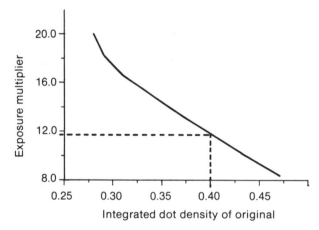

Figure VIII-5. Nomagram to determine correct exposure for Hard Dot Gravure CROMALIN proof. The graph shows how to determine the exposure multiplier for a hard dot positive with shadow density of 0.40. The multiplier is 11.8 which is the number by which the dot for dot exposure must be multiplied to obtain the correct exposure for the spread positive on the proof. (DuPont)

The nomagram indicates the multiplier, or number of times the standard exposure must be multiplied, to obtain the correct exposure for original positives of specific integrated dot densities to produce positives with the proper dot spread for proofing. The example shown is for an original positive with integrated dot density of 0.40 (measured with a densitometer on the shadow area) indicating a multiplier of 11.8. If the dot-for-dot exposure of the positive was 5 seconds, the exposure for the spread positives is 5 x 11.8 = 59 seconds. This exposure time should produce a 96% to 97% (1.30 to 1.50 integrated density) dot in the shadow area of the spread positive. A test run should be made to confirm this. This then becomes the proper exposure for all work using positives with the same integrated dot densities and the same lot of BLE-4 film. The densities or dot percentages of each of the steps on the HARD DOT GRAVURE target should be recorded for checking and control.

Making the Proof: After the films are registered and punched a HARD DOT GRAVURE DuPont Cromalin target is attached to the edge of each halftone positive. A contact negative is made from each color positive on BLE-4 film, emulsion-to-emulsion, and adjusting the exposure to produce dot-for-dot reproduction from positive to negative. The negatives are used to make the spread positives for the proof by exposing through the base (emulsion up) on BLE-4 film as shown in Figure VIII-6 using the exposure determined in the calibration (59 seconds for positives with integrated solid density of 0.40).

The spread positives are used to make the CROMALIN proof in the regular way. The inks used in gravure packaging are close to offset inks in hue, so the use of Standard Offset Positive (SOP) toners are generally satisfactory. Other colors can be mixed if needed.

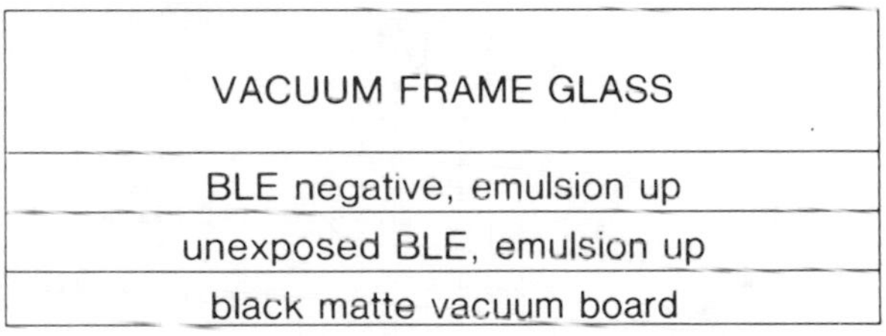

VACUUM FRAME GLASS
BLE negative, emulsion up
unexposed BLE, emulsion up
black matte vacuum board

Figure VIII-6. Orientation of films to obtain correct dot gain on the spread positives in the proof. (DuPont)

SPECTRA Gravure Color Proofing System

The K&E SPECTRA Color Proofing System described in Chapter VI has been modified for use as an off-press proofing system for the positives used in conventional and variable area/variable depth gravure. The modifications involve (1) the matching of SPECTRA toners to the GTA Group I and Group V inks and (2) the conversion of gravure continuous tone color separation positives to halftone negatives that produce proofs with dot size ranges corresponding to the tone range of inks on gravure prints. Keuffel and Esser has been experimenting with contact screens for several years and has found one that comes very close to duplicating the tone reproduction of gravure prints as displayed in the GTA Group V color standard book for coated paper. These studies were reported by Dr. R.M. Lazarus, Keuffel and Esser, at the GRI Annual Meeting, November 3 – 6, 1982.

An example of the tone reproduction curve of a magenta SPECTRA proof on 34 lb. (51 gsm) gravure coated stock compared with the densities of the same tones on a magenta sheet in the GTA Group V color book is shown in Figure VIII-7. Yellow, cyan and black toners have been matched to Group V inks and Group I toners are also available. SPECTRA is engaged in field testing of this gravure color proofing system. In the meantime work is progressing on the development of a positive color proofing system for use with halftone gravure processes.

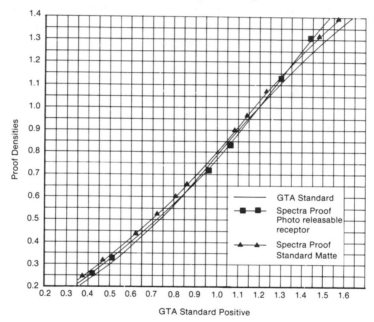

Figure VIII-7. Plot of magenta curves showing correlation between tone reproduction curves of GTA V standard magenta and magentas produced on SPECTRA proof. (GRI)

Photographic Color Proofing Systems for Gravure

As already mentioned several photographic color proofing systems have been developed and investigated for checking continuous tone separation positives for gravure. These have included Ciba-Geiby

CIBACHROME, Kodak EKTACHROME RC-14 and EKTAFLEX PCT, which are described and discussed in this section.

CIBACHROME Gravure Color Proofing System

CIBACHROME Gravure is a color reversal, silver dye-bleach color print paper manufactured by Ciba-Geigy in Switzerland and marketed in the U.S. by Ilford, Inc. The colored image is formed by *azo* dye layers which are very stable and have high resolution. In a silver dye–bleach process like CIBACHROME Gravure each silver halide emulsion layer contains an azo dye corresponding to the color represented by the silver halide layer. After exposure of all the color separation positives and during development of the film, black and white negative silver images are formed in each layer. Wherever silver is developed in the negative image a chemical reaction with the silver destroys the dye in contact with it so that after development, bleaching, fixing and washing, which removes all the silver and other soluble materials in the film, the result is a composite color proof with a stable azo dye image in each of the three emulsion layers.

The materials needed for making CIBACHROME Gravure proofs are:

- Cibachrome P-18 chemicals, consisting of developer, bleach, and fix solution.
- Pre-exposed control strips for monitoring fog level, contrast, and maximum density in processing.
- K&M type tungsten light source for exposure.
- Special 175 line/inch (69 1/cm) 50% copy screen which is placed in contact with the positives during each exposure and is used to reduce contrast.

Because Cibachrome film has dyes with fixed spectral characteristics multiple, or split, exposures must be used to approximate a match between the colors in the proofs and the standard GTA Group V colors. A comparison of the color characteristics of GTA Group V inks and unshifted Cibachrome dyes on a proof is shown in Table VIII-I. The proof was made by GRI with single exposures through each positive, using color separations and press prints of a Macbeth Color checker and Wratten Filters No. 47B (blue) for the yellow positive, No. 58 (green) for the magenta positive and No. 25 (red) for the cyan positive.

These colors are shown plotted on a GATF color circle in Figure VIII-8. There are wide, unacceptable discrepancies between these colors and their overprints — all CIBACHROME colors are grayer, or dirtier, than the Group V inks and the color gamut is smaller.

TABLE VIII-I

COLOR CHARACTERISTICS OF GROUP V INKS
VS. UNSHIFTED CIBACHROME DYES

		Hue Error	Grayness
Yellow	Group V	19.0%	7.7%
	CIBACHROME	16.7%	18.2%
Magenta	Group V	67.6%	20.4%
	CIBACHROME	32.4%	47.9%
Cyan	Group V	34.4%	32.6%
	CIBACHROME	8.8%	37.4%

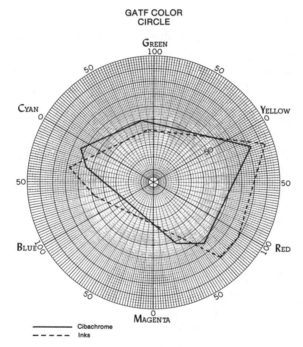

Figure VIII-8. Plot on GATF Color Circle of CIBACHROME proof without color shifts. (GRI)

Hue shifts in the CIBACHROME proof colors are produced by sandwiching yellow and magenta positives during part of the blue filter exposure and magenta and cyan positives during part of the green filter exposure. Tests run by GRI indicated that Wratten Filter No 46 (blue) worked better than No. 47B on sandwiched exposures and that close

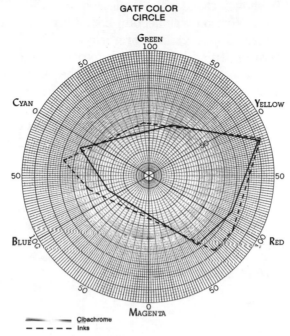

Figure VIII-9. Plot on GATF Color Circle of CIBACHROME proof with color shifts. (GRI)

correspondence between the hues of the CIBACHROME proof and Group V inks was obtained when sandwiched positives were used for 90% of the blue and green filter exposures. Table VIII-II shows the hue shifts obtained with 70% split exposures.

TABLE VIII-II

70% CIBACHROME (SPLIT) GRAVURE COLOR SHIFT

		Hue Error	Grayness
Yellow	Group V	19.0%	7.7%
	CIBACHROME	20.9%	8.5%
Magenta	Group V	67.6%	20.4%
	CIBACHROME	59.7%	31.4%
Cyan	Group V	34.4%	32.6%
	CIBACHROME	13.9%	52.2%
Red	Printed Group V	97.2%	20.3%
	CIBACHROME	90.2%	27.3%
Green	Printed Group V	88.9%	58.1%
	CIBACHROME	59.6%	56.9%
Blue	Printed Group V	75.9%	51.8%
	CIBACHROME	85.0%	67.2%

Figure VIII-9 shows these colors plotted on a GATF color circle. Considerable color correction was accomplished but the cyan and blues in the proof still require subjective interpretation.

With split exposures an additional flash exposure is required to reduce contrast and make the tone reproduction of the proof correspond with that of the press print. The GRI tests indicated that a flash exposure of aproximately 0.50% produced the desirable correction. Table VIII-III shows a comparison of the tone reproductions of the press print and the 70% split exposure CIBACHROME proof with a 0.50% flash.

TABLE VIII-III

TONE REPRODUCTION WITH 0.50% FLASH EXPOSURE

Press Print	70% CIBACHROME (Split)
0.15	0.16
0.29	0.29
0.46	0.52
0.73	0.84
1.13	1.23

With the proper use of split exposures and flash, CIBACHROME proofs can produce a reasonable simulation of gravure press prints and can be a useful aid to retouchers without other visual guides.

Kodak EKTACHROME RC-14 Gravure Color Proofing System

Kodak Ektachrome RC-14 is a color reversal print paper originally developed for applications in commercial photography. It has been used successfully for color proofing of gravure continuous tone positive color separations in Europe and the U.S. for several years. The process for making gravure color proofs on Ektachrome RC-14 paper were described by William A. Rocap, Jr., Technical Director, Meredith/Burda, Inc., in a report at the GRI Annual Meeting November 11–14, 1981.

The equipment and materials used for the process are:

- Vacuum frame and K&M point light source for exposure with light integrator to control exposure.
- Wratten Filters Nos. 47B (blue), 58PM (green) and 25 (red).
- Simmons Drum Processor with rotator and timer for one-shot processing.
- Temperature controlled sink for processing with provision for maintaining solution temperatures within $\pm \frac{1}{2}°F$.

- Kodak EKTACHROME RC-14 paper.
- Chemicals for Kodak Ektaprint R-100 process.

The procedures for making continuous tone gravure color proofs on EKTACHROME RC-14 paper are:

- Separation film positives and Ektachrome RC-14 paper are punched for register during multiple exposures.
- Light intensity is set at 50% pointlight for all colors — the black positive is included for part of the exposure with each separation.
- Exposure times: 5 units yellow separation (47B); 3.8 units magenta separation (58PM); 6 units cyan separation (25); and 0.1 unit for black separation in contact with each of the other separations. No flash exposure is used.
- Processing is done using the 14 step Kodak EKTAPRINT R-100 process and chemistry.

After the process was put into production at Meredith/Burda, an automatic processor was used for processing the proof to assure uniformity and reduce cost of the finished proof. The Kodak Ektaprint R-100 Control Strips are used to monitor the Ektaprint R-100 processing. The factors controlled in the processing are maximum density (D-max.), contrast, speed, color balance, and stain. A plot of the EKTACHROME proof colors on a GATF color circle compared with corresponding colors in a Meridith/Burda color book, and a CROMALIN gravure color proof is shown in Figure VIII-10. A plot of a gray scale on the proof compared with the same scale on the original is shown in Figure VIII-11. A 45° line would indicate exact tone reproduction between original and proof.

The EKTACHROME RC-14 off-press color proof is used at Meredith/Burda to determine what corrections are necessary in the positives in order for the proof to match the color and contrast of the original copy, and to check the effects of retouching after it is done. The process, according to Rocap, has simplified the task of producing positives with the proper color and tone corrections for making the cylinders, thereby reducing cylinder making time and costs, increasing productivity and improving print quality.

Kodak EKTAFLEX PCT Gravure Color Proofing System

The process is the same as the one described in Chapter VI. It has the same dye set as Kodak EKTACHROME RC-14 and because of the simplicity and repeatability of its processing and matching colors with the programmable multiplex 9100 exposure unit, the EKTAFLEX PCT process is being recommended by Kodak to replace EKTACHROME RC-14 for gravure color proofing.

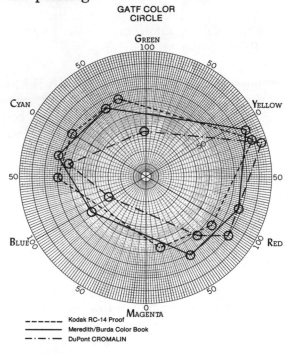

Figure VIII-10. Comparison of plots on GATF Color Circle of colors on EKTACHROME proof, CROMALIN and Meredith-Burda Color Book. (GRI)

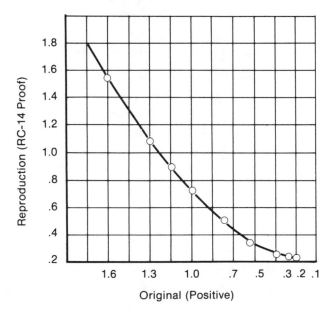

Figure VIII-11. Plot of EKTACHROME proof vs. original. (GRI)

Projection Proofing

This is not a new proofing system. It is a new means or method of making multiple exposures for current proofing systems. It is included in this chapter because it will be applied more to making proofs for gravure than for other processes.

Projection proofing is a method of making proofs of subjects using a combination of separate exposures of the intermediate films before they have been assembled into composite final films. The term projection is used because the *Opti-Copy* projection step and repeat system has been recommended for making these proofs.

Many color jobs, especially magazine advertising, are composed of a number of separate pieces of art consisting of color transparencies, flat art, line drawings and text. It is often desirable to produce a composite proof of the subject before all the films are completely assembled into a single film for each color as it is easier and less costly to make corrections, if needed, on the individual films than on the composite films.

The means recommended for accomplishing this is by successive projection of the individual elements onto the proofing materials using a projection device like the Opti-Copy. This is a means with high energy illumination and precision optics for projecting multiple images at same size in register at fairly high speed and with copy-dot resolution (2% dots on 150-line screen images). Combination exposures of all the elements for a color separation are made in succession on the color proofing medium: Cromalin film for CROMALIN proofs; the appropriate Transfer Key films for MATCHPRINT proof and Color Key or NAPS/PAPS films for COLOR KEY and NAPS/PAPS proofs. The films for the individual elements of the final separation must be properly silhouetted and masked as they would be for making the composite separation films for each color plate.

The Opti-Copy is also used for making fast projection proofs of film subjects of color page makeup systems like the Scitex Response 300. Proofs can be made in position on a plate or 2-page layout using the digital data for position from the page makeup or electronic layout system. Exposure times for the proofs are long but are being shortened by increasing the power of the illumination on the Opti-Copy and the speed of the coatings in the proofing systems.

In making KC-Color Composite Proofs, projection exposures are not possible or necessary. Multiple exposures for each color can be made successively directly on the KC-Crystalplate before each plate is toned or inked. The KC-Crystalplate has the necessary high speed and resolution for making the composite proofs in reasonable time. With other proofing systems exposure times are long which make proofing times for systems using multiple exposures excessive. Proofs for gravure have been made on the KC-Analog Color Proofer using up to 16 separate exposures of as many as 40 films in total proofing times of 30 to 40 minutes.

Chapter IX

Electronic Color Proofing

The invasion of graphic arts by electronics and computers especially in the pre-press areas has logically spread to color proofing. The widespread use of electronic color scanners has multiplied the need for fast color proofing. The new sophisticated computerized pre-press systems have replaced intermediate films that can be used for proofing with digitized composite images displayed on video screens. These situations have spawned the development of electronic means for proofing color images to be sure they are correct for reproduction. These images are called "soft proofs" and though very useful for internal checking they suffer from the main limitation that while they have the appearance of printed subjects, they are without substance, do not have the feel of press prints and cannot be signed for approval and reference. Electronic proofing has advanced to digital proofing in which the digitized images are converted to "hard proofs" that can be used and handled like press prints.

This chapter covers electronic previewers which are used for "soft proofing" to increase the productivity of electronic color scanning, improve its quality and reliability and reduce the necessity for rescanning; and the digital color proofing systems that have been developed to produce "hard proofs" to complement soft proofs and enhance the effectiveness of the expensive, sophisticated electronic color pre-press page makeup systems.

Electronic Previewers — Soft Color Proofing

The introduction of electronic dot generation in color scanners in 1972 has been responsible for more than a tenfold increase in speed of producing direct color corrected color separation halftones which has both reduced the cost of color reproduction and increased its quality. These two factors have been the main reasons for the tremendous growth of color printing. The expansion in the use of color, coupled with the increased speed of producing color separations have created unprecedented demands for fast color proofing. The increased speed of scanning left much room for error and it has been estimated that 25% to 50% of the separations made on a scanner have to be remade — resulting not only in increased cost but reduced productivity. In an effort to reduce the error ratio and make color separation and correction more predictive and productive, the electronic color previewer was introduced in 1971 in a joint venture by Hazeltine and DuPont.

The first color previewers were introduced before direct screening on scanners was generally accepted and their main purpose was to determine the optimum screening conditions for continuous tone color separations. Three color previewers were built and installed on trial in two trade shops and one printing plant. In the course of determining screening requirements for specific printing conditions much was learned about the variability of the printing process and ways to control it. While the previewers were not entirely successful in their primary mission of establishing optimum screening conditions, they were very effective in pinpointing printing variables and determining procedures for controlling them. The information gained has been useful in programming the previewers for process variables.

By 1972 when Hell introduced electronic dot generation on the DC 300 scanner and direct screening became established on scanners the need for, and interest in, previewers for determining halftoning conditions diminished. DuPont dropped out of the venture and Hazeltine continued to work on the previewer, improve it and explore new uses for it. Gravure was especially in need of a means for evaluating continuous tone positives used for cylinder making and found the electronic previewer helpful in this evaluation. In 1976 TOPPAN introduced a similar system for previewing gravure positives prior to cylinder making.

Color previewers are now being used to check scanner output before proofing, and for compatibility proofing for publication printing of advertising subjects from different agencies and engravers. The term "soft proofing" has been applied to this type of proofing that uses video screens for full color displays of the composite images of the corrected color separation films.

The electronic color previewing systems described in this section are those made by Hazeltine and TOPPAN which can be used with the output of any scanner. There are others by Crosfield (Pro-Edit), Hell (Scanskop) and Scitex (PreSponse) but these are proprietary and are designed for use only with the manufacturer's systems. The principles of their operation are similar to the Hazentine and TOPPAN systems.

HAZELTINE Electronic Proofing System

The HAZELTINE Electronic Proofing System consists of two peripherals and the HAZELTINE Model SP 1620 Separation Previewer which is an electro-optical system that can simulate the color printing process from color separation through press and produce an electronic color video display of the ink-on-paper result. The color previewer has two units: a video camera and digital image processing unit and a video display unit as illustrated in Figure IX-1. It is simple to operate. Each separation film is placed in register on the light table; the button corresponding to the separation film's color on the console is pressed for the exposure; the film is removed; and the operations are repeated for the next film until all four separations are exposed. Within 30 seconds a four-color proof as it would look printed with ink on paper appears on the video screen of the display unit.

Figure IX-1. Hazeltine Separation Previewer Model #SP01620 showing electronic camera and video display unit. (Hazeltine)

System Capability

The system is pre-programmed to simulate all the characteristics of the color printing process including all photographic and photomechanical processes such as color separation, color correction, contacting and platemaking, and mechanical and optical characteristics of transferring ink to paper on a printing press. Besides displaying a full color press result the previewer has the capability of displaying progressives in any combination. To simplify image analysis and assist in the evaluation of subtle gradations, the individual separations can be displayed in black and white without changing the tone scale.

The previewer has an internal color computer which allows a choice of up to seven programs for process/ink/paper/press combinations. It works with either positive or negative separations, screened separations for lithography or letterpress, and continuous tone or halftone separations for gravure. The system has built-in comprehensive color correction features which allow the operator to do *flat etching* or *local etching* using a *digital zoom* to frame and magnify (four times) portions of the image to be corrected. A movable cursor with a built-in densitometer provides readings of any color in any image area. A digital meter displays dot percentage for screened separations and density for continuous tone separations. The system also has controls for *midtone gradation* which can be used to compensate for dot gain, *ink level* to simulate the effect of changing the amount of ink run on the press, and *total ink density* to assist in analyzing the picture for undercolor removal. If corrections are needed the specific changes required to produce the desired result with ink-on-paper are read from the digital meter.

Peripherals

The two peripherals added to the previewer to make it the HAZELTINE Electronic Color Proofing System are: *Multi-Stor* — a high-speed retrievable storage system: and *Scanner Interface* for pre-scan and pre-viewing.

The *Multi-Stor* is used to store the 4-color images on video tape in video cassettes as they are recorded. A hard copy printer compiles a directory of all the images on the cassette tape by key numbers which are used for almost instant recall of the color images on the video tape. The Multi-Stor allows two images to be viewed alternately. It can be used for comparing (1) a corrected set of separations with the original set; (2) a subject's color with a reference color in storage; and (3) the color balance or compatibility of images that will print on the same form. This last feature makes this system ideally suited for compatibility proofing for magazine printing where films for advertising subjects come from many different sources.

The *Scanner Interface* permits linking the previewer to a scanner and previewing the output of the scanner before films are made. After all the settings are made on the scanner to produce a set of separations a fast scan is used to feed the color data through the Scanner Interface directly to the Previewer which displays a proof on the video screen corresponding to the scanner settings. If corrections are desirable the operator can utilize the correction features of the previewer and transfer the new settings to the scanner controls. The new settings can be previewed with a fast scan through the Scanner Interface and the Previewer before committing the scanner to the production of film separations.

TOPPAN Color Proofer

The TOPPAN CP525-MKII Color Proofer is very similar in design and function to the HAZELTINE Electronic Color Proofing System. There are some differences. The TOPPAN system consists of four units: video camera for inputting separations; digital image processing console for manipulation and correction of images; video display monitor for displaying the color proof; and viewing booth for viewing the original transparency or reflection print (Figure IX-2). TOPPAN has a sophisticated *undercolor removal matrix* to handle the display of "problem colors" like deep shadows and dark colors requiring undercolor removal.

Figure IX-2. TOPPAN CP 525-MK II Color Proofer showing electronic camera, operator panel, image conductor and display unit. (P&J)

Peripherals

TOPPAN has added an *Image File System* which allows a user to record an image onto a floppy disc memory. The disc records the image in digital mode as opposed to the analog images of the Hazeltine Multi-Stor system which are on video tape. Each 4-color image is on a separate disc which is filed for future use such as comparing images before and after correction or for use by a customer on another TOPPAN unit or a satellite station.

The *TOPPAN Satellite Station* consists of a video monitor and a floppy disc reader. It can be set up in a pressroom to provide the pressman with a visual proof of the subject being printed to compare the press print with it. It can also be used in a customer's shop or client's office to improve communications.

Summary

Electronic Previewers or Soft Proofing Systems are becoming established components of color printing systems especially for compatibility proofing by advertising agencies and publication printers. They are also finding use for internal checking and quality control proofing. They have the advantages of speed and low cost by producing proofs at each step in the color reproduction process, whereas conventional proofs take time and are expensive to produce. The effect of corrections can be viewed before committing them to film so that the first corrections can be the last. Also the first "hard" proof will not need to be made until all corrections have been made and approved so it should win customer approval without much rework. The savings in material costs and labor of making conventional proofs can help to offset the costs of the system.

The Scanner Interface for the previewer is a popular feature of the HAZELTINE Electronic Color Proofing System. If and when scanners go all-digital and record images in a colorimetric space, as in the EIKONIX Designmaster 8000, color previewers will not be needed, as the image in these systems will not be committed to film until all manipulations and corrections have been made and approved as displayed on the color monitor which is really a dedicated previewer. In effect, the modular color previewers are filling a void in the transition from analog to digital scanners. What all these systems need to make them complete is a means of converting the soft proofs to hard proofs, which is the subject of the next section of this chapter.

DIGITAL PROOFING — HARD COPY PROOFS

The sophisticated electronic color pre-press, or page makeup systems like the Hell Chromacom, Scitex Response 300 and 350, Crosfield Studio 800 Series, Dianippon Screen Sigmagraph 2000 and KC-Digital System, which go from copy to film, or to plate, directly, without any intermediate films, use soft proofing extensively in all phases of their operation. A major limitation of the systems, however, has been the lack of subsystems to produce a "hard proof" from the digital data in the system — i.e., an image writer or recorder that can use the digital data in the system to produce a color proof on paper, or other substrate.

Conventionally, proofs are made from the output films from the systems which will be used to make the printing plates or cylinders. If changes are needed they must be made in the pre-press system from which new films are made for new proofs. This procedure is time-consuming and expensive, especially for gravure where most proofing is done on a press. The direct digital color proof made before the digital data is committed to film (or plate or cylinder) can save considerable time and expense by eliminating the need for multiple proofings. Oversimplified block diagrams in Figure IX-3 show comparisons between digital color proofing (A) and conventional color proofing (B) in color pre-press systems. Also the direct copy to plate or cylinder systems which are being used in gravure and are being developed for lithography do not use films so that off-press proofing by conventional means becomes impossible or exceedingly expensive especially for gravure.

HARDCOPY PROOFING FOR DIGITAL PRE-PRESS

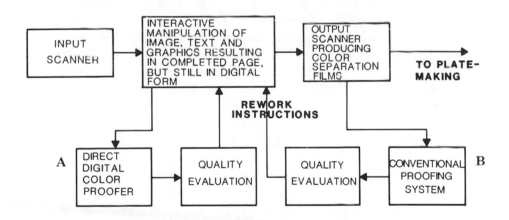

Figure IX-3. Oversimplified block diagram for digital color proofing using digital techniques (A) and conventional proofing (B). (MDA)

The digital color proof in pre-press systems is needed mainly for the customer or client to use to see what the printed job will look like. The customer can approve and sign it as a record of acceptance after which it can be used as the customer approved proof for printing on the press. Or the customer can indicate changes on the proof which can be used as a guide for corrections and a reference with which a new proof can be compared.

The first digital color proofs were shown at DRUPA '82 by Hell and Crosfield. Hell showed proofs on color photographic paper made on its CPR 403 Color Proof Recorder from data in its Chromacom system. Crosfield showed color photographic proofs of images on the video monitor of its Studio 860 system made on a LogE/Dunn VersaColor Camera which is being considered for hard proofing in other digital systems. These systems are described in this section. Also described are two digital color proofing systems in development: one by Polaroid Corporation using a MacDonald Dettwiler Film Recorder and Polaroid Diffusion Transfer Color Paper; and the other by Coulter Systems Corp. using the Laser Printer of the KC-Digital Pre-Press System and the KC-Color Proofer.

Hell CPR 403 Color Proof Recorder

The Hell Chromagraph CPR 403 Color Proof Recorder is a means of producing a continuous tone color proof from digital data in the Hell Chromacom color page makeup system in size up to 21 x 29 inches (540 mm x 735 mm) on color photographic paper in less than 20 minutes. The proof is a facsimile of the soft proof on the Chromacom's color monitor incorporating the characteristics of the process/plate/ink/paper/press combination by which it will be printed. The proof is intended to represent the press print with the distinguishing characteristics of the printing process — lithography or gravure — and duplicating the effects of plate or cylinder type; hue, saturation and purity of the inks; paper brightness, gloss and ink absorptivity; and press variables such as dot gain, slur, trapping, etc.

The system is illustrated in Figure IX-4. It consists of an operator terminal with a VDT (video display), keyboard, dual floppy disc drives and an electronics cabinet with an R-10 minicomputer or CPU; exposure cabinet housing the recording subsystem with two lasers (Argon ion and Helium/Neon), three modulators, mirrors, beam splitters, filters and lens; on-line color photographic processing unit; and a 300 megabyte (MB) disc drive for picture or page storage data. Also included in the system is an automated robotic subsystem consisting of a magazine of 50 sheets of color photographic paper, means for extracting one sheet at a time,

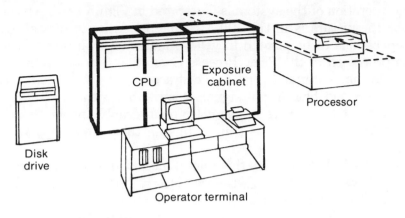

Figure IX-4. Hell CPR 403 Color Proof Recorder. (HCM)

punching it for register, mounting it in precise position for exposure, detaching and transporting it to the on-line processor.

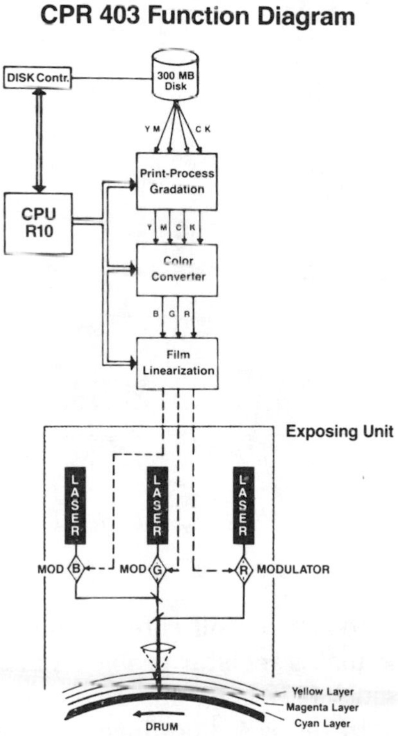

CPR 403 Function Diagram

Figure IX-5. Operation of CPR 403. (HCM)

The operation of the system is illustrated in Figure IX-5. All the color data for the picture is in the 300 MB magnetic disc in digital form for four separations to be printed in yellow, magenta, cyan and black. This data is processed in the Print Process Gradation Station to incorporate all the printing, material and process characteristics and is then converted to red, green and blue (r,g,b) signals compatible with the colors of the paper, inks and dye layers in the color photographic paper through the color converter that contains transformation tables on floppy discs in a terminal and keyboard.

The data is balanced in the Film Linearization Station so that it controls the exposure through the two lasers. In the Exposing Unit the light from the Argon ion laser is split into blue and green portions using interference filters. These beams pass in parallel paths through continuous tone modulators and are combined with the modulated light from the He/Ne laser to form a single beam that goes through a lens and exposes the three emulsion layers on the color photographic paper mounted on a rotating cylindrical drum. The efficiency of the two lasers for exposing a typical negative color photographic material is shown in Figure IX-6.

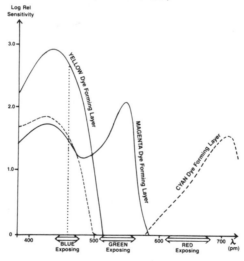

Figure IX-6. Efficiency of two lasers for 3-color exposures. (HCM)

The simultaneous exposure of all three emulsion layers on the color photographic paper eliminates register problems in the image. Resolution capability is 1200 lines/inch (472 l/cm) and recording times are 10 minutes for full 21 x 29 inch size at 300 lines/inch (120 1/cm) resolution — 4 minutes for an A4 size (8¼ x 11⅝ inch) image. Processing on-line is 11–

14 minutes depending on the print material used. The CPR 403 can be operated in daylight and step and repeat recording can be done along the circumferential direction of the scanner drum. A comparison of the spectral characteristics and color gamuts of a color proof, printing inks (European Eurostandard) and the phosphors on the Chromacom color video monitor are illustrated in Figure IX-7.

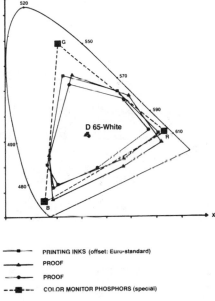

Figure IX-7. Comparison on a CIE Chromaticity diagram of the spectral characteristics of printing inks (Offset: Eurostandard), two-color proof materials and the color monitor phosphors. (HCM)

LogE/Dunn VersaColor Camera System for Digital Color Proofing

The LogE/Dunn VersaColor Camera System produces hard copy color proofs from digitized computer generated images using an exposure method based on color separation principles. It is a stand-alone camera system (Figure IX-8) with a wide range of electronic and photographic functions consisting of the following features:

- Intelligent terminal with RS-232C Interface for user programming of camera control to store *red, green* and *blue* exposure calibrations for various inks and papers and photographic and film types.

- 64-character liquid crystal display and 96-character alphanumeric keyboard for user interactivity and feedback.
- High performance electro-optical components including a special flat-face, high resolution monochrome (black and white) video monitor for reduced exposure times.
- Color corrected, on-axis lenses and microprocessor electronics.
- Switch selectable raster smoothing for image enhancement.

Systems Interconnect

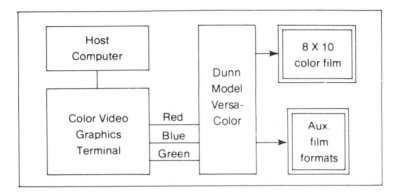

Figure IX-8. Block diagram of LogE/Dunn VersaColor Camera used by Crosfield in Magnaproof digital color proofing system. (LogE/Dunn)

In operation, the digital signals from the color monitor in the color pre-press system corresponding to the red, green, and blue video components, or separations, are fed to the camera where they are displayed sequentially on the high resolution black and white monitor. Each component is exposed through the corresponding red, green, and blue filter which is automatically placed in the on-axis optical path. Proper exposure times for each color are determined and set automatically by the intelligent terminal depending on the color paper or film used. After processing, the proof, or print, is a color composite of the superposed red, green and blue exposures corresponding to the image on the pre-press system monitor. Total exposures and processing is about 12 minutes using Kodak EKTAFLEX PCT negative paper.

Crosfield Magnaproof System

The LogE/Dunn VersaColor Camera has been modified for use in the Crosfield Magnaproof Hardcopy Preview System which is capable of producing fast, inexpensive preview prints of any image or page produced in the Crosfield Studio 860 Image Processing System. The output of the camera has been enlarged from its normal 8 x 10 inch (203 x 254 mm) size to 11 x 14 inch (279 x 356 mm) so that a full A4 page size subject can be proofed. In use full color correction and gradation control of the preview proof print is automatically carried out by the Studio 860 System using a simple menu command calibrated with the customer's requirements. The data is transferred to the Magnaproof (LogE/Dunn VersaColor Camera) and the exposure sequence is automatically handled by the camera's computer through red, green and blue filters. An important feature is that the proof can be made without affecting the work flow on the Studio 860. Also the Magnaproof can be used with the Crosfield ProEdit System to allow the designer maximum flexibility with layouts and color changes with hard proofs for customer review and approval.

Polaroid Digital Color Proof System

First announced at the 1983 Lasers in Graphics Conference, the Polaroid Digital Color Proof System in development consists of (1) a MacDonald Dettwiler Color FIRE 240 Film Recorder to convert the data from a digital imaging system like a scanner or pre-press system into a recordable image and (2) Polaroid Industrial Instant Color Film to accept and record the color proof image. It is an example of the synergy possible by combining the unique properties of products by two leaders in their respective fields to produce a product that satisfies a need in another field.

MacDonald Dettwiler is a small high technology company in British Columbia that has had extensive experience designing and manufacturing high performance remote sensing equipment for Landsat satellites data receiving and processing stations around the world. Its Color FIRE 240 Film Recorder, which is the quality standard of the remote sensing industry and received an IR-100 Award in 1982 for technical significance, has been redesigned as the image engine for the Polaroid Direct Digital Color Proof System. A schematic of the optical characteristics of the Color FIRE 240 Film Recorder is shown in Figure IX-9. Its design and operational features are:

- *Xenon arc-lamp light source* which is a cost efficient light source that allows recording of up to 5000 images before replacement (inexpensive).
- *Electro-Prism™ modulating system* which performs the dual functions of (1) selecting the desired color primaries and (2) modulating the intensities of the primaries as a function of the input digital data. The three primaries are inherently coaxial thus

providing perfect color registration.

- *On-axis optical system* which allows the use of inexpensive off-the-shelf optics to produce a scanning spot as small as 25 m in diameter.
- *Single-faceted spinner mirror* which avoids the problems of expensive multifaceted mirrors and their "spinner signature" microbanding (patterns) and line-start jitter.
- *Air-bearing spinner support* which assures "camera-quality" images free of patterns (microbanding). The support provides rigorous rotational repeatability and smoothness with unlimited life.
- *Precision micropositioner* which is powered by a stepper-motor and drives the spinning mirror assembly across the film with digital accuracy and a precision limited only by the lead screw (2 μm).
- *Curved film platen* which allows data recording during 180° of the spinner rotation and dramatically reduces light requirements and demands on system electronic bandwidth.
- *Intensity servo* which monitors light level to provide accurate feedback for intensity control.
- *Roll film supply* which eliminates need for darkroom loading by the operator.

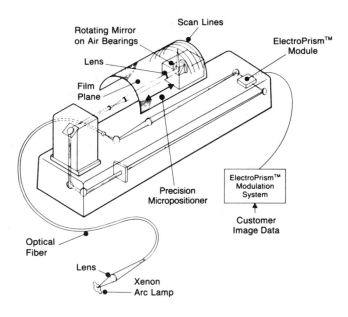

Figure IX-9. Optical schematic of MacDonald Dettwiler Color Fire 240 Film Recorder. (MDA)

The performance characteristics of the Color FIRE 240 system claimed for color proofing are:

- *Image quality:* no visible artifacts; "camera quality" images; good saturated colors.
- *High resolution:* up to 1000 pixels per inch (394/cm).
- *Geometric accuracy:* no visible color misregister; pixel placement accurate to 0.02%.
- *Hands-off operation:* full control via host computer; hundreds of images made with no operator interaction.

The system is being modified to accommodate a larger format size than 8 x 10 inch (203 x 254 mm), sheet output, and a built-in color transform to compensate for pigments in the inks, paper characteristics, scanner sensitivity, dyes in the film, dot gain, trapping variations, film and recorder variability.

The MacDonald Dettwiler Color FIRE 240 Film Recorder imposes some demands on the type of photographic material that will produce optimum results in a digital color proofing system. These are:

- *Light sensitivity* must be higher than for systems using lasers. The use of a conventional light source like the Xenon arc-lamp avoids the cost, complexity, light sensitivity and reliability problems associated with laser light sources.
- *Large color space:* The color space of the color paper must be able to come close to the full gamut of the printed color inks.
- *Resolution* must be high enough to accurately represent images printed at screen densities of 150 l (60 l/cm) for lithography and 175 l (69 l/cm) for gravure.
- *Processing* must be simple with a minimum number of chemicals, repeatable, low sensitivity to ambient conditions, low maintenance and low operator interaction.
- *Cost* must be less than conventional off-press proofing materials.

Polaroid Industrial Instant Color Paper more than satisfies these requirements. Regular instant photography with a completely integrated sandwich of film negative, positive receiver paper and developer chemicals is more expensive than conventional color proofing materials (excluding labor). After intensive research lower priced industrial films have been produced that do not sacrifice the unique convenience of instant photography. A system has been developed that uses a roll of light-sensitive material, a roll of positive print material and a tray of pods containing the development reagent. Unlike amateur products in which all these elements are integrated into a single unit or sandwich, in the industrial products they are all loaded separately into a special processor (Figure IX-10) which makes the combination lower in cost and very competitive with conventional off-press color proofing materials. In addition there are substantial savings in labor costs.

With the proper color transform developed by Polaroid and used in the MacDonald Dettwiler Color film Recorder color proofs have been made of a number of subjects on speical Polacolor materials that match ink-on-paper press proofs of the same subjects well enough to be acceptable for customer approval.

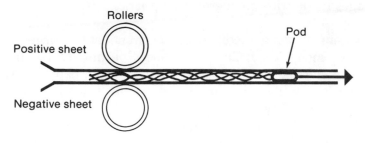

Figure IX-10. Diagram of Polaroid processing system. Viscous processing agent is squeezed out of **Pod** when rollers break it and agent is spread evenly by rollers in layers between positive and negative. (Polaroid)

KC-Digital Color Proof System

The KC-Digital Pre-Press System is in development by Coulter Systems Corporation. It consists of input scanners which send the colorimetric data for the original in digital form; data processing terminals which perform the usual functions of color correction, image enhancement, magnification, sizing, cropping, rotation and positioning; and an output laser printer. The laser printer can be used independently of the pre-press system to process digital data from scanners and other page makeup systems to produce film color separations that are used to make proofs on the KC-Color Proofer (Chapter VII).

Chapter X

How To Compare Color Proofs And Press Prints

It was Lord William Thompson Kelvin, noted English physicist and mathematician, after whom the absolute temperature and color temperature units are named, who was the first to propose that, "If you can't measure something, you can't control it." One of the major difficulties encountered in comparing off-press color proofs with press prints is that regardless of how many objective measurements are made on the proof and the print the final decision usually rests on a subjective visual examination. The eye is a very accurate and precise measuring instrument when it is used to compare two similar objects under the same conditions; but there are no common physical or mathematical units in which to accurately express differences in visual appearance.

The language of color differences is very colloquial and filled with "buzz words." At a Research and Engineering Council of the Graphic Arts Roundtable Discussion of Color Prepress Operations in October 1976 a total of 126 buzz words used in the description of color deviations were generated during the one-day session. These are listed in Table X-I. There are surely many more in use.

In all fairness, most of these are concerned with problems of matching a proof with the original. Here some compromises must be made because most originals are transparencies and the tone or density ranges of these (2.6 – 3.0) are far in excess of what can be printed on a press (1.5 – 2.0) corresponding to brightness ranges of 400:1 – 1000:1 vs. 30:1 – 100:1. The answer to this problem has been cleverly described by Jean Chevalier, a French graphic arts consultant, as quoted by Gordon O.F. Johnson (LogE) in a paper he presented on Color Proofing at the Lasers in Graphics Conference in September 1982, "Color separation is like the big man in a small coffin. Someone in the family must decide where to cut to make him fit." The proof must duplicate what the press can print as well

TABLE X-I

BUZZ WORDS*

Add Contrast
Add Density
Add Snap
Air Out
Balance the Neutrals
Beef up Color
Blown-Out
Blue Out
Burn Down
Burner
Chalky
Chocked Up
Choppy Midtones
Clean Up
Color Too Skinny
Color O.K. but More Density
Colors All Jammed Up
Color O.K. but Flat
Color O.K. but Thin
Color O.K. but Too Heavy
Colors Too Strong
Commercially Acceptable Color
Contrasty
Cooler
Crisp Color
Delete a Little Red
Dirty and Flat
Do a Little Better Here
Does Not Have Shine
  of Transparency
Dull Down
Eliminate the Hot Spots
Exaggerate the Condition
Fleshier Face Tones
Flesh Needs Weight & Color
Flick Less
Give It a Kiss Wash
Give Me a Pretty Picture
Give Me More Shape
Give Me Pleasing Color
Give It a Strong Wash
Give the Reds a Bump
Grainy

Greek Out
Harsh
Hold Highlight
Improve the Fleshtones
Increase contrast
  in Middletones
Increase Detail
Increase-Highlight-
  Separation
Increase Saturation
Increase Sharpness
It's Got To Be Livelier
It's Got To Jump
I Want the Reds to
  Jump Off the Page
Lacks Snap
Livelier
Make it Brighter
Make Colors Cleaner
Make Colors Warmer
Make Colors Colder
Make it Glossier
Make it Sing
Make it Sky Blue
Make it Pop
Maintain Gray Balance
Match Attached
Match Copy
Match the Crossover
Moire!!!
More Guts or Gutsier
More Metallic
More Neutral
More Punch
More Sock
More Texture
Muddy
Mushy
Needs Dimension
Needs More Depth
Needs Luminosity
Needs Warmth
N.G.

N.G. Reseparate
N.G. Try Again
Neutral Brown
O.K.!!!
O.K.???
O.K. With Correction
Over-Etched-See 1st Proof
Open Shadows
Open Up Shadows
Out of Color Balance
Plugged
Pushy
Raw
Redder Reds
Refer to First Proof
Reduce Blue 2½%
Reduce One More Step
Reduce Overall
Reduce 2%
Ruddy
Seems Cloudy
Seems Fuzzy
+ Shape
Soften Back
Strengthen
Subdue
Tad Less
Tone down
Too Dull
Too Flat
Too Hot or Cold
Too Jumpy
Too Much Internal Contrast
Too Muddy
Too Piny
Too Weak
UGH!
Whew
Whisper More
Whiter Whites but Hold Detail
Wrong Shade of Red
Yellow O.K. but See the Proofs
You Went Too Far

*Generated at the Research & Engineering Council Roundtable Discussion, Chicago, October, 1976.

as satisfy the customer's expectation of what he thinks the job should look like. Once agreement has been reached on this score, the only way to be sure the press can print what is in the proof is by setting standards and making objective measurements and comparisons of the proof and the print.

The secret of producing proofs that match press prints, or vice versa, is to know what to measure in the proof and print; how the measurements relate; and how they can be used to control the proof and the print. No attempt at making off-press color proofs should be made until the proofing process and the printing process that produces the prints the proofs are expected to match are both under control. For both processes to be under control they must be predictable, which means they must produce proofs and prints that are consistent and repeatable. It must be known exactly what tone values, 10%, 20%, 40%, 60%, 80% or any other dot size on the film or plate will print on the press. When this is known the reproduction curves for both processes can be drawn and these are used to determine what dot values are needed in the proof for it to match the press print or vice versa.

Problems will be encountered whenever the tone reproduction curve changes. There are myriads of factors and combinations of them that can affect tone reproduction on the press as a review of Chapter III and Appendix C will quickly reveal. How can these factors be measured and controlled so color proof and color print can be correlated? The answer on "what to do" is simple — special printing targets, scales and color bars are used on films and the plates; they are measured on the proofs and the printed sheets with a densitometer and magnifier; the results are studied and interpreted. "How to do it" is what's difficult and tedious. The most critical step in the production process is printing so this must be stabilized and controlled before off-press proofing can be effective.

This chapter is divided into three parts. The first part is devoted to descriptions and discussions of ways and means to control printing on the press, so the characteristics of the print can be determined and stabilized. The second part describes ways and means to control color proofs. Some of the same means such as color targets are used for both, so it may appear that some of the information is redundant, but the same targets are used and interpreted differently. The third part is what this book is all about — how to compare color proofs with color prints. This part may appear to have some redundancies, but these are necessary in order to emphasize the significance of the targets, what they show, and how to analyze them.

HOW TO MEASURE AND CONTROL THE PRESS PRINT

Printing is a mechanical process that involves inertia, stresses, strains, phase equilibria, distortions, harmonics and a number of other complicated physical and some chemical phenomena. Running a press is like driving a car. The biggest strain on the engine, drive-train, fuel consumption and the driver is getting the car started, shifting the gears and adjusting the accelerator so the engine runs at a reasonably constant speed, with minimum fuel consumption and strain on the driver and the drive-train. This is when everything is in phase equilibrium and the car is running at maximum efficiency and minimum wear and tear. But contaminated oil in the engine, improperly or insufficiently lubricated bearings and joints, improperly inflated tires, overheating and alternate braking and accelerating all have deleterious effects on the efficiency and economy of operation. The car runs best when everything is in equilibrium. So does the printing press.

No attempt at standardizing printing operations should be made unless everything is in phase, or in equilibrium — when the press is running at reasonably constant speed, the ink and water (lithography) feeds are constant, and ink densities are consistent from sheet to sheet. It can take up to 15 minutes for a new job to settle down and reach equilibrium on a press which is equivalent to about 1000 sheets on a sheet-fed press and up to 2500 signatures on a web press. This is called the "makeready" — the period during which the pressman is trying to get everything in phase. A number of attempts have been made to shorten this period and reduce the waste of spoiled paper and signatures. Some success has been achieved with the press pre-makeready systems that most press manufacturers have introduced for new presses and are available as conversions and accessories for presses in use.

Besides the pre-makeready systems, presses can be equipped with means for color measurement and control to assure consistent results during the run. There are off-press color measurement and control systems with high-speed color measurement (densitometers) and recording (CRT or printers) and operator intervention for setting of press controls; one has remote control of inking; and several incorporate on-press densitometers.

Pre-Makeready Systems

Pre-makeready systems for presses were developed in the middle 1970's by MGD Graphic Systems Division of Rockwell International and by Harris Corporation. These were based on scanning across a flat of positive or negative films from which a press plate was to be made; recording the average light transmission according to ink fountain key zones; and using the information to pre-set the ink fountain keys on the press for each color prior to the start of printing. The systems were not very popular, primarily because of unreliability due to the large number of variables that could affect the reproduction of tone values in the platemaking operation. In other words, the measurements made on the films were not predictable representations of the tone values on the plate and consequently, those printed on the press.

At DRUPA '82 a number of press-makeready systems were introduced that use plate scanners, in place of film scanners, to measure the ink profiles of the plates, and microprocessors for recording the data which is then used to preset and control the ink fountains during printing. These new systems have corrected the limitations of the earlier film scanners and all claim savings in makeready waste of up to 50%. Some of these systems have special ink fountain controls in place of the conventional ink keys. The interest in these systems is demonstrated by the seven technical papers describing different plate scanning systems at the 1983 Annual Conference of the Technical Association of the Graphic Arts (TAGA).

Typical systems are by Heidelberg known at the CPC-3 Plate Image Reader (Figure X-1) which is a plate scanner that can be used in the plateroom to produce tape cassettes of the density profiles of the plates that are used on the CPC1-02 at the press to preset the ink fountains and

Figure X-1. Heidelberg CPC-3 Plate Scanner. (H-E)

control them during printing. Roland (MAN-Roland) has a plate scanner as part of its RCI and CCI Color Control Systems on the press. These systems are proprietary and can be used only on the manufacturer's presses.

Dainippon Printing Company, the largest printing company in Japan, has introduced a plate scanner unit for any press called DEMIA (*Device for Measuring Image Area*) which consists of a scanner and an input and output device for the ink preset controller and an ink fountain mechanism. The information from the DEMIA is transferred to the input and output device which uses a magnetic card to automatically preset the ink supply. The Perretta Control System I-77 uses a special EEPROM computer chip that can be used on any press to preset a special patented leak-proof segmented ink fountain blade. Besides the special ink fountain blade the system consists of a console with microprocessor to which each fountain blade is linked and connection for the EEPROM chip which contains the digital data from the plate scans. The data is transferred to the computer when the chip is plugged into the keyboard socket of the press console providing the computer with the information it needs to set the ink fountain segments.

All the systems have provisions for manual override by the pressman to fine-tune the ink settings. These units not only speed up makereadies and reduce waste, they improve the consistency and reproducibility of the printing by controlling the inking function. In addition they provide a permanent record of the ink settings for the job in case a new makeready is needed or the job is rerun.

Color Measurement and Control Systems

Off-Line Systems

More important for consistency of the printed product than the ink presetting and pre-makeready systems are the numerous systems for color measurement and control on the press during printing. All of them depend on the use of special color targets, scales and bars across the press sheet and high speed densitometers for making the readings so that if corrections are needed, they can be made before too many sheets are wasted. Roland presses can be equipped with CCI and RCI Color Control systems (Figure X-2, page C-6). Both can be programmed so they can measure color strips or bars in x,y, positions allowing the strips to be placed and measured in waste or trim areas thereby eliminating waste when larger sheets must be used to make room for color bars placed at the gripper or back edge of the sheet. This can help conserve expensive board in packaging.

Heidelberg has a whole family of CPC color measurement and control systems. CPC1 is a basic control system (Figure X-3 page C-6); CPC1-01 is used for inking and register; CPC1-02, as already mentioned, is used for ink presetting on the press; CPC1-03 is an automatic follow-up system for fast response ink correction when combined with the CPC-2 which is a color quality control unit for several presses and different control strips; CPC-3 as already mentioned in the previous section is a plate image reader that can be set up in the plateroom away from the presses and produces tape cassettes for ink presetting using the CPC1-02. Both the Roland and Heidelberg systems are off-line, i.e., sheets or signatures must be taken from the delivery of the press and measured on a table or console. Also the units are dedicated for use only with the manufacturer's presses.

There are other off-line systems that can be used with any presses. The Tobias SCR Scanning Densitometer (Figure X-4) scans a sheet 40 inches (1016 mm) wide, off-press, and records density readings for as many as 54 predetermined locations on a sheet in less than 8 seconds using a computer directed program. The readings are displayed on one or more video terminals showing for each color scanned, the ink fountain position on the press, ink color, actual density, reference density, and a bar chart comparing the results with two tolerance levels set in the instrument. Other functions such as dot size, dot gain, trapping, print contrast, hue shift, grayness, etc., can be calculated. Positions to be measured are indicated by a magic marker on a pre-scan and are retained in computer memory. Reference densities can be set by using density values of colors and overprints from a color proof or by scanning the OK sheet.

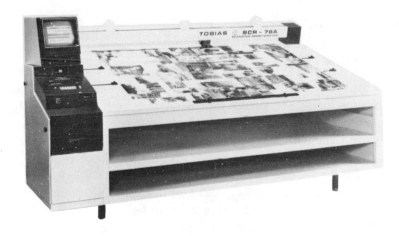

Figure X-4. Tobias SCR Scanning Densitometer. (Tobias)

At DRUPA '82 Gretag showed an even faster unit — the Scanning Densitometer D732 (Figure X-5). This is claimed to be capable of making 200 color measurements, 3840 pieces of data, in 6 colors across a 40 inch (1016 mm) sheet in 6 seconds! It measures solids, screened areas and overprints, and records density, density difference, dot percentage, dot gain, relative print contrast, trapping, grayness, hue and statistical production data. Like the Tobias unit it has a measuring table with densitometer and video display.

Figure X-5. Gretag High Speed Scanning Densitometer D-732. (H-E)

On-line Systems

As microprocessors increase the speed of measuring and recording, on-line systems using on-press densitometers are being developed in increasing numbers. Macbeth has had an on-press densitometer system for some time which measures color densities of all four colors on both sides of a printed web on a web press and displays the readings on two CRT's for the pressman's judgment and control (Figure X-6). The densitometer measures not only solid and halftone ink densities but also dot size, dot gain, trapping and other color data.

At DRUPA '82 three on-press densitometers were introduced; one by Color Metal on its Chromaprint 4074 sheet-fed color proof press, which press is no longer manufactured; the second Densidyne, by AEG Telefunken with 30 measuring heads across a 40 inch (1015 mm) sheet

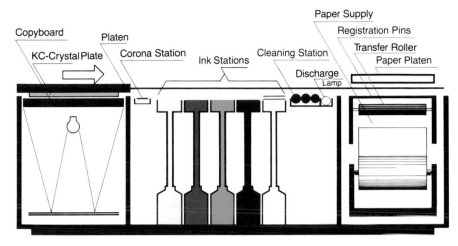

Figure VII-1. Schematic of the KC-Analog Color Proofer, ACP III.

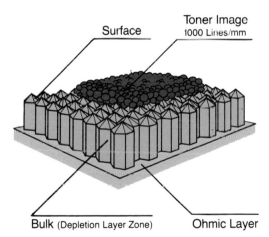

Figure VII-3. Structure of KC-Crystalplate — the imaging component of the KC-Color Proofer shown partially colored with toner ink after exposure and inking.

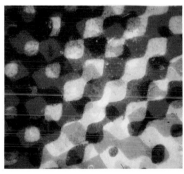

Figure VII-8. Enlargement of multiple deposits of color toner inks on KC-Proof showing transparency of pigments to produce subtractive color mixtures.

Figure X-2. Roland CCI and RCI
Color Control Systems.
(Rockwell)

Figure X-3. Heidelberg CPC
Print Quality control console.
(H-E)

C6 PRINCIPLES OF COLOR PROOFING

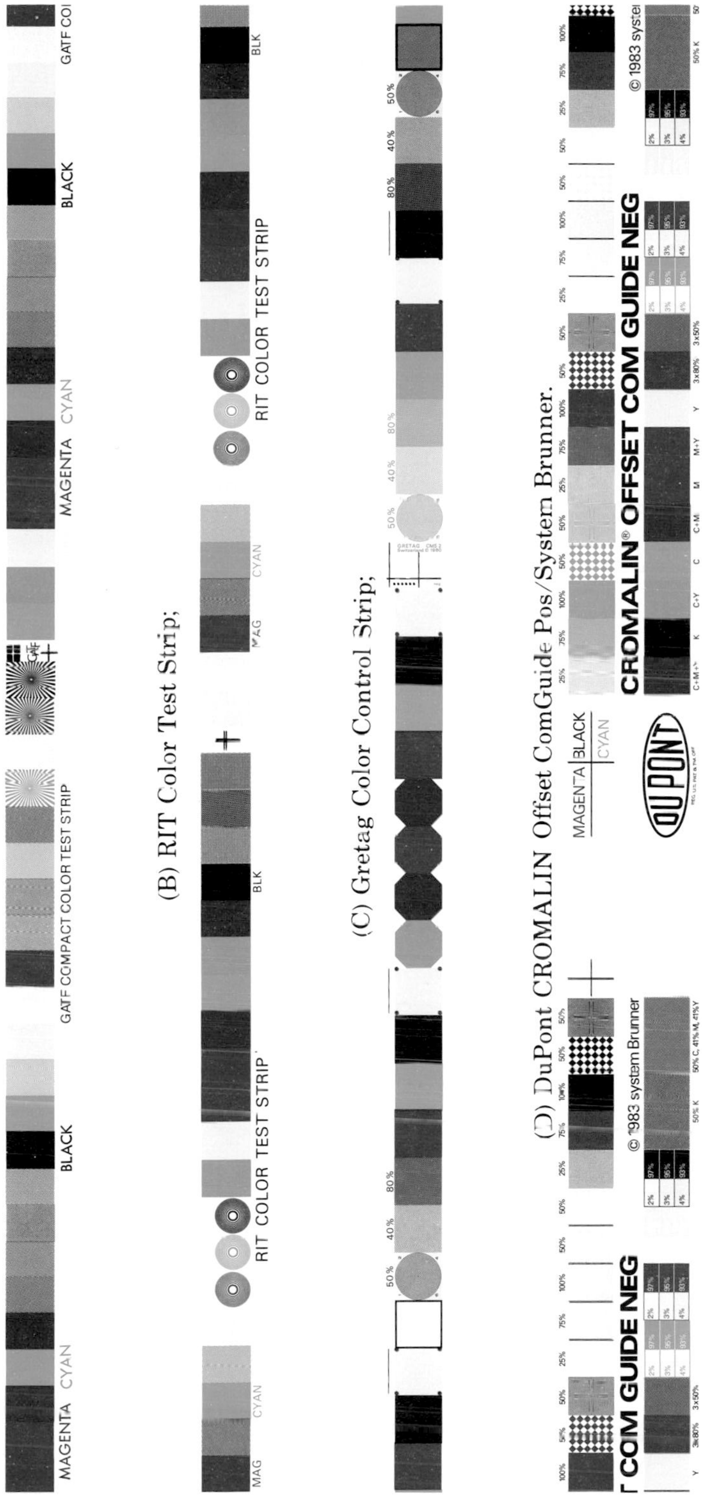

(A) GATF Compact Color Strip;

(B) RIT Color Test Strip;

(C) Gretag Color Control Strip;

(D) DuPont CROMALIN Offset ComGuide Pos/System Brunner.

Figure X-9. Four commonly used press control strips:
(GATF, RIT, H-E, DuPont)

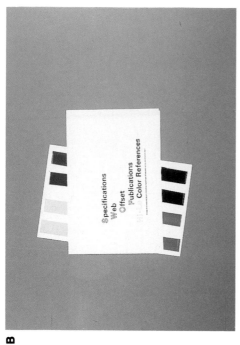

Figure X-15. (A) SWOP Standard Color References; (B) SWOP High-Low Color References. (IPA)

Figure X-16. Partial Color Proofing bar for SWOP Specifications. (GATF)

claimed to be capable of recording the 30 measurements at press speeds up to 3000 feet (915 meters) per minute; and the third, the IGT Press Densitometer by IGT, the former Graphic Arts Research Institute of Holland. A multi-channel on-press densitometer was described in a paper by the Technical Research Center of Finland at the 1982 Annual TAGA Conference.

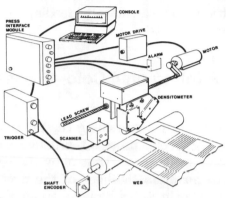

Figure X-6. Macbeth On-Press Densitometer. (TAGA 1983)

The IGT On-Line Press Densitometer illustrated in Figure X-7 not only measures densities on a control strip at press speed but it averages them over a number of sheets, shows trends in variation, in what direction and at what speed so the pressman can determine when and

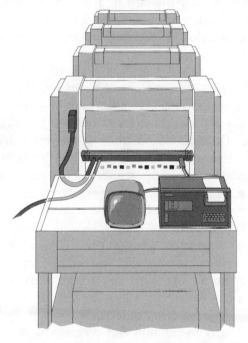

Figure X-7. IGT On-line Press Densitometer. (Reprotest)

what corrections are needed. The measurements are made at a number of points on the control strip as the sheet is transported from the last printing unit to the delivery. On a 28 inch (710 mm) sheet, 20 measuring heads are used, five for each color of which four are for solids and one for halftone areas. In order to measure correctly, the distance between measuring head and paper must be constant and the heads must be clean. Both conditions are satisfied by feeding filtered compressed air through the measuring heads.

Printing on 4-Color Presses

While a densitometer is used to measure solid ink densities during makeready on the press when matching the press print to the proof for an *OK* and in printing 4-color process reproductions on single- and two-color presses, the most widely used control by the pressman on 4-, 5-, and 6-color presses is to maintain the hues of the overprint colors visually. The visual appearance of pictures remains about the same, even though their strengths and saturation change. It appears that both printers and customers are in general agreement as to what the overprint colors red, green, and blue should look like. This has been verified in a number of recent studies described by Miles Southworth in the Quality Control Scanner, Volume 3, Numbers 4 and 7. This concept was proposed by Frank Preucil at GATF many years ago and is described later in this chapter. It is now substantiated by extensive testing done for the Graphic Communications Association (GCA) and reported at SPECTRUM '82 in September 1982.

The tests were part of a GCA Study of 16 web offset publication presses, described in the Quality Control Scanner, Volume 3, Number 4. Its purpose was to determine the influence of paper, ink, press and printing order on color reproduction for magazine printing. GCA supplied each printer with a standard set of films for a job being printed in the plant. The printers were asked to print the test so that the advertising on the test form matched the appearance of the subject on the printed job. No proofs were supplied and the crews were instructed to operate the presses normally or as they would on a regular job. Results of the 16 tests are shown in Table X-II.

Despite the wide variation among the 16 printers in densities of solids, dot gain, hue error and trapping, the *red, green* and *blue* overprints had visually similar hues, although the colors varied in strength and saturation. A plot of the overprint colors for the 16 test runs on a GATF Color Hexagon (see Appendix A), illustrated in Figure X-8, shows that the overprints were similar in hue but varied in strength. The GCA SPECTRUM 1983 tests showed similar results.

TABLE X-II

GCA SPECTRUM TEST RUN ON 16 PRESSES — 1982

	Cyan	Magenta	Yellow	Black
Solids				
Average	1.11	1.18	.94	1.56
High-Low	1.44-.86	1.48-.93	.96-.69	1.95-1.30
Range	.58	.55	.29	.63
Dot Gain %				
Average	19	20	23	28
High-Low	34-12	30-12	42-13	46-18
Range	22	18	29	28
Hue Error %				
Average	26	49	5	
High-Low	46-23	63-43	8-3	
Range	23	20	5	
Trapping %	Red	Green	Blue	
Average	63	84	71	
High-Low	76-45	102-65	79-67	
Range	31	37	.12	

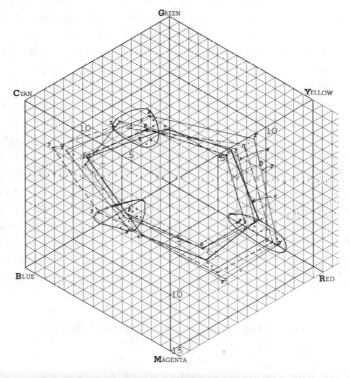

Figure X-8. Plot on GATF Color Hexagon of overprint colors
in 16 press test runs for 1982 GCA Spectrum Conference
—Quality Control Scanner, Vol. 3, No. 4. (GAP)

Pressmen intentionally vary color ink densities to compensate for printing factors like dot gain, trapping, and ink rheology which changes the hues of overprinting colors because ink feed is the easiest adjustment to make on the press while it is running. Pressmen know that as soon as a web offset press starts printing, ink tack, viscosity, water pick-up, trapping, and dot size start changing; but those are variables that cannot easily be changed while the press is running so he resorts to compensating for them by changing ink densities.

Fortunately for printer and customer the system works but it is critical and fraught with dangers. The major factors causing color changes on the press are dot gain and trapping. Both are mainly affected by changes in ink rheology or tack during running on the press. There is no easy way to control ink tack while the press is running so pressmen resort to changing ink feed. Running more ink makes a color stronger but it can compound the problem of color change since it can cause more dot gain which affects the hues of tint mixtures and can change trapping which affects the hues of solid overprints. The way presses are being run, constant attention must be given to the control of overprint colors or the printing can very quickly get out of hand.

It is very easy to make a wrong decision on a hue change visually. The hue of a red overprint can change to an orange-red if there is too much yellow or not enough magenta ink. If magenta is increased when the hue change is due to too much yellow it could start a chain reaction that could cause serious variations in dot gain, trapping, ink-water balance and eventually considerable waste and downtime.

There are new densitometers that measure all these components of a. process color and display them simultaneously. In the case of the red overprint hue change, the densitometer could be used to determine the color composition of the red overprint on the OK sheet and compare it with the printed sheet. The readings tell the pressman which color(s) change and by how much. This type of measurement would reinforce visual control and help to stabilize printing and make the printed results more consistent. What would help the pressman are (1) color control strips and targets that tell him when the hues of overprint colors are changing and what is causing the changes and (2) means for quickly analyzing the information and making the necessary corrections.

Analysis of Color Control Strips

There are four commonly used systems of color strips or bars used for color control in printing: GATF system represented by the Compact Color Strip; RIT Color Test Strip; Gretag Color Control Strip; and the

Brunner System represented by CROMALIN Offset ComGuide/System Brunner. These are illustrated in Figure X-9, page C-7. Each has distinguishing targets that identify specific printing defects. As stated in Chapter III printing control strips must be as small as possible with targets that are more sensitive to variations and defects in printing than the line and halftone images being printed so they serve to warn the pressman before the variations or defects have a noticeable effect on the printing. To accomplish this objective the pressman must know what the targets measure, or show, and how to interpret them quickly so they are a help to him rather than a hindrance. All the strips have solids and one or more tints of each color; overprints of two-color and three-color solids and three-color tints; and register marks in each color. Each strip has additional distinguishing targets which are described in the following sections.

GATF Compact Color Test Strip

This strip has 27 separate steps consisting of:

- 3 cyan, 2 magenta, 2 yellow and 2 black solid blocks.
- 1-50% tint block of each of the 4 colors.
- 3 solid overprints, red (M + Y), green (C + Y) and blue (C + M).
- 3-50% tint overprints — (M + Y), (C + Y) and (C + M).
- 3 3-color tint blocks.
- 1 star target in each of the four colors.
- Register marks.

The critical targets in this strip and what they are designed to show are:

- *Star targets* show dot gain, slur and doubling. The effects of these defects on the appearance of the targets are shown in Figure III-27, page 77.
- *2- and 3-color tint overprints* are very sensitive to dot gain which causes very noticeable changes in the hues of the overprints.
- *Solid overprints* are sensitive to trapping variations which change the hues of overprint colors.

RIT Color Test Strip

This color strip consists of 22 separate steps:

- 2 solid blocks of each of the 3 primary colors and 1 black solid.
- 1-60% tint of each of the 4 colors.
- 1 solid overprint each of red (M + Y) and blue (C + M); 2 of green (C + Y); and 1 3-color solid overprint.
- 2 3-color tint overprints.
- 4 Bull's-eye targets — one in each color.

The critical targets in the strip and what they are designed to show are:

- *Bull's eye targets* are for fast visual checking of dot gain, slur and doubling. The effects of these defects on the appearance of the bull's eye targets is shown in Figure X-10.
- Like the GATF Strip the solid and tint overprints are sensitive to trapping and dot gain changes respectively.

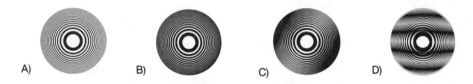

A)   B)   C)   D)

Figure X-10. Enlarged view of RIT Bull's Eye targets showing (A) no gain; (B) dot gain; (C) slur; (D) doubling. (RIT)

Gretag Color Control Strip OMS-1

This color strip consists of 32 separate steps:

- 3 solid blocks of each of the 4 colors.
- 1-70% tint of each of the 4 colors.
- 1 2-color solid overprint each of red (M + Y), green (C + Y) and blue (C + M).
- 1 4-step continuous tone gray scale of each color.
- 1-40% tint 3-color overprint: 1-70% tint 3-color overprint and 1-80% tint 3-color overprint.
- 4 circular elements, one in each color, with 50% coverage concentric rings with 1%, 2%, 4%, and 6% tints in the corners of the blocks.
- 1 blank block for the addition of a fifth color or for zeroing a densitometer.

The critical targets in this strip and what they are designed to show are:

- *Circular elements* show slur and doubling (Figure X-11) which are forms of unsymmetrical dot gain. Note the directional pattern for slur and the random pattern for doubling which also shows in the dots and numbers in the corners.
- *Continuous tone gray scales* with densities of 0.6, 0.9, 1.2 and 1.5 in the four steps are like the sensitivity guide described in Chapter III and are used to check plate exposures which can affect dot gain.
- *Overprint tints,* like the GATF and RIT strips, are sensitive targets for indicating dot gain in individual colors which changes the hue of the overprint tint.

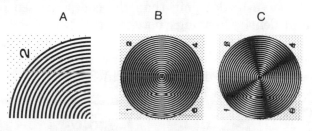

Figure X-11. Enlarged view of Gretag circular elements showing (A) no gain; (B) slur; (C) doubling. (II-E)

Brunner Control System

System Brunner offers a family of positive and negative control strips and test forms for print control and analysis. A compact version of the positive strip 1 x 5 inches (25 x 127 mm) was adapted for Eurostandard CROMALIN. In North America negative and positive versions of the compact strip are available under the name CROMALIN Offset Com (Communications) Guide/System Brunner. The long print control strips are now also available in both negative and positive and in special formats required for the Heidelberg, Roland and Tobias scanning densitometers.

The Brunner Control System shown was adapted specifically for CROMALIN proofing but is very useful for measuring and analyzing press operation. It is wider but can be made longer than the other strips and consists of 36 separate steps:

- 2 solid blocks of patches of each of the 3 primary colors and 1 black
- 1-25% and 1-75% tint of each of the four colors plus a 50% tint of black
- 3 2-color solid overprints, red (M + Y), green (C + Y) and blue (C + M); 1 3-color solid and 1 4-color solid overprint
- 1 3-color 80% tint overprint; 1 3-color 50% overprint; one tint

overprint with 50% C, 41% M and 51%Y
- 4 coarse and fine screen patches
- 4 highlight dot and microline patches

The critical steps in this strip and what they are designed to show are:

- *Coarse and Fine Screen patches* enlarged in Figure X-12, are sensitive measures of dot gain. The principle is similar to the GATF Dot Gain Scale (Chapter III). The coarse and fine screen patterns both occupy 50% of the area but the fine screen (60 l/cm – 150 l/in.) is more sensitive to dot gain than the coarse screen pattern. The difference in density readings between the two areas is a relative measure of the dot gain that can be made with most densitometers with an aperture of at least 3.5 mm. This method of monitoring dot gain tends to eliminate densitometer differences.

Figure X-12. Enlarged view of Brunner Coarse and Fine Screen Patches. (DuPont)

- *Highlight Dot and Microline* patches shown enlarged in Figure X-13, represent the effect of exposure on dot size on the plate. The color strip for negative plates and proof has different highlight dot and microline particles.

0,5%	1%	6µ		0,5%	1%	6µ		0,5%	1%	6µ		
		8µ				8µ				8µ		
2%	3%	11		2%	3%	11		2%	3%	11		
		13				13				13		
4%	5%	16		4%	5%	16		4%	5%	16		

Original   Correct   Too Sharp   Too Full

Figure X-13. Enlarged view of Brunner Highlight Dot and Microline patches. (DuPont)

- *25% and 75% Screen* patches are used to draw simple characteristic curves for tone reproduction and dot gain. Typical curves are shown in Figure X-14.
- *Gray Balance* patch is used for visual examination of printing. The combination of 50% cyan, 41% magenta and 41% yellow should produce a neutral gray in printing with European offset scale inks.

Any change in dot gain will change the hue of the overprint which can be readily detected visually.

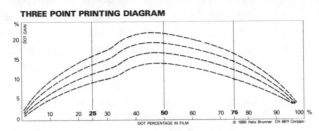

THREE POINT PRINTING DIAGRAM

Figure X-14. Typical tone reproduction curves drawn from the Brunner 25% and 75% patches. (DuPont)

Summary

While color control in printing is accomplished by visual examination of the hues of overprinted colors, there are numerous targets available to assist the pressman in this judgment. The GCA studies indicated that even with wide tolerances in densities of individual inks acceptable quality could be produced as long as the hues of the overprints, especially overprint tints, were consistent. The hues of overprint tints are affected much more by dot gain than by solid ink densities. It is, therefore, much more important in printing to control dot gain than solid ink densities which can change by as much as ± 0.10 in density without affecting the acceptability of the prints as long as the overprints match or look the same. The concept of using overprint colors to evaluate color reproduction fidelity and quality is being programmed into closed-loop computer controlled systems on newer presses to satisfy customers at lower cost with less waste and higher productivity.

This discussion of printing has concentrated on the lithographic process. As explained in Chapter III once makeready is complete letterpress is not plagued by all the variables of the lithographic process and produces reasonably consistent results as long as the ink and paper remain the same. The rheology of the ink, especially, is important as it affects trapping and the overprint colors. Similarly once a gravure run is started the main variables affecting the consistency of the output are ink viscosity and doctor blade wear. There are automatic controls for ink viscosity; and doctor blade wear can be monitored without much effort. These processes, therefore, are more amenable to control than lithography and their products are more consistent and predictable so comparisons between press prints by letterpress and gravure and proofs should be easier to make than for press prints by lithography.

A color printing process is under control when it produces consistent color reproductions with similar appearance, which, in lithographic printing occurs when the overprint colors look the same from sheet to sheet. The same definition applies to letterpress which can have serious problems with trapping that can affect overprints of solid and dark colors. Gravure is not affected appreciably by trapping but it is dependent on dot spread or gain for extending its tone scale which can affect overprints of tints and lighter colors. Flexography is not affected much by trapping but it has dot gain effects and other problems that keep it from serious competition with the other processes in high quality printing markets. Lithography is the most difficult process to control because there are many more variables in the printing process and more factors affect the hues of overprint solids and tints.

HOW TO CONTROL COLOR PROOFS

Matching a color proof to a press print, or vice versa, is a matter of having the same amount of control of overprint colors in the color proofing system as in the printing process. The overprints become the benchmarks for control and the densities of the printed solids are secondary. In lithography the overriding printing characteristic that affects the hues of overprinting colors, particularly tints, is dot gain, so color proofing systems for lithography must have the ability to duplicate press dot gain and control all the factors that affect it. In letterpress the important printing property affecting overprint colors is ink trapping, so . proofing systems for letterpress must be able to duplicate ink trapping and its control. In gravure, including the new halftone gravure conversion processes, the main characteristic that affects the colors of the overprints is spread of the ink during printing to extend the tone scale of the printed reproduction, so color proofing systems for gravure must be able to simulate the optical result of the ink spread and predict its effect on the gravure printed image.

The distinguishing characteristic appearance defects of the printing processes described and illustrated in Chapter III: *embossing* and *mottle* in letterpress, *highlight skips* and *mottle* in gravure, and *mealy solids* in lithography do not need to be reproduced in proofs as they are inconsistent and usually unpredictable. They are, however, image defects that affect the visual appearance of the reproductions and can interfere with the comparisons between proof and prints; so the printer and proofer should be able to recognize them and know how to control them or deal with them in comparisons of proof and print.

Another factor that needs to be considered in the comparison of proof and prints is that for many uses, particularly customer and advertising agency approval, the proof is not required to simulate the exact structure of the printed image; it does not have to duplicate the exact size and shapes of the dots, or have dots at all; but it *must* reproduce the *optical effects* and *appearances* of the printed image. This has been a widely debated issue that is being fueled by new digital color proofing systems most of which use continuous tone color photographic images as output. The concept is gaining acceptance in gravure with the introduction of the special proofing processes for gravure described in Chapter IX. How it will be received by lithography is debatable.

At the 1983 Lasers in Graphics Conference three advertising agency executives, Klaus Schmidt, Young and Rubicam (New York), Donald Greifenkamp, J. Walter Thompson (Chicago) and William Joyce, Ogilvy-Mather (Toronto) agreed that the primary mission of the hard proof is to simulate the optical appearance of the press print and it does not need to have the exact structure of the press print to accomplish this goal.

Production supervisors and craftsmen in lithography and letterpress, particularly, have been so accustomed to examining images with magnifiers, up to 20X, that it will be difficult for them to evaluate and, consequently, accept proofs that do not have the same structure as the press prints. For them, press proofs will continue to be made and used. To take advantage of the economics of time and costs inherent in off-press color proofs, compromises must be made. Eventually with sufficient use and experience results will become more dependable and predictable and optically correct proofs will become generally accepted.

As mentioned in Chapter III the same dot sizes in letterpress and lithography produce different visual or optical effects. The letterpress image is lighter in tone value, crisper in sharpness, and slightly mottled. The lithographic image is darker in tone but smoother in appearance. These are optical effects that must be compensated for when converting letterpress halftones to lithography, and vice versa. Attempts at duplicating the image structure of the three different gravure cylinder making processes would be impossible and unnecessary or useless in a proofing system unless it could also reproduce the effect of variable amounts of ink in the conventional and variable area/variable depth gravure processes, and the lateral spread of the very soft inks in all three gravure processes.

What are needed to correct these anomalies are comprehensive image analyses of each printing process and proofing systems that can consistently match the optical effects of the integral image traits or innate characteristics of the printing processes. Then the proofs produced will look like the reproductions and be acceptable as reliable predictions of what the press prints will look like when the image carriers representing the different printing processes are printed on the presses.

Color Proofing Standards

To produce valid image analyses of the printing processes, color standards are needed for both the printing and proofing processes. Publication printing is the first segment of the printing and publishing industries which has tackled the issue of industry-wide standard color specifications for proofing colors and papers that match those used in the printing processes. Such specifications have been developed and adopted for all three major printing processes, letterpress, lithography and gravure. While the specifications have not solved all the problems of matching proofs to prints, they have been very helpful in improving communications between publishers, advertising agencies, color separators and printers.

In 1967 when letterpress was still the dominant printing process for publication printing, the Magazine Publishers Association (MPA) and the American Association of Advertising Agencies (AAAA) jointly published "Standard Specifications for Letterpress" which with minor revisions are still observed and used. The standard specifications, championed by F.E. (Al) Church, then with *Readers Digest*, were designed for use by photoengravers who produced plates for the many printers of magazines to assure that all the plates were balanced for, and proofs were printed with, the same ink colors and papers so plates from different engravers could be combined on the same runs with the same ink and paper and get acceptable results. The specifications have worked very well for letterpress publication printing.

In the early 1970's when lithography (web offset) was gaining prominence in publication printing, attempts were made to use the letterpress standards for web offset but they were unsuccessful. In 1973 a joint committee of the AAAA and American Business Press (ABP) was formed to study the situation. The study had imputs from other interested groups which included: the Association of National Advertisers (ANA), Business/Professional Advertising Association (B/PAA), Graphic Arts Technical Foundation (GATF), International Pre-Press Association (IPA), MPA, National Association of Printing Ink Manufacturers (NAPIM), Printing Industries of America (PIA), and Research and Engineering Council of the Graphic Arts (R&EC). The results of the study were incorporated in what was first called the "Recommended Standards for Web Offset Publications" (SWOP) issued in 1975. The name has since been changed to "Recommended Specifications — Web Offset Publications."

A review board consisting of one representative of each of the endorsing groups was established to keep the specifications current with process changes. Three minor revisions of the SWOP specifications have been issued since 1975: in May 1977, July 1978, and February 1981. The SWOP specifications have been reasonably successful and have helped to make web offset the dominant printing process for publication printing. Cooperative studies of magazine printing based on the SWOP specifications have been conducted by the Graphic Communications Association (GCA) of PIA since 1979. These have shed much light on the web offset printing process for publication printing and the requirements of proofing for it. They have also helped to stabilize the printing process and improve its consistency.

SWOP Specifications

The SWOP specifications are designed to provide the web offset publication printer with separations, or films, of process color, single color, or other multicolor subjects and proofs made from the films using the same ink colors and paper. The specifications are used by trade photoplatemakers and the printers' prepress departments to assure a uniform input to the printer especially when films from a number of different sources and made at different times (as for advertising subjects) must be printed together on the same plate with the same inks and paper. They specify: film requirements; screen rulings; tone densities and amount of undercolor removal (UCR); register; gray balance; proofing requirements including paper; inks; color references for inks (Figure X-15 page C-8), ink densities and tolerances; sequence of colors; types of color scales or color bars (Figure X-16, page C-8); combinations for progressives; viewing conditions for comparing copy with proofs; and off-press color proofing alternativese to press proofing. Also included is a standard offset inspection form to record the conformity to, or deviation from, specifications (Figure X-17). Copies of the SWOP booklet are available from AAAA, ABP, and MPA (addresses are listed under "References" at the end of the book).

Several problems have been encountered with the use of SWOP specifications. One of the main ones has been the selection of a proofing paper that matches the optical and physical characteristics of the printing paper. Consolidated Paper Company's 60 pound (90 grams/sq. meter-g/m^2) Fortune Gloss has been recommended but it does not match the appearance and feel of 30 to 50 pound (45 to 75 g/m^2) #5 publication grades of web offset papers generally used. Trials have been made with an Appleton paper which seems to match the optical appearance of web offset publication grades better. A subcommittee has been studying this matter and a decision is expected soon.

Another problem has been the strengths of the proofing inks. Proofing inks used in establishing the specifications and printing the SWOP Color

PUBLISHER'S STANDARD OFFSET INSPECTION FORM

Publication _____ Issue _____ Printer _____ Engraver _____

Size _____ Advertiser/Product _____ Agency _____

Headline _____ Ad No. _____

Date Received _____ Date Inspected _____ By _____

MATERIALS RECEIVED _____

VIEW ALL FILM "RIGHT READING" *P2*

☐ Positives   ☐ Emulsion Up   Other: _____

☐ Negatives   ☐ Emulsion Down   _____

_____

☐ Offset Proof   ☐ Cromalin *P6*   ☐ Color Control Bar *P4*   Comments: _____

☐ Offset Progs   ☐ Transfer Key *P6*   ☐ SWOP Stock *P3*   _____

☐ Letterpress Proof   ☐ Other Proof: _____   ☐ Head to Foot   _____

☐ Letterpress Progs   ☐ Color Corrections on Proof   ☐ Side to Side   _____

_____

MATERIAL EVALUATION _____

	YELLOW	MAGENTA	CYAN	BLACK
Proof Density Deviation *P5* High	_____	_____	_____	_____
Low	_____	_____	_____	_____
Screen Ruling *P2*	_____	_____	_____	_____
Tonal Density (Film) Total: _____ *P2*	_____	_____	_____	_____
Reverse Type Spread: ☐ Yes ☐ No *P2*	_____	_____	_____	_____

Film Match Prog: ☐ Yes ☐ No. Explain: _____

SWOP Ink Hue: ☐ Yes ☐ No. Explain *P3* _____

Gray Balance in UCR Areas: ☐ Yes ☐ No, Explain *P2* _____

Register OK: ☐ Yes ☐ No. Explain *P2* _____

PRINTER'S EVALUATION _____

Materials: ☐ Acceptable ☐ Unacceptable, replace for following reasons: _____

_____

☐ Reproduction will be different from proof (**must** comment): _____

_____

Comments and Suggested Corrections: _____

_____

_____

_____

_____

ITALICS REFER TO PAGE NUMBER IN SWOP BOOKLET AVAILABLE FROM AAAA's, ABP AND MPA.

Figure X-17. Copy of Publisher's Standard Offset Inspection Form. (IPA)

References (Figure X-15) by IAP were provided by Borden Chemical Company and are designated as series 5001OP and 5002OP. If inks from manufacturers other than Borden are used, an evaluating service is available, at a fee, from NAPIM Technical Institute and GATF to verify conformity to the standard series Borden inks. Ink strengths, in particular, are important since ink film thickness in printing has such an enormous effect on dot gain. As pointed out in Chapter III and Appendix C, *dot gain varies as the square of the ink film thickness!* A 2x change in ink film thickness produces a 4x change in dot gain!

The SWOP specifications have been developed primarily for the control of advertising materials that appear in magazines. The same ads by national advertisers appear in many magazines so numerous sets of films and proofs must be made for distribution to the many printers. For such large quantities of films and proofs press proofing is used predominantly especially for large advertising agencies in New York and Chicago. It is estimated that if more than 10 proofs, or progressives are needed press proofs are more economical than off-press proofs.

According to a summary of SPECTRUM 1983 in the Quality Control Scanner, Volume 3, Number 11, Hearst reported that in a ten month survey over 96,000 pages sent to Hearst for inclusion in offset-printed magazines, 96% were accompanied by press proofs and 4% by off-press proofs. Hearst also reported that 653 or 9% of the proofs (the same ads appeared in many different magazines) submitted did not meet SWOP standards. In contrast, of 1345 pages submitted to Hearst for gravure-printed magazines, 43% were rejected, of which 30% were acceptable after correction and the remaining 13% were rejected again.

The effectiveness of SWOP was also demonstrated in a report by W.A. Krueger Company. Of over 98,000 4-color advertising pages printed in 1982 there were only 145 complaints, or less than 1.5 in 10,000! On the other hand, Knapp Communications reported that 18% of the films supplied by color separators arrived without color proofs. Obviously, there are wide variations in the practices of some trade shops regarding SWOP specifications. There were a number of suggestions at the SPECTRUM 1983 meeting that communications between printers, color separators, advertising agencies and publishers be improved and that adherence to the SWOP specifications be more stringently exercised by all.

As already mentioned GCA has conducted a number of cooperative tests to check the validity of the SWOP specifications and develop means for improving their utility and reliability. Results of the tests reported at SPECTRUM 1983 and described in the Quality Control Scanner, Volume 3, Number 11, indicated that some additions and modifications to the SWOP specifications would be desirable and could improve their effectiveness. It was suggested that SWOP should consider including:

- A middletone control step in the color bar.
- Recommendations on acceptable dot gain for films and proofs.
- Pressroom parameters when establishing printing tolerances.

• A contacting/proofing control guide to accompany each generation of film up to platemaking

The tests also developed *GCA Average Required Separation Curves* which were derived from Kodak's *Customized Color System* and were calculated by Kodak. If adopted, they could save on scanner make-overs, proofing and press makeready times, and overall printing waste. They could also result in improved quality of reproduction as all films would be in better balance and compromises for compatible proofing would be easier to make. These separation curves and their relation to color proofing are described in another section.

GTA Color Specifications

The gravure industry was actually the first of the major printing processes to establish specifications and standards for printing. Until the advent of electromechanical engraving and now halftone gravure conversions, the gravure industry was, like letterpress, almost completely dependent on engravers to produce cylinders or films, and on press proofing to predict what the job would look like. Through the Gravure Technical Association (GTA) in a cooperative program among printers, publishers, engravers and advertising agencies, the industry has established an intensive system of gravure printing standards encompassing proofing stock, proofing inks, lighting and viewing conditions, positive densities and screen rulings. The most important elements of the system are the Standard Color Charts which have been the communication tool between agency and engraver, printer and publisher, and publisher and agency for over 20 years.

The first GTA Color Charts were printed in 1960 from engraved copper plates on sheet-fed proof presses. In 1973, GTA printed the first Color Charts on a production press using a standard stock and cylinders made from hard dot positives conforming to GTA positive density standards and established GTA Standard reproduction curves. The Color Charts were printed again in 1981 from cylinders made by the Hell Helioklischograph System. The latest revision of the Color Charts in 1983 incorporated many innovations.

In the 1983 Color Charts, the tone scale has been expanded from 12 to 18 steps with all the new steps in the highlight and middletone sections of the charts. There are 324 color squares per page, compared with 144 in the former books, and 26 pages of charts with a total of 8,353 color combinations. The charts are interleaved with blank sheets to minimize show-through and there is a calibration page for users to calibrate their densitometers to the color chart book they are using. There are also two pages of color illustrations to provide examples of the wide color ranges in the reproduction of highlights, flesh tones and fine detail. The back cover contains the reproduction curves, continuous tone positive film values and corresponding reflection density print values for both wide and narrow band densitometers.

Two Color Chart books are available:

- *Group I — Supplements:* Charts printed on a roto newsprint stock using GTA Standard Group I Inks. The charts are typical of printing on Sunday newspaper supplements, newspaper inserts, some magazines and catalogs.
- *Group V — Magazines:* Charts printed on coated stock using GTA Standard Group V Inks. The charts are typical of printing on most magazines, catalogs and similar publications.

The GTA Standards Program is recognized as a dependable method of checking gravure proofs and positives. It includes specifications for positive density ranges, total positive densities, lateral hard dot tolerances and screen ruling, reproduction curves, color bars, proofing inks, proofing stocks and lighting and viewing conditions.

- *Positive Density Ranges.* The standard density ranges for continuous tone positives are 0.35 to 0.90 (midtone) to 1.65 (within recognized tolerances) measured on a transmission densitometer. The 0.30 value prints as a fade-off and 0.25 is white paper (no tone).
- *Total Positive Density.* The GTA Standards Committee recommends a total positive density value in four colors of 4.70 ± .10 corresponding to an undercolor reduction with 290% total density of ink on paper. Only one solid value of 1.65 (contone density) is advisable where more than one color is used for overprinting.
- *Lateral Hard Dot.* The scale and tolerances are: tone positive - 0.35 ± .02 to 1.65 ± .05; screen positive — 0.05 ± .01 to 0.30 ± .02. Fade-off tones are: 0.30 tone positives equivalent to 0.04 screen positive.
- *Screen Ruling.* 150 l. lateral dot screen is GTA Standard for publication printing.
- *Reproduction curves.* Standard GTA Reproduction Curves have been established for each color. These are illustrated on the back covers of the Color Chart books and in Figure X-18 for Group V printing.
- *Color Bars.* New GTA Color Bars were developed for the 1983 Color Charts. The basic bar consists of a contone film with 19 steps from 0.25 to 1.65 density with numerical identification provided for step 0.35, 0.90 and 1.35. It prints at 18 steps as the 0.25 step is white

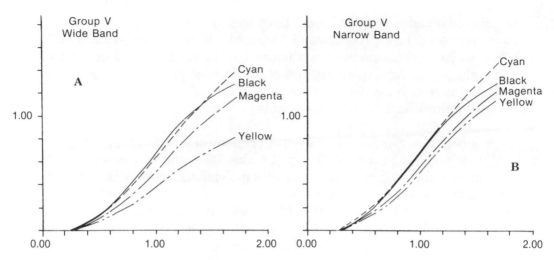

Figure X-18. Standard GTA Reproduction Curves for Group V inks as shown on the back covers of the GTA Color Chart Books. (A) Wide band densitometer; (B) Narrow band densitometer. (GTA)

paper. Two bars are printed on the proof or print: one with black ink and the other consisting of a composite of the three colors, yellow, magenta (red) and cyan (blue). The inks in Group V have been modified to produce a gray balance when the three colors are overprinted. The bars are used by the engravers to check etching of the cylinders and by the engraver and printer to check gray balance in proofing and printing.

- *Proofing Inks.* Two sets of standard proofing inks have been developed through ink manufacturers: *Group I Inks* — for proofing on roto newsprint, provided by Inmont Corp. *Group V Inks* — for proofing on GTA coated stock, provided by General Printing Ink Division, Sun Chemical Corp.
- *Proofing Stocks.* The standard proofing stock for Group I is 30 lb. (45 g/m²) non-premium, grain long, to be printed on the wire side. The standard proofing stock for Group V is 34 lb. (51 g/m²) lightweight machine coated #5, grain long.
- *Lighting and Viewing Standards.* GTA has adopted the American National Standards Institute (ANSI) recommended standard of 5000 Kelvin and a Color Rendering Index of 90 (see Appendix B) as the standard for viewing reflection art and/or transparencies [35 mm to 8 x 10 inch (203 mm x 254 mm)] when comparing them with proofs or progressive prints. A booklet describing the Lighting and Viewing Standards is available from GTA.

All these standards are used for evaluating and controlling proofs and prints from the conventionally used gravure processes which use continuous tone and lateral dot halftone positives. The newer halftone gravure conversion processes use full-scale halftone positives and electomechanical engraving machines like the Hell Helioklischograph to convert the halftones into quasi-continuous tone images for producing the engraved cylinders. For these processes, off-press color proofing systems can be used which have been correlated to the reproduction curves of the gravure process. These systems are so new that techniques for their optimum use are just evolving.

HOW TO EVALUATE COLOR PROOFS AND PRESS PRINTS

A color proof to be used as a color guide for prints should satisfy the following conditions:

- It should be made from the same set of separation films as the plates.
- The solid ink densities should correspond to those printable on the press with the inks to be used at ink film thicknesses on the press vibrator rollers between 0.0002 to 0.0004 inch (0.005 to 0.01 mm).
- The color scales or color bars should print so that *visually* all the overprints of solids and tints have the correct hues and strengths.
- The overprints of the tints should have the same relative dot gains as the press print will have when the job is printed on the press.

Ideally the proof should be on the same base stock and feel like the final press print. These last two requirements are highly desirable and would make a proofing system that has them preferable over one that hasn't but they are not mandatory. The most important characteristic, or quality attribute, of the proof is that it *look like* the printed job. It must have the same optical characteristics as the press production print so that when the two are laid side by side they are nearly indistinguishable.

In all types of proofing the proof should be a reliable, reproducible and consistent representation of the separations from which it is made and yet it must predict how the print on the press will look when the films are used to make plates and the plates are printed on the press. Whether the proof is made for customer approval or to check color correction, color balance, size, fit, ink and paper compatibility, or any other image characteristics, the craftsman or checker must be sure that what he sees in the proof is a faithful composite reproduction of what is in the films and not the result of a combination of the film characteristics modified by process variables. This is a main reason why off-press color proofing is gaining in use and preference at the expense of press proofing.

Most off-press color proofing systems are photomechanical processes in which the image characteristics are predictable and controllable. On the other hand, in addition to being expensive and time intensive, press proofing is subject to all the unpredictable variables of the platemaking and printing processes. The color separator, dot etcher, art director and quality control checker cannot be sure whether the changes in optical appearance they see in press proofs are caused by modifications or deficiencies in the films or the many unpredictable and some uncontrollable variables in the way the plates are made and printed on the press. It is estimated that close to 70% of the color proofs made for lithographic printing are by the many off-press color proofing systems described in Chapters V, VI, VII, VIII, and IX and their share of the total color proofing market is increasing, especially since the introduction of halftone gravure conversion processes which use the same off-press color proofing systems.

Special Color Proofing Targets

The targets described in this section are designed mainly for use in evaluating proofs for lithographic and web offset printing. They are also applicable for use in evaluating proofs for halftone gravure conversion processes. Targets for color proofing are similar to the color scales, bars and test strips used for color control in printing and described in the section in this chapter on color strips. The targets for color proofing are not, however, restricted by space limitations so they can be larger. Examples are the three-row GATF Standard Offset Color Control Bars used in the SWOP specifications; the two-row DuPont/System Brunner CROMALIN Offset Com Guides/System Brunner (Pos and Neg) for positive and negative CROMALIN proofs; and the new GCA/GATF Proof Comparator for quick visual comparisons of proofs and prints.

Regular press color control strips can also be used as long as they have provision for measuring solids, overprints, tints, tint overprints and gray balance steps, like the GATF Compact Color Test Strip, RIT Color Test Strip and Gretag Color Test Strip. The standards and tolerances used in the color proofing processes are dependent on the characteristics of the printing process. The limits of solid ink densities (SID) and overprint colors of the proofs are determined by the press inks and their press performance and not vice versa. In many instances presses are required to match proofs based on arbitrary standards which do not necessarily correlate with the printing process and press used to print the job. SWOP specifications had been in use over five years before GCA designed and conducted comparative tests to see how well SWOP proofs correlated with prints from a number of presses and how closely the presses correlated with each other.

In the GCA tests reported at SPECTRUM 1982, in the Quality Control Scanner, Volume 3, Number 4, and on page 239 in this chapter, there were wide variations in the solid ink densities of all colors run in the 16 press tests as shown in Table X-III which is a summary of the solid ink densities in Table X-II.

TABLE X-III

GCA PRESS TEST RUN ON 16 PRESSES IN 1982

Solids	Cyan	Magenta	Yellow	Black
Average	1.11	1.18	.94	1.56
High	1.44	1.48	.96	1.95
Low	.86	.93	.69	1.30
Range	.58	.55	.27	.63

The condition persisted in the 1983 tests in which a range of solid ink densities for magenta from .81 to 1.68 were reported!

Such wide ranges of solid ink densities for each color indicate a wide spread in ink pigment strengths in the inks. As already pointed out in Chapter III, for an ink to print properly on an offset press it must have film thicknesses, measured on the vibrator roller above the ink form rollers, between 0.0002 and 0.0004 inch (0.005 and 0.01 mm). If ink film thicknesses are below this range, plate wear is accelerated as the amount of ink on the image areas is insufficient to lubricate the impression between the plate and blanket; if they are above this range, dot gain increases as the square of the increase in ink film thickness and other print defects such as slurring, doubling, poor trapping and changes in ink-water balance are intensified.

These wide variations in ink densities are caused by the printers' desire to save on ink costs by buying cheaper inks. Since pigments are the most expensive ingredients in inks, any reduction in ink costs *must* be accompanied by a reduction in ink pigment, or the substitution of cheaper pigments which are weaker and could have impurities and less transparency. The purchase of cheaper inks is a false economy which can be responsible for many problems causing variations in printing, particularly in dot gain, slur, doubling, trapping, ink-water balance and print contrast, all of which can interfere seriously with print quality and consistency on the press and matching press prints with proofs and vice versa.

Typical color bars and targets and how they can be used to evaluate color proofs and press prints are described in the following sections.

GATF Standard Offset Color Control Bar

This color bar was developed in cooperation with the AAAA/MPA Joint Committee on Advertising Reproduction. The consistency and standardization of 4-color offset magazing proofing was the objective of the bar but it has since found wide acceptance by platemakers and pressmen as an effective color test strip for evaluating platemaking, process inks and press performance for all offset process color printing. All sections of the bars are recommended for use on proofs and various elements of the strip can be used on production runs depending on the available trim space. The complete strip provides comprehensive and concise means of controlling primary and overprint colors, tints (120-line and 150-line screens) gray balance, dot gain, slur, doubling, ink and water feed both visually and with a densitometer.

Components of the bars, their use and interpretation are:

- *GATF "QC" Strip* which is an effective visual control of ink film thickness, ink-water balance and dot quality. Because of its compact size and simplicity of use it is used extensively on web offset printing. The strip on the OK sheet is compared with the strip on a printed inspection sheet. Any difference in appearance in any of the steps in the strip alerts the pressman to look for the cause of the difference in his press conditions. Typical variations in the appearance of the strip are shown in Figure X-19.
- *GATF Compact Color Test Strip:* All the components of this strip are in the color bars except that the steps are larger, are arranged differently and are in 120-l (47 l/cm) as well as 150-l (60 l/cm) screen. These targets are used to measure the hues and densities of printed inks; their hue error and grayness; the hues of overprinting colors, both solids and tints; uniformity of inking across the sheet; and dot gain or loss, slur, and doubling (star targets).
- *GATF Star Target* is a very sensitive and versatile quality control device for the pressman to quickly and visually detect ink or dot spread, slur and doubling on the press. Its design is such that it magnifies ink and dot spread or gain about 23 times making it readily visible and easily calculated. Typical examples of star target depictions are shown in Figure X-20.
- *GATF Dot Gain Scale and Slur Gauge* visually indicates dot area changes by observing displacement of an invisible number to a

higher or lower value, and slur by the appearance of the word *"SLUR."* The visual movement of the invisible number is a reliable measure of the degree of dot size changes. The slur gauge also indicates dot doubling. Typical changes in appearances of the Dot Gain Scale are shown in Figure III-26. The GATF Star Target and Dot Gain Scale and Slur Gauge are also used as controls in platemaking, which uses are described in Chapter III.

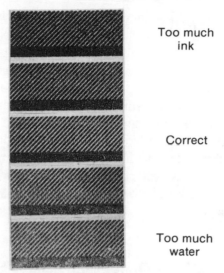

Too much ink

Correct

Too much water

Figure X-19. Enlarged view of GATF QC strip showing effects of ink-water balance on printing. (GATF)

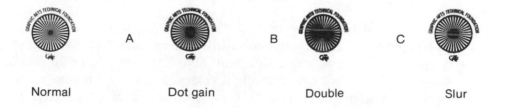

Normal   A   Dot gain   B   Double   C   Slur

Figure X-20. Enlarged view of GATF Star Targets showing dot spread or gain, slur and doubling. (GATF)

• *GATF Midtone Dot Gain Scale II* is a new quality control device, introduced in 1984, used in halftone printing and proofing for visually determining changes in dot area of the 50% tones in the reproduction. The new scale is illustrated in Figure X-21 which shows (A) the scale printed without dot gain and (B) the appearance of the scale when there is an increase in dot gain of 10% in the 50% tints.

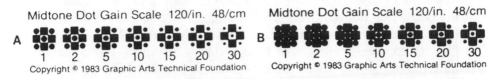

Figure X-21. Enlarged view of GATF Midtone Dot Gain Scale II. (A) no gain and (B) 10% gain in midtones. (GATF)

For setting printing standards and tolerances for comparing proofs with press prints the complete strip should be run on several production jobs. Densitometric measurements of the color control bars on the press sheets will determine the consistency and reproducibility of inherent printing characteristics like dot gain, slur, doubling, trapping, ink-water balance, solid ink density and their fluctuations. Analysis of the data will help set standards and tolerances for solid ink densities, dot gain, trapping and color balance of overprint solids and tints so there can be reasonable assurance that the color proof can match the press prints and vice versa.

DuPont CROMALIN Offset Com Guides/System Brunner

In the Brunner System special printing test forms are used to analyze the printing conditions to determine the tolerances of the printing/proofing system. Key elements of the test forms are:

- *Two color pictures:* one of a girl's face against a low contrast background — a combination which is very sensitive to process deviations like dot gain, slur and doubling; the other of wool samples with a wide range of bright colors, grays and browns which represent fine detail, tone and color rendition which are affected by the contrast of reproduction.
- *26-step halftone scales* in series, consisting of as many units of scales that fit across the sheet. Each unit consists of four scales; a neutral black scale and three 3-color scales in combinations of tints calculated to produce neutral gray scales if printed correctly on the press. With the Brunner Eurostandard inks the combination in the 50% tint consists of 50% dots in the cyan films, 41% dots in the magenta films, and 41% dots in the yellow films. The percentage tint of each color varies with the pigments used in the inks. These scales are very sensitive to dot size changes across the press.

- *Tolerance frame charts* from which are derived the standard deviation s for the printing and the proofs. These are illustrated in Figure X-22, page C-9. According to DuPont/Brunner data CROMALIN proofs have a standard deviation of $\sigma = 1.2\%$; good printing on sheet-fed presses have a $\sigma = 2.4$; and good printing on web offset presses shows standard deviations below 3.0.
- A group of four Brunner System 5 x 5 blocks for each color (yellow, magenta, cyan and black) consisting of 25 precise halftone steps from 4% to 100% dot area from which Isocontour curves are drawn for each color on the press prints and proofs. These curves show the acceptable ranges of dot size changes on the press prints and proofs. Typical Isocontour curves for press prints and proofs are shown in Figure X-23.
- A group of three Brunner System 5 x 5 blocks of 2-color overprints consisting of solids and calibrated tints for visual judging of trapping.
- Two groups of three Brunner System 5 x 5 blocks of 4-color overprints: one of near solids and the other of 50% tints for visual judging of trapping, overprint colors and undercolor removal.
- Numerous Brunner System print control strips for checking uniformity of printing or proofing across the sheet.

Once correlation is established between press prints and proofs and tolerances are determined CROMALIN Offset Com Guides/System Brunner strips are used for controlling proof making. As previously stated, there are two types of Com Guides — *Pos* and *Neg* for use with proofs made from positive films and negative films. The Pos guide is illustrated in Figure X–9D, page C-7. The main difference between the two guides is in the type of target used to visually indicate correct exposure. These are shown in Figure X-24. The Pos guide has *highlight dot and microline* patches similar to the ones illustrated in Figure X-13 and the Neg guide has *highlight and shadow dot* patches. Recommended guidelines for using the two color guides are:

- A photopolymer light source with Kokomo filter and integrator is used for exposure.
- Vacuum frame and pump must be in good condition. Roller vacuum frames which expel air with a roller action are preferred.
- For positive CROMALIN proofing stocks are Champion Kromekote or SPR-15; for negative CROMALIN they are PRS-12 or SNR-15. SPR-15 and SNR-15 provide improved registration but require additional drawdown time to assure proper contact during exposure.
- CROMALIN process toners in Y-M-C-K sequence are used for positive CROMALIN; the same toners are used in K-Y-M-C

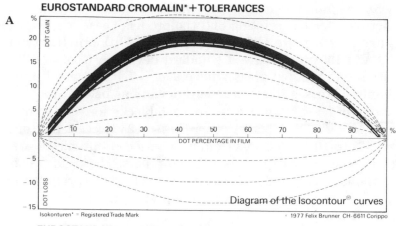

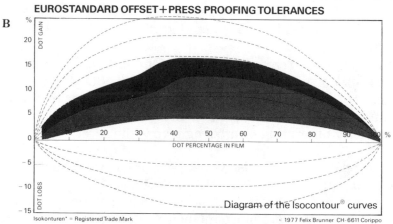

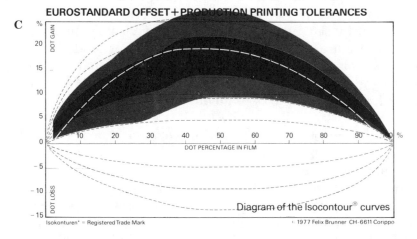

Figure X-23. Typical Isocontour curves from the four groups
of 5x5 blocks of 25 halftone steps from 4% to 100% dot areas
for (A) CROMALIN proofs; (B) press proofs; (C) press prints.
(DuPont)

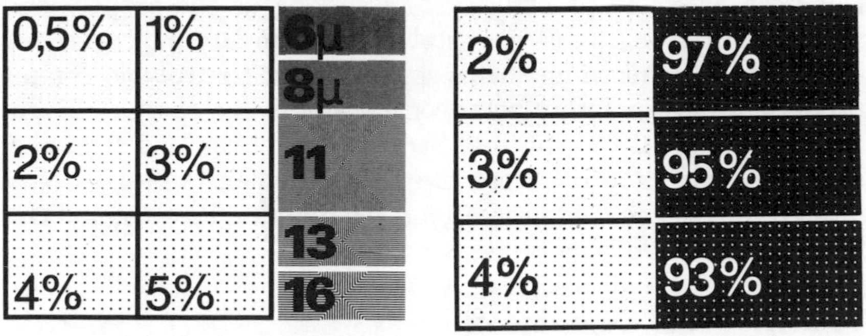

A   B

Figure X-24. Highlight dot and microline patch to monitor
exposure on positive CROMALIN proofs (A); Highlight and
shadow dot patches for negative CROMALIN proofs (B).
(DuPont)

sequence for negative CROMALIN. Recommended techniques for
hand toning are followed. For automatic toning room temperatures
should be maintained at 72°F ±2°F (22.2°C ±1.1°C) and RH at
55% ±5%.

- For optimum results with balanced dot gain for all colors, each
  Cromalin layer may require a slightly different exposure.
- For *positive CROMALIN* proofs the 0.5% and 1% highlight dot
  patches are dropped out while the 2% patch is barely maintained.
  (This corresponds to dropping out the 6 and 8 microline patches and
  retaining most of the 11 microline patch.) For *negative CROMALIN*
  optimum exposure is achieved in each layer when the 2% highlight
  patch is uniformly retained and the 1% is broken or ghosted. The
  95% shadow patch should be completely open while the 97% patch
  is partially open.
- When exposures are properly established and densities are
  maintained in a balanced relationship, CROMALIN proof
  consistency will permit critical assessment of color separations.
- System Brunner print control strips are recommended for
  monitoring dot gain and other critical variables in printing for
  consistent print runs that closely match approved proofs.
- For finishing techniques refer to the CROMALIN instructions in
  Chapter VI.
- As in the use of all control strips, it is imperative that only original
  strips be used which can be identified, in the case of Brunner strips,
  by the embossed serial number or each strip.

While these instructions apply to the use of the Brunner strip for the
comparison of CROMALIN proofs with press prints, the Brunner strip

can be used with any proofing system as long as the proper conditions and correlations for its use are established, The Brunner system is well conceived and organized and helps simplify color control and comparisons of proofs and prints. Other color control strips like the GATF Compact Color Test Strip, RIT Color Test Strip and Gretag Color Test Strip can also be used with any color proofing system when the strips have been calibrated for the printing process and the proofing system, and the press print and proof have been properly correlated.

GCA/GATF Proof Comparator

This new control device introduced at SPECTRUM 1983 has been in development and testing for several years. It is designed to enable printers, color separators, color proofers, publishers, advertising agencies and customer personnel to make quick visual judgments to check proofs for adherence to specifications and consistency from proof to proof, subject to subject on the same job, and job to job. It is similar to the GATF Standard Offset Color Control Bars shown in Figure X-16, with the addition of several new elements that increase sensitivity to quality changes so they enhance the acceptability and reliability of quick visual judgments.

The GCA/GATF Color Proof Comparator is illustrated in Figure X-25, page C-9. Note that besides eliminating the GATF "QC" Strip and differences in the placement of the component elements of the GATF Standard Offset Color Control Bars, there are three new targets in the GCA/GATF Color Proof Commparator and all halftone elements are in 133-line (152 l/cm) screen. The new elements are:

- *Exposure Control Target* which consists of blocks of 5% and 95% halftone tints of each color situated next to the GATF Dot Gain Scale and Slur Gauges and the GATF Star Targets. These show visually and under 10x magnification whether highlight dots have been lost and/or shadow dots plugged, which conditions are related to incorrect exposures.
- *Gray Balance Target* which consists of two rows of gray bars on each side of the comparator. The bottom bars have one block of 4-color 75% tints and two blocks of black tints: one 25% and the other 75%. The upper bars have one block of 4-color tints, like the bottom bar, and two blocks of 3-color tints that approximately match the neutral gray color of the black tints in the bottom bars. The dot values of each of the colors in the 3-color tints are calculated to produce neutral grays with the SWOP inks.
- *Pictorial Subject* which is the comparator's centerpiece consists of two pictures; one of a girl's face illustrating flesh tones; and the

other of wool skeins and knitting accessories with fine detail and a range of difficult-to-reproduce colors. These pictorial subjects are useful for non-technical personnel to identify deviations between proofing and master comparators.

According to Frank Benham, Vice Presidend, Marketing, of American Color Corp. and Chairman of the recent GCA SPECTRUM conferences, the GCA/GATF Color Proof Comparator helps to identify proofing variations and visually evaluate the accuracy of films used to produce the proofs. Any visual differences between a proof comparator on a proof and a master comparator indicate immediately that there are differences between the proofed image and the films from which it was made.

In some cases the proof may look good but the comparator is off. This means the proof is not an accurate rendition of the separation film and another proof should be made with correct rendition of the comparator. Or, the comparator may reproduce accurately and the proof is off, which means the films should be corrected before another proof is made. When such differences are observed the comparator bars can be studied and analyzed visually and densitometrically for fidelity of dot reproduction including dot gain, slurring and doubling, trapping, register, ink densities and hues of printing inks and overprinting colors. Corrections can then be made to bring the proof into closer correspondence with the proof comparator.

HOW TO CORRELATE COLOR PROOFS AND PRESS PRINTS

The hierarchy of color proofing involves a long and arduous series of steps. The color proofing series starts as a part of the color separation process. Color proofs are made from the color separation films to determine (1) how closely they reproduce the original, (2) whether plates made from the films will produce an acceptable print on the press, and (3) if either or both conditions are not met, whether corrections can be made in the films to help them satisfy the requirements, or whether new separations should be made. After the separations are corrercted or remade, a new proof is made, which if it satisfies the requirements is shown to the customer for approval. Several internal proofs may be necessary before reaching the point of submission for approval. If further corrections are indicated these are made and a new proof is submitted for approval.

When the proof is OK'd and signed by the customer it becomes the guide or target for the finished printed job and is the master used in the pressroom to establish the OK sheet for the press run. Once the OK sheet has been signed, the proof has completed its function and the OK sheet becomes the guide used by the pressmen and quality control inspectors with which the printed sheets are compared during the press run.

Many other proofs, known as scatter proofs, are made, for checking work in process, which are not intended for customer approval, but are, nevertheless, needed to complete the production function.

While the approved proof is the target for satisfying the customer and for printing on the press, it should have printing characteristics and defects typical of the printing process and type of press to be used, and in some instances the actual press on which the job will be printed. The proof should be capable of being duplicated easily on the press when it is running with near optimum settings at close to maximum speed. Matching the proof on the press should impose no restrictions on the pressman or limit the tolerances on his settings. To accomplish this objective the press print characteristics for normal, optimum, consistent operation should be determined and incorporated in the specifications for the proofs. These are types of specifications that are evolving from GTA for gravure and from the GCA SPECTRUM tests for web offset publications (SWOP).

Control of Overprint Colors

As the GCA SPECTRUM 1982 and 1983 tests have indicated, the most important criteria on the press for matching press prints to the OK sheet are the hues of the overprint colors and the most effective control is for the pressman to try to keep them from varying. This concept had previously been proposed in 1976 in a master's thesis by an RIT student, John G. Gaston III. The thesis entitled "An Investigation of Solid Ink Density Variations as Determined by the Acceptability of Overprints in Process Color Printing" and its results are described in the Quality Control Scanner, Volume 3, Number 4. The study was conducted in several Rochester printing plants doing high quality printing. It was found that quality control inspectors were less concerned with changes in solid ink densities than with shifts in overprint colors. Table X-IV summarizes the variations in solid ink density ranges using solid overprints and solid ink patches to evaluate the printing.

The results of the GCA SPECTRUM 1982 tests shown in Table X-II drew similar conclusions, as did the GCA SPECTRUM 1983 tests. The variations in ranges of solid ink densities of the individual colors was almost twice those of the overprint colors (trapping) and yet the prints from all 44 press tests were considered acceptable — they varied in print contrast but were in reasonable color balance.

TABLE X-IV

ACCEPTABLE SOLID INK DENSITY RANGES

Colors	Using Overprints to Evaluate Printing	Using Solid Ink Patches to Evaluate Printing
Yellow	0.13	0.19
Magenta	0.12	0.22
Cyan	0.13	0.16

How to Produce Press Prints and Color Proofs with Proper Overprint Colors: Actually the first one to propose the concept of maintaining the hues of overprint colors for color control in printing was Frank Preucil at LTF/GATF. He taught the concept in his color seminars which started in 1958 and first published it in LTF Research Progress No. 67 (Nov. 1964) entitled *The Color Reproduction Guide.*

According to Preucil the solid ink densities of the individual colors are related to their hues, or hue errors. Regardless what pigments are used in the inks the pressman can control the hues of the overprints by varying the strengths, or densities, he runs on the press (Figure X-26, page C-10). The hues of green can be varied from bluish-green to yellowish-green by varying the strengths of the yellow and cyan inks. The same is true of reds and blues. The strength of the yellow depends on the blueness of the magenta. A typical yellow strength or density* to produce a satisfactory red overprint with a Lithol Rubine magenta is about 0.90 and with a Rhodamine Y magenta, about 1.0. Setting the strength of the yellow establishes the strengths of cyan and magenta to produce the proper overprints of green, blue and red. The pressman controls these by the amounts of inks he prints.

Using the GATF Color Circle to depict the hue and grayness levels of the overprint colors the pressman prints a strength or density of cyan ink that plots the overprint color of cyan and yellow, *green,* at a position on the color circle about 10% to the cyan side of the green line (see Appendix A for instructions on how to plot colors on the GATF Color Circle and other color diagrams)(Figure X-27, page C-10.) The magenta is printed at a strength so the overprint of magenta and yellow, *red,* plots exactly opposite the cyan on the circle so the line joining the positions of cyan and red goes through the center of the circle. The overprint of cyan and magenta, *blue,* then plots slightly to the magenta side of the blue

---

*All densities are for densitometers using wide band Wratten Filters #25, #58 and #47.

line on the circle. With different ink-sets the hues of the overprints will be the same but their saturation or grayness (distance from the center of the circle) will vary. Grayness or saturation are related to brightness and print contrast.

The plots on the GATF Color Circle determine the positions of the overprint solids with good trapping. Since trapping is affected by color sequence on the press the tests should be run with the color sequence used in printing. If there is poor trapping of the second color over the first one the hue of the overprint will be dominated by the first down color. If cyan is printed over yellow and there is poor trapping the green will be yellowish. If yellow is printed over the cyan and there is poor trapping the green will be bluish. These effects are characteristic of the printing process and the inks and papers used. They should therefore be duplicated in the proof by adjusting the strengths of the overprinting colors to match the final overprint hue achieved in the press print.

The hues of overprinting *tints* are affected only slightly by the strengths of the solid inks. The dominant factor affecting the hues of overprinting tints is variable dot size, or dot gain. The hues of overprinting tints are controlled by varying the dot sizes of the individual tints. For example, equal dot sizes of yellow, magenta and cyan produce a brown tint and not a neutral gray. To make the tint gray the cyan tint must have a larger dot size than yellow and magenta. In addition, to produce a neutral gray with a Rhodamine Y magenta the dots in the yellow tint must also be slightly larger than the dots in the magenta tint. As long as a press print has consistent dot gain, as determined by the test methods described in previous sections, the hues of the overprint tints can be adjusted by changing their component dot sizes. It is imperative, therefore, that press conditions are stabilized so that dot gain is consistent and predictable. Otherwise the printing process is uncontrollable and any attempts to match proofs to prints made under such conditions are useless. If dot gain varies, it becomes impossible for the pressman to control the hues of the overprint tints with the controls readily available to him while the press is running. These are varying ink feeds to change ink density which has little effect on the hues of tints, or varying the water feed, unless too much water is causing apparent dot sharpening by reducing the densities of the dots, or too little water is causing fill-in or dot gain.

If the printing process is consistent and predictable the proofmaking process has reliable targets for hues and strengths of the overprint solids and tints. The ability to produce and maintain correct overprint hues becomes a critical condition for the acceptability of the proofing process. A proofing process must reproduce the hues and strengths of the *printing* colors, but, what is more important, it must also reproduce the hues and strengths of the *overprint* colors, *solids* and *tints*, since most of the

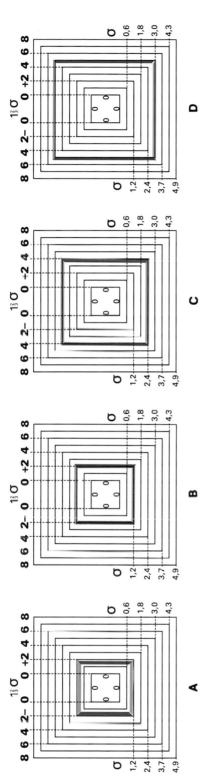

Figure X-22. Enlarged view of Tolerance Frame charts for (A) CROMALIN proofs; (B) Proof press with automatic inking and dampening; (C) Good sheet-fed printing; (D) Good web offset printing. (DuPont)

Figure X-25. GCA/GATF Color Proof Comparator for visual judgment and objective measurement of proofs and prints. (GATF)

C9

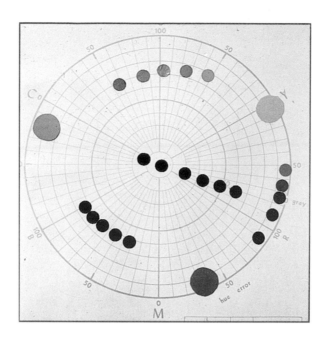

Figure X-26. Plot of ink colors on GATF Color Circle showing pressman's ability to change the hues of overprint solid colors by varying the strengths or amounts of the primary inks run on the press. (GATF)

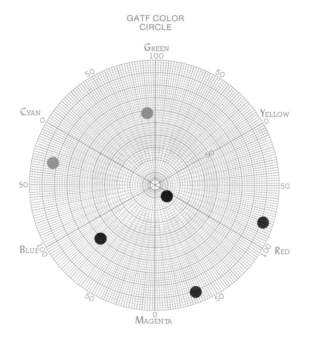

Figure X-27. Plot of solid ink colors on GATF Color Circle for optimum color reproduction. (GATF)

pictorial scene is made up of mixtures of colors and not just the single printing colors. In addition, it must duplicate the *dot gain* of the printing process, including both platemaking and printing, or the overprints will not reproduce correctly.

Print Contrast

At the 1984 GCA SPECTRUM Conference, in addition to equivalent dot gain (optical plus mechanical), overprint hues and ink strength, or solid ink density, *print contrast* was cited as an important printing control. Print contrast was defined as follows:

$$PC = \frac{D_s - D_{75}}{D_s} \times 100$$

where PC = Print Contrast
D_s = Solid Ink Density
D_{75} = Density of 75% Tint

It was stated that print contrast values of 25 or more are characteristic of reproductions with good shadow detail and visual impact.

Also at the 1984 GCA SPECTRUM Conference it was proposed that a satisfactory *dot gain window* for the GATF 50% 120-line screen tint is 18-26% on No. 5 grade coated web offset paper. The recommended window for the Brunner 50% 150-line screen tint is 22-29% on the same paper. The dot gain window of 18-26% was subdivided as follows:

Optical	4-8%
Press (mechanical)	5-10%
Register	5-10%
Negative plates	+4%
Positive plates	-2%

These were suggested guidelines. It was recommended that each printer assemble a data base of experience with all press conditions and supplies for each press to assure greater accuracy in predicting a desirable combination of equivalent dot gain, solid ink density and print contrast for future jobs.

Standard Color Separation Curves

The dot gain characteristics of the printing process have an effect on more than the proofing process and print contrast. They determine the tone reproduction characteristics of the color separation films so that the plates made from them will be compensated for the physical dot gain on the press and the proof will have the advantage of the same dot gain input as the plates. The proofing process will then only be required to reproduce the same dot gain as the press instead of having to compensate also for any plate/press discrepancies.

The *Kodak Customized Color Test Form* was used in the GCA Run Tests for SPECTRUM 1983 to determine the printing characteristics of the 28 presses involved in the tests, as reported in the Quality Control Scanner, Volume 3, Number 11. Using a spectrophotometer to measure the results of the printing of the Kodak Customized Color Test Form in Phase I of the tests and a computer to determine the average printing characteristics for all the participating printers a set of "GCA Average Required Separation Curves" were derived based on a 280% maximum total printing dot area (UCR) and a skeleton black. These curves were used to modify the separations used in Phase II of the tests. Only four printers had completed the Phase II tests, which is not a significant sample, but there were indications that printing was improved and that the use of the "GCA Average Separation Curves" or similar tone reproduction characteristic curves, could extend the effectiveness of the SWOP specifications.

Once consistent printing is achieved on the press the Kodak Customized Color System could be an effective way to analyze the printing conditions and image characteristics on the press. The data could be used to set specifications for color separation and color proofing tone reproduction curves, dot gain, ink strengths and overprint hues for solids and tints. The color proofing curves will be different from the color separation curves as they will incorporate the dot gain incurred in platemaking and printing. Checks on the specifications should be run frequently to determine continuity of consistency and they should be run every time paper, inks, ink tack, ink strength, color sequence, fountain solutions, or other press conditions change.

Similar results could be achieved by the intelligent use, interpretation and analysis of the data from any one of the many color bars and targets described in this chapter. This, however, will require formulating a system and verifying it, which could be more lengthy, expensive and less accurate than using an available system with an established track record.

Conclusion

A great number and variety of off-press color proofing systems have been described in this book. Not all are acceptable for customer approval but all have found some uses and users, or they would not be in the marketplace. Besides the obvious requirement of consistency and reproducibility of results and the ability of proofs to match the hues and strengths of overprints of solids and tints in press prints there are a number of other characteristics or color proofing systems that are important to their use and should be evaluated when choosing a system.

In a private communication from Frank Benham, Vice President, American Color Corp., he listed a number of additional factors to consider when evaluating an off-press color proofing system for use in color reproduction. They are:

- Do the inks match the industry aim points for printing inks in hue, saturation and brightness, i.e., SWOP for web offset and GTA Group I and Group V for gravure?
- What should the densitometer readings (wide band and narrow band) be for the different colors on the proof to match *visually* the correct ink densities on the press print?
- Does the manufacturer have density levels of the imaging materials to match the ink density levels on paper?
- Can the proof be made on the printing stock or does it have a means to visually simulate ink on paper?
- What is the mid-tone dot gain — physical and optical?
- Is a test bar or object available for the proofmaker to establish, maintain and reproduce a standard — both visually and densitometrically?
- Can the system produce a neutral gray throughout the gray scale?
- How long does it take to make a proof and what does it cost?
- What is the reputation of the manufacturer and/or supplier and the dependability of their services?

Comparisons between off-press color proofing systems for these characteristics are desirable and necessary but the proof of the pudding is in how well the systems work, i.e., how easily, quickly, consistently and economically they produce proofs that predict and/or match the printing.

It must also be remembered that proofs are made for many different purposes and the specifications should suit the purposes for which the proofs are intended; and these do not always include customer approval. Therefore, each use, or system, may be judged by different criteria.

The important tools needed to satisfy the different criteria are:

- Sensitive targets for visual and objective examination.
- Reliable means for measuring the targets or evaluating them visually.
- Standard viewing conditions under which all visual examinations and comparisons are made.
- Realistic tolerances acceptable to the printer and customer.
- Sound analytical procedures for interpreting and evaluating the data.

A well organized program will lead to valid conclusions that will (1) strengthen the confidence of all concerned; (2) detect and clarify deviations in procedures and results; and (3) identify success — or recognize when conformity to objectives has been achieved — or show when the color proof and color press prints match within acceptable tolerances.

UPDATE

In the interval between the time when the text of this book was completed and the illustrations were finished some changes occurred in color proofing processes and markets, and in the database of tone and color reproduction information which need updating.

The number of studies of the factors affecting color reproduction have been accelerating and the information developed has led to a better understanding of color printing and the role of color proofing in it. The main studies have been the GCA SPECTRUM tests to check SWOP specifications. These have been expanded to include halftone gravure and gray component replacement (GCR). In addition, there have been some changes in color proofing systems; the manufacturing and marketing of one process has been changed; and six new processes have been introduced.

Many of the results of the SPECTRUM studies were anticipated and were reported in the text related to the measurement and control of tone and color reproduction mainly in Chapters III and X. These parts of the book, therefore, will need a minimum of additions except for the effects the SPECTRUM studies have had on the revision of the color specifications for web offset and gravure periodical printing. The GCR studies are in early organizational stages and it is too soon to report any significant results.

This UPDATE summarizes the changes these studies and effects have produced. Rather than disturb the text, which would have caused additional delays, it was decided to prepare a separate section for all the additions and changes to the text. These are described and discussed in this section by chapter and subject in the order in which they apply to, or modify, the text.

Chapter II — The Color Reproduction Process

The demand for color printing of all types continues to accelerate as single color printing declines. This trend has significantly increased the use of electronic scanning for color separation and correction. The number of electronic scanners in use worldwide has grown to over 8,000. About 25% of them are in the U.S.A., accounting for almost 80% of the color separations made; about the same number of scanners are in Japan doing over 90% of the color separations there; and almost 45% are in Europe, where over 80% of the separations are made on scanners. They are an important part of the prepress equipment of practically all trade shops, and large and medium size printing plants.

New lower cost, entry level electronic color scanners, that can be upgraded later, have been introduced by Crosfield, Hell, and Dainippon Screen for use by smaller printing plants, newspapers, and in-plant printers. Lower cost, entry level color electronic prepress systems (CEPS) have also been introduced by Crosfield, Hell, Scitex and Dainippon Screen. This proliferation of scanners and CEPS will not only expand the use of color reproduction but will greatly increase the demand for off-press color proofing systems and operators who can use them properly and interpret the proofs and their comparisons with press prints correctly.

Chapter IV — Press Proofing

There have been no changes in press color proofing equipment and systems for lithography, letterpress and flexography. Meanwhile, press proofing for gravure is undergoing many changes generated by the introduction and increased use of halftone gravure. GTA has made a change in ink standards for printing on coated magazine paper. The GTA Group V standard has been supplemented with the GTA Group VI standard which uses inks with *hues* similar to those of SWOP inks. Practically all press proofing for halftone gravure is being done by trade shops on offset presses using SWOP inks and Fortune Gloss paper.

The matches between gravure press prints made with cylinders produced from halftone prints on electromechanical engravers and offset press proofs using plates made from the same halftones and printed with SWOP inks have been acceptable to most users. In fact, many users consider the matches superior to those possible with gravure press proofs. There are some occasional problems with dot gain on offset press proofs. Gravure printing does not have dot gain, per se, but has ink spread which is similar to dot spread, or gain, but is proportional throughout the tone scale. On the other hand, dot gain in offset printing reaches a maximum in the middletones (See Appendix C). This causes a slight distortion in the match between the tone reproduction curves of the gravure and offset press prints resulting in poor matches between some pairs of offset and gravure prints that have critical detail and contrast in the middletones.

Chapter VI — Integral (Single Sheet) Color Proofing Systems

This chapter is divided into four sections: Sensitized ink, direct transfer, adhesive polymer dry toner, and photographic processes. Changes have occurred in all the categories.

Sensitized Ink Color Proofing Systems

The sensitized ink color proofing systems discussed in the text are *Watercote*, *Kwik-Proof*, and *dr Color Proof* by Direct Reproduction Corp., and *Final Proof* by American Photo-Graphics Corp. There are no changes in the Watercote, Kwik-Proof and dr Color Proof processes. Final Proof, on the other hand, has been discontinued. A new process *Quadracolor* has been announced.

Quadracolor: At PRINT 85 Castcraft Industries, Inc. (Chicago, IL) introduced a new process similar to Final Proof called **Quadracolor**. It is produced on the actual printing paper using a special sealant. Like Final proof it uses Meyer Rods to accurately control the coating thicknesses of the ink/photopolymer mixtures on the sealed paper. After the coating is dried the base is exposed to the appropriate separation negative, developed with a water spray, dried and recoated with the next color ink/photopolymer mixture. This process is repeated for as many times as there are colors. Photopolymer inks can be mixed and matched from 62 base colors. Besides color proofing, the process is being promoted as a low cost design tool for decorating sample packages.

Direct Transfer Color Proofing Systems

The direct transfer systems described in the text are *Gevaproof* by Agfa Gevaert and *TransferKey* and *Matchprint* by 3M. There are no changes in any of these systems. Three new systems have been introduced: Matchprint II by 3M; Trans-Naps by Enco Printing Products; and Fuji Color Art.

Matchprint II: At Print 85, 3M introduced **Matchprint II** which produces prints that look the same whether they are made from negatives or positives of the same separations. Matchprint II differs from Matchprint in the base sheets used and the way the imaging films are transferred to the base sheets. Matchprint uses pressure sensitive coatings to adhere the color film to the yellow sheet and the composite of the four color films to the printing substrate. In Matchprint II the yellow color film is laminated with heat and pressure directly to a special base sheet, exposed to the appropriate separation film and processed. The sequence of operations is repeated with each color film until the proof is completed.

The order of color sequence is yellow, magenta, cyan and black — YMCK. Two special mounting bases are available: *Publication Base* which has the color and brightness of a publication grade printing paper with a brightness of about 72; and *Commercial Base* which simulates the color and brightness of a premium coated offset paper with a brightness of 81. SWOP pigments are available for both positive and negative processes. Average dot gain on the proofs is 24% for the 40% dot on a GATF 120 line screen color target. 3M also introduced Matchprint II for gravure at Print 85. This will be described in the section on Chapter VIII.

Enco Trans-Naps: This is a new off-press color proofing system introduced at Print 85 by Enco Printing Products Division of American Hoechst Corp. It is a single sheet transfer system that uses pigmented light sensitive coatings on films that are laminated to a special receiver sheet 0.007 inches thick dimensionally stable white polyester. The laminated film is exposed emulsion/emulsion to the appropriate separation negative using a photopolymer exposing lamp with a Kokomo filter after which it is processed by hand or in a NAPS/PAPS processor using a water base, non-combustible and odorless developing solution. The steps of laminating, exposing and processing are repeated with each separation film until the proof is complete.

Pigment hues and densities match SWOP specifications and proofs can be made with any sequence of colors. Dot gain is 20%-22% on the 40% step of the GATF 120 line color target. A second brighter base has been developed for commercial printing. Enco Trans-Naps is a simple color proofing system to execute as only three steps are involved: laminate, expose and process.

Fuji Color Art Proofing System: This is a new transfer type single sheet color proofing process developed by Fuji Photo Film Co. Ltd. and introduced at JP-85 Printing Equipment Exhibition in Japan in March 1985. It consists of individual pigmented photosensitive films which are exposed and processed and can be viewed like an overlay proof. The single sheet proof is produced by laminating the images from each separate film in succession onto a receiving sheet and from it to the actual printing paper. The final proof is a sandwich of the pigmented images in the light-hardened photosensitive layers on the actual printing base. A matte surface can be simulated by casting a matte pattern with a special matte cover film over the proof. The whole process takes about ten minutes for a B2 size (20x28 inches) proof.

The equipment and materials for making a Fuji Color Art Proof are:

- *Photosensitive Color Films:* CN-4, negative yellow; CN-M, negative magenta; CN-C, negative cyan; and CN-K, negative black. These consist of a polyester base, a stripping layer, a pigmented photosensitive color layer, and a protective film.
- *Intermediate Receiving Base:* CR-T Receiving film which consists of a polyester base, a photo adhesive polymer layer, and a protective film.
- *Proof Base:* Actual printing paper or other substrate. Sizes of bases are from A4 to B2 (8.3x11.7 inches to 20x28 inches).
- *Exposure frame* for room light exposure.
- *Fuji Color Art Processor CA 600P* with Color Art Developer CA-1 and Replenisher CA-1R.
- *Fuji Color Art Laminator CA 600T.*
- *Fuji Color Art Technical Kit* with Color Art control wedge CLD to calibrate and control exposures.

Procedure for making Fuji Color Art Proofs: There are five steps for making Fuji Color Art proofs. These are (1) exposure; (2) processing; (3) transfer of the color images from the individual films to the receiver base; (4) transfer of the composite image from the receiver base to the printing paper; and (5) overall exposure of the laminated sandwich of receiver sheet and printing substrate. There is a sixth optional step in case a matte surface is desired on the proof.

- *Exposure:* Color separation negatives are exposed in room light emulsion/emulsion on the Color Art films with the protective films in place. Dot gain can be controlled by exposure.
- *Processing:* After exposure the protective film is removed and the pigmented photosensitive coating is processed in an alkaline developer CA-1 in the Color Art Processor CA 600P. The processing removes the unexposed coating leaving the light hardened pigmented image and the stripping layer on the polyester base. Total processing time (dry to dry) including developing, masking and drying is one minute.
- *Transfer I:* The protective film is removed from the CR-T receiver base. The base is registered with the black Color Art film and the

black image is transferred to the base with heat and pressure in the Color Art Laminator CA 600T. The cyan, magenta and yellow images are transferred in succession and in that order to the receiver base in a similar manner.

- *Transfer II:* After all the images are transferred to the receiver base it is registered with the printing substrate and fed into the laminator where the composite four images are transferred to the printing substrate.
- *Post Exposure:* After transfer an overall exposure is given to the sandwich of the receiver base and printing substrate. This exposure hardens the photo adhesive layer in the receiver base which facilitates removal of the film support of the receiver base from the proof.
- *Matte Surface:* The surface of the proof is glossy after the base is removed. It can be converted to a matte finish by casting a matte pattern with a special matte film to the surface of the proof using the laminator.

The total time to carry out all these steps to produce a Color Art proof is ten minutes.

The system, which is in use in Japan is negative and is balanced for Japanese standard inks. A positive system has been developed as well as pigments to match inks for the U.S. and European markets. Also, special products are being developed for use by package designers, and for special markets like small lots of displays, signs, advertising panels, counter cards and point-of-purchase displays.

Adhesive Polymer/Dry Toner Color Proofing Systems

The adhesive polymer/dry toner systems described in the text are *Cromalin* and *Spectra*. Significant changes have occurred in both systems. At PRINT 85 DuPont introduced two new *Cromalin* products: *Masterproof* and *Quickproofer*. *Spectra* manufacturing and marketing have been changed from Keuffel and Esser and Heidelberg Eastern to Sage Technology (San Diego, CA).

Cromalin Masterproof: This is the name for a new color proofing system to replace the present positive and negative Cromalin processes. The new system is a balanced combination of sensitized films, toners and receptors to produce nearly identical color proofs from positive and negative separations of the same subject. Current sensitized films are used for both the positive and negative processes. Present toners are used for the positive process and new toners have been produced for the negative process. The biggest change is in the receptor base. A new brighter base is used for both processes which produces better highlights, matched backgrounds and higher contrast. This base provides a good match for commercial printing. A new base has been developed for publication printing.

The **Quickproofer** introduced at Print 85 is a prototype machine for expanding the automation of the Cromalin proofing process. The new machine was shown to test the market demand for such a product. It automates the laminating and exposure steps of the Cromalin process. Combined with the automatic toning machines the Cromalin proofing process can now be almost completely automated, thus cutting Cromalin proof-making time almost in half.

Spectra was sold by Kratos, parent company of Keuffel and Esser, to Sage Technology (San Diego, CA) in January 1985. At the same time marketing of the color proofing system was transferred from Heidelberg Eastern to Sage. In the meantime Polaroid Corporation has invested in Sage Technology; new equipment is being designed for coating Spectra films; and plans are being developed to automate some of the steps in the production of the Spectra proofs. As soon as these plans are completed the process will return to its former potential.

Photographic Color Proofing Systems

Only one photographic color proofing process is described in Chapter VI of the text. It is the Kodak Ektaflex PCT Color Proofing System. No significant changes have been made in this process, its materials or equipment. A new photographic color proofing process that eliminates many of the deficiencies of other photographic processes was mentioned but could not be described because of patent restrictions. Since the text was written, a patent has been issued on the process, so it can now be described.

TM Color Proof Process: This is a new photographic color proofing system developed by J. Tom Morgan, Jr. who wrote the Foreword to this book. It is marketed by his new company, Morgan Enterprises (Columbus, Georgia 31901). The process uses color paper like Kodak Ektacolor, or similar color papers by 3M and Fuji Photo Film Company. It utilizes ingenious combinations of photographic negatives and positives, and special dye transfer images, to produce color proofs with a full extended range of tones, midtone dot gain and color hues that match the press print.

The materials and equipment for making a TM Color Proof are:
- Color photographic papers like Kodak Ektacolor, Fuji Color Paper and 3M.

- Diffuser sheet for diffusing image during exposure.
- Vacuum frame with register pins for exposure.
- Model 232 EP-2/DURA by Hope or similar processor.
- LogE Multiflex 9100 programmable light source described in the text with equipment used for exposing Kodak Ektaflex color proofs. The light system has been modified with a different light source and a shutter for more accurate short exposures and gear track for easy access.
- Dye transfer matrices, dyes and trays for correcting hue errors of dyes to match printing inks.

Procedures for making TM Color Proofs: The main deficiencies of photographic color proofing systems are: (1) They are continuous tone so they cannot reproduce the structure of halftone images; and (2) The yellows are too orange, magentas too blue and cyans too yellow, so they cannot match SWOP and other printing ink colors. The TM Process corrects these deficiencies in ingenious ways: using multiple exposures to extend the tone range of halftone subjects and dye transfer images to correct for the hue errors in the dye-coupled dyes in photographic color images. To accomplish the correction for these two deficiencies, the process uses a number of materials and steps not necessary in other processes but still can, after punched negatives and/or positives are contacted, produce proofs easily in not much more than twenty minutes, ten minutes of which are for color processing.

Following are the steps used to produce a TM Color Proof not requiring ink hue corrections beyond the range of hues in the dye-coupled dyes. Most of the steps are carried out in a dark room in total darkness.

- *Color Separations:* Pin register is used throughout the process. Both negative and positive of the same separations are used. Type and necessary cropping can be added when contacting. If a camera is used to make the separations, contact positives are made from the separation negatives. If a scanner is used, contact negatives are made from the separation positives.
- *Calibration and Programming of Exposures:* Filter exposures of the programmable light source are derived by comparing the 3x3 color sets (densitometer readings of the yellow, magenta, and cyan colors through the red, green and blue filters) of each of the three printing inks with that of the dye-coupled dyes in the color paper. Required hue changes are obtained by split-filter and neutral density filter combinations.
- *Exposure of Color Photographic Paper:* The blue filter or yellow printer negative is placed in emulsion/emulsion contact with the color photographic paper in the vacuum frame. The frame is closed,

the vacuum is drawn and an exposure is made with the calibrated programmed light source. The frame is opened, the diffuser sheet is placed over the negative and the yellow positive is placed on the register pins over the diffusion sheet. The frame is closed, vacuum is drawn and an exposure is given to the multiple films of sufficient length to produce the proper amount of dot gain in the midtones. The main purpose of the multiple exposure is to extend the range of the halftone tints into the highlight area of the tone scale without closing of the dots in the shadows.

After the two exposures are made for the yellow layer of the color paper, the yellow negative and positive are removed from the frame and the magenta negative is placed on the pins in register with the color paper. The frame is closed, vacuum is drawn and the proper exposure is made for the magenta after which the frame is opened, diffusion sheet and magenta positive are inserted over the negative and the extended range and dot gain exposure is made for the magenta. The same procedure is followed for the cyan. If a short range or skeleton black is used, the secondary positive exposure for the black is not necessary.

- *Processing:* After all exposures are made, the color paper is processed in the automatic processor. After ten minutes in the processor, the proof is completed.

If the ink hue correction needed for the proof is beyond the range, or gamut of hues of the dye-coupled dyes in the color paper, a dye transfer technique has been added to the TM Color Proof procedure. The dye transfer soluble dyes are used to correct for the hue errors in the insoluble dye-coupled dyes. These are the steps to make such a proof.

- *Color Separations:* In addition to the full range negative and positive of each color separation, a short range positive or negative separation is made of the color to be corrected which is usually the yellow. The range of dots in the short range separation is from 66% to 100%. Contact negatives or positives are made of the short range separations.
- *Exposure:* Calibration of the exposing light is made as in the previously described procedure. Exposure of the colors that will not be corrected is also done exactly like the previously described procedure. Exposure of the colors to be corrected is done by first placing the short scale halftone positive on top of the negative and then the diffusion sheet, closing the frame, drawing the vacuum and switching on the calibrated light. After the first exposure, the frame is opened and the full range positive is placed over the sandwich of the full range separation negative, short range positive, and diffusion sheet. The frame is closed, vacuum is drawn and the exposure is made for the extended range and dot gain. This

procedure is used for all the colors that need to be corrected which are usually the yellow, sometimes the magenta to match SWOP specifications, and occasionally the cyan.

- *Processing:* The processing is done the same as previously described. Examination of the print shows unusual shadow areas of the colors corresponding to the short range positive. What the short range positives do is provide a descending tone value in the dye-coupled print at 66% to no color at all in the solids. The proper color tone values are then inserted in these areas by dye transfer

- *Dye Transfer:* A dye transfer matrix of the color to be inserted is made from the short range halftone negative of the color and it is immersed in the appropriate dye for the proper time. The dye transfer matrix is squeegeed in register with the dye-coupled print. The dye transfers from the matrix to the print in the areas corresponding to those that were not exposed in the dye-coupled print. The dye transfer dyes are soluble and blend with the coupled dyes which are insoluble. The gelatin of the color paper acts as an imbibition surface for the dye transfer dyes. If more than one color is corrected, a dye transfer matrix is made for each color and the dyes are all transferred in succession onto the dye-coupled print.

Despite the large number of steps, most of which are automated and take longer to describe than to carry out, the TM Color Proof Process is easily taught and takes only twenty minutes to do, half of which are for the automatic processing. Materials and equipment costs are nominal. The process is simple to use and well suited to the needs of medium and smaller size commercial and in-plant printers and the trade shops that serve them. It should find considerable use in these important and growing segments of the printing industry.

Chapter VII — Electrostatic Color Proofing Systems

KC-Color Proof: The name of the KC-Color Proofing System has been changed to COULTERcolor. The ACP-III COULTERcolor Proofing system was formally introduced and demonstrated at PRINT 85. A number of systems are operating in the U.S., Australia and Germany.

Kimoto Kimofax Color Proof: This is an electrostatic single sheet color proofing system by Kimoto (Japan) using an organic photoconductor and dry toners. It has limited resolution and is used mainly for color proofing line subjects such as maps.

Chapter VIII — Gravure Proofing

As already stated in the section on Chapter IV, color proofing for gravure has changed radically since the introduction of halftone gravure. One of the main reasons halftone gravure is so popular and successful is its ability to use conventional offset press and off-press color proofing systems with minor modifications. Another reasons is its coupling with electromechanical engraving and the design of new scanning heads that eliminate moire at screen rulings as low as 120 lines per inch (48 lines per cm). In addition, compatibility between lithography and gravure has been improved by the adoption of new color standards for magazine printing on coated stock by GTA which are similar to SWOP specifications. The new standards are known as GTA Group VI Color Inks. These new inks will eventually replace the GTA Group V Color Inks. The new standards are described in the section on Chapter X.

DuPont has modified its Cromalin toners to match gravure standards. 3M has introduced a new Positive Matchprint II Gravure Proof System that matches Group V inks. They already have the Positive Matchprint II that matches SWOP inks. The Gravure Matchprint II is similar to the Matchprint II Positive process except that the recommended color sequence for gravure is cyan, yellow, magenta, and black — CYMK.

Chapter IX — Digital Color Proofing

The area of most intensive action in off-press color proofing has been in direct digital color proofing, particularly hard copy proofing. At a conference on Direct Digital Color Proofing in February 1985 sponsored by the Research and Engineering Council of the Graphic Arts, the systems for soft and hard copy proofing were discussed and it was universally agreed that soft proofs were not adequate simulations of the press print. They are very useful as internal quality control and verification tools in the preparation of color reproductions but are not acceptable to the customer or the trade shop/printing plant as predictions of the press prints. All agreed, there is no substitute for a hard proof on a substrate like paper, in pigments or dyes similar to the colors of the printing inks, yellow, magenta, cyan and black, in place of the red, green and blue pixels of the video display screen. It should be a proof that can be signed by the customer and used by the pressroom as the guide for arriving at an OK sheet for the printed job.

The digital color proofing systems described in Chapter IX are Hazeltine SP1620 and TOPPAN SC525 soft proofing systems and Hell Color Proof Recorder CPR 403, LogE/Dunn VersaColor Proof Camera, and MacDonald-Dettwiler/Polaroid Instant Fire 240 Color Proofing System. No changes have occurred in the TOPPAN SC525, Hell CPR 403, and LogE/Dunn VersaColor Camera proof processes. Hazeltine

SP1620 has been sold to W&B Commercial Graphics Ltd. and is part of the PagePlanner Color Systems Division.

The PagePlanner Scanalyzer 2001 scanner presetting and soft color proofing system was introduced at PRINT 85. The MacDonald-Dettwiler/Polaroid Instant Fire 240 was used both as a digital hard copy proofing system by Crosfield and a means of producing hard copy color and press corrected second originals. A new larger format digital color proof system was introduced by MacDonald—Dettwiler/Polaroid called the Instant Fire 300. This was demonstrated at the Scitex booth at PRINT 85 along with a Matrix QCR color camera and an ink-jet color proofing system by Tektronix. IRIS Model 2044 Ink Jet Color Printer was introduced in November, 1985 for making off-press color proofs of images as large as 34x44 inches.

PagePlanner Scanalyzer 2001 Scanner Pre-setting and Soft Color Proofing System

The Scanalyzer 2001 is a lower cost replacement for the Scanner Interface in the Hazeltine system. It has a console with high resolution CRT that is claimed to reproduce the color gamut of most printing inks and interface with most scanners to provide the scanner operator a reasonably accurate preview of the scanned image before committing the scanner to film. After setting the scanner, a fast scan (30 seconds) is made and viewed on the Scanalyzer CRT. If not satisfactory, settings can be adjusted and another fast scan made and viewed. This process can be repeated until the image is satisfactory before making the separation films. The Scanalyzer can also be used to simulate paper, ink and printing conditions to produce a soft proof of what the scanned image will look like when printed on the press.

Several levels of software sophistication are available to allow the Scanalyzer 2001 to interface with: (1) multiple scanners of different manufacture; (2) "Multi-Stor" video tape for storage and retrieval of up to 99 color images; (3) mag tape storage for set up information of up to 99 images with LED readout; (4) line printer for hard copy transfer, remote monitors, gradation and ink density controls; and (5) split screen images to compare corrections. A design and development effort has been undertaken to add a hard copy output device to the Scanalyzer 2001.

Polaroid/MacDonald-Dettwiler Instant Fire 300 High Speed Color Proofing System

Like the Polaroid/MacDonald-Dettwiler Color Fire 240 described in Chapter IX, the Instant Fire 300 accepts digital data from a color electronic prepress system (CEPS) and produces one- or two-page color proofs ready for evaluation in less than 10 minutes. With a larger format size (12.2x18.5 inches — 310x470 mmm) the system's main components are: a high-quality direct digital film recorder similar to the one for the Color Fire 240 described in the text; a real-time color transform circuit, an automatic film processor, and Polaroid Polacolor Instant Color Proofing Film.

The film recorder, designed by MacDonald-Dettwiler, reads ink-on-paper image data stored in the CEPS' disk and writes it onto the proofing film. The color transform circuit, by Polaroid, resides in the film recorder and calculates the red, green and blue exposure values for each picture element (pixel) of the image in real-time as it is being read off the disk and written onto the color film. The color transform assures accuracy of the color match between the proof and press print by compensating for the color characteristics of the inks, paper, proofing film, film recorder's filters, light source, press conditions and spectral properties of the viewing illumination.

After the film is exposed it passes into the instant film processor and the finished proof is ready in less than two minutes. The whole process for a one- or two-page proof requires less than ten minutes, in which time the system processes over 100MB of information. It has the speed and accuracy to process data relayed from a satellite and received in multiple locations around the country. This system has the same limitations as the Hell CPR403 Color Proof Recorder. The images are in 3-color continuous tone so they lack the structure of press printed images, and the dyes have different color gamuts than the printing inks. The yellows especially, are too orange.

Matrix QCR D4/2 Quality Color Recorder

This is a compact color film recorder manufactured by Matrix Instruments, Inc. (Orangeburg, NY 10962). It is similar in design and operation to the LogE/Dunn VersaColor camera described in the text. The recorder can produce color slides and continuous tone color prints from digital data. At PRINT 85 it was in the Scitex booth and produced digital color proofs on Polacolor Instant color paper of comparable quality to other color photographic proofs. The system on display had a size limitation of 8x10 inches (203x254 mm) and, like other digital color proofing systems using color photographic papers, the proofs were in three colors and continuous tone.

Ink Jet Color Printers

Ink jet printing is a means of producing images on plain paper or other substrates using drops of very fluid inks, like fountain pen inks, and some type of digital image transform to control the flow of the drops from nozzles to form images on the paper. Common examples of such systems are A.B. Dick Videojet and Kodak Diconix which are used for addressing and coding. There are two main types of ink jet printing systems in use: (1) *continuous jet* and (2) *drop-on-demand*. In the continuous jet type electrostatic charges modulated by digital data are used to control the drops so they print in the proper place on the paper. In the drop-on-demand type, the drops are formed and eject from a nozzle on demand according to digital commands from a computer or digital storage medium. Both these types of ink-jet systems have been used to design ink jet color proofing systems.

Tektronix 4692 Color Ink Jet Printer: This is an ink-on-demand type of ink-jet printer at a reasonably low OEM cost that can convert digital data to a 4-color proof in A4 size (8¼x11⅝ inch — 210x297 mm) in less than one minute. The ink drops, projected at 40,000 per second, produce color images in which colors, register, color breaks, crossovers and other critical image characteristics can be readily identified and verified. Specially coated paper is used in which the coating reacts with the dye in the ink to increase its light fastness. The image is produced by dots which all have approximately the same size but vary in spacing to create the illusion of gradient tones. This is not the same structure as a printed image but it creates a similar visual effect.

The Tektronix ink jet printer was operating in the Scitex booth at PRINT 85. The prints appeared grainy which was blamed on the digital data used to produce them. Despite this, the speed with which the print can be made, its relatively low cost, and its ability to discriminate colors and other critical image characteristics can make it a valuable tool for many verification and internal quality checking applications in prepress systems and as a communication medium between remote terminals.

IRIS Model 2044 Ink Jet Color Printer: This is a continuous binary ink jet type of color printer with four nozzles (yellow, magenta, cyan, and black) issuing 1,000,000 droplets per second per nozzle from digital data capable of producing 4-color images in sizes up to 34x44 inches (864mmx1118mm) in 2 to 30 minutes depending on size, color saturation and resolution of the image. Output can be on plain paper, mylar and flexible materials. The inks are water soluble, non-toxic dyes. Drop size is claimed to be 15 to 20 micrometers (0.0006-0.0008 inch). The drops, however, spread when they hit the paper so the drop size in the image is much larger (up to 100 micrometers or 0.004 inch). Two resolutions are available: **high** which is 240 dots per inch; and **medium** which is 120 dots per inch. This is the order of resolution in high quality copying machines, which is somewhat coarse for high quality (magazine) graphic arts picture and typographic quality. The speed of the system, size of image and digital imaging capability make this an attractive system for many uses for hard copy color proofs.

Prospects for Digital Color Hard Copy Proofing Systems

Other Digital hard copy color proofing systems are in various stages of development. There are not many color imaging technologies that can be activated digitally or electronically and can produce images with the structure of printed subjects and the necessary resolution [at least 1,500 lines per inch (600 lines per cm) for 150 line screen (60 lines per cm)]. Color imaging technologies that can be activated digitally include photography, ink jet, impact ribbon, thermal transfer, mechanical ink plotter, ion deposition, photoencapsulation, and electrophotography (electrostatics). Of these, only photography has the light-sensitivity and resolution to satisfy printing requirements but all existing color photographic processes are 3-color dye images on gelatin coated paper which do not have the feel of printed images and all but one are continuous tone which do not match the structure of printed images.

Electrophotographic systems have the light sensitivity but at present only one system has the necessary resolution. It is the COULTER-color ACP III process which uses vacuum sputtered cadium sulfide as the photoconductor. This has the spectral sensitivity for exposure by blue lasers like Argon ion or Helium/Cadium (He/Cd), high exposure speed, and very high resolution potential — over 500 lines pairs/mm which is equivalent to halftone reproductions with screen rulings over 1,000 lines/inch (400 lines/cm) that are way beyond the capability of any printing system. Coulter Systems Corp. is developing a laser engine to transform digital data from any CEPS into input to a modified ACP III color proofer. At the R&E Digital Color Proofing Conference in February 1985 both DuPont and 3M representatives admitted publicly that their companies were working on digital color proofing systems but they declined to discuss any details about them.

Chapter X — How to Compare Color Proofs and Press Prints

Chapter X contains information on how to analyze and standardize printing and proofing so that proofs and press prints can be matched with reasonable consistency, reproducibility and predictability. This involves the use of color control strips, their measurements, analysis and interpretation and the setting of industry segment standards and specifications.

Since Chapter X was written, a number of new systems and instruments have been introduced for measuring and controlling color measurements on and off the press; new SWOP specifications and GTA color ink standards have been adopted; the GCA/GATF Proof Comparator has been revised; another GCA/SPECTRUM test has been run and reported; and DuPont has reported on a North American Print Survey conducted over a two year period.

Color Measurement Systems

The systems described in Chapter X are plate scanners and press ink-setting and pre-makeready systems by Heidelberg, MAN-Roland, Dainippon Printing Co., and Perretta; off-line color measurement and control systems by Heidelberg, MAN-Roland, Tobias, and Gretag; and on-line systems by Macbeth and IGT. At PRINT 85, improvements and modifications were shown in all these systems and new ones were introduced by Macbeth, Cosar, Hunterlab and Graphics West Micro Systems.

Macbeth: Macbeth (Newburgh, NY) introduced three new systems at PRINT 85 based on the use of the new PXD981 scanning densitometer head. One was the *Microdot* for scanning sheets from a sheet-fed press; the other two included the *Press Control System* for web offset printing which can be fitted with an auxiliary *Ink Activation Module* that converts it to an *Automated Closed-Loop Press Control System*.

The *Macbeth Microdot* is a rugged console instrument that can read press targets or images on sheets up to 55 inches (1,400 mm) wide. (A larger version for sheets up to 78 inches [1,980 mm] is available.) It is programmed for most of the control strip formats and displays the information on density, dot gain, trapping, and other press factors on a color monitor. The heart of the system is the new scanning densitometer head PXD981 which has exclusive narrow band (SPI) responses that match the spectrophotometric curves of the process inks. Also it is the only scanning densitometer head to use a pulsed xenon light source for non-contact measurement, that freezes movement and eliminates the effects of ambient light.

The *Macbeth Press Control System* is similar to the *Microdot* except that it is an on-press system and the readings are made in real-time directly on the press while the job is running. There are two PXD981 scanning densitometers arranged to read targets on both sides of the web. The system is claimed to speed up makereadies, improve run consistency, and reduce waste. It measures and alerts the pressman to variations in (1) *ink film thickness* which are claimed to produce 25% of all print defects; (2) *ink trapping* which account for 15% of print defects; and (3) *ink/water balance* which cause 20% of all print defects.

The *Macbeth Ink Activation Module* is an accessory for the Press Control System that uses *artificial intelligence* (AI) to convert it to a fully automatic closed-loop press control system. The module is programmed with specific parameter information about the offset process and calculations pertaining to a range of color variables derived from a database of over ten years' experience with an on-press densitometer on web offset presses.

By using an array of optical and electronic sensors and adding exploratory problem solving routines an artificial intelligence approach has been developed which allows the Ink Actuation Module to drive the press to what Macbeth calls a *True Production Balance* by the most direct path possible. This is equivalent in most cases to the *Color OK* which can be overridden by the pressman to accommodate inferior separations or to satisfy a customer's personal color preference. This is the first approach to closed loop operation of an offset press that shows some promise of success.

Cosar Autosmart Densitometer is a new high speed scanning densitometer which has the unique feature of being programmable to measure both color strips and anywhere within the image on the printed sheet and the ability to calculate and analyze the printing for defects that affect its quality and consistency. The capability to make readings in critical image areas allows analysis and control of color printing on sheets where color bars or strips are not used or possible because of space limitations.

Graphics West Micro Systems (Van Nuys, CA) has introduced a set of new instruments including a plate scanner and a closed loop ink setting device that can be used on any sheet fed press. The ink setter automatically sets ink fountain keys according to measurements made on printed sheets and compares them with preset values or densities measured on the *Color OK sheet*.

Hunterlab (Hunter Associates Laboratory, Reston, VA 22090) has introduced the first colorimeter for measurement of color specifically aimed at graphic arts. 85. This system, known as the Process Image Color Control System (PICCS 2200), consists of an IBM PC/XT computer; a spectrophotometer, which measures the reflectance of the color [spot size from 0.25 inch (6.35 mm) to 1.75 inch (44.5 mm)]; and a data processor with CRT display. The instrument is provided with an external printer for permanent records, as well as a number of illuminants (including 5000°K) and color scales. Measurements are made in critical printing areas using a method of area averaging which has been successful in analyzing color variations in printing.

The color space used is CIE Lab, in which colorimetric measurements are more accurate for comparing colors than a densitometer, as the colorimeter measures color as the eye sees it. Such an instrument is very useful in applications where the accuracy of logo, trademark and product colors is important. It is almost indispensable for the measurement of subjects with dissimilar colorants such as in the comparison of an off-press color proof made with toners or dyes and a press print made with printing inks which situation happens when an off-press color proof is used as the color guide for a press OK sheet.

SWOP Specifications

As pointed out in Chapter X, SWOP (Specifications for Web Offset Publications) were adopted in 1975 and there have been three minor revisions since, in 1977, 1978 and 1981. A new major revision has been developed based on recommendations resulting from the GCA/ SPECTRUM Tests of 1982, 1983 and 1984. These recommendations include limits for overall ink coverage, density, screen rulings, dot gain, gray balance, print contrast and viewing conditions.

Dot gain is the most important printing characteristic not included in the present specifications. Dot gain windows have been recommended for proofs and web publication printing; for proofs and prints made from negatives and from positives; and for images with 133 and 150 lines per inch screen rulings. This includes limits for allowable variations in dot gain between colors in the same subject to maintain gray balance. In addition to these parameters, one set of viewing conditions (5000°K) is being considered along with density limits commensurate with GCA/SPECTRUM test results.

It is interesting to note that the recommendations include limits for all parameters that agree closely with proposed European specifications by FIPP (International Federation of the Periodical Press) and FOGRA (the West German Graphic Arts Research Institute, Munich, W. Germany). Agreement between these groups suggests that consistency in dot gain and other print parameters is a goal that can be realistically achieved by specification and control.

GTA Color Specifications

Since the GTA Color Charts were first introduced in 1960 they have had major revisions in 1973, 1981, and 1983. With the advent of *Halftone Gravure* they have had another major revision in 1985. There have been two sets of color specifications for publications: Group I for newspaper supplements which are printed on newsprint with GTA Standard Group I Inks; and Group V for magazines which are printed on coated stock using GTA Standard Group V Inks.

Printers and tradeshops working with halftone gravure soon found that offset press proofs made with SWOP inks and off-press proofs made with SWOP pigments or toners produced a better match with gravure press prints than press or off-press proofs made with inks, pigments or toners that match Group V inks. It was, therefore, decided to develop a new standard for halftone gravure known as GTA Standard Group VI Inks. These inks have hues which closely resemble the pigments in SWOP inks.

The use of the cleaner SWOP colors will provide halftone gravure with an additional asset as it will be capable of printing brighter cleaner colors than web offset even though both use inks with the same hues. This is because the ink-spread in gravure printing allows the inks to cover more of the area of the paper thus eliminating much of the light absorption in the paper between the image elements (dots) that causes dirtying of the colors of halftone tints in printing by lithography and letterpress (flexography).

GCA/GATF Proof Comparator

The GCA/GATF Proof Comparator described in Chapter X has been gaining acceptance. It has been used in the GCA/SPECTRUM tests for 1984 and 1985. Significant changes have been proposed as a result of these tests. The screen ruling in the picture and color bars will be changed from 120 to 133 lines per inch and the color bars will contain four levels of tints instead of three — 25%, 50%, 75% and 100% instead of 10%, 40% and 100%. In addition a reference comparator subscription service is being considered that will provide new reference color proofs of the pictures and color bars at six month intervals, like the SWOP Standard Color and High-Low References.

DuPont North American Print Survey

The flood of new technology in the printing industry has prodded all segments of the industry to get a better understanding of the printing process and the factors that affect it. Proofing and printing have been particularly affected as these are where the final results are predicted and produced. Recognizing the need for more understanding of the printing process and the factors that can affect the correlations between proofing and printing, the Technical Resource Group of The Printing Systems Division of DuPont undertook a most extensive two year survey of the printing industry in North America. The survey provides average values of ink properties, solid ink densities, and midtone dot gain for the proofing and production aspects of sheet fed and web printing derived from the analysis of over 700 printed sheets.

Measurement Techniques: Measurements were based on the CRO-MALIN Offset Com Guide/System Brunner Test Form together with the Brunner Print Control Strip. All halftone elements measured had a 150 line screen ruling. Densities were read with a Macbeth RD-918 densitometer with SPI narrow band filters and 4mm aperture. Effective dot area and dot gain were calculated using the Murray-Davies equation which integrated both mechanical and optical dot gain. All information on printing conditions and type of market served were supplied by the printer. In particular, the printer declared if he was printing proofs according to SWOP specifications. Table U-1 shows the breakdown of the number of sheets analyzed, by industry segment. The web publication data was largely obtained by cooperation with GCA during the SPECTRUM print property tests.

TABLE U-1
Types of Printing Analyzed

Printing Segments	Types of Plates	
	Negative	Positive
SHEET-FED		
Proofing	125	70
SWOP	88	54
Production	154	32
WEB OFFSET		
Commercial	23	27
Publication	72	37

Ink Color Properties: All colors were plotted for hue and grayness on the GATF Color Circle according to the procedure outlined in Appendix A. The cyan, magenta and yellow inks used to print SWOP proofs and web publication prints were fairly tightly clustered showing good adherence to SWOP specifications. The overprints, on the other hand, showed a fairly wide distribution, due to effects of differing solid ink densities, ink transparency and trapping. As expected, sheet-fed production and commercial web printing which were not printed to SWOP specifications showed wider distributions of ink and overprint hues particularly in the greens and blues. Ink sequence was also studied. Table U-2 shows the comparison between the sequences: yellow, magenta, cyan (YMC), and cyan, magenta, yellow (CMY) with black (K) printed anywhere in the sequence, usually either first or last.

TABLE U-2
Ink Sequence

Printing Segments	Sequence	
	(YMC)K	(CMY)K
SHEET-FED		
Proofing	25%	62%
Production	6%	84%
WEB OFFSET		
Commercial	—	100%
Publication	3%	97%

Solid Ink Densities: Solid Ink Densities were measured across the sheet on the Brunner Print Control Strip. Density variations over the sheet ranged from 0.066 for proofs to 0.088 for web publications and approximately 0.10 between printers. Solid ink densities for SWOP proofs were mostly within the SWOP High-Low ink references. Deviations were usually on the side of higher densities.

Dot Gain: The midtone dot gain values in this survey were measured on a 150 line per inch elliptical dot screen. The dot gain measurements were found to vary proportionally with the screen ruling: e.g. a dot gain of 26% on a 150 l. screen was equivalent to a dot gain of 21% on a 120 l. screen. Studies were made for all the segments using plates made from negatives and plates from positives. Isocontour drawings were made of the all the tests. The results for the averages of midtone (50% dot) dot gain in all the segments are shown in Table U-3.

TABLE U-3
Midtone Dot Gain Averages by Segment

Printing Segments	Types of Plates	
	Negative	Positive
SHEET-FED		
All Proofs	18.6	17.2
SWOP Proofs	19.0	16.6
Production	20.2	17.2
WEB OFFSET		
Commercial	24.7	19.3
Publication	26.8	18.9

The ranges of variation in dot sizes from the averages in all instances was about +/- 4%. The differences in dot gain between printing from negative and positive plates is due to plate characteristics.

Images on plates made from positive films are sharper because light undercuts the image during exposure. Images on plates made from negative films are fuller as the light spreads during exposure. This difference between the two types of plates accounts for some of the increasing popularity of positive plates — they print with less dot gain. Another reason is that positive photopolymer plates are capable of longer runs on the press by baking the polymer after exposure and processing of the plate.

One important factor in the control of color printing was not covered in this survey. This is the variation in dot gain between colors on the same subject which, if too great, upsets *gray balance* and causes color hue shifts. A total variation of 8% in midtone dot gain such as was found in these studies, is too large and can cause serious gray balance and color hue shift problems. It has been found in the GCA/SPECTRUM tests that if the variations in midtone dot gain between colors on the same subject does not exceed 4% or +/- 2% from the average, gray balance and color hue shifts are barely noticeable and should not cause serious color matching problems.

More information on the DuPont North American Print Survey is available from the DuPont Technical Resource Group, Printing Systems Division, Wilmington, DE 19898.

Elementary Principles of Color For Color Reproduction

Color reproduction by a printing process consists of converting a color original into separate elements, which when made into printing surfaces or plates and printed with colored inks on a substrate, usually white paper, produce a reproduction that resembles the original from which it was made. To accomplish this the photographer who converts the original into the color separations, the printer who makes the plates and prints them with colored inks on the substrate, and the color proofer who tries to predict the end result, must all be thoroughly familiar with the basic principles of color and how they relate to the products and processes used in the reproduction system.

The photographer uses color sensitive photographic films, color filters, and lights of varying color temperatures — all of which affect the color responses of the operations he performs. The printer uses colored inks and substrates, whose color absorptions and reflections also affect the color of the reproduction. The color proofer tries to match all these color responses with materials that often differ widely from those used in the printing. Therefore, the understanding of color principles and the control of color functions by measurement are indispensable to the successful and efficient operation of any color reproduction system.

Color and Light

Color is as important a discriminating feature or physical property of objects as linear dimensions, area, volume, or mass. It is impossible to have color without light. Therefore, many of the characteristics of color depend on the properties of light.

Light is a form of radiant energy which occupies a narrow band in what is known as the electromagnetic spectrum that includes all forms of radiant energy, from the very short cosmic, gamma, and x-rays to the longer ultraviolet rays, visible light, infrared, and radio waves (Figure A-1, page C-11). All radiant energy consists of tiny bursts of electromagnetic energy that behave as particles, called quanta or photons. The waves are transverse, similar to those produced when a stone is thrown into water.

The different types of electromagnetic energy vary in *wavelength* (the distance from the crest of one wave to the crest of the next) and *frequency* (the number of waves that pass a point in a given period of time), but they all travel at the same speed in a vacuum — 30 billion centimeters (cm) per second or 186,284 miles per second. As the wavelength increases, the frequency decreases, and vice versa. Wavelengths of electromagnetic radiation range from less than one trillionth of a centimeter for cosmic rays to over 500 million centimeters or 3100 miles for the waves from a 60-cycle (hertz) electric motor. The wavelength range from 380 to 760 nanometers (nm) is the visible portion of the electromagnetic spectrum (1 nm = 0.0000001 cm). The angstrom unit (Å) is another unit of wavelength, equal to 0.1 nm (1000 Å = 100 nm).

As visible light varies in wavelength and frequency it changes in color from violet for the shortest wavelengths to blue, green, yellow, orange, and finally red for the longest visible wavelengths (Figure A-2, page C-11). The violet end of the visible spectrum is bordered by the shorter invisible ultraviolet (UV) rays and the long red wavelength end is bordered by the longer invisible infrared (IR) rays. Wavelengths from about 4 nm to 380 nm are in the ultraviolet region of the spectrum. The waves in the range from 210 nm to 300 nm are useful in the absorption of Vitamin D by the body and can cause sunburn. The range from 300 nm to about 450 nm is useful in exposing UV and blue light-sensitive photographic and photomechanical (platemaking) emulsions or coatings.

Radiant energy having wavelengths from 760 nm to about 10 micrometers (μm) is known as infrared energy. (A micrometer, formerly known as a micron, is equal to one millionth of a meter, 1,000 nm, or 0.00004 inch.) Infrared rays with wavelengths up to 3.4 μm are used to set or dry inks.

Properties of Light

Light has a number of important properties. It can be transmitted, reflected, absorbed, and polarized — all properties which are important to the appearance of objects and to photography and graphic arts. The glass elements in lenses and the glass or plastic used for making light filters for photography transmit and absorb light.

Lens Coatings

Special thin coatings of metallic fluorides with thicknesses of about half a wavelength of light, are applied to the exposed glass elements of lenses to minimize the reflection of light by these surfaces. These coatings reduce the interreflections between lens elements, which cause lens flare. The bluish or gold color of the surface of a glass lens element is an indication that the element is coated.

Index of Refraction

When light passes at an angle from one medium into another of different density, its speed is changed and the beam is bent; in going from air into glass, for example, the speed is reduced almost one-third. The ratio of the speed of light in a medium to that in a vacuum is known as the *index of refraction* of the medium. In lens making, glasses for the various elements in the lens are specially selected with different indices of refraction to help correct for aberrations (errors) in the image-producing properties of the lenses.

Polarized Light

Light from a frosted incandescent lamp is made up of electromagnetic waves showing no particular preference for plane of vibration. Such illumination is said to be *non-polarized*. When such light is reflected from a shiny surface, such as glass, the reflection process removes some of the random rays, leaving a beam tending to oscillate more in one plane than another. A beam showing such preferred direction produces specular reflection and is polarized. Some natural crystals and some man-made sheet materials can cause an unpolarized beam to become polarized. Such a device is called a polarizer or polarizing filter, which can be used to eliminate unwanted reflections in photography.

Light Intensity

For photography and graphic arts applications, one of the most important properties of a light source is its intensity. The luminous flux, expressed in lumens per unit area on an illuminated surface is called the *illumination,* which depends on the intensity of the source and its distance from the source. Illumination is very important in photography because photography is a recording on a light-sensitive surface of the spatial pattern of variations of light intensities reflected from or transmitted through a subject. The higher the level of illumination, the shorter is the exposure time needed to produce a developable image. A light meter can be used to measure incident or reflected light. When electric light sources are used, a change in voltage can alter the intensity of the source. In such cases, a light integrating meter is needed to control the exposure, especially when exposures are long.

Color Temperature

When a black body radiator like iron is heated in a forge, its color changes as its temperature increases. It goes from red hot to yellow hot to white hot, when it is very soft and malleable before it melts. A substance like iron, when heated, gives off a continuous spectrum of all the wavelengths of visible light. The temperature of the source is expressed in degrees *Kelvin*. The Kelvin temperature is equivalent to the absolute temperature of the source (°C + 273.1°C).

A color temperature of about 5,500° Kelvin shows an approximately equal distribution of all wavelengths of light and looks nearly white. Light having a color temperature lower than this is richer in yellow light and poorer in blue so it looks yellowish. Light of a higher color temperature is richer in blue and poorer in red and looks bluish. This is shown in Figure A-3. Mean noon sunlight in a temperate zone about mid-June has a color temperature of about 5,600°K, which means that it has nearly equal amounts of radiant energy in equal wavelength intervals over the visible spectrum. A tungsten light bulb gives off light with a color temperature of about 2,800°K, so it appears yellowish in comparison with daylight. North sky light is usually about 7,500°K, appearing bluish in comparison with direct sunlight, and blue sky can have a color temperature of 20,000°K or more.

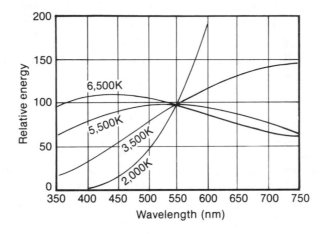

A-3. Spectral power distributions of light sources emitting continuous spectra at various color temperatures. (GAM)

The method of light production in fluorescent lamps is a combination of glow discharge and fluorescence. Neither of these produces a continuous spectrum like that of a glowing black body radiator (see Figure A-4). For this reason the light emitted from fluorescent lamps cannot be described by a simple color temperature but is equated to a

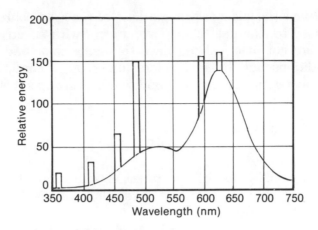

A-4. Spectral power distribution of a fluorescent lamp. Narrow peaks superimposed on continuous curves of phosphor radiation represent the contribution of mercury lines emission. (GAM)

black body radiator which makes a white (non-selective) surface look the same as it does when illuminated by the fluorescent light.

When incandescent electric lamps are used, not only does the intensity of the light source vary when the voltage changes but also its color temperature. The higher the voltage, the higher the intensity and color temperature, and vice versa. An example of this is the photoflood lamp, which has a filament like an ordinary tungsten lamp designed to operate at about 70 volts. When the lamp is operated at 110 to 120 volts, the tungsten is heated to a higher temperature, so the intensity is increased and the color temperature rises from 2,800°K to about 3,400°K. The life of the bulb, of course, is shortened because of the overload on the tungsten filament. The variation in color temperature due to voltage changes is a serious problem in photography because films are color sensitive and their exposures depend on the illumination, color temperature of the light source, and color transmission of the filters, all of which can vary if the voltage on the light source changes. This makes the need for light integrators doubly important for color photography when exposures are long as when making plates, halftones and proofs.

Metamerism

One of the most accurate ways to specify a color of any object is to measure it in a spectrophotometer. This produces a spectrophotometric curve for the color which is a measure of the reflection and absorption of the color at selected wavelengths across the visible spectrum (see Appendix B). If two objects have the same spectrophotometric curves, they always have the same color regardless of the light source or viewing conditions used to examine them. Two objects with spectrophotometric curves that are not identical can have the same color under one set of viewing conditions but different colors under other conditions. This is called a metameric match, and the condition is known as metamerism.

Color

Color is a combination of the physical sensation of light and the psychological interpretation of it. Physically, visible light is radiant energy having wavelengths in the range from about 380 nm to 760 nm. The equal combination of all wavelengths of visible light produces the sensation of white light. Many different spectral distributions produce white light. When the radiation is separated into individual wavelengths — as when it is passed through a prism (Figure A-5, page C-11) or in a rainbow — each wavelength causes a different color sensation. The shorter wavelengths in the blue end of the spectrum are bent more in passing through a prism than the longer wavelengths in the yellow, orange, and red end of the spectrum.

Physically, the color spectrum consists of almost 10 million perceptibly different colors. Psychologically the eye has receptors which are sensitive to three broad bands of color — blue, green, and red (Figure A-6, page C-11). The receptors which are on the surface of the retina are rods and cones. Only the cones are sensitive to light and color. The eye is sensitive to very great differences in intensities of light, ranging from the light of the bright sun to a dim moonlit night (a range of about one million to one in intensity). The rods in the retina are sensitive to the broad range of light intensities but do not sense color. The cones are sensitive not only to light but also to color (Figure A-7).

There are three types of cones. Simply expressed, some cones are sensitive to long wavelengths of light (red), others to medium wavelengths (green), and a third kind to short wavelengths (blue). When the eye views a scene, the long wavelengths of light from the scene affects the cones which produce the sensation of red light, and the cones send impulses to the brain. The medium wavelengths of light affect the green-sensitive cones, and these transmit their impulses to the brain. The same happens to the short wavelength (blue) light. The brain then recreates the scene based on the signals the various cones have sent to it. What the brain sees is the result of the experience of the viewer and the condition of the cones on his retina. If some are diseased, the viewer's interpretation of some colors will be affected, and color blindness may result. Some individuals are born with color vision anomalies.

Figure A-1. Electromagnetic spectrum. (GAM)

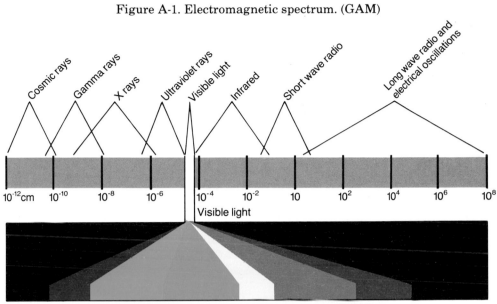

Visible light

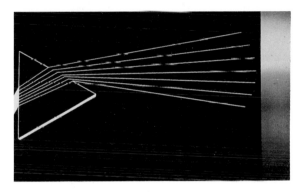

Figure A-2. Visible light spectrum. (GATF)

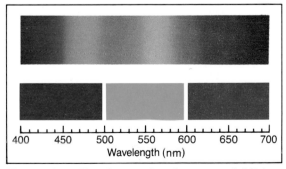

Figure A-5. Dispersion of white light passing through a prism producing a rainbow spectrum.

Figure A-6. The three color theory — Additive primaries.

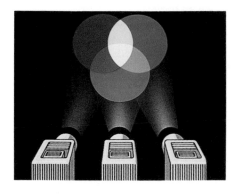

Figure A-8. Additive color combinations using light from three projectors covered with broad band filters.

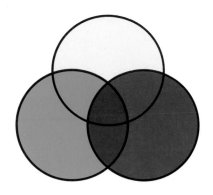

Figure A-9. Subtractive color combinations using printing inks.

A

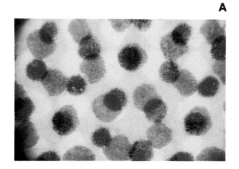

Figure A-10. Enlargement of overlap of halftones showing additive and subtrac-

B

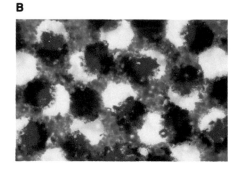

tive color combinations in (A) highlight (B) middletone areas. (Preucil)

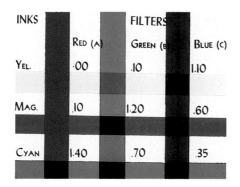

Figure A-11. Production printing ink colors showing impurities due to presence of other colors. (GATF)

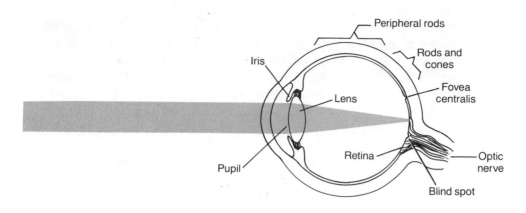

A-7. Cross-section of human eye showing position of rods and cones on retina.

Additive Primaries

The broad band short wavelength colors blue, medium wavelength green, and long wavelength red are called additive primaries. When lights of these broad band colors are superimposed they add to form white light. This can be easily proved by taking three projectors and covering the lens of one with a broad band blue filter, the second with a broad band green filter, and the third with a broad band red filter. (The Wratten A-25, B-58, and C5-47 filters come close in transmission to a set of additive primaries consisting of broad band red, green and blue light respectively. There are a lot of sets of additive primaries.) Shining all three projectors onto a white screen would show white light where the three colors overlap. Where blue and green overlap, a new color is seen which is a combination of blue and green and is called *cyan.* where blue and red overlap, another new color is seen which is *magenta.* Where red and green overlap, the new color seen is *yellow.* This is what is known as additive color mixture and is shown in Figure A-8, page C-12.

The mixture of red and green light to form yellow is the most difficult concept for most people to understand in the theory of color, because most people's experience with color has been with paints or crayons and not with light. It is easy to understand that a mixture of red and blue pigments can produce a magenta color and blue and green can produce cyan but red and green pigments can never produce a yellow pigment. It can be easily shown, however, that *red and green light* produce *yellow light* as seen in Figure A-8, page C-12.

Subtractive Primaries

The new colors — *yellow, magenta,* and *cyan* — are called subtractive primaries. They are the colors which are used to print process color reproductions. Each color represents the two colors which remain when one additive primary is subtracted from white light. When the additive primary color, red, is subtracted from white light, the colors left are blue and green light which produce cyan. Cyan, therefore, is the complement of red light, and during printing, the blue and green in the subject are reflected to the eye wherever the cyan ink is printed.

When green light is subtracted from white light, the colors left are red and blue, and the additive mixture of these is magenta. Magenta, therefore, is the complement of green, and wherever magenta ink is printed the red and blue in the subject are reflected to the eye.

When blue light is subtracted from white light, the colors left are red and green, and this mixture produces yellow. Yellow, therefore, is the complement of blue, and wherever yellow is printed, the red and green in the subject are reflected back to the eye.

Red, blue, and green, the additive primaries, are the colors of the filters used in color separation photography. Cyan, magenta, and yellow, the subtractive primaries, are the colors of the printing inks with which color reproductions are printed.

Process Color Printing

Most printing inks are transparent; that is, they allow light to pass through them to the paper. As the light passes through the ink, it is modified according to the spectral characteristics of the ink. The paper then acts as a reflecting surface which reflects the light back through the ink to the eye. Each process color ink ideally absorbs one of the components of the light passing through it and transmits the other two components to the paper so that they may be reflected back to the eye.

Inks that are not transparent — that is, opaque inks — do not have this property. They reflect light directly back to the eye and are independent of the substrate. When two opaque inks are overprinted or overlapped, the color the eye sees is that of the top layer as only the top layer reflects light back to the eye.

When two transparent inks are overprinted, light can go through both layers and produce a new color. If cyan and yellow are overlapped, for example, both the red and blue components are absorbed, leaving only green to be reflected back to the eye. The combination of all three process color inks can absorb all three components of white light and produce black. This is known as subtractive color mixture, which is illustrated in Figure A-9, page C-12. Combinations of colors are also produced by tiny halftone dots of two or more colors placed adjacent to each other as in light colors and highlight areas of the reproduction. This is an additive rather than a subtractive mixture. Where dots overlap as in middletone and shadow areas, there is a combination of additive and subtractive mixtures (Figure A-10, page C-12.) If the inks are not completely transparent, the colors can be different in the additive and subtractive mixtures.

Three-color Theory

The three-color theory of light described above would work very well if ink pigments were completely transparent and matched the theoretical subtractive primaries. If printing inks were ideal, they would produce pure colors without contamination with other colors. Because inks are not ideal — that is, they do not reflect and transmit the colors they should and are contaminated with other colors — the colors they produce are not pure, and considerable manipulation or correction must be done in color reproduction to compensate for the color errors in the inks.

The inadequacy of printing inks to reproduce the proper colors is shown in Figure A-11, page C-12. As demonstrated in the illustration, the yellow inks are quite good, but the magentas and cyans are very poor. This is not a fault of the three-color theory of color reproduction; the problem lies in the incorrect absorption and transmission of colors by the pigments of the inks that are used. Fluorescent pigments are better in their spectral properties than conventional pigments, but they are not quite ideal, so they still require corrections.

Ink Color Errors

The color errors in inks can be determined by measurement of solid prints of the inks on white paper with a densitometer through three broad band color filters corresponding in color to the three additive primaries red, green, and blue. A densitometer is useful for these measurements because it has a response similar to the photographic emulsions used to make the color separations. The readings of three-process color inks when plotted together form a matrix. An ideal set of process color inks would have densitometer readings similar to those shown in Table A–I. (The numbers in parentheses correspond to the numbers of the Wratten filters used in the densitometer.*)

Table A-I begins on the next page

---

*Narrow band filters such as are used in some densitometers for measuring ink densities on the press cannot be used to make the readings and calculations described in this chapter.

TABLE A-I

DENSITOMETER READINGS FOR IDEAL INKS

	Filters		
Printing Inks	Red (25)	Green (58)	Blue (47)
Yellow	0.0	0.0	2.0
Magenta	0.0	2.0	0.0
Cyan	2.0	0.0	0.0
Red	0.0	2.0	2.0
Green	2.0	0.0	2.0
Blue	2.0	2.0	0.0
3-color	2.0	2.0	2.0

This matrix shows that the yellow ink absorbs 99% of the blue light and reflects or transmits all the red and green light. The magenta ink absorbs 99% of the green light and reflects or transmits all of the red and blue light; and the cyan ink absorbs 99% of the red light and reflects or transmits all of the green and blue light. The overprint colors, red, green, blue, and three-color show completely additive densities.

An actual set of production process color inks have densitometer readings as shown in Table A–II.*

TABLE A-II

DENSITOMETER READINGS FOR PRODUCTION INKS

	Filters		
Printing Inks	Red (25)	Green (58)	Blue (47)
Yellow	0.01	0.06	0.95
Magenta	0.10	1.15	0.46
Cyan	1.20	0.50	0.20
Red	0.10	1.08	1.30
Green	1.20	0.50	1.13
Blue	1.25	1.48	0.56
3-color	1.28	1.51	1.48

This matrix illustrates the extent of the color errors in the inks used for printing which is the most serious problem in color reproduction. The yellow ink absorbs almost 90% of the blue light and absorbs a small amount of the red and green light which it should reflect or transmit completely. The yellow ink, however, is the best of the inks from the standpoint of having the least color errors. The magenta ink absorbs

*Examples shown are from the "Graphic Arts Manual," J.M. Field, Editor, published by Arno Press, New York, 1980, pp. 19-21.

green light well but it also absorbs some red light and about 70% of the blue light it should reflect. Blue absorption is equivalent to yellow reflectance so the magenta appears too reddish. The cyan has good red light absorption but absorbs about 75% of the green light and about 30% of the blue light it should reflect. These unwanted absorptions make the appearance of the cyan too bluish and dirty (lacking saturation).

Additivity Failure

For ideal color reproduction the densities of overprinting colors should be additive. Additivity failure is characteristic of all color reproduction and is due to *first surface reflection, multiple internal reflections, ink opacity, trapping, back transfer, spectral characteristics, halftone structure,* and *light scatter in paper.* These factors are too involved to be defined or discussed in this brief treatment of color reproduction. They are discussed in detail in Yule's *Principles of Color Reproduction* pages 220 – 231.

In color reproduction the overprint colors are as important as, if not more important than, the actual printing colors, as most of the picture consists of mixtures of colors rather than pure colors. The red overprint (magenta and yellow) shows slight additivity failure (0.06 + 1.15 > 1.08 and 0.95 + 0.46 > 1.30) and the hue is redder as the blue is scattered more. The green overprint shows additivity failure and is quite dirty (green absorption = 0.50) and slightly bluish (red absorption > blue). The blue overprint shows additivity failure and is very dirty (blue absorption is almost 75%) with a purplish hue. The three-color overprint also has additivity failure and is brownish in hue (high red reflectance).

The fourth color, black, has been added to the three-color process to help compensate for the additivity failure and color errors in inks which cause brownish grays and shadows. The color or spectral errors in the inks are also responsible for most of the color correction needed in color separations for color reproduction and are the main reason for the large number of different sets of four-color process inks in use. Efforts at standardization of four-color process inks have failed because ideal inks or pigments do not exist and some sets of inks produce better results with less correction for some jobs than others. Also different types of paper (coated vs. uncoated) and other substrates can affect the hue, grayness and strength of the inks printed on them so they complicate the reproduction process still further. With modern inks and coated papers additivity failure is not as serious a problem as it was formerly.

A thorough understanding of these effects and how to measure and control them is important not only to achieve the desired result in the printing process but also to produce proofs that simulate the result of the printing process. Standards for particular applications can be very useful like the Specifications for Web Offset Publications (SWOP) adopted by the American Association of Advertising Agencies (AAAA) and the Magazine Publishers of America (MPA) and the GTA Gravure Ink Standard Color Charts for Group I and Group V inks.

Analyzing Inks for Color Reproductions

In studying inks or comparing pigments or toners for reproduction, it is helpful to plot combinations of densitometric data of the inks, pigments, or toners on simple diagrams using a system like the one developed by Frank Preucil of the Graphic Arts Technical Foundation. There are three simple diagrams — the Color Circle, Color Triangle, and Color Hexagon — for plotting this data to analyze ink color characteristics and determine their suitability for color reproduction. These diagrams should not be confused with or used in place of the color order systems discussed in Appendix B. While densitometric data cannot replace colorimetry (because the densitometer does not respond to colors as the eye sees them), the diagrams are useful devices for analyzing the suitability of inks for printing, comparing pigments, dyes or toners for proofing and comparing proofs and press prints.

Color needs three dimensions to describe its sensations — hue, grayness, and strength in the case of the Preucil/GATF color diagrams (see Appendix B). The GATF color diagrams, however, are two-dimensional. The GATF Color Circle and Color Triangle are used to plot the same two dimensions — hue and grayness. An advantage of the Color Triangle is that the mixtures of two colors fall on straight lines joining the two colors, whereas on the Color Circle the lines are curved. The Color Hexagon is used to plot hue and color strength. The description and use of all three diagrams is contained in the GATF Research Progress Bulletins Nos. 38, 53, and 81. These bulletins and blank chart forms for plotting colors are available from the Graphic Arts Technical Foundation.

GATF Color Circle: As an example of how the GATF Color Circle can be used to analyze color reproduction, consider the color matrix in Table A-II. To plot the colors in this matrix on the Color Circle, the hue error and grayness of each of the colors must be determined. to do this the following formulas are used:

$$\text{Hue error} = \frac{M\text{-}L}{H\text{-}L}$$

$$\text{Grayness} = \frac{L}{H}$$

where, for each color:

H = high density reading
M = medium density reading
L = low density reading

For the yellow ink, the low reading is 0.01, the medium reading is 0.06, and the high is 0.95. The formulas would therefore read as follows:

Yellow: $\qquad$ Hue error $= \dfrac{0.06 - 0.01}{0.95 - 0.01} = \dfrac{0.05}{0.94} = .05 = 5\%$

$\qquad$ Grayness $= \dfrac{0.01}{0.95} = .01 = 1\%$

New "smart" densitometers are available from Cosar, X-Rite, Brumac, and most other densitometer manufacturers that have microcomputers which are programmed to solve the Preucil hue error, grayness, and other color function equations so the operator does not need to calculate the functions to plot the diagrams.

The hue error of the yellow is plotted on the circle opposite the color corresponding to the high reading (blue) and toward the color with the low reading (red). Grayness is plotted as the distance in from the outer perimeter of the circle.

The same procedure is used for plotting all colors. The values for the magenta and cyan hue errors and grayness in the sample color matrix are:

Magenta: $\qquad$ Hue error $= \dfrac{0.46 - 0.10}{1.15 - 0.10} = \dfrac{0.36}{1.05} = .34 = 34\%$

$\qquad$ Opposite green — toward red

$\qquad$ Grayness $= \dfrac{0.10}{1.15} = .09 = 9\%$

Cyan: $\qquad$ Hue error $= \dfrac{0.50 - 0.20}{1.20 - 0.20} = \dfrac{0.30}{1.00} = .30 = 30\%$

$\qquad$ Opposite red — toward blue

$\qquad$ Grayness $= \dfrac{0.20}{1.20} = .17 = 17\%$

The values for the overprint colors are:

Red: Hue error $= \dfrac{0.98}{1.20} = 82\%$

                Opposite blue — toward red

                Grayness $= \dfrac{0.10}{1.30} = 8\%$

Green: Hue error $= \dfrac{0.63}{0.70} = 90\%$

                Opposite red — toward green

                Grayness $= \dfrac{0.50}{1.20} = 42\%$

Blue: Hue error $= \dfrac{0.69}{0.92} = 75\%$

                Opposite green — toward blue

                Grayness $= \dfrac{0.56}{1.48} = 38\%$

3-color: Hue error $= \dfrac{0.20}{0.23} = 87\%$

                Opposite green — toward red

                Grayness $= \dfrac{1.28}{1.51} = 85\%$

These seven colors are plotted on the color circle in Figure A-12, page C-13. The plot of these colors on the circle shows what is considered to be optimum color reproduction with this set of inks (see Chapter X).

GATF Color Triangle: The same colors in Table A-II, page 304, can be plotted on the Color Triangle using the same calculations for the color circle and in much the same way (Figure A-13, page C-13). *Hue error* is plotted opposite the color representing the high filter density reading and toward the low; and *grayness* is plotted from the outer perimeter toward the center. Next to the advantage that mixtures of two colors fall on a straight line, the Color Triangle's main use in color reproduction is to indicate characteristics of the photographic masks required for color correction in photographic color separation processes.

GATF Color Hexagon: Each point, or color, in the GATF Color Hexagon is plotted using only two numbers. Since the Hexagon plot is not concerned with grayness, the gray component of each color, or the *lowest* density reading for that color, is subtracted from the high and medium density readings. The higher number for each color (H-L) is stepped off from the center of the Hexagon in the direction opposite the color of the filter with the high density reading (*blue* for yellow, *green* for magenta, and *red* for cyan). From this point the other number (M-L) is stepped off in the direction opposite the middle density reading (away from *green* toward red in plotting yellow, away from *blue* toward red for magenta, and away from *green* toward blue for cyan). The same procedure is used for all the colors plotted. The plotted colors are shown in Figure A-14, page C-14.

As already stated, the main use of the Color Hexagon is to plot *hue* and *strength* so it is useful in printing for the pressman or quality control inspector to check variations in hue and ink strength on the press and in color proofing for the proofer or supervisor to compare pigment or toner hues and strengths on the proof with those of the inks on the press print.

Measurement of Ink Trapping

Ink trapping is an important characteristic of printing on multi-color presses which affects the appearance of the printed product, as it determines the hue and strength of the overprinted solid colors, red, green, blue, and black. If ink trapping is correct (i.e., the same amount of ink transfers to previously printed ink as transfers to plain unprinted paper), the overprints will have the correct hue and strength. If the ink is undertrapping as in letterpress (i.e., less ink is transferred to previously printed ink than to plain paper) the overprint will be weak in strength and its hue will be distorted toward the underlying color. If ink is overtrapping as in gravure (i.e., apparently more ink is transferred to previously printed ink than to plain paper) the overprint is strong and the hue is slightly distorted toward the overprinting color. These statements are not strictly correct because some of the visual effects of under- and overtrapping are due to ink opacity and changes in gloss of the ink layers as they overprint other ink layers. Therefore, the phenomenon of trapping is more correctly referred to as "apparent trap."

Apparent trap can be calculated from the densitometer readings in the color matrix shown in Table A-II, using the GATF/Preucil Trapping Equations.

GATF/Preucil Trapping Equations: These equations are based on the precept that the apparent trap of an overprint of two colors is the quotient of the difference of the densities of the overprint color measured through the filter complementary to the overprinting color minus that of the bottom color through the same filter divided by the density of the top color measured through the same filter.

Red Trap: The formula for measuring the apparent trapping of the *red* overprint if magenta was printed over yellow for the case in Table A-II is:

$$\% \text{ Apparent Trap } R_{(M/Y)} = \frac{R_G - Y_G}{M_G}$$

where R_G = density of red solid overprint through green (58) filter
$\quad\;\; Y_G$ = density of yellow solid through green filter
$\quad\;\; M_G$ = density of magenta solid through green filter

Using the data in Table A-II
$$\% \text{ Apparent Trap } R_{(M/Y)} = \frac{1.08 - .06}{1.15} = \frac{1.02}{1.15} = 89\%$$

This shows slight undertrapping of magenta over yellow.

If the red was produced by yellow printing over magenta the formula is:

$$\% \text{ Apparent Trap } R_{(Y/M)} = \frac{R_B - M_B}{Y_B}$$

where R_B = density of red overprint through blue (47) filter
$\quad\;\; M_B$ = density of magenta solid through blue filter
$\quad\;\; Y_B$ = density of yellow solid through blue filter

Using the data in Table A-II
$$\% \text{ Apparent Trap } R_{(Y/M)} = \frac{1.3 - .46}{.95} = \frac{.84}{.95} = 88\%$$

Apparent trap of the red overprint is about the same.

Green Trap: The formula for measuring the apparent trapping of the *green* overprint if cyan was printed over yellow is:

$$\% \text{ Apparent Trap } G_{(C/Y)} = \frac{G_R - Y_R}{C_R}$$

where G_R = density of green solid overprint through red (25) filter
$\quad\;\; Y_R$ = density of yellow solid through red filter
$\quad\;\; C_R$ = density of cyan solid through red filter

Using the data in Table A-II

$$\% \text{ Apparent Trap } G_{(C/Y)} = \frac{1.2 - .01}{1.2} = \frac{1.19}{1.2} = 99\%$$

This is essentially perfect trapping.

If green was produced by printing yellow over cyan the formula is:

$$\% \text{ Apparent Trap } G_{(Y/C)} = \frac{G_B - C_B}{Y_B}$$

where G_B, C_B and Y_B are the densities of the green solid overprint and the cyan and yellow solids through the blue filter.

Using the data in Table A-II

$$G_{(Y/C)} = \frac{1.13 - .2}{.95} = \frac{.93}{.95} = 98\%$$

This is very good trapping.

Blue Trap: The formula for measuring the apparent trapping of the *blue* overprint if cyan was printed over magenta is:

$$\% \text{ Apparent Trap } B_{(C/M)} = \frac{B_R - C_R}{M_R}$$

where B_R, M_R, and C_R are the densities of the blue solid overprint and the magenta and cyan solids through the red filter.

Using the data in Table A-II

$$B_{(C/M)} = \frac{1.25 - .1}{1.2} = \frac{1.15}{1.2} = 96\%$$

This is very good trapping.

If the blue overprint was produced by magenta printing over the cyan the formula is:

$$\% \text{ Apparent Trap } B_{(M/C)} = \frac{B_G - C_G}{M_G}$$

where B_G, C_G, and M_G are the densities of the blue solid overprint and the cyan and magenta solids through the green filter.

Using the data in Table A-II

$$B_{(M/C)} = \frac{1.48 - .5}{1.15} = \frac{.93}{1.15} = 81\%$$

This is undertrapping which is typical of the poor trapping obtained when overprinting magenta inks on cyan inks on multicolor presses.

Black Trap: It is also possible to measure the apparent trapping of black ink on cyan which is equivalent to the black over the three color combination. The formula for this function is:

$$\% \text{ Apparent Trap Bk/C} = \frac{\text{Bk/C}_B - \text{C}_B}{\text{Bk}_B}$$

where Bk/C_B, C_B, and Bk_B are densities of the black solid overprint on the cyan, the cyan and black solids through the blue filter.

The densities of the black ink and overprints with black are not recorded in Table A-II so this calculation was not carried out.

As can be seen from the calculations in this section the basic rule in making measurements of % Apparent Trap of color inks is to use the filter which gives the highest density to the top color. With black on top use the filter which gives the lowest density to the bottom color.

These overprints are plotted on the GATF Color Circle in Figure A-12, page C-13.

Other trapping equations have been proposed by Felix Brunner and Warren Childers. All three formulae show trapping in the same direction but the amounts are different. Brunner trapping calculations are always close to 100% while Childers' calculations are farthest from 100% and Preucil's are in between.

Plotting Trapping on GATF Color Triangle: A graphic means of checking trapping is to compare actual measured apparent trapping with ideal trapping on the Color Triangle. The values for ideal trapping are derived from the densitometer readings of the colored inks and overprints in the color matrix as in Table A-II.

To derive the values for ideal trapping other sets of numbers need to be added to the color matrix. These are the combination of yellow and magenta solids (Y + M); the combination of yellow and cyan solids (Y + C); the combination of magenta and cyan (M + C); and the combination of all three colors (Y + M + C). For the matrix in Table A-II the values

	Filters		
	Red (25)	*Green (58)*	*Blue (47)*
Y + M (Red)	0.11	1.21	1.41
Y + C (Green)	1.21	0.56	1.15
M + C (Blue)	1.30	1.65	0.66
Y + M + C	1.31	1.71	1.61

When these values are plotted on the GATF Color Triangle, they indicate the positions of the proper (ideal) overprints depending on the densities of the solid inks. As shown in Figure A-15, page C-14, these overprints for (Y + M), (Y + G), and (M + C) lie on the straight lines joining the Y, M, and C points. They are indicated with an (x) which shows the position of the ideal or correct overprint or perfect trapping. The position of the actual printed colors red, green, and blue are plotted on the same triangle using the densities listed for these colors in Table A-II.

Plotting Trapping on GATF Color Hexagon: Another graphic means of analyzing trapping is to plot ideal and apparent trapping on the GATF Color Hexagon as described in the section on the GATF Color Hexagon on page C-15. The Hexagon is the most useful of the color diagrams for indicating press factors as it plots the two important color attributes affected by variables on the press, hue and strength. A plot of the printed overprint colors is shown in Figure A-16, page C-15. These represent typically good sheet-fed printing by lithography.

Figure A–17A, page C-15 represents typical printing by letterpress showing apparent undertrapping and in Figure A-17B, page C-15 printing by gravure showing apparent overtrapping. Figure A-18, page C-16 indicates graphically how to interpret plots of apparent trapping on the GATF Color Hexagon showing the effects of undertrapping, overtrapping and opacity on the hues and strengths of the overprinted colors.

The Specification and Measurement of Color

The properties of light and color and their effects on color reproduction have been covered in Appendix A. In addition to these properties there are many other characteristics of color that need to be considered when specifying certain colors to produce a special color match or to make sure that a new lot of paper or ink matches the previous one. Just as there are instruments to measure and units in which to express physical properties like length, area, volume or mass so must color be measured and expressed in units that permit accurate description and duplication and the ability to record and communicate it properly. A densitometer is a convenient instrument for measuring some attributes of color but color has a number of unique characteristics which cannot be adequately specified or measured with a densitometer. Densitometers are useful mainly for comparing colors with identical spectral characteristics. The proper measurement of color requires other instruments. The process of measuring color and specifying color matches is called colorimetry, which like color, is a complicated science involving physics, psychophysics and psychology.

As pointed out in Appendix A, color is three-dimensional, and in measuring it three characteristics of the color must be taken into account. This is due to the structure of the eye, which acts as if it contains three different kinds of light-sensitive elements that respond to different wavelengths of light. The most obvious characteristic is that of *hue,* which distinguishes blue from green, red from blue, green from yellow, etc. The rainbow and the spectrum provide familiar examples of the

Violet	Blue	Green	Yellow	Orange	Red

B-1. Spectrum colors can be arranged in a line.

arrangement of colors (not object colors) in order of hue or wavelength; — violet, indigo, blue, green, yellow, orange, and red. The colors of the spectrum can be arranged in a line (Figure B-l); but object colors which include purple and magenta that are not in the spectrum, are represented more naturally in the form of a circle (Figure B-2). The number of subdivisions of the hue circle is quite arbitrary. Many more hues than seven can be easily recognized even without comparison with a standard.

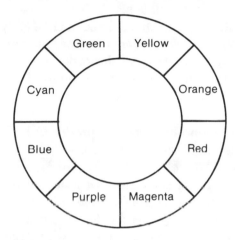

B-2. Object colors cannot be arranged in a line and fall more naturally in a circle.

In the Munsell System (a system of color notation widely used in the United States) five basic hue names are used (yellow, red, purple, blue, and green). This number is increased by the use of combination names such as purple-blue and blue-purple.

When arranging objects by hue, there are some with colors like white, gray, and black to which no hue can be assigned. These are called *achromatic colors,* and they are placed in the center of the circle. This suggests the second characteristic according to which colors can be arranged — namely, color *saturation* or colorfulness. This is known as *chroma* in the Munsell System. The saturation of the achromatic colors is zero, and all colors can be arranged according to saturation, with gray at one end of the scale and a saturated color at the other. Or they can be arranged according to both hue and saturation, by putting the grays in the center of the circle and the more saturated colors out from the center.

The third characteristic is *darkness* or *lightness.* Lightness is known as *value* in the Munsell System, with a scale of numbers going from zero (dark) to ten (light). All the colors can be arranged in order of lightness, although there may be some difficulty in deciding on the relative lightness of colors differing widely in hue. All three characteristics of colors, however, cannot be arranged in a plane. To add lightness to the hue-saturation circle, a third (vertical) dimension is needed. Such three-dimensional arrangements are clumsy to construct and use (Figure B-3, page C-16). More common are charts in which two of the characteristics are varied and the third is constant, such as chroma-value charts of constant hue in the Munsell System.

Hue, saturation (chroma), and lightness (value) have been used as an example of a set of three characteristics for classifying and arranging color. This is not the only possible set. Colors can be arranged in terms of hue, grayness and strength, as in the Preucil/GATF System.

These are known as *color order* systems, of which there are many using different sets of attributes. A color order system based on the three appearance attributes, hue, saturation (chroma), and lightness (value) is called a *color-appearance system*. Examples of such systems are *Munsell* and *DIN*.

The colors in color photographs are produced by various amounts of three dyes, and painters obtain a wide gamut of colors by mixing a few well-chosen pigments. A color order system based on the systematic variation of the amounts of colorants in the mixture is called a *colorant-mixture* system. An example is the *Pantone Ink Matching System* (PMS).

In the usual ink-printing process, colors are produced by overprinting yellow, magenta, cyan, and black inks on white paper, using halftone images with varying percentages of dot area. The dot patterns are combinations of additive and subtractive mixtures of light, so a color order system based on a systematic variation of halftone dot percentages is not like any of the other types. It is called a *halftone-mixture* system. Examples are the color charts used by printers.

Color Measurement

There are three basic methods of measuring color: (I) visual comparison (a) with a standard set of colored materials or (b) with mixtures of standard color lights; (II) measurement through three color filters as in densitometers and colorimeters; and (III) measurement of the amount of each wavelength of light reflected or transmitted by an object as in spectrophotometry.

In method Ia (comparing the color with a set of standard colored materials) the Munsell, DIN, Ostwald or other systems of classification can be used. The Munsell System is most commonly used in America; DIN and Ostwald systems are widely used in Europe. Method Ib (comparison of the color with a mixture of three colored lights) is mostly used in research on color vision and is not commonly employed for routine color measurement. Method II (measurement of reflectance or density through three color filters) is simple and satisfactory provided

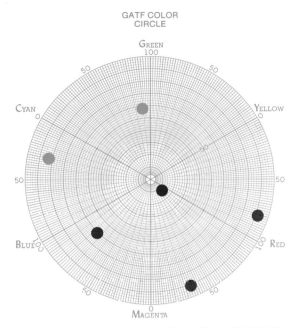

Figure A-12. Plot of color inks in Table A-II on GATF Color Circle. (GATF)

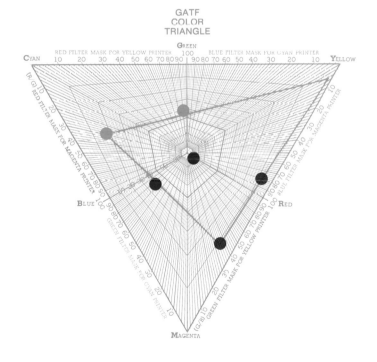

Figure A-13. Plot of color inks in Table A-II on GATF Color Triangle. (GATF)

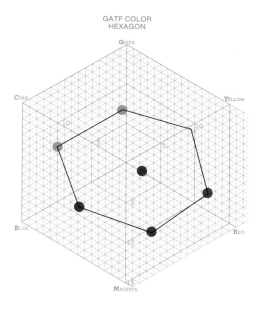

Figure A-14. Plot of color inks in Table A-II on GATF Color Hexagon. (GATF)

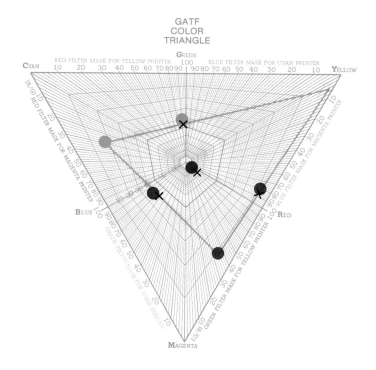

Figure A-15. Plot of trapping of color inks in Table A-II on GATF Color Triangle. (GATF)

C14   PRINCIPLES OF COLOR PROOFING

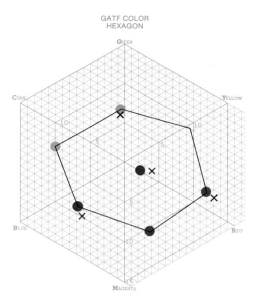

Figure A-16. Plot of trapping of color inks in Table A-II on GATF Color Hexagon. (GATF)

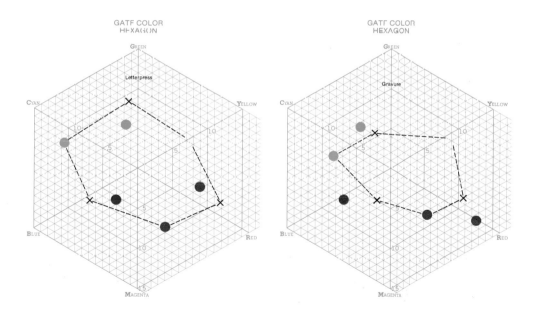

Figure A-17. Graphic analysis of trapping on GATF Color Hexagon showing (A) typical undertrapping in letterpress printing; (B) apparent overtrapping in gravure. (GATF)

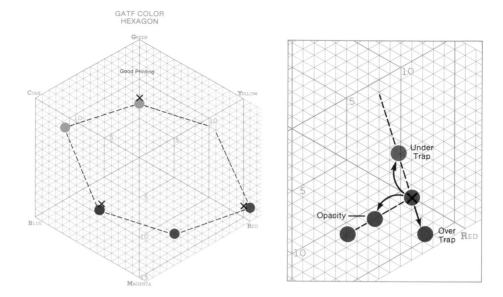

Figure A-18. Graphical analysis of trapping on GATF Color Hexagon showing differentiation between correct trapping, undertrapping, overtrapping and opacity. (GATF)

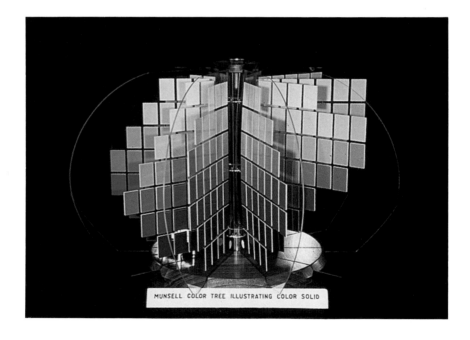

Figure B-3. Munsell Color Tree is an example of a 3-dimensional color space. The various **hues** radiate at different angles from the center. Color increases in **value** (lightness) from bottom to top, and **chroma** (saturation) increases from center outward. (GAM)

the sensitivity or "spectral response" of the instrument to the various colors of the spectrum is properly related to that of the eye. Method III (spectrophotometry) is the most widely used for accurate specification and measurement of colors.

To measure a color means to apply three numbers to it so that any two colors which look the same will be represented by the same set of numbers, and any two colors which look different will have different numbers. This is a limited objective. No attempt is made to evaluate what the observer sees — the "perceived color" — in absolute terms. The perceived color is greatly influenced by many factors, especially in live scenes. Fortunately, these factors are not very important in color reproduction because it involves viewing a printed reproduction or comparing it with an original or proof which are also in color.

Color Order Systems

Munsell System :   In measuring color, it is desirable, but not essential, that equal visual differences in the colors should be represented by equal differences in the measurements, and that the numbers should correspond to recognizable characteristics such as hue. This is the basis of the Munsell System whose parameters (hue, chroma and value) have already been described. In this system all colors with a chroma of 5.0, for example, appear equally saturated, whether they are light or dark, and whatever their hue; and the visual difference between values two and three is the same as the difference between values five and six. Hue differences, however, are less distinguishable for the less saturated colors.

The Munsell notation of a color can be determined approximately by comparing the sample with the standard colors given in the Munsell Book of Color (Munsell Color Co., 1929). A more modern method is based on first determining the color's chromaticity and luminance (from spectrophotometric readings) which can be converted to hue, value, and chroma using a series of charts. In the Munsell notation : 4.5YR 6.9/2.1, the 4.5YR is the hue, and the other two numbers represent value and chroma respectively. This color would be a light brownish-gray.

DIN-Color System:

This is the system adopted by the Deutsche Industrie Norm, the national standards institution of West Germany. The color solid is described in terms of hue, saturation, and relative degree of darkness, which is a logarithmic function of relative lightness (DIN-Farbton, DIN-Sattigung, and DIN-Dunkelstufe). Colors of the same DIN-Farbton have the same dominant wavelength which corresponds roughly to their hues. The hue circuit is divided into 24 perceptually equal steps. DIN-Sattigung is correlated with saturation or colorimetric purity, independently of DIN-Dunkelstufe. DIN-Dunkelstufe is a logarithmic function of luminous reflectance or lightness (Y) relative to the luminous reflectance of the optimal color having the same chromaticity or hue and saturation as the sample. Painted chips are available each identified by the DIN notation (F:S:D), the chromaticity coordinates which define the position of the color on the chromaticity diagram, dominant or complementary wavelength, colorimetric purity, Munsell notation, and Ostwald notation.

Ostwald System: This is a color-mixture system represented by 30 triangular arrays of chips, one for each of 30 hues. The neutral series is arranged vertically, forming one side of a triangle, and a saturated color, the full color, lies at the opposite vertex. The graded series between the full color and white is called the light clear series, and the series between full color and black is the dark clear series. Other series are arrayed in parallel to the light and dark clear series so that those that fall in a vertical line have the same saturation, but vary only in reflectance or percentage of light reflected. Such a vertical series is called a shadow series and is said to lie along an isochrome of the space. Colors are described in terms of hue, white content, and black content. The system is used more in Europe than in the United States.

Pantone Matching System: This system by Pantone, Inc. (Moonachie, New Jersey) closely resembles a colorant-mixture system. The company provides 564 colored samples, each of which bears a serial number. The color specified by that number can be obtained with proprietary inks, colored papers, colored overlay film, or marking pens. The inks are used for printing and the others are artists' materials which are generally used for preparatory art work or specifying colors. An ink of prescribed color is obtained by mixing specified amounts of any of ten basic inks. Pantone licenses ink manufacturers to use its name on inks and monitors the colors produced. The company also provides physical standards for control of the printing of corporate and packaging colors, viewing booths for judging colored samples under controlled conditions, a four-color reflection densitometer designed for the measurement of solid colors produced by printing, and a compact proofing press.

The Pantone 4-Color Process Guide is a chart of 15,000 colors created with combinations of screen-tint values of the four Pantone Balanced Process Colors on coated and uncoated paper. The Pantone Color Data System provides equipment and computer services for precise measurement of color at the printing plant, rapid transmission of color data, remote computation of the formula for an ink to match the color submitted, and direct transmission of the formula to the plant. A similar ink system, including numbered color catalog, ink formulary, and proprietary inks, is offered by Metricolor Ink Systems. There are also other companies supplying computer services for matching colors of inks.

Visual Comparisons: For systems requiring visual comparisons, the illumination under which the comparisons are made must be standardized. Usually artificial daylight is used, because it is consistent all day, from day to day, and from one place to another. Viewing booths with such standard illumination are commercially available. The interior of the booth is neutral gray to standardize the visual field in which comparisons are made. Judgments are often made in simulated daylight and by incandescent lamplight to assure that the colors in question match under both illuminants and are not metameric.

Visual judgments are commonly used in industry because they are fast, cheap and generally very sensitive to small differences. They are, however, subject to the kinds of errors and uncertainties usually associated with human judgments. There are individual differences in color vision; the angular conditions of viewing are often poorly controlled; and inspectors become fatigued. The inevitable small errors in making the color standards also contribute to the overall error. For all these reasons the need for completely objective methods of colorimetry was recognized over fifty years ago, and such methods have been developed.

Filter Method

The objective or instrumental measurement of color involves photometry, that is, measurement of the amount of light. The light reflected by the sample, expressed as a fraction or a percentage of the light reflected by a white object, is known as the *reflectance*. The corresponding term for transparent materials is *transmittance*. In the control of a color reproduction process, it is more useful to express the measurements of light in terms of optical density which increases with the amount of colorant and evaluates it as the eye would. Density is the negative logarithm of the fractional reflectance or transmittance and is a measure of the light absorption or opacity of an object. The instrument used to measure it is a *densitometer*. The higher the red density, for example, the less red light is transmitted or reflected by the sample. A density of zero means 100% transmittance. Reducing the transmittance in half increases the density by 0.3; dividing it by ten increases the density by 1.0. Thus transmittances of 50%, 25%, 10% and 1%

correspond to densities of 0.3, 0.6, 1.0 and 2.0, respectively. The same relationship holds between reflectance and reflection density. Conversion tables relating density with reflectance are in Appendix D.

As already mentioned, in the process of vision, the eye responds to the amount of stimulation of three different types of receptors. These receptors respond to the red, green, and blue regions of the spectrum. This process is related to the filter method of color measurement, which consists of measuring the amount of red, green and blue light reflected by an object. This is usually done in a densitometer with a photoelectric cell over which red, green, and blue color filters are placed. A reading is made through each of the three filters. The three numbers obtained in this way do not, or course, tell what the actual visual sensation is, but they can be used for comparing colors with the same spectral characteristics.

The more closely the measuring instrument corresponds to the eye in spectral sensitivity, the more accurately the resulting readings will indicate the color. For some purposes, in studying color reproduction, it is preferable to use an instrument whose spectral sensitivity corresponds to that of the photographic materials used in the color separation process or to measure the photographic response to the colors directly. The readings obtained in this way are called *actinic* densities, which do not correlate very well with the visual appearance, but they supply very useful information about the characteristics required in the photographic and printing process for good color reproduction. Densitometer readings made through Wratten A-25, B-58 and C5-47 filters are such densities.

Besides the inability of densitometers to respond to color stimuli as the eye sees them they suffer from other limitations:

- Poor agreement between instruments because of spectral variations in light sources, photomultiplier tubes and filters. Newer densitometers are being designed with new features such as photodiodes and microprocessors which have improved consistency, higher speed and the ability to calculate color functions quickly.
- No widespread color standards exist and measurements cannot be related in any way with the CIE system which is the accepted standard language of color.

Colorimeters are like densitometers in that they, too, are filter instrumets except that they use special filters with three broad bands of color responses that are related to the eye and a standard illuminant. Newer types of colorimeters use photodiodes in place of color filters that make measurements at 18 wavelengths across the visible spectrum from which colorimetric measurements are computed. These measurements are in tristimulus values which can be converted to chromaticity coordinates or the parameters for the color order systems.

Spectrophotometric Curves and the CIE System

The third method of measuring color gives a more detailed description of the light-reflecting properties of the object. In this method the light reflected or transmitted at each wavelength of the spectrum is measured and plotted to give a spectrophotometric curve, illustrated in Figure B-4. The reflectance, transmittance, or density is plotted against the wavelength (in nanometers). This curve does not directly specify the color, but the plotted information can be used to calculate a set of three numbers which do represent the chromaticity of the object.

Recording spectrophotometers are available which plot the spectrophotometric curve directly in a few minutes. By inspecting the curve of Figure B-4, it can be readily seen that it represents a yellow object, since it absorbs blue light only (400 to 500 nm). The curve does

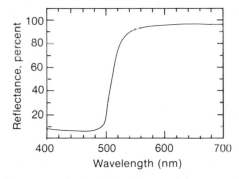

B-4. Spectrophotometric curve of a yellow ink. (Wiley)

not show exactly what variety of yellow is represented, but the visual response can be calculated from the curve by means of the CIE System. This system is named after the International Commission on Illumination (abbreviated CIE for Commission Internationale de l'Eclairage) which in 1931 adopted the red, green, and blue weighting values which are the tristimulus values that define the standard observer as shown in Figure B-5.

A number of methods are available for converting spectrophotometric data to the CIE System. Three numbers are obtained, corresponding roughly to the amounts of red, green, and blue light reflected or transmitted by the sample under a given illuminant. These are the tristimulus values, X, Y, and Z, which are analogous to the red, green, and blue measurements obtained by the filter method. Y corresponds to the lightness or luminance of the sample. Three more numbers, the trichromatic coefficients x, y, and z, are usually derived from the tristimulus values by means of the formulas:

$$x = \frac{x}{x + y + z}; \qquad y = \frac{y}{x + y + z}; \qquad z = \frac{z}{x + y + z}$$

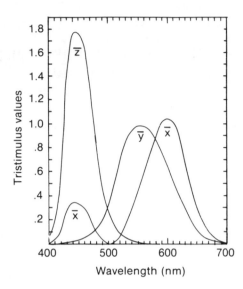

B-5. Tristimulus curves that define a standard observer adapted by the International Commission on Illumination (CIE) in 1931. (GAM)

Since $x + y + z = 1$, only x and y are needed to identify the chromaticity of a color. The coefficient x can be regarded as the redness and y the greenness of the sample. When the redness and greenness are low, the sample is blue. These two numbers which define the chromaticity of the sample are plotted on a chromaticity diagram (Figure B-6). The position of the point (x,y) is related to the hue and saturation of the sample. The curve in Figure B-6 represents the chromaticities of monochromatic (single color) light of the wavelengths indicated, and is called the spectrum locus. The straight line at the bottom of the spectrum locus represents magentas and purples, which cannot be produced by a single wavelength of light. These are non-spectral colors obtained by mixing short (blue) and long (red) wavelength light from the extreme ends of the spectrum.

The point marked "Illuminant C" represents the chromaticity of an illuminant similar to daylight. Any neutral black, gray or white sample viewed by illuminant C will also have this chromaticity and will, therefore, plot at this illuminant point. The chromaticity of the yellow material whose spectrophotometric curve is given in Figure B-4 is shown in Figure B-7. A straight line drawn from the illuminant point through the point

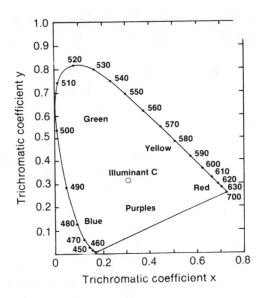

B-6. CIE Chromaticity Diagram. (GATF)

representing the material in question meets the spectrum locus at the *dominant wavelength* (575 nm for the yellow ink). The dominant wavelength corresponds roughly to the hue of the material — yellow in this case. The ratio of the distance of the sample point from the illuminant

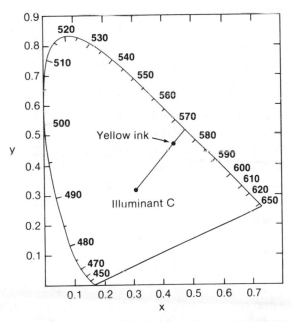

B-7. CIE Chromaticity Diagram showing the chromaticity of the yellow ink illustrated in Figure B-4. (Wiley)

point to the length of the dominant wavelength line gives the value for the *excitation purity* of the sample (85%), which is a rough indication of its *saturation*.

An important advantage of the CIE System and of other systems which are based on it is that the data correlate well with visual matches. That is, two samples with identical tristimulus values will look alike under the illuminant in question. This is essential in color specifications. Another advantage, which is useful in dealing with colored lights, is that chromaticities of mixtures of two colored lights will fall on the straight line joining the points representing these lights on the chromaticity diagram.

The chromaticity depends not only on the color of the material, but also on the spectral composition of the light with which it is illuminated. *Illuminant C* is most widely used in these calculations and corresponds to simulated overcast sky daylight. Three other illuminants have been defined: *Illuminant A* represents simulated tungsten light (2854°K); *Illuminant B* represents simulated direct sunlight; and Illuminant D65 represents average natural daylight at 6500°K.

A very important point about spectrophotometric curves is that two objects with identical spectrophotometric curves always have the same color; but the converse is not true. Two objects of the same color do not necessarily have identical spectrophotometric curves, although they are usually similar in their general shape, except near neutral. Objects of the same color but with different curves are termed *metameric*. They do not match when viewed with a different illuminant, and they can cause trouble in color reproduction processes, especially when trying to match a color proof to a print if the pigments or dyes used to make the proof are metameric or do not have the same spectrophotometric curves as the pigments in the printing inks.

Any method of plotting on paper in two dimensions will only represent two of the three attributes of color. The chromaticity diagram, for example, gives no information as to how dark the material is. White and black, therefore, plot at the same point. This may be misleading, for example, when studying the accuracy of color reproduction on a chromaticity diagram. To specify the color completely, the luminance, Y, must be given as well as the trichromatic coefficients, x and y, which are plotted on the diagram.

In the CIE System equal distances on the chromaticity diagram unfortunately do not represent equal visual differences, and points on a straight line connecting two points are not exactly visually intermediate between the colors represented by these two points. Moreover, two samples of the same chromaticity (x, y) but differing in luminance (Y) will not appear equally saturated; the lighter one will appear the more saturated and, when specified by the Munsell System, will have a higher chroma. For example, a sample whose CIE specification (x, y, and Y) is 0.500, 0.416, and 43.06, has a chroma of 12.0; but a darker sample (Y = 12.00) of the same chromaticity has a chroma of only 7.7. Consequently, the positions of points on the chromaticity diagram often give misleading impressions of the colors of the samples they represent and of the color differences between two samples.

Other Color Measurement Systems

A number of color measurement systems have been devised to avoid the limitations of the CIE System. Any color can be specified precisely by the three tristimulus values x, y and z in the CIE System. By the use of simple equations all other parameters for at least 20 color systems can be derived from these values. The important ones related to graphic arts are the Munsell System which has already been described, CIELAB, and CIELUV which are transformations of the CIE (1931) System (with 1976 revisions) into good perceptual color spaces.

CIELAB and CIELUV are variations of the Hunter System introduced in 1947 which is widely used in industries outside the graphic arts. The principles of these systems are illustrated in Figure B-8 which appeared in a paper on "Color Measurement for Graphic Arts" by Richard E. Maurer (Eastman Kodak) in the 1979 TAGA Proceedings.

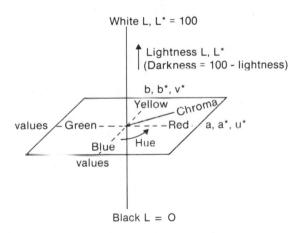

B-8. Principles of Hunter, CIELAB and CIELUV color spaces. (TAGA)

Plots of the same ink colors are shown in Figures B-9, B-10, B-11 and B-12 by these three color systems and the GATF/Preucil Color Triangle. (These are not the same inks listed in Table A-II in Appendix A.) The plot of the color inks on the GATF/Preucil Color Triangle in Figure B-9 indicates this is a typical set of process color inks with the green and blue (violet) overprints showing slight undertrapping and the red overprint

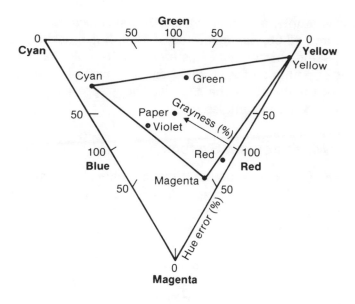

B-9. Color inks plotted on GATF Color Triangle. (TAGA)

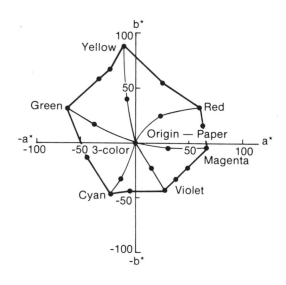

B-10. Same color inks plotted on Hunter color space. (TAGA)

slightly overtrapping.

The Hunter Lab space plot (Figure B-10) and the CIELAB space plot (Figure B-11) have similarities in the direction and curvature of the connecting lines. In fact, these two systems are very similar and, according to Maurer, the CIE commission hopes the CIELAB system will replace many Hunter applications and become the standard. When

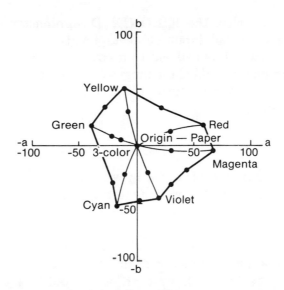

B-11. Same color inks plotted on CIELAB color space. (TAGA)

samples with equally perceived chroma, or saturation, are plotted by the CIELAB system the points form better circles than with other systems.

The plot of the colors in the CIELUV space (Figure B-12) is quite different from the Hunter and CIELAB plots. The main differences are: (1) mixtures of the lights or pigments fall on much straighter lines; and (2) perceived differences in hues are more equally spaced. These are characteristics that are very important to graphic arts and it appears that this may become the preferred system for graphic arts use. It is

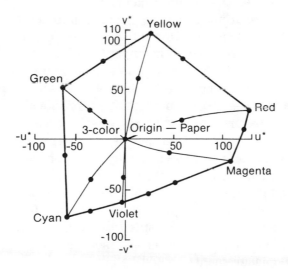

B-12. Same color inks plotted on CIELUV color space. (TAGA)

interesting to note that the EIKONIX Designmaster 8000 all-digital color scanner records all input subjects for the scanner in CIELUB colorimetric data, which is claimed to account for the relative ease with which color corrections and color changes can be made on this system as compared with existing systems using C-M-Y-K data derived from densitometer readings.

Color Measurement in Color Reproduction

There are a number of ways in which color measurements and densitometer readings made through color filters are used in graphic arts and color reproduction.

1. A most important use for color measurements is to determine whether the proper amount of ink has been printed or whether a print has the same ink strength as a proof. For this use density readings are made through complementary color-separation filters on color bars which are placed outside the picture area. For example, a blue-filter measurement would be used to check the relative amount of yellow ink. For this purpose, the exact characteristics of the filters do not matter as long as neither the filters nor the inks are changed and proof and press colors have identical spectral curves. These readings are sometimes called "ink-film thickness measurements," but this is not correct because the density is not proportional to the thickness. The density depends on the filter, the color strength of the ink, the paper, and other factors besides the ink film thickness.

2. Density measurements of the printing inks and their two-color and three-color overprints through all three of the color-separation filters are of great value in understanding the color-reproduction process and matching color prints to color proofs. They are useful in detecting printing defects like dot gain and trapping variations which affect the consistency of color reproduction.

3. Density measurements of corresponding areas in the original and the proof or reproduction can be made through color-separation filters. Although the results may not correspond to the visual sensation the measurements are useful in analyzing and tracking the possible causes of inaccurate color reproduction.

4. Color measurements of printed ink swatches (usually in one of the CIE systems) are used for specifying ink colors. The shape of the spectrophotometric curve is also specified to avoid metamerism. Similar measurements should be made on the pigments, dyes, and toners used in color proofing systems to make sure they match the pigments in the printing inks.

5. Color measurements of the inks and their combinations can be used to determine the gamut of colors covered by a set of inks. For this purpose the CIE specifications are usually converted to another system, such as the Munsell System or one of the CIE systems like CIELAB or CIELUV. The GATF/Preucil system provides a simpler but less accurate method of evaluating color gamut, because the densities are measured through filters that do not correspond to the spectral sensitivities of the eye. This system, however, is useful and recommended for comparing color gamuts of inks and color proof colorants especially if the color proof colorants are similar to the pigments used in the inks and the comparisons are made with the same filters and illuminants. When more experience is gained with colorimetric instruments, systems like CIELUV will be used for making these comparisons.

Viewing Conditions

A color printing job, or comparison of proof with the original, or proof with the press print, passes or fails on the basis of visual comparisons and judgments. Such comparisons and judgments are made by artists, photographers, engravers, pressmen, advertising agencies, publishers, and customers. Rarely, if ever, are all these people in the same place at the same time. If they judge the product under different viewing conditions, that is, under lights with different spectral distributions, they may reach different conclusions and make erroneous decisions that can be costly and time-consuming.

Most of these problems are avoided by the use of standardized viewing conditions for comparing the original art or transparency with the proof and the proof with the printed reproduction. Standard conditions for viewing are specified in "American National Standard Viewing Conditions for the Appraisal of Color Quality and Color Uniformity in the Graphic Arts," ANSI Standard PH2.32 – 1972, and "American National Standard Projection Viewing Conditions for Comparing Small Transparencies with Reproductions," ANSI Standard PH2.45 – 1979. The first standard deals with two separate functions: (1) the appraisal of color quality and comparison of a photomechanical reproduction (proof or print) to the original art or transparency; and (2) the appraisal of color uniformity in printing by comparing press sheets with approved proofs or OK sheets. The transparencies covered by the first standard are limited to 4 × 5 inch (102 × 127 mm) to 11 × 14 inch (279 × 356 mm) in size. The second standard covers viewing conditions for small transparencies such as the 2 × 2 inch (51 × 51 mm) slides from 35 mm photography or the 2¼ × 2¼ inch (57 × 57 mm) films from Hasselblad type cameras.

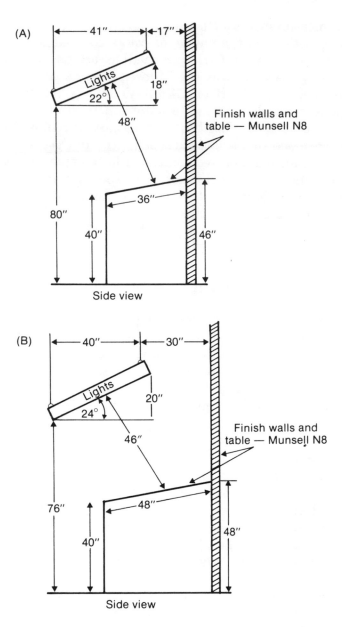

B-13. Diagrams for standard color viewing booths (A) for 36 inch (914 mm) deep table; (B) for 48 inch (1220 mm) deep table. (GATF)

For judging the color quality of reflection materials the original art, reproduction and/or proof are illuminated with light having a color temperature of 5,000°K with adequate amounts of power in all parts of the visible spectrum to provide good color rendition equivalent to a color rendering index of between 90 to 100. A booth is recommended in which the background area surrounding the samples to be viewed is painted a matte, neutral gray with reflectance factor of about 60% (Munsell notation N8). The light is mounted so that the illumination is diffuse and even over the subjects to be examined. Diagrams for typical viewing booths are illustrated in Figure B-13.

Large transparencies are viewed on special transparency illuminators, with the same kind of illumination and color rendering index (5,000°K and 90 – 100 CRI) as the reflection standard. Small transparencies are judged on special projection viewers which project an enlarged image of the transparencies for easier viewing. Transparency viewers are shown in Figure B-14.

The appraisal of the color uniformity of press sheets during a run and the comparison of these sheets to OK sheets poses a slightly different problem. In this type of comparison it is important to be able to detect small color shifts in the printing before they become unacceptable. A problem occurs with the discrimination of yellow and colors containing yellow under 5,000°K illumination. The use of illumination with a color temperature of 7,500°K provides a higher proportion of light in the blue end of the spectrum, which allows better visual discrimination of greens and warm colors like yellow, orange, and red, which are more difficult to

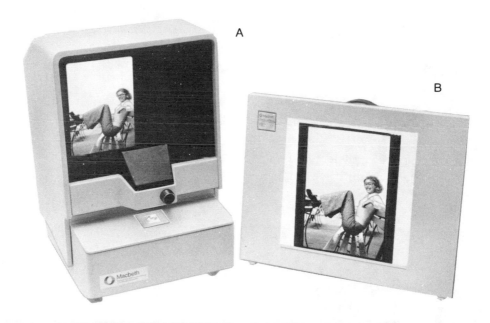

B-14. Standard transparency viewers: (A) for 35 mm and 2¼ inch (57 mm) films; (B) for 4x5 inch (102 mm x 127 mm) to 11x14 inch (279 mm x 356 mm). (GAM)

differentiate at the lower color temperature (5,000°K). Most viewing booths used in production are equipped with both types of illumination.

No visual comparisons of colors between originals and proofs, proofs and OK sheet, and press prints and OK sheet should be attempted without a viewing booth equipped with controlled illumination and a neutral background. Comparisons made under any other conditions are even less reliable than comparing apples and oranges.

Measurement and Control of Dot Gain

The types of dot gain — optical and physical — and the factors affecting them, especially in lithographic printing, are discussed in Chapter III. As mentioned there a number of press studies have been made to learn the mechanism of dot gain in offset lithographic printing and isolate the factors that affect it. These studies include those made by RIT (Sigg, 1970); DuPont (Brunner, 1979); and PIRA (Johnson, 1980). These are summarized and evaluated here. They are not considered in chronological order, but are reported in the order of their relevance and significance. One of the first studies of dot gain was made by Frank Preucil in conjunction with the first LTF/GATF Color Survey in 1958. Preucil taught the concepts of control of dot gain in the many LTF/ GATF Color Seminars he conducted from 1958 to 1967 when he left GATF to join RCA.

A. Johnson/PIRA Study (1980)

Anthony Johnson and his group at PIRA, the British graphic arts research institute, made a thorough study on "Correlating Proofs to Production Prints" in 1980 and found that the controlling factor in lithography affecting the matching of proofs with press prints was dot gain. They found that dot gain is characteristic of the lithographic process. It defies standardization and is exceedingly elusive, varying from plant to plant, press to press, and even from run to run. They studied the parameters affecting dot gain on proof and production presses and determined their relative importance.

In the study, they likened the action of the ink in the nip between the plate and blanket cylinders on a printing press, mathematically, to a parallel plate viscometer in which the force required to compress the liquid is defined by Stefan's equation (Figure C-1).

$$F = \frac{3\pi \eta\, a^4 u}{4h^3}$$

where F = force on plates
η = viscosity of liquid (ink)
a = radius of liquid (ink)
u = velocity of approach of the two plates
h = plate separation

By making several assumptions, which were not specified in the report, they showed that the dot gain Δq is expressed by:

$$q - q_0 = \Delta q = \frac{4\pi k}{3d^2} \left(\frac{h_0^2 t}{\eta} \right)$$

where Δ q = dot gain or difference between the area of ink before (q_0) and after impression (q)
d = reciprocal of screen ruling
h_0 = ink film thickness before impression
t = time of dwell between plate and blanket
η = viscosity of ink

Thus this model predicts that dot gain is a function of the screen ruling, press speed, ink film thickness, and ink viscosity. The equation was tested by plotting values of q against ho^2 for a range of inks and tone values, and the correlation coefficient in each case was greater than 0.9. This establishes a definite relation between dot gain and the square of the ink film thickness. This means that any change in the amount of ink on the press results in a change in dot gain which is equal to the square of the difference in ink film thicknesses!

A similar definite relation between dot gain and the reciprocal of the viscosity (η) of the ink could not be established (correlation coefficient was 0.826). Slightly better correlation was obtained when dot gain was plotted against the yield value of the ink. The fact that q_0 seems to depend on the yield value of the ink indicates that ink transfer is visco-elastic in nature, which will require more elaborate techniques or rheological measurement. Also a wider range of ink viscosities than those used in the test may be needed to show significant differences to test the simple theory.

No attempt was made in the experiment to study the relation between dot gain, press speed, and impression pressure. The equation predicts that dot gain is a function of pressure and inverse speed which agrees with experience. This relation between dot gain, impression pressure, and press speed helps to explain the difficulty in matching press proof with production press prints, especially those made on flatbed and rotary proof presses. Proofs are generally sharper with less dot gain than production

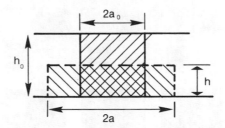

C-1. Principle of parallel plate viscometer as a model for dot gain in printing. (PIRA)

prints. The customary solution has been to make the plates with fuller images to simulate dot gain, but the gain is not proportional on fuller plate images and causes variations in the ends of the tone scale. The PIRA study indicates that the better answer is to vary the concentration of the ink so that higher ink film thicknesses are used which cause greater dot gain. An addition of 5% gel reducer to the ink resulted in 7 to 10% increased gain in the middletones. This has been standard practice employed by many press proofers.

Next to inks, the blankets had the most significant effect on dot gain. The total spread of dot gain in the middletones for six different blankets was 6% (16 to 22%) although variations between the same types of blankets (compressible and non-compressible) were less.

Another variable studied in the PIRA experiment is the effect of the substrate on ink transfer and dot spread. Substrates differ considerably in these characteristics which necessitate changes in ink film thickness, impression pressures, blankets, etc., in order to print properly. These items cannot be standardized but experience generally supplies the proofer with information on typical dot gain occurring with different paper/press combinations.

The effect of screen ruling on dot gain was studied by Rosen at RIT and is reported in Chapter III. The PIRA model shows dot gain as an inverse function of the square of the reciprocal of the screen ruling. This was not checked in the experiments, but if it is valid it explains the big differences in dot gain between 65-line, 120-line, and 150-line screen tints illustrated in Figure III-36 in Chapter III.

The study concluded that while ink properties are not the only parameters affecting dot gain, they are a major factor, especially ink film thickness, which can be used as the variable to modify when other press conditions are different and cannot be reconciled.

Franz Sigg RIT Study (1970)

Franz Sigg's study at RIT, reported in the TAGA Proceedings of the

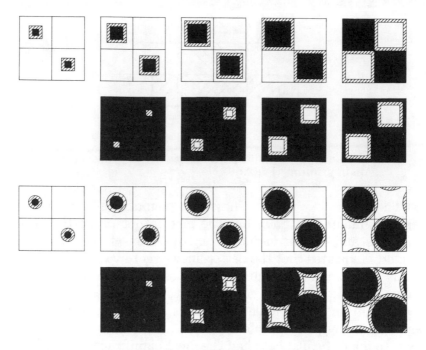

C-2. Comparison of perimeters of (A) square dots and (B) round dots. (TAGA)

1970 Annual Conference, described a special target, adapted by RIT and Gretag, for measuring and evaluating dot gain; and results of press tests to produce dot gain and validate the target. A most significant part of this study was an investigation to determine which dot area and dot shape was most sensitive to dot gain. He compared two gray scales, one with square dots and the other with round dots. Making two simplifying assumptions that (1) all dots have an even amount of dot gain and (2) the ink density of each dot is the same as the solid ink density, he found that the dot gain was a function of the perimeters or circumferences of the dots.

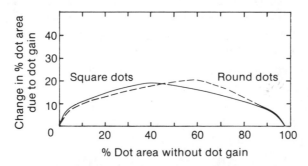

C-3. Changes in dot area due to dot gain with both square dots and round dots. (TAGA)

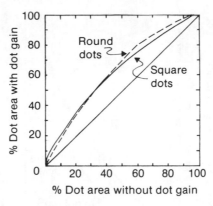

C-4. Curves showing the effects of dot gain with square dots and round dots. (TAGA)

Under conditions that cause dot gain, square dots gain more in the lower percentages than round dots because the perimeters of the square dots are larger than the round dots (Figure C-2). For square dots the dot size that experiences the largest gain is approximately 45% (for round dots it is about 60%). This is shown in Figure C-3. Curves showing the effect of dot gain in percent dot area are illustrated in Figure C-4. The conversion of the data in these two figures to density values using the Yule-Nielsen equation (see section on Measurement of Dot Area), with a solid density of 1.5 and an n value of 1.6 is shown in Figures C-5 and C-6. Lack of agreement between theoretical and experimental curves is believed due to the simplifying assumptions not being completely valid, especially in the highlights. Elliptical or chain dots were not considered in the study. Their dot gain characteristics can be calculated from their perimeters.

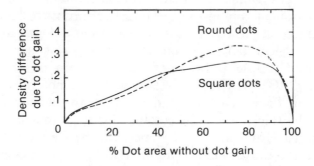

C-5. Data of Figure C-3 plotted in density. (TAGA)

DuPont/Felix Brunner Study (1979)

A most interesting and significant study of dot gain was made in 1979 by Felix Brunner (Corippo, Switzerland) for DuPont Eurostandard

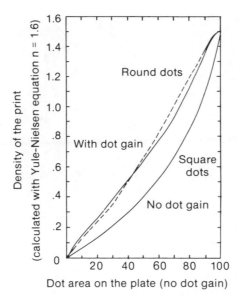

C-6. Data of Figure C-4 plotted in density. (TAGA)

CROMALIN. Brunner is known for his printing control targets using *microline* images to control plate exposures and color printing by lithography. The study has developed a precise procedure for making Eurostandard CROMALIN proofs using a special control strip and test form with microline targets that closely match the press prints produced by the offset printing systems used in Europe. This approach has been extended to the SWOP CROMALIN requirements based on continuing research into North American printing characteristics by DuPont/Brunner.

A most exceptional feature of the Brunner System is that it has been able to equate optical gain in the CROMALIN proof to the combination of dot sharpening on positive plates (or dot gain on negative plates) plus optical and physical dot gain on the press print controllably and reproducibly. CROMALIN proofs made from positives, as the Eurostandard CROMALIN proofs are made, cannot have physical or mechanical gain. They have optical gain caused by the shadows the dots cast through the thickness of the combined transparent films (Figure C-7). According to Brunner, when properly controlled by exposure the optical gain on the Eurostandard CROMALIN proof can be held to closer tolerances than press gain on the production print and is closer to the production print than a proof produced on a proof press.

The DuPont/Brunner Eurostandard CROMALIN Control Strip is composed of Brunner control patches used extensively in Europe, in press control systems. It consists of 36 measuring patches arranged in two rows 6 mm (¼ inch) wide and 4 mm (3/16 inch) apart with a width of 16 mm (11/16 inch) without the lettering. This strip is similar to the DuPont CROMALIN Offset Com Guide (Pos) illustrated in Chapter X, Figure X-10. Length of the bar with register marks and DuPont logo is 125 mm (5 inches).

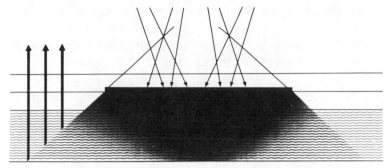

C-7. Mechanism of optical dot gain on CROMALIN proofs. (DuPont)

The 36 measuring patches are divided into 7 control groups:

- Solid density patches for monitoring the solid densities of the four printing colors.
- Coarse screen and fine screen patches of 50% dot area for measuring dot growth in the proof and the press print using the difference between coarse and fine screen readings as a characteristic value. For coated papers typical characteristic values are yellow 0.08, cyan 0.10, magenta 0.12, black 0.14 with tolerances of ±0.02 for proofs and ±0.04 for press prints (Figure C-8).
- Halftone patches in 25% and 75% dot areas which are used to plot simple characteristic printing or dot gain curves to indicate irregular distortions in cases when proof does not match the press print; trapping patches to determine if poor trapping on press print is the cause of a poor match between proof and press print.
- Highlight dot and microline patches which are the most important controls in the Brunner system used to control and monitor dot

C-8. Characteristic values for yellow, cyan, magenta and black in coarse screen and fine screen patches in Brunner target. Same as X-12, pg. X-21. (DuPont)

sizes. Figure C-9 illustrates the appearance of the targets for *correct, sharp,* and *full* CROMALIN proofs.

- Gray balance patch which consists of 50% cyan, 41% magenta, and 41% yellow dots that should appear neutral with Eurostandard inks — any shift in color indicates variation in dot gain in one or more colors.
- Tolerance measuring patches used to determine the amount of deviation from standard in the case of gray balance variations.

The seven control groups of targets are used in four control systems:

(1) Use of the highlight dot and microline patches to control dot sizes.
(2) Gray balance.
(3) Use of the coarse screen/fine screen halftone patches to measure and control dot gain.
(4) Measurement and control of solid density.

There are two additional controls when visual differences exist between proof and print despite good agreement in the four standard controls. This can happen when there are irregular distortions of the characteristic printing curve which can be determined by plotting new curves using the 25% and 75% dot size readings for the control strip along with the 50% reading. Another cause of poor agreement between proof and print is improper trapping which is the reason for the inclusion of these targets in the control strip. The measurement of trapping is described in Appendix A.

The Eurostandard CROMALIN test form incorporates other elements like pictures, gray scales, and other targets in addition to the control strips in order to optimize and standardize the printing process, determine its tolerances, and allow accurate comparisons between the proof and press print. Results of proofing and press tests run with the Eurostandard CROMALIN test form are shown in Figures C-10, C-11 and C-12. The

0,5%	1%	6μ
2%	3%	8μ
		11
4%	5%	13
		16

Original   Correct   Too Sharp   Too Full

C-9. Appearance of Highlight Dot and Microline Patches (A) unexposed; (B) too sharp; (C) correct exposure for CROMALIN proofs; (D) too full. (DuPont)

legend accompanying each illustration explains its significance. The dotted lines in each plot are called "isocontours" by Brunner which indicate regular characteristic printing curves as distinguised from irregular curves caused by printing aberrations such as ink emulsification with dampening solution or excessive dot gain due to high ink film thickness.

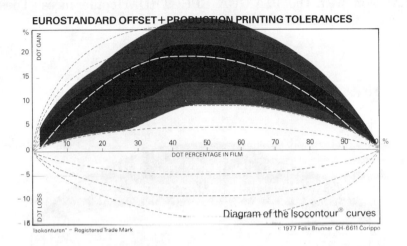

C-10. **Eurostandard Offset — Production Printing Tolerances.** Dark gray area shows optimum printing (+/- 4%). In practice curves are generally found in the medium gray area. Broken white line is the standard curve for Eurostandard CROMALIN. (DuPont)

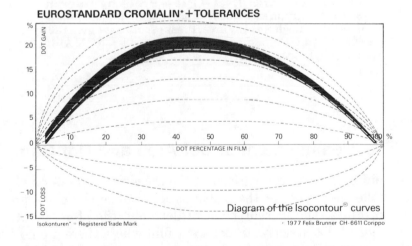

C-11. **Eurostandard CROMALIN plus tolerances.** CROMALIN proof curves lie close to standard printing curves with narrower tolerances than press proofing and production printing. (DuPont)

Brunner and DuPont are to be congratulated on this significant study of dot gain, its measurement and control. The standardization and control of printing will be a boon to all proofing systems, and the principles of this system of control are sure to be applied to other means of proofing besides CROMALIN.

A number of other press tests of dot gain have been run particularly in connection with the PIA/GCA SPECTRUM conferences. These are discussed in Chapter X.

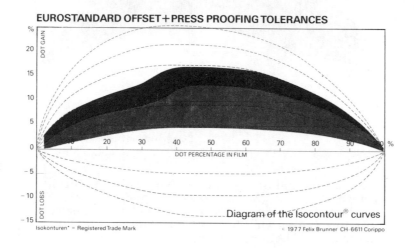

C-12. **Eurostandard Offset — Press Proofing Toleran-
ces.** Dark gray area is ideal range but in practice many proofs fall in medium gray area. Press proofs have generally less dot gain than production prints and CROMALIN proofs. (DuPont)

The Measurement of Dot Area and Dot Gain

Dot gain involves a comparison of the areas of the dots on the films used to make the proofs or the plates used to make the press proofs or production prints. The measurement of dot gain, therefore, involves the measurement of dot areas on transparent film where there are no surface and internal reflections, and on reflection prints on paper in which surface and internal reflections and diffusion of light play an important part. A comprehensive discussion of the measurement of dot area is included in the Quality Control Scanner, Volume 2, Number 9.

Halftone Film: The measurement of dot area on halftone film is done with a transmission densitometer. The densitometer is zeroed on the film base or on the dot fringe, (in the case of a soft-dot halftone) and the density of the halftone tint area is read using an aperture large enough to integrate about 200 dots. The equation for calculating the percent film dot area is:

$$a = 100 - T = 100 - 10^{-Dt}$$

where: a = % dot area

T = transmittance

D_t = transmission density of the dot tint

Tables for converting density readings to transmittance and reflection are in Appendix D. A number of transmission densitometers are equipped with microcomputers which are programmed to read dot areas directly. A programmable calculator can also be used to make the conversion or it can be read directly on a scientific calculator with a 10^{-x} function.

Reflection Print: The measurement of dot area on a printed reproduction or reflection proof or print is much more complex. The optical dot area (ODA) or effective dot area (EDA) as it is also called, is a measure of the total amount of light absorbed by the printed halftone pattern which is the combination of the press dot gain and/or the optical dot gain. Press proofs and prints have both types of dot gain — off-press proofs like positive CROMALIN and positive MATCHPRINT have only optical dot gain. From density measurements of the halftone tint and the solid, the Murray-Davies equation is used to calculate the ODA or EDA;

$$D_t = -\log [1 - a(1 - 10^{-Ds})]$$

Solving this equation for a

$$a = \frac{1-10^{-Dt}}{1-10^{-Ds}}$$

The total dot gain can be calculated from the ratio of the dot areas on the print or proof and the film positive or negative. As pointed out in the DuPont/Felix Brunner study optical gain is the result of inefficient light reflection on the printed substrate, the light diffusion from the substrate surface, light scatter within the substrate, and extra absorption of the ink. A 45% dot printed on paper under normal printing conditions could have the same density as a 65% dot. If the dot was printed on coated metal it could have a density equivalent to a 55% dot as the metal does not have the inefficient light reflection of the paper. Under examination with a 10x – 20x magnifier, the dot tint showing the 65% dot density would appear more like 55% dots as the effect of the optical dot gain disappears.

Optical dot gain on press proofs or prints is a function of the substrate and screen ruling. Under normal printing conditions on any particular job these would be constant. Therefore, to determine the actual physical dot area (PDA) the optical dot gain due to these factors must be factored out of the equation. This is done in the Yule-Nielsen equation:

$$D_t = -n \log [1-a(1 - 10^{-Ds/n})]$$

Solving this equation for a

$$a = \frac{1-10^{-Dt/n}}{1-10^{-Ds/n}}$$

where a = physical dot area PDA
D_t = density of halftone tint
D_s = density of solid
n = paper/screen ruling factor

When $n = 1$ this equation reduces to the Murray-Davies equation. The determination of the "n-value of General Conditions" was described by M. Pearson (RIT) in the 1980 TAGA Proceedings. He recommended a value of 1.7 for *n for most calculations. Typical values of n are listed in Table C-I from the Quality Control Scanner, Volume 2, Number 9.*

TABLE C-I

	Typical n Values
Coated paper	1.65
Uncoated paper	2.70
DuPont Cromalin	2.60
Agfa Gevaert Gevaproof	1.40
3M Color Key	4.00
3M Transfer Key	1.90

To measure dot area, zero the densitometer on the paper. Measure the solid ink density and halftone tint density. Some densitometers read out dot area directly from these two readings. A calculator can be programmed to make the calculation. Using an *n* value of 1.0 will give total optical dot area (ODA); using another value of *n* will give the physical dot area (PDA) for the paper/screen ruling combination used to produce the press proof or print.

Miscellaneous Information

DIAMETER OF HALFTONE SCREEN DOTS
FOR COMMONLY USED SCREENS

Diameter in micrometers (μM)

L = Line Screen Spacing inches^{-1} (cm^{-1})	P = Percent Dot Size								
	1	2	3	5	10	20	30	40	50
300 (120 lines/cm)	9.55	13.5	16.5	21.4	30.2	42.7	52.3	60.4	67.5
150 (60 lines/cm)	19.1	27.0	33.1	42.7	60.4	85.4	105	121	135
133 (52 lines/cm)	21.5	30.5	37.3	48.2	68.1	96.4	118	136	152
120 (47 lines/cm)	23.9	33.8	41.4	53.4	75.5	107	131	151	169
110 (43 lines/cm)	26.0	36.8	45.1	58.2	82.4	116	143	165	184
100 (40 lines/cm)	28.7	40.5	49.6	64.1	90.6	128	157	181	203
85 (33 lines/cm)	33.7	47.7	58.4	75.4	107	151	185	213	238
65 (26 lines/cm)	44.1	62,4	76.4	98.6	139	197	242	279	312

$$D = \sqrt{\left(\frac{25.4}{L}\right)^2 \times \frac{P}{100} \times \frac{4}{\pi}}$$

$$D = \frac{2866}{L} \sqrt{P}$$

where D = dot diameter (micrometers)
       L = line screen spacing (lines per inch)
       P = percent dot size

DOT AREA VS. DENSITY

Integrated Halftone Density to % Dot Area

Integrated Halftone Density	Percent Dot Area	Integrated Halftone Density	Percent Dot Area
0.00	0	0.36	56
0.01	2	0.38	58
0.02	5	0.40	60
0.03	7	0.42	62
0.04	9	0.44	64
0.05	11	0.46	65
0.06	13	0.48	67
0.07	15	0.50	68
0.08	17	0.54	71
0.09	19	0.58	74
0.10	21	0.62	76
0.11	22	0.66	78
0.12	24	0.70	80
0.13	26	0.74	82
0.14	28	0.78	83
0.15	29	0.82	85
0.16	31	0.86	86
0.17	32	0.90	87
0.18	34	0.95	89
0.19	35	1.00	90
0.20	37	1.10	92
0.22	40	1.20	94
0.24	42	1.30	95
0.26	45	1.40	96
0.28	48	1.50	97
0.30	50	1.70	98
0.32	52	2.00	99
0.34	54		

Calculated from Murray Davies Equation:

$$\text{Dot area} = \frac{1-10^{-D_t}}{1-10^{-D_s}}$$

D_t = density of tint
D_s = density of solid

CONVERSION TABLE

Optical Density vs. Percent Transmission and Reflection

Density	Transmission or Reflection Percent	Density	Transmission or Reflection Percent	Density	Transmission or Reflection Percent	Density	Transmission or Reflection Percent	Density	Transmission or Reflection Percent	Density	Transmission or Reflection Percent
0.00	100.00	0.50	31.62	1.00	10.00	1.50	3.162	2.00	1.000	2.50	0.3162
0.01	97.72	0.51	30.90	1.01	9.772	1.51	3.090	2.01	0.9772	2.51	0.3090
0.02	95.50	0.52	30.20	1.02	9.550	1.52	3.020	2.02	0.9550	2.52	0.3020
0.03	93.33	0.53	29.51	1.03	9.333	1.53	2.951	2.03	0.9333	2.53	0.2951
0.04	91.20	0.54	28.84	1.04	9.120	1.54	2.884	2.04	0.9120	2.54	0.2884
0.05	89.13	0.55	28.18	1.05	8.913	1.55	2.818	2.05	0.8913	2.55	0.2818
0.06	87.10	0.56	27.54	1.06	8.710	1.56	2.754	2.06	0.8710	2.56	0.2754
0.07	85.11	0.57	26.92	1.07	8.511	1.57	2.692	2.07	0.8511	2.57	0.2692
0.08	83.18	0.58	26.30	1.08	8.319	1.58	2.630	2.08	0.8318	2.58	0.2630
0.09	81.28	0.59	25.70	1.09	8.128	1.59	2.570	2.09	0.8128	2.59	0.2570
0.10	79.43	0.60	25.12	1.10	7.943	1.60	2.512	2.10	0.7943	2.60	0.2512
0.11	77.62	0.61	24.55	1.11	7.762	1.61	2.455	2.11	0.7762	2.61	0.2455
0.12	75.86	0.62	23.99	1.12	7.586	1.62	2.399	2.12	0.7586	2.62	0.2399
0.13	74.13	0.63	23.44	1.13	7.413	1.63	2.344	2.13	0.7413	2.63	0.2344
0.14	72.44	0.64	22.91	1.14	7.244	1.64	2.291	2.14	0.7244	2.64	0.2291
0.15	70.79	0.65	22.39	1.15	7.079	1.65	2.239	2.15	0.7079	2.65	0.2239
0.16	69.18	0.66	21.88	1.16	6.918	1.66	2.188	2.16	0.6918	2.66	0.2188
0.17	67.61	0.67	21.38	1.17	6.761	1.67	2.138	2.17	0.6761	2.67	0.2138
0.18	66.07	0.68	20.89	1.18	6.607	1.68	2.089	2.18	0.6607	2.68	0.2089
0.19	64.57	0.69	20.42	1.19	6.457	1.69	2.042	2.19	0.6457	2.69	0.2042
0.20	63.10	0.70	19.95	1.20	6.310	1.70	1.995	2.20	0.6310	2.70	0.1995
0.21	61.66	0.71	19.50	1.21	6.166	1.71	1.950	2.21	0.6166	2.71	0.1950
0.22	60.26	0.72	19.05	1.22	6.026	1.72	1.905	2.22	0.6026	2.72	0.1905
0.23	58.88	0.73	18.62	1.23	5.888	1.73	1.862	2.23	0.5888	2.73	0.1862
0.24	57.54	0.74	18.20	1.24	5.754	1.74	1.820	2.24	0.5754	2.74	0.1820
0.25	56.23	0.75	17.78	1.25	5.623	1.75	1.778	2.25	0.5623	2.75	0.1778
0.26	54.95	0.76	17.38	1.26	5.495	1.76	1.738	2.26	0.5495	2.76	0.1738
0.27	53.70	0.77	16.98	1.27	5.370	1.77	1.698	2.27	0.5370	2.77	0.1698
0.28	52.48	0.78	16.60	1.28	5.248	1.78	1.660	2.28	0.5248	2.78	0.1660
0.29	51.29	0.79	16.22	1.29	5.129	1.79	1.622	2.29	0.5129	2.79	0.1622
0.30	50.12	0.80	15.85	1.30	5.012	1.80	1.585	2.30	0.5012	2.80	0.1585
0.31	48.98	0.81	15.49	1.31	4.898	1.81	1.549	2.31	0.4898	2.81	0.1549
0.32	47.86	0.82	15.14	1.32	4.786	1.82	1.514	2.32	0.4786	2.82	0.1514
0.33	46.77	0.83	14.79	1.33	4.677	1.83	1.479	2.33	0.4677	2.83	0.1479
0.34	45.71	0.84	14.45	1.34	4.571	1.84	1.445	2.34	0.4571	2.84	0.1455
0.35	44.67	0.85	14.13	1.35	4.467	1.85	1.413	2.35	0.4467	2.85	0.1413
0.36	43.65	0.86	13.80	1.36	4.365	1.86	1.380	2.36	0.4365	2.86	0.1380
0.37	42.66	0.87	13.49	1.37	4.266	1.87	1.349	2.37	0.4266	2.87	0.1349
0.38	41.69	0.88	13.18	1.38	4.169	1.88	1.318	2.38	0.4169	2.88	0.1318
0.39	40.74	0.89	12.88	1.39	4.074	1.89	1.288	2.39	0.4074	2.89	0.1288
0.40	39.81	0.90	12.59	1.40	3.981	1.90	1.259	2.40	0.3981	2.90	0.1259
0.41	38.90	0.91	12.30	1.41	3.890	1.91	1.230	2.41	0.3890	2.91	0.1230
0.42	38.02	0.92	12.02	1.42	3.802	1.92	1.202	2.42	0.3802	2.92	0.1202
0.43	37.15	0.93	11.75	1.43	3.715	1.93	1.175	2.43	0.3715	2.93	0.1175
0.44	36.31	0.94	11.48	1.44	3.631	1.94	1.148	2.44	0.3631	2.94	0.1148
0.45	35.48	0.95	11.22	1.45	3.548	1.95	1.122	2.45	0.3548	2.95	0.1122
0.46	34.67	0.96	10.96	1.46	3.467	1.96	1.096	2.46	0.3467	2.96	0.1096
0.47	33.88	0.97	10.72	1.47	3.388	1.97	1.072	2.47	0.3388	2.97	0.1072
0.48	33.11	0.98	10.47	1.48	3.311	1.98	1.047	2.48	0.3311	2.98	0.1047
0.49	32.36	0.99	10.23	1.49	3.236	1.99	1.023	2.49	0.3236	2.99	0.1023
0.50	31.62	1.00	10.00	1.50	3.162	2.00	1.000	2.50	0.3162	3.00	0.1000

$$D = \text{Log}_{10} \ \frac{1}{T} \quad \text{or} \ \text{Log}_{10} \ \frac{1}{R}$$

METRIC-ENGLISH CONVERSION TABLES*
(Units of Length)

Metric-English										English-Metric					
Cm.	In.	Cm.	In.	Cm.	In.	Cm.	In.	Cm.	In.	In.	Cm.	In.	Cm.	In.	Cm.
0.1	.039	31	12.20	70	27.56	109	42.91	148	58.27	1/64	.040	23	58.42	62	154.48
0.2	.079	32	12.60	71	27.95	110	43.31	149	58.66	1/32	.079	24	60.96	63	160.02
0.3	.118	33	12.99	72	28.35	111	43.70	150	59.06	1/16	.159	25	63.50	64	162.56
0.4	.157	34	13.39	73	28.74	112	44.09	151	59.45	1/8	.318	26	66.04	65	165.10
0.5	.197	35	13.78	74	29.13	113	44.49	152	59.84	3/16	.476	27	65.58	66	167.64
0.6	.236	36	14.17	75	29.53	114	44.88	153	60.24	1/4	.635	28	71.12	67	170.18
0.7	.276	37	14.57	76	29.92	115	45.28	154	60.63	5/16	.794	29	73.66	68	172.72
0.8	.315	38	14.96	77	30.31	116	45.67	155	61.02	3/8	.953	30	76.20	69	175.26
0.9	.354	39	15.35	78	30.71	117	46.06	156	61.42	7/16	1.113	31	78.74	70	177.80
1.0	.394	40	15.75	79	31.10	118	46.46	157	61.81	1/2	1.27	32	81.28	71	180.34
2	.787	41	16.14	80	31.50	119	46.85	158	62.21	9/16	1.43	33	83.82	72	182.88
3	1.18	42	16.54	81	31.89	120	47.24	159	62.60	5/8	1.59	34	86.36	73	185.42
4	1.57	43	16.93	82	32.28	121	47.64	160	62.99	11/16	1.75	35	88.90	74	187.96
5	1.97	44	17.32	83	32.68	122	48.03	161	63.39	3/4	1.91	36	91.44	75	190.50
6	2.36	45	17.72	84	33.07	123	48.43	162	63.78	13/16	2.06	37	93.98	76	193.04
7	2.76	46	18.11	85	33.46	124	48.82	163	64.17	7/8	2.22	38	96.52	77	195.58
8	3.15	47	18.50	86	33.86	125	49.21	164	64.57	15/16	2.38	39	99.06	78	198.12
9	3.54	48	18.90	87	34.25	126	49.61	165	64.96	1	2.54	40	101.60	79	200.66
10	3.94	49	19.29	88	34.65	127	50.00	166	65.35	2	5.08	41	104.14	80	203.20
11	4.33	50	19.69	89	35.04	128	50.39	167	65.75	3	7.62	42	106.68		
12	4.72	51	20.08	90	35.43	129	50.79	168	66.14	4	10.16	43	109.22		
13	5.12	52	20.47	91	35.83	130	51.18	169	66.54	5	12.70	44	111.76		
14	5.51	53	20.87	92	36.22	131	51.58	170	66.93	6	15.24	45	114.30		
15	5.91	54	21.26	93	36.61	132	51.97	171	67.32	7	17.78	46	116.84		
16	6.30	55	21.65	94	37.01	133	52.36	172	67.72	8	20.32	47	119.38		
17	6.69	56	22.05	95	37.40	134	52.76	173	68.11	9	22.86	48	121.92		
18	7.09	57	22.44	96	37.80	135	53.15	174	68.50	10	25.40	49	124.46		
19	7.48	58	22.83	97	38.19	136	53.54	175	68.90	11	27.94	50	127.00		
20	7.87	59	23.23	98	38.58	137	53.94	176	69.29	12	30.48	51	129.54		
21	8.27	60	23.62	99	38.98	138	54.33	177	69.69	13	33.02	52	132.08		
22	8.66	61	24.02	100	39.37	139	54.72	178	70.08	14	35.56	53	134.62		
23	9.06	62	24.41	101	39.76	140	55.12	179	70.47	15	38.10	54	137.16		
24	9.45	63	24.80	102	40.16	141	55.51	180	70.87	16	40.64	55	139.70		
25	9.84	64	25.20	103	40.55	142	55.91	181	71.26	17	43.18	56	142.24		
26	10.24	65	25.59	104	40.95	143	56.30	182	71.65	18	45.72	57	144.78		
27	10.63	66	25.98	105	41.34	144	56.69	183	72.05	19	48.26	58	147.32		
28	11.02	67	26.38	106	41.73	145	57.09	184	72.44	20	50.80	59	149.86		
29	11.42	68	26.77	107	42.13	146	57.48	185	72.83	21	53.34	60	152.40		
30	11.81	69	27.17	108	42.52	147	57.87	186	73.23	22	55.88	61	154.94		

1 inch = 2.54 centimeters (cm) = 25.4 millimeters (mm)
1 cm = .3937 in.

*GATF Publications #507, "Black and White Stripping." p. 324.

Illustration Codes, Credits and References

Many of the illustrations in this book have been adapted from other books and manufacturers' literature. In order to keep from cluttering the Figure captions with long credit lines, codes have been used to identify the sources of the illustrations. The codes are listed below alphabetically along with the credits, figure references and sources. The author wants to take this opportunity to thank all who contributed illustrative materials and gave permission to use copyrighted illustrations as they help immeasurably to explain the text and make it more understandable to the reader. Figures without codes have been drawn or photographed from existing knowledge or materials without legal restrictions as far as the author knows.

Codes	Credits and References
A-G	Courtesy: Agfa-Gevaert Inc. Figure VI-3 of the Gevaproof process redrawn from the Gevaproof instruction booklet.
Bobst	Courtesy: Bobst Group Inc. Figures IV-3 and IV-5 from photographs of F.L.A.G. Lithographic Proof Presses.
Crosfield	Courtesy: Crosfield Electronics Inc. Figures III-9 Magnascan 640 scanner and III-41 Lasergravure from slides from Crosfield.
D.R.	Courtesy: Direct Reproduction Corp. Figures VI-1 and VI-2 Watercote and Kwik-Proof processes drawn from Direct Reproduction Corp. literature.
DuPont	Courtesy: DuPont Photo Products Figure III-12 Optical Dot gain and III-29 Total Dot gain from DuPont/Brunner Eurostandard CROMALIN booklet; V-6 CROMACHECK from DuPont literature; Figures VI-7 and VI-13 Cross-section of Cromalin film and proof; and VI-8-VI-12 Cromalin laminator, and Cromalin manual toning patterns from **Cromalin Process Manual**; VIII-2 Cromalin gravure proof from

Cromalin Process Manual; VIII-3-VIII-6, Cromalin Hard Dot gravure from DuPont literature; X-9(D), X-12, X-13, X-14, X-22, X-23, X-24, C-7-C-12, CROMALIN Com Guide/System Brunner, Targets and Tolerances from DuPont literature.

Enco   Courtesy: Enco Printing Products, American Hoechst Corp. Figures V-1B, V-4 and V-5 NAPS/PAPS Processing and Processor drawn from Enco literature.

Fuji   Courtesy: Fuji Photo Film Co. Figure VI-18 Fujichrome color film structure, drawn from Fuji literature.

GAM   Courtesy: Graphic Arts Manual, Irving E. Field, Musarts Publishing Co., New York, NY Figures II-16 Pin Register (Figures 9.24, 9.26 and 9.27), II-22 (Figure 11.9), II-23 (Figure 11.11), II-24 (Figure 11.12), II-25 (Figure 11.13) Diagrams of Printing Presses; III-17 Powderless Etching (Figure 10.5), III-18 Letterpress Dot (Figure 10.4); A-1 Electromagnetic Spectrum (Figure 2.1); A-3 (Figure 2.2), A-4 (Figure 2.3) Color Temperature diagrams of typical light sources; A-9 Subtractive color combinations (Figure 2.7), B-3 Munsell Color Tree (Figure 2.11), B-5 Tristimulus curves (Figure 2.12) and B-14 Standard Transparency viewers (Figure 2.17); all from original art or redrawn from the book (Figure numbers indicated).

GAP   Courtesy: Graphic Arts Publishing Co., Livonia, NY Figures III-6 and III-7 Color separation processes, Color Reproduction Guide, pp. 20, 21; III-31 Effect of Screen ruling on dot gain. Quality Control Scanner, Vol. 2, No. 9; X-8 Hexagon plot of overprint colors — Quality Control Scanner, Vol. 3, No. 4.

GATF   Courtesy: Graphic Arts Technical Foundation Figures III-23 - III-27 GATF Quality control targets from actual targets and illustrations in GATF Research Progress Bulletins and promotional literature; III-28 Printing defects from slides made from technical service samples used in GATF seminars; III-30 Dot gain study from slide made from LTF/GATF First Color Survey; III-32, III-33 from slides used by Frank Preucil in GATF color seminars; III-36 and III-37 from slides used in GATF Paper and Ink Seminar. X-9A GATF Compact Test Strip from actual strip; X-16 GATF Standard Color Bars; X-19 QC Strip and X-20 Star targets from Research Progress Bulletin and slides used in GATF press seminar; X-21 Midtone Dot Gain Scale from GATF folder; X-25 GCA/GATF Proof Comparator from actual guide; X-26 and X-27 Ideal color reproduction from slides used by Preucil in GATF Color seminars. A-2, A-8, A-10, A-16 Color information from slides used by Preucil in GATF Color Seminars; A-17, A-18 Graphical Analysis of trapping from slides used by Preucil in GATF Color Seminars; B-6, CIE diagram from illustration in **Lithographer's Manual** page 7:16; B-13 Standard Viewing Booths from illustrations in **GATF Handbook for Graphic Communications: Illumination**, pages 3-4.

GRI
Courtesy: Gravure Research Institute
Figures III-42 and III-43 Electrostatic Assist from slides provided by GRI; VIII-1 Tone Reproduction Curves by R. de Master (3M) from GRI Report No. M-253 Nov. 1983; VIII-7 Spectra curve from GRI Report No. M-199 Nov. 1982; VIII-8, VIII-9 Plots of Cibachrome proofs on GATF Color Circle from GRI Report No. T&C 34 Nov. 1979; VIII-10, VIII-11 Plots of Ektachrome Proofs by W.A. Rocap from GRI Report No. M-189 Nov. 1981.

GTA
Courtesy: Gravure Technical Association
Figures II-18 Gravure cylinder types from **GTA Gravure Technical Manual**; III-40 Helioklischograph principles from **GTA Gravure Technical Manual**; IV-6 and IV-7 Gravure proof presses from **GTA Gravure Technical Manual**; X-18 Standard GTA Reproduction Curves from **GTA Bulletin** Spring 1983.

Hazeltine
Courtesy: Hazeltine Corporation
Figure IX-1 Separation Previewer from photograph supplied by Hazeltine.

HCM
Courtesy: HCM, U.S. representative of Dr. Ing Rudolph Hell, Gmbh
Figures II-11 Skeleton and full blacks from HCM slide; II-14 DC-300 scanner from HCM slide; III-8 Control panel of DC-300 from HCM slide; IX-4 - IX-7 Illustrations of CPR403 Digital Color Proofs, original art supplied by HCM.

H-E
Courtesy: Heidelberg-Eastern — U.S. representative of Heidelberger Druckmaschinen Aktiengesellschaft
Figures III-45 CPC-2 photo by Heidelberg-Eastern; VI-14 - VI-17, Spectra illustrations supplied by Ed Riggs, Heidelberg-Eastern; X-1 and X-3 CPC units from photograph and slide supplied by Heidelberg-Eastern; X-5 Gretag D-732 from photograph supplied by Heidelberg-Eastern; X-9C Gretag Color Strip supplied by Heidelberg Eastern; X-11 Gretag Elements, photographed and drawn from Gretag brochure.

IP
Courtesy: International Paper Company, publisher of "Pocket Pal"
Figures II-3, Lithography adapted from illustration in Pocket Pal, 13th Edition, page 29; II-6, Halftone, adapted from illustration in Pocket Pal, 13th Edition, page 67; II-13 Scanner redrawn from illustration in Pocket Pal, 13th Edition, page 81; III-4 Moire patterns adapted from Pocket Pal, 13th Edition, page 82.

IPA   Courtesy: International Pre-Press Association
Figures X-15 SWOP Color References from slides supplied by
IPA; X-17 Inspection Form from SWOP booklet.

K-C   Courtesy: Coulter Systems Corporation
Figures VII-1 - VII-9 Illustrations of KC-Analog Color Proofer
and Process from original art by Coulter Systems Corp.; IX-11
KC-LP610 from photo by Coulter Systems Corp.

LogE   Courtesy: LogEtronics Inc.
Figures VI-19 Programmable Light Source from photograph by
LogEtronics; IX-8 LogE/Dunn Color Camera from slide supp-
lied by LogEtronics.

MDA   Courtesy: MacDonald Dettwiler and Associates
Figures IX-3 Block diagram and IX-9 Schematic from art supplied by MDA.

P&J   Courtesy: Phillips & Jacobs, U.S. representative of TOPPAN
Color Proofer
Figure IX-2 TOPPAN CP 525 from photograph supplied by P&J.

PIRA   Courtesy: PIRA, Printing, Packaging and Paper Industries
Research Association (ENGLAND)
Figure C-1 reproduced from PIRA Paper No. 8, 1980.

Polaroid Courtesy: Polaroid Corporation
Figures IX-10 Polaroid processing system produced from a
reproduction of the original art.

Reprotest Courtesy: Reprotest BV (IGT)
Figure X-7 IGT On-line densitometer.

RIT   Courtesy: Rochester Institute of Technology
Figures X-9B RIT Color Test Strip from the actual strip; X-10
Bull's Eye targets from actual samples.

Rockwell Courtesy: Rockwell International, Graphic Systems Division
Figures III-44 and X-2 Color Control Systems from photographs
supplied by Rockwell International.

TAGA   Courtesy: Technical Association of the Graphic Arts
Figures X-6 Macbeth On-Press Densitometer from illustration in
paper by Dr. S.J. Kishner in **1983 TAGA Proceedings** page
160; B-8 - B-12, Diagrams of color spaces reproduced from illustrations in paper by R.E. Maurer in **1979 TAGA Proceedings**
pages 218 and 219; C-2 - C-6 Illustrations from paper on Dot Gain
by F. Sigg in **1970 TAGA Proceedings** pages 209-211.

3M   Courtesy: Printing Products Division, 3M
Figures V-2, V-3 Color Key Proofs drawn from information in 3M
literature; VI-4 - VI-6 Transfer Key and Matchprint Proofs,
drawn from information in 3M literature.

Tobias   Courtesy: Tobias Associates
            Figure X-4 Scanning Densitometer from photography supplied
            by Tobias Associates.

Wiley   Courtesy: John Wiley and Sons, publisher of **Principles of
            Color Reproduction** by J.A.C. Yule
            Figures II-5, II-7 Printing steps from Figure 1.01 and 1.02 in
            Principles of Color Reproduction, page 4; II-12 Color Sepa-
            ration redrawn from Figure 4.05 in **Principles of Color
            Reproduction**, page 57; B-4 and B-7 Spectrophotometric Curve
            and CIE plot drawn from Figures 2.01 and 2.02 in **Principles of
            Color Reproduction**, pages 22 and 23.

Glossary and References

The information in this and succeeding sections relates to the text in the ten chapters, conclusion and four appendices and is listed alphabetically. This section refers to products, processes, reports, published articles and other items mentioned in the text but not otherwise defined.

Acigraf — A controlled etching process for making gravure cylinders made by Engravers: Andreotti, 38 Via Bovisaca, Milan, Italy.

ACR — Achromatic Color Reduction — Now called Gray Component Replacement (GCR), it is a process for substituting black for the third color in a color requiring three colors for its rendition.

Additive Primaries — Red, Green and Blue light which when added together as colored lights produce white light. White light consists of approximately equal proportions of red, green and blue light.

A-G — Agfa-Gevaert — Manufacturer of Gevaproof color proofing system.

ANSCO Printon — The first photographic color proofing process used for proofing line maps during World War II.

ANSI — Acronym for American National Standards Institute.

ANSI-PH 2.32-1972 — American National Standard Viewing Conditions for the Appraisal of Color Quality and Color Uniformity in the graphic arts. See pages 329-332 for discussion.

ANSI-PH 2.45-1979 — American National Standard Projection Viewing Conditions for Comparing Small Transparencies with Reproductions. See pages 329-332 for discussion.

Bobst Group — Manufacturer of Lithographic proof press.

Dr. Willem Brouwer — System of printing in which no color is produced with more than two colors and black, accomplishing it by modifying the Neugebauer equations and calculating the amount of black and the other colors to produce each color using look-up tables.

Brownprint paper — A print-out photographic paper sensitized with silver nitrate used for single color proofs. It is developed in plain water and can be fixed with a weak hypo solution. Also called Van Dyke, Solar or silver paper.

Brunner — Felix Brunner is a manufacturer of printing control strips in Corippo, Switzerland who has produced special test targets and strips for calibrating and controlling DuPont CROMALIN off-press color proofs. See pages 243-244 and 260-264.

Brunner/DuPont Study — Study conducted by Felix Brunner (Corippo, Switzerland) for DuPont in 1979 to determine correlation of dot gain between CROMALIN proofs and printing done with plates made from positives. Similar studies were made later with proofs and plates made from negatives. See pages 337-342.

Chevalier, Jean — Well-known graphic arts consultant and owner of a color reproduction trade shop in Paris, France, that produces covers for 15 of France's most prominent weekly magazines.

Chrome Guide — Off-press color proofing system of the overlay type made and marketed by Polychrome Corp., discontinued in July 1984.

Church, F.E. (Al) — Pioneer in the development of color specifications for magazine printing as a representative of MPA. He was active in the establishment and promotion of the original Standard Specifications of Letterpress in 1967 and the **SWOP** Specifications in 1975. He is now retired and writes a monthly column on printing specifications for Graphic Arts Monthly magazine.

Cibachrome — A dye-bleach color photographic paper used for making color proofs from gravure continuous tone positives. It is made and marketed by Ciba-Geigy Corp.

Colex 520 — The first off-press color proofing process of the adhesive polymer-dry powder type produced and marketed by A-E Staley Co. It was withdrawn from the market after about a year.

Color Key — Off-press color proofing process of the overlay type made and marketed by 3M.

Color Separations — The products in negative or positive form of the process of separating color originals into the subtractive color components, yellow, magenta, cyan and black. They are made photographically or by electronic scanning.

Coulter Systems Corp. — Manufacturer of KC-Color Proofing systems.

CPR 403 Color Proof Recorder — Digital system for producing "hard" color proofs from the Chromacom electronic color page makeup system. See pages 220-223.

Cromacheck — Off-press color proofing system of the overlay type by DuPont using peel-apart technology. The process was developed by and is marketed by DuPont. See pages 142-144.

Cromalin — Off-press color proofing process of the adhesive polymer-dry powder type made and marketed by DuPont. See pages 161-171 and 197-203.

Crosfield Electronics — Manufacturer of Magnascan electronic scanners, Studio 800 systems of electronic color page makeup systems, Lasergravure, Data Systems Datrax laser platemaking systems and data compression systems for image data transmission.

Crosfield Studio 800 — A series of electronic color page makeup systems consisting of the Studio 820, 840 and 860 systems made and marketed by Crosfield Electronics Corp.

Dainippon Screen Co. — Manufacturer of electronic scanners, Sigmagraph 2000 electronic color page makeup system and numerous products and machines for use in prepress operations.

DEMIA — Plate scanner to measure image areas on plates to use for presetting ink fountains on the press. Name is acronym for **DE**vice for **M**easuring **I**mage **A**reas. The equipment is made by Dai Nippon Printing Company (Japan). The system was described in a paper presented at the 1983 TAGA Conference and published in 1983 TAGA Proceedings, pp. 74-88.

Diazochrome-Tecnifax — An overlay off-press color proofing system first made by Tecnifax Corp. which is now James River Graphics.

Dijit — Ink-jet printer using multiple jets to do variable printing like addressing, computer letters, package coding, etc. Formerly produced by Mead Corp., now made and marketed by Eastman Kodak Co. and called Diconix.

DIN Color System — A color order system used in Germany for the specification of colors.

Direct Reproduction Corp. — Manufacturer of Watercote, KWIK-Proofs and dr Proofs.

DRUPA — Acronym for **D**ruck und **Pa**pier (Print and Paper) — The largest international exhibition of printing equipment, machinery and techniques held in Dusseldorf, W. Germany about every five years since 1952 until 1982 when it announced a four year schedule.

Dot Gain — Changes in dot size that occur in platemaking and in printing especially in lithographic printing.

D.R. — **Direct Reproduction Corporation** — Manufacturer of Watercote, Kwik-Proof and dr Color Proof Systems.

dr Color Proof — Off-press color proofing process of the sensitized-ink type produced by Direct Reproduction Corp. It is an improvement over the Watercote process using a drum coating technique.

DuPont — Manufacturer of CROMALIN, CROMACHECK, DYLUX,

MYLAR and LASTIK.

Dylux — A single color proofing material using a free radical process and organic dyes with exposure to UV light to produce a blue image on white paper.

Eastman Kodak — Manufacturer of EKTAFLEX PCT and EKTA-CHROME RC-14 used in color proofing systems.

Edelman, M. — As Technical Director of C.H. Lorilleux Ink Co. (Paris, France) he suggested the concept of **Vivacite** described by Frank Preucil (LTF/GATF) in an article entitled "How Strong to Run the Colour" that appeared in **Penrose Annual No. 58**, 1965. This attribute of color is related to Preucil's function **Paper Surface Efficiency (PSE)**.

Ektachrome RC-14 — A color photographic paper for making color proofs from continuous tone gravure positives. It is made and marketed by Eastman Kodak.

Ektaflex PCT — A color photographic diffusion transfer system used to make color proofs from continuous tone and halftone negatives. Also used as the output for digital systems like Hell CPR403 and Crosfield MagnaProof (LogE/Dunn VersaColor camera). Made and marketed by Eastman Kodak. See pages 177-180 and page 209.

Electrostatic Assist (ESA) — Process developed by GRI to reduce skips in the highlights during printing on gravure presses using electrostatic forces to assist the ink transfer from the wells in the light tones to paper with irregularities in the surface. See pages 108-109.

Enco NAPS — Off-press color proofing process of the overlay type made from negatives — produced and marketed by Enco Printing Products, American Hoechst Corp.

Enco PAPS — Same as Enco NAPS except proofs are made from positives.

Final Proof — Off-press color proofing process of the superposed sensitized-ink type made and marketed by American Photo-Graphics Corp.

Flexo-Mounter-Proofers — Special presses for mounting flexographic plates on the actual printing cylinders in correct position for printing, and proofs are pulled in a special paste ink to make sure plates are in register for printing. See page IV-6.

Flexo Proof Press — BIEFFEBI (Preprint) — Special press for mounting 4-color process plates in which the precision of mounting is monitored with a microprocessor.

Flexo Proof Press, Geo Moulton Successors (GMS) — Special press for proofing flexographic and gravure cylinders.

Flexo Proof Press, D. Timmons & Sons — Special press for proofing flexographic and gravure cylinders.

Fuji — Fuji Photo Film Co.

GAM — Graphic Arts Manual.

GAP — Graphic Arts Publishing Co.

GATF Dot Gain Scale — A target with numbers 1 to 9 in fine screen ruling against a coarse screen background used to indicate dot size changes in platemaking and printing.

GATF Dot Gain Scale II — A special target for measuring dot gain in 50% tints in printing.

GATF Sensitivity Guide — Also called Stouffer Scale, it is a continuous tone grey scale with density differences between the numbered 21 steps equal to the square root of 2 or 1.4, used to measure and control exposures in photography and platemaking. A change in exposure of two steps amounts to double, or half, the exposure oif the preceding or succeeding step depending on whether the exposures are increasing or decreasing.

GATF Star Target — A 3/16-inch (9.5 mm) pinwheel target with 36 spokes emanating from the center used to indicate dot size changes in platemaking and printing and their causes.

Gevaproof — Off-press color proofing process of the direct transfer type made and marketed by Agfa-Gevaert Co.

Graph-Expo — The largest printing machinery exhibition held annually in the U.S.A. sponsored by the Graphic Arts Show Company which consists of representatives of PIA, NAPL and NPES (National Printing Equipment and Supply Association).

Gravure Cylinder Making — Information from **Rotogravure** by H.W. Cartwright and Robert MacKay which was published by the MacKay Publishing Co. Inc., Lyndon, KY in 1956.

Gravure Cylinder Making — Information from GTA **Gravure Technical Guide** which was published by the Gravure Technical Association in 1955 and was edited by Oscar Leiding. The latest edition in 1975 was revised by Oscar Smiel who also included new material.

Gray Component Replacement (GCR) — See ACR.

Gretag D-732 — Off-line system for color measurement and control using a high speed densitometer to make as many as 200 color measurements across a 40 inch (1016 mm) sheet in 6 seconds as well as recording 3840 pieces of color data. The system is made and marketed by Gretag Ltd. (Switzerland). See page 236.

GRI — Gravure Research Institute.

GTA Group I Inks — Color charts produced by Gravure Technical Association (GTA) with inks for printing on roto newsprint stock used for Sunday newspaper supplements, newspaper inserts, some magazines and catalogs.

GTA Group V Inks — Color charts produced by Gravure Technical Association (GTA) with inks for printing on coated stock used for magazines, catalogs and similar publications.

Gutenberg, Johann — Credited with the invention of printing with movable type in Mainz, Germany about 1440 AD.

Halftone Gravure — Means for making gravure cylinders using halftone positives or negatives on electromechanical engravers like Helioklischograph and special reading heads to convert the halftone images to variable area/variable depth engravings on the cylinders. See pages 105-106 and 194-196.

Hazeltine Color Previewer SP1620 — Digital system for making "soft" proofs from color separation films. It is made and marketed by Hazeltine Corp.

HCM — North American dealer of Hell products and systems.

Heidelberg CPC Systems — A family of systems for the off-line measurement and control of color printed sheets on Heidelberg presses.

Helioklischograph (EME) — An electromechanical engraving machine to produce gravure cylinders by using photoelectric scanning heads to transmit data from continuous tone black and white positive or negative prints on a white plastic ("bromide") to a data processor that sends impulses to engraving heads fitted with diamond styli that produce diamond shaped cells of the variable area/variable depth type in the copper surface of the printing cylinder. The machines are made by Dr. Ing. Rudolph Hell Gmbh and marketed in the U.S.A. by HCM Corp.

Hell, Dr. Ing. Rudolph, Gmbh — Manufacturer of Chromagraph scanners, Chromacom electronic color page makeup systems, flat-field scanners, facsimile transmission systems, digital color proofing system and Helioklischograph electromechanical engraving machine for making gravure cylinders.

Hell Chromacom — Electronic color page makeup system made by Dr. Ing. Rudolph Hell Gmbh in Kiel, W. Germany and marketed in the U.S.A. by HCM Corp.

IBM 3800-6670 — High speed electrostatic copiers, also known as intelligent copiers, used for electronic laser printing systems. They are made and marketed by IBM Corp.

IP — International Paper Co. — Publisher of **Pocket Pal**.

IPA — International Pre-Press Association.

Johnson, Gordon O.F. — Chairman of LogEtronics Corp. and popular speaker, panelist and chairman of sessions on the impact of new technology on printing.

Jung, Dr. Eggert — of Dr. Ing. Rudolph Hell Gmbh; accomplished achromatic color reduction (ACR) by a combination of UCR and calculation.

KC-Color Proof — Off-press color proofing process using an electrostatic, completely inorganic photo-conductor and liquid toners made by Coulter Systems Corp. marketed in Europe by Coulter-Stork Corp. and in the U.S.A. and the rest of the world by Coulter Systems Corp. See Chapter VII.

Kleeberg, Fred — Book production specialist and consultant who provides book production management and supervisory functions and services for smaller publishers.

Klietsch, K. — Credited with the invention of gravure printing in Germany about 1880 AD.

Klimsch — Manufacturer of cameras and other prepress equipment. Products marketed in U.S.A. by Heidelberg Eastern.

Kodak Customized Color Service — is a means of analyzing color printing developed and offered as a service by Eastman Kodak Co. The mechanism of the service is described in the paper R.E. Maurer (Kodak) presented at the 1982 Annual TAGA Conference on "Customized Color Computer Printing Analysis" and published in the 1982 **TAGA Proceedings**, pp. 518-550. See page 270.

Kolor-Kote — Off-press color proofing process of the sensitized ink type similar to Watercote. It was produced by Teitelbaum Sons, Inc., but is no longer available.

Kunz, Dr. Werner — His paper "Ink Transfer in Gravure Process" presented at 1975 TAGA Conference and published in 1975 **TAGA Proceedings**, pp. 151-176 discusses four factors that influence ink transfer and the parameters that affect them.

Kuppers, H. — Accomplished ACR in Europe by the process of undercolor removal (UCR), i.e. removing equal amounts of the third color from each color and substituting a corresponding amount of black.

Laser Assisted Engraving — Also called Laser Assisted Deplating (LAD) — A new system of producing gravure cylinders being developed by GRI which combines laser imaging and chemical etching.

Lasergravure — A process for producing gravure cylinders by coating the cylinder with an epoxy resin, curing it, and imaging it with wells in helical grooves produced by laser impingement in the plastic modulated by impulses from a Crosfield color scanner or Crosfield Studio 860 electronic color page makeup system. The process was developed and is marketed by Crosfield Electronics Corp.

Lasers In Graphics — Annual conferences sponsored by Dunn Technology devoted to reports on developments in Pre-Press systems. There has been five conferences up to 1983 and published proceedings of each conference are available from Dunn Technology.

Leekley, R.M. — At the Institute of Paper Chemistry, Leekley, R.F. Tyler and J.D. Hultman studied Preucil's PSE factor and concluded that surface reflection was a more reliable measure of the effect called Paper Surface Efficiency by Preucil. Their study and conclusions are contained in the paper "The Effect of Surface Reflection on Color" published in the 1978 **TAGA Proceedings**.

Lithographic Proof Press, Flatbed-FLAG Offset Press 104 — Special motorized proof press in which dampening control is assisted by a refrigerated plate platen. The press is manufactured and marketed by Bobst Inc. See page 121.

Lithographic Proof Press, FLAG-Speedproof 4C — A common impression cylinder press with four independent plate and blanket cylinder couples positioned around a large central impression cylinder. Manufactured and marketed by Bobst Inc. See pages 121-122.

Lithographic Proof Press, Production Press, OMCSA-Aurelia — Small production press with electronic drive used extensively for color proofing in trade shops and large plants. Manufactured by OMCSA in Italy.

Lithographic Proof Press, Rotary, Vandercook-RO4 — Compact 4-color proof press of unique design with three cylinders — a large cylinder on which the four color plates are mounted, a large blanket cylinder with four blankets and a single size impression cylinder. Manufacture has been discontinued.

LogE/Dunn Versacolor Camera — Digital system for producing "hard" color proofs from electronic color page makeup systems. It is used in the Crosfield MagnaProof system for making "hard" proofs from the Crosfield Studio 860 electronic color page makeup system.

M.A.N.-Roland RCI-CCI — Off-line systems for color measurement and control of printed sheets off Roland sheet-fed presses. The RCI system allows manual setting of ink fountain keys. The CCI system is a closed loop system for automatic setting of the ink fountain keys.

MATCHPRINT — Off-press color proofing process of the direct transfer type using a spacer between the actual printing substrate as a base and the sandwich of laminated color films to duplicate dot gain on web offset presses. It is made and marketed by 3M.

Maurer, R.E. — Consultant on color reproduction controls and techniques. Retired from Kodak Research Lab, ex-president of and prolific contributor to TAGA annual conferences on color reproduction subjects. Originator of the Kodak Customized Color System.

MDA — MacDonald Dettwiler — Manufacturer of image processing systems.

Moire — An undesirable enlarged screen or beat pattern caused by overprinting two or more halftones at incorrect screen angles. Minimum moire patterns are caused when angles of 30 degrees are used between halftones. Moire patterns can also be caused in single color printing between the halftone and the screen pattern of the wire screen on the paper machine which sometimes leaves an embossed screen pattern on the wire, or bottom side, of the paper. See pages 58-59.

Morgan, J. Tom Jr. — Noted authority on and printer of high quality color and black and white reproductions. He was owner of the Litho Krome Co. in Columbus, GA, which he sold to Hallmark Cards in 1979. He is the originator of the double black technique which he announced and described at the 1960 NAPL convention and is the inventor of a new color photographic proofing process which is capable of correcting the orange-yellow hues of color photographic print paper to hues that match yellow ink pigments.

Munsell Color System — A color order system used extensively in the U.S.A. for specification of colors.

Murray-Davies Equation — is used to calculate Optical or Equivalent Dot Area (ODA or EDA) from measurements of the halftone tint and the solid. It is described and discussed on pages 342-344.

Neugebauer Equations — Simultaneous equations representing the colors produced when halftone tints of colors are combined. They were derived by Hans Neugebauer in 1937 and are useful in the mathematical analysis of color reproduction.

Ohio Electronic Engraver — An electromechanical engraving machine to produce gravure cylinders similar to the Hell Helioklischograph, manufactured by Ohio Electronic Engravers, Inc.

Ostwald System — A color order system used in Europe for the specification of colors.

Ozachrome — One of the first off-press color proofing processes of the overlay type produced by Ozalid Corp., a division of GAF Corp. Products are no longer produced.

Peretta Control System 1-77 — A plate scanning system using a special EEPROM computer chip to preset special ink fountains. See X-7 and the paper by B.L. Quilliam, "Development of a System for Computerized, Automatic Ink-Flow Control" in the 1983 **TAGA Proceedings**, pp. 89-103.

P&J — Phillips & Jacobs — U.S. representative of TOPPAN CP525 soft color proofing system.

PIRA — See Research Institutes.

Polaroid/MacDonald Dettwiler — A digital color proofing system to produce hard copies of digital data from scanners or color page make-up systems using an image digitizer by MacDonald Dettwiler and Polaroid Industrial color print paper. See pages IX-17 - IX-21 and **Proceedings of Lasers in Graphics 1983 Conference**, Vol. 2, pg. 327-336.

Polytrans — An early off-press color proofing process by Kodak using pigmented films which were laminated by heat and pressure. It was discontinued after about a year in the marketplace.

Press Control Strips and Targets — Special bars containing color strips and targets used to help color proofers and pressmen maintain consistency in quality of color proofs and press prints.

Preucil, Frank M. — Color reproduction specialist, consultant, lecturer and seminar chairman with experience in letterpress, lithography and gravure; former supervisor of color reproduction studies at LTF/GATF (1957-1967). Originator of LTF/GATF Color Diagrams, Color Reproduction Guide, Paper Surface Efficiency function and Trapping Equations.

PRINT 85 — Second largest international exhibition of printing machinery (next to DRUPA) held in Chicago at intervals of about four years.

Proof-Kote — Off-press color proofing process of the sensitized-ink type similar to Watercote. It was produced by Lith-Kemco, now part of Anchor/-LithKemCo but is no longer manufactured.

Proof Presses for Letterpress — Vandercook — There are three Vandercook proof presses for letterpress color proofing: the single color test press; the 2-color proof press and the 4-color proof press.

PSE — Paper Surface Efficiency is a function which describes the visual effect or efficiency of a paper-ink combination. It was developed by Frank Preucil at LTF/GATF. It is related to the gloss of the paper or ink film and the ink absorptivity of the paper. The more absorptive the paper the lower is the PSE; the higher the gloss and lower the absorptivity the higher the PSE. It is described in **GATF Research Progress** No. 60, 1963.

REMAK — The first off-press color proofing system using an electrostatic photo conductor and liquid toners.

RIT — See Research Institutes.

Rocap, William A., Jr. — Prolific writer on quality control procedures and color proofing processes. He was responsible for the use of the Kodak Ektachrome RC-14 process by Meredith-Burda Co. which he described in a report presented at the 1981 Annual Meeting of the Gravure Research Institute, Nov. 11-14, 1981.

Rockwell — Rockwell International, Graphic Systems Division, U.S. representative of MAN-Roland presses and color control systems.

Scitex — Manufacturer of electronic color page makeup systems and peripherals.

Scitex Response 300, 350 — Electronic color page makeup systems made by Scitex in Israel and marketed in the U.S.A. by Scitex America Corp.

Screenless Printing — A process for printing without a halftone screen. Special plates are used which are printed with ink and dampening solution on lithographic presses. The process had limited use because of restrictions imposed by a U.S. patent owned by Milton Ruderman. This patent has expired so the process is free of restrictions.

Senefelder, A. — Credited with the invention of lithography in Germany about 1800 AD.

Shipley, Edd — Retired director of industry relations at Kingsport Press, now head of Southeastern Graphics Group, Kingsport, Tenn., which provides book design and production management and supervisory services and functions for publishers. He prepared the comprehensive layouts for the front matter, chapter openings, text pages and back matter and the cover design, and handled the production details of this book at Kingsport Press.

F. Sigg/RIT Study — Study of dot gain in 1970 to determine which dot area and dot shape was most sensitive to dot gain. Results showed that dot gain was a function of the perimeter of the dots. Square dots gained more than round dots.

Sigmagraph 2000 — Electronic color page makeup system made by Dainippon Screen Co., Japan and marketed in the U.S.A. by D.S. America Inc.

PECTRA — Off-press color proofing process of the adhesive polymer-dry der type made by Keuffel and Esser Co. and marketed by Heidelberg rn.

RUM — A series of annual conferences started in 1979 and spon- CA in which the results of cooperative studies of magazine printing e SWOP specifications are reported. See pages 238-240 and

ifications for Web Offset Publications — See pages

ries — Yellow, Magenta and Cyan which when added produce black. Each is the mixture of the two colors mary color is subtracted from white light. **Yellow** is d green when blue is subtracted from white light. on of red and blue remaining when green is sub- n is the combination of green and blue remain- m white light.

s and Associations.

, TRANSFER KEY and MATCHPRINT

r measurement and control using a y as 54 readings across a 40 inch or functions are also displayed on keted by Tobias Associates. See

Digital System for making

"soft" proofs from color separation films. It is made by TOPPAN in Japan and marketed in the U.S.A. by Phillips and Jacobs Co.

Transfer Key — First off-press color proofing process of the direct transfer type introduced in 1968, made and marketed by 3M.

Trapping — Good Trapping is achieved when the same amount of ink appears to transfer to a previously printed ink image as to the unprinted paper. When less ink appears to transfer it is **undertrapping**; when it appears as though more ink has transferred it is called **overtrapping**.

Trapping Equation-Brunner — Equation to calculate trapping conditions in printing.

Trapping Equation-Childers — Same definition as Trapping Equation-Brunner.

Trapping Equations-Preucil — Equations developed by Frank Preucil (GATF) to determine conditions for correct trapping, over- and under-trapping.

True Rolling — The concept of adjusting the packing of the plate, blanket and impression cylinders on an offset press to compensate for the distortion of the rubber blanket in printing is known as "True Rolling" and was invented in 1933 by Miehle Printing Press Co. (now Rockwell International, Miehle Div.). The principles are described in a paper presented at the 1953 TAGA Conference entitled "True Rolling and Cylinder Packing" by A.T. Kuehn and B.T. Sites and published in the 1953 TAGA Proceedings, pp. 72-77.

Van Dyke paper — Same as Brownprint paper.

Videojet — Ink-jet printer using a single jet to do variable printing, lik addresses, computer letters, package coding, etc. It is made and marketed b A.B. Dick Co.

Watercote — The first commercial off-press color proofing process. It superposed sensitized ink color proofing process made and markete Direct Reproduction Corp.

Waterless Lithography — A process using planographic plates in the image and non-image areas are essentially on the same plane. Th areas consist of ink and the non-image areas consist of silicone ru water or dampening solution is needed in printing. 3M called thei **Driography** introduced in 1970 and withdrawn in 1977. TORA has introduced both positive and negative plates for waterless li which are running in limited markets in Japan, Europe and the pages 97-98.

Wiley — John Wiley and Sons, publisher of "Principles of Color J.A.C. Yule.

Xerox 8700 & 9700 — High speed electrostatic copiers, so **intelligent copiers** used in electronic printing systems. A cated Xerox 9900 has been introduced. These are produced and marketed by Xerox Corp.

Yule, J.A.C. — Research Chemist and recognized authority on Color reproduction employed at Eastman Kodak Research Labs for over 20 years. Author of **Principles of Color Reproduction**, John Wiley & Sons, New York, 1967 and Chapter 17, **Color Reproduction in the Graphic Arts**, pp. 466-480, **Neblette's Handbook of Photography and Reprography**, edited by John M. Sturge, Van Nostrand-Reinhold, New York, 1977.

Yule-Korman-Ventures Research & Development Corp. — J.A.C. Yule and Dr. N.I. Korman (formerly with RCA) were the first to produce an all digital scanner in 1970 using a printed color chart and look-up tables for color correction. The company was underfinanced and ran out of money before a sponsor could be found. The system was described in the **Proceedings of the 11th Annual IARIGAI Conference**, pp. 93-106 published in 1973.

Yule-Nielsen Equation — is used to calculate the physical dot area by factoring out the effects of the substrate and the screen ruling. It is similar to the **Murray-Davies equation** with the introduction of an **n-factor**. It is described on pages C-14 and C-15 and in a paper by M. Pearson entitled **n-Value for General Conditions** in the 1980 TAGA Proceedings, pp. 415-425.

Directory

This section lists names and addresses of manufacturers, suppliers, individuals, associations and research institutes mentioned in the text or related to the references.

Companies and Individuals:

A.B. Dick Co., 5700 N. Touhy Ave., Chicago, IL 60648, Tel.: (312) 647-8800.

Acigraf Sp. A., Via T. Moneta 41 20161 Milano, Italy.

Agfa-Gevaert, Inc. Graphic Systems, 150 Hopper Ave., Waldwick, NJ 07463, Tel.: (201) 444-7700.

American Photo-Graphics, 700 Bonnie Lane, Elk Grove Village, IL 60007, Tel: (312) 640-7721.

Ansco, formerly a division of GAF Corp. and now Anitec Image Corp., One Paragon Dr., Montvale, NJ 07645, Tel.: (201) 573-6900; Laboratory and Manufacturing: 40 Charles St., Binghamton, NY 13902, Tel.: (607) 774-3333, Telex: 93461.

Azoplate Corp., now ENCO Printing Products, American Hoechst Corp., 3070 Highway 22 W., P.O. Box 3700, Somerville, NJ 08876, Tel.: (201) 231-3875.

Baldwin-Gegenheimer, Div. Baldwin Technology Corp., 417 Shippan Ave., Stamford, CT 06902, Tel.: (203) 348-4400, Telex: 643697.

Bobst Group, 146 Harrison Ave., Roseland NJ 07068, Tel.: (201) 226-2800.

Burda-Meredith/Burda, P.O. Box 289, Newton, NC 28658, Tel.: (704) 464-8810.

Chemco Photoproducts Co., Charles St., Glen Cove, NY 11542, Tel.: (516) 676-4000.

Chevalier, Jean, Consultant, 93, Ave Des Champs Elysees, 75008, Paris, France.

Ciba-Geigy Corp., Pigments Div., Lower Warren St., Glens Falls, NY 12801, Tel.: (518) 761-2215; Also Ilford Cibachrome, West 20 Century Rd., Paramus, NJ 07652, Tel.: (201) 265-6000.

Consolidated International Corp., 4501 S. Western Blvd., Chicago, IL 60609, Tel.: (312) 376-5600.

Coulter Systems Corp., 35 Wiggins Ave., Bedford, MA 01730, Tel.: (617) 275-2300.

Crosfield Electronics Inc., 480 Central Ave., East Rutherford, NJ 07073, Tel.: (201) 438-4550.

Dainippon Printing Co., 12, Ichigaya-Kagacho 1-Chome, Shinjuku-ku, Tokyo, 162 Japan, Tel.: (266) 2111, Cable: DNPRINT TOKYO.

Dainippon Screen — D.S. America, 5110 Tollview Dr., Rolling Meadows, IL 60008, Tel.: (312) 820-1960.

Direct Reproduction Corp., 835 Union St., Brooklyn, NY 12115, Tel.: (212) 857-6116.

Dunn Technology Inc., 759 Vista Way, Vista, CA 92083-4197, Tel: (619) 758-9460.

DuPont — E.I. DuPont DeNemours Co., Photo Products Dept., Chestnut Run, Wilmington, DE 19898, Tel.: (302) 774-1000.

Eastman Kodak Co., Graphics Markets, 343 State St., Rochester, NY 14650.

Eikonix Corp, 23 Crosby Lane, Bedford, MA 01730, Tel.: (617) 275-5070.

Fuji Photo Film U.S.A., Inc., Graphic Arts, 1000 Pratt Blvd., Elk Grove, IL 60007, Tel.: (312) 569-3500.

Gerber Scientific Instrument Co., 83 Gerber Rd., South Windsor, CT 06074, Tel.: (203) 644-1551.

GMS Ltd., 33 Moss Lane, Walkdon, Manchester M285WD, England, Tel.: 061-7903714. Telex: 668288. U.S. Agent: Daetwyler, 75 Davids Dr., Hauppauge, NY 11787, Tel.: (516) 231-3232.

Grapho-Metronic, Mess -und Regeltechnik GmbH & Co., Postfach 800726, D-8000, Muenchen 80, Federal Republic of Germany, Tel.: (089) 470-2091, Telex: 528042 rsgmd.

Gretag Ltd., Althardstrasse 70, CH-8105, Regensdorf/Zuerich, Switzerland, Tel.: 018421111, Telex: 53950. U.S. representative: Heidelberg Eastern, Inc.

Hazeltine Corp., Pulaski Rd., Greenlawn, NY 11740, Tel.: (516) 261-7000.

Heidelberg Eastern Inc., 73-45 Woodhaven Blvd., Glendale NY 11385, Tel.: (212) 896-5500.

Heidelberger Druckmaschinen AG, D-6900 Heidelberg 1, Federal Republic of Germany, Products distributed in U.S.A. by Heidelberg Eastern Inc., 73-45 Woodhaven Blvd., Glendale NY 11385, tel.: (212) 896-5500.

HCM Graphic Systems Inc., 300 Rabro Dr. East, Hauppauge, NY 11788, Tel.: (516) 582-6520.

Hell — Dr. Ing. Rudolph Hell gmbH, Kiel, W. Germany. All Hell products are marketed in the U.S.A. by HCM Graphic Systems Inc., 300 Rabro Dr. East, Hauppauge, NY 11788, Tel.: (516) 582-6520.

Hell Colormetal — See HCM.

IBM Corp., National Marketing Div., P.O. Box 2150, Atlanta, GA 30055, Tel.: (404) 238-2000.

James River Graphics, 28 Gaylord St., South Hadley, MA 01075, Tel.: (413) 536-7800.

Keuffel & Esser Co., 20 Whippany Rd., Morristown, NJ 07960, Tel.: (201) 285-5000.

Kleeberg, Fred, consultant, 109 E. 79th St., New York, NY 10021.

Lith-Kem Co ;— Now Anchor/LithKemKo, 50 Industrial Loop N., Orange Park, FL 32073, Tel.: (904) 264-3500.

LogE/Dunn Instruments Inc., 544 Second St., P.O. Box 77172, San Francisco, CA 94107, Tel.: (415) 957-1600.

MacDonald Dettwiler and Associates, 3751 Shell Rd., Richmond, B.C., Canada V6X 2Z9, Tel: (604) 278-3411, Telex: 04-355599.

M.A.N.-Roland U.S.A., Inc., 333 Cedar Ave., Middlesex, NJ 08864, Tel.: (201) 469-6600.

Mead Corp., Digital Systems Div., P.O. Box 3230, Dayton, OH 45431, Tel.: (513) 898-3644. Now Diconix, owned by Eastman Kodak.

Misomex Corp. Sweden is represented in the U.S.A. by Royal Zenith Corp., 2101 Jericho Tpke., P.O. Box 860, New Hyde Park, NY 11040, Tel.: (516) 488-3200.

Morgan, J. Tom, Jr., 1914 Stark Ave., Columbus, GA 31906, Tel.: (404) 322-2194.

Mosstype Corp., 150 Franklin Tpke., Waldwick, NJ 07463, (201) 444-8000.

Munsell Color Division, Kollmorgen Corp., P.O. Box 950, Newburgh, NY 12550.

Ohio Electronic Engravers, Inc., 3193 Plainfield Rd., Dayton, OH 45432, Tel.: (513) 253-3004.

OMCSA Advertising, Baranzata di Bollate, Via Manzoni, 45, Milano, Italy, Tel.: 02-3560-425.

Opti-Copy Inc., 10930 Lackman Rd., Lenexa, KS 66219, Tel.: (913) 492-3322.

Ozalid Corp., 1000 McArthur Blvd, Mahwah, NJ 07430, Tel.: (201) 529-3100.

PDI — Printing Developments Inc., 6 Prowitt St., East Norwalk, CT 06855, Tel.: (203) 853-8385.

Perretta Graphics Corp., 40 Violet Ave., Poughkeepsie, NY 12601, Tel.: (914) 476-0550.

Phillips and Jacobs Inc., Fox St. & Roberts Ave., Philadelphia, PA 19129, Tel.: (215) 221-8850.

Polaroid Corp., 784 Memorial Drive-2C, Cambridge, MA 02139, Tel.: (617) 577-2000.

Polychrome Corp., On The Hudson, P.O. Box 817, Yonkers, NY 10702, Tel.: (914) 965-8800.

Preucil, Frank M., Consultant, 735 Sheridan Rd., Evanston, IL 60202, Tel.: (312) 328-6938.

Rockwell International Graphic Systems Div., Miehle Products, 800 E. Oak Hill Dr., Westmont, IL 60559, Tel.: (312) 920-2000.

Scitex America Corp., 8 Oak Park Dr., Bedford, MA 01730, Tel.: (617) 275-5150.

Shipley, Edd, Consultant, Southeastern Graphics Group 2324 Brandon Lane, Kingsport, TE 37660, Tel.: (615) 246-5179.

Shukosha Co. Ltd., International Business Div., 40-10 Ohtsuka 1-Chome, Bunkyo-Ku, Tokyo 112, Japan.

Tietelbaum Sons Inc., 1575 Bronx River Ave., P.O. Box 444, Bronx, NY 10451, Tel.: (212) 892-3838.

3M Printing Products Div., Bldg 223-2N-01 3M Center, St. Paul, MN 55144, Tel.: (612) 733-6785.

Tobias Associates, 50 Industrial Dr., P.O. Box 2699, Ivyland, PA 18974, Tel.: (215) 322-1200. Telex: 510-667-1738.

Toppan Printing Co. Ltd., 5-Itaito-1-Chome, Taito-Ku, Tokyo, Japan 110 represented in the U.S.A. by Phillips and Jacobs Inc., Fox St. & Roberts Ave., Philadelphia, PA 19129, Tel.: (215) 221-8850.

TORAY Industries (America) Inc., 280 Park Ave., New York, NY 10017, Tel.: (212) 697-8150.

Vandercook, now Vandersons Corp., 2020 S. Carboy Rd., Mt. Prospect, IL 60056, Tel.: (312) 437-6143.

Ventures R&D Corp., formerly in Princeton, NJ — no longer in existence.

Xerox Corp., Business Systems Group, Xerox Sq.-006, Rochester, NY 14644, Tel.: (716) 423-3539.

Associations and Research Institutes:

AAAA — American Association of Advertising Agencies, 200 Park Ave., New York, NY 10017, Tel.: (212) 682-2500.
Director: L.S. Matthews

American Business Press, 205 East 42nd Street, New York, NY 10017, Tel.: (212) 661-6360.
Director: T.N. King

ANSI — American National Standards Institute, 1430 Broadway, New York, NY 10021, Tel.: (212) 752-0813.

ANPA-RI — American Newspaper Publishers Association-Research Institute, P.O. Box 17407, Dulles Int'l Airport, Washington, DC 20041.
Director: W.O. Rinehart

ERA — European Rotogravure Association, Streitfeldstr. 19 D-8000 Muenchen 80, Federal Republic of Germany, Tel.: (089) 433010, Telex: 523 349 eraevd.
Director: Anders Bjurstedt

FOGRA — Deutche Forschungsgesellschaft fur Druck-und Reproducktionstechnik ev Streitfeldstr. 19, Postfach 800 469,D-8000 Muenchen 80, Federal Republic of Germany, Tel.: (089) 403045. Telegraph Address: A Muenchen.
Director: Dr. H.J. Falge

FTA — Flexographic Technical Association, 95 W. 19th St., Huntington Station, NY 11746, Tel.: (516) 271-4224.
Director: George J. Parisi

GATF — Graphic Arts Technical Foundation (formerly Lithographic Technical Foundation [LTF]), 4615 Forbes Ave., Pittsburgh, PA 15213, U.S.A., Tel.: (412)

621-6941. Cable GATFWORLD
Director: G.W. Basset

GCA — Graphic Communications Association (an affiliate of PIA), 1730 North Lynn St., Arlington, VA 22209, Tel.: (703) 841-8100.
Director: Norman W. Scharpf

GRI — Gravure Research Institute, 22 Manhasset Ave., Port Washington, NY 11050, Tel.: (516) 883-6670.
Director: Harvey F. George

GTA — Gravure Technical Association, 60 East 42nd St., New York, NY 10017, Tel.: (212) 661-8936.
Director: McKinley M. Luther

IPA -- International Pre-Press Association 552 West 167th St., South Holland, Il 60473, Tel.: (312) 596-5110.
Director: R.A. Harris

IARIGAI — International Association of Research Institutes for the Graphic Arts Industry, 18, The Ridgeway, Fetcham Park, Leatherhead, Surrey, KT22 9AZ, U.K.
Director K.N. Hoare

IPC — Institute of Paper Chemistry, P.O. Box 1039, Appleton, WI 54912, Tel.: (414) 734-9251.

IGT — Instituut voor Grafische Technick TNO (Research Institute for the Printing and Allied Industries-Holland) Closed in 1983. Most of the instruments and service on them has been taken over by Reprotest BV, P.O. Box 4672, 1009 AR Amsterdam, Holland, headed by Fer A. DeVox and represented in the U.S.A. by Werner F. Gerlach, Techno-Graphic Instruments, 5321 Bentwood Dr., San Angelo, TX 76904, Tel.: (915) 944-4102.

ISCC — Inter-Society Color Council, Dept. of Chemistry, Rensselaer Polytechnic Institute, Troy NY 12181, Tel.: (518) 270-6000.

MPA — Magazine Publishers Association, 575 Lexington Ave., New York, NY 10022, Tel.: (212) 752-0055.
Director: Kent Rhodes

PIA — Printing Industries of America, 1730 N. Lynn St., Arlington, VA 22209, Tel.: (703) 841-8100.
Director: Rodney L. Borum

PIRA — Paper and Board, Printing and Packaging Industries Research Association, Randalls Road, Leatherhead, Surrey KT22 7R4, England. Telephone Leather 76161, Telex 929810.
Director: Dr. Keith Bridge

R&EC — Research and Engineering Council of the Graphic Arts, P.O. Box 2740, Landover, MD 20784, Tel.: (301) 577-5400.
Director: Harold Molz

RIT — Rochester Institute of Technology, School of Printing and Photography, 1 Lomb Memorial Drive, Rochester, NY 14623-0887.
Director: Dr. Mark F. Guldin

TAGA — Technical Association of the Graphic Arts, RIT T&E Center, 1 Lomb Memorial Drive, P.O. Box 9887, Rochester, NY 14623-0887, Tel.: (716) 475-6662.
Director: Michael H. Bruno

UGRA — Verein zur Foerderung Wissenschaftlicher Untersuchungen im Graphischen Gewerbe, c/o Eidy. Materialpruefungs-und Versuchsanstalt (EMPA): Unterstrasse 11, CH-9001 St. Gallen, Switzerland, Tel.: 071 2091 41.
Director: Prof. Dr. P. Fink

Collateral Reading

This section includes suggestions on other sources of information relating to the subjects in this book and lists books, newsletters, magazines and periodicals

Books:

Advances in Printing and Technology, Vols. 1-17
> Proceedings of Biennial *IARIGAI* Conferences
> Editor: Dr. W.H. Banks
> Publisher: Pentech Press, Estover Rd., Plymouth, Devon PL6 7P2 ENGLAND

Color Reproduction Guide
> Author: Professor Miles Southworth
> Publisher: Graphic Arts Publishing Co., Livonia, NY 14487, 1979

Color Separation Techniques, Second Edition
> Author: Professor Miles Southworth
> Publisher: Graphic Arts Publishing, Livonia, NY 14487, 1979

Flexography: Principles and Practices, Third Edition
> Publisher: FTA, Huntington Station, NY 1983

GATF Publications
> Lithographers Manual
> What The Printer Should Know about Paper
> Handbook for Graphic Communications
> Research Progress Bulletins
> Publisher: GATF, 4615 Forbes Ave., Pittsburgh, PA 15213

Graphic Arts Manual
> Editor: Janet N. Field
> Publisher: Musarts Publishing Corp., New York, 1980

Gravure Technical Guide, Third Edition
> Editor: Oscar Smiel
> Publisher: GTA, New York, Third Edition, 1975

Lasers in Graphics Proceedings, Six Annual Editions to 1984
> Editor: Dr. S. Thomas Dunn
> Publisher: Dunn Technology, 759 E. Vista Way, Vista, CA 92036-4197

Neblette's Handbook of Photography and Reprography
> Editor: John M. Sturge
> Publisher: Van Nostrand Reinhold Co., New York, 1977

Pocket Pal
> Editor: Michael H. Bruno
> Publisher: International Paper Co., New York, 13th Edition, 1983

Principles of Color Reproduction
> Author: J.A.C. Yule
> Publisher: John Wiley & Sons, Inc., New York, 1967

TAGA Proceedings, 1949-1984
> Proceedings of Annual TAGA Conferences
> Publisher: TAGA, Rochester, NY

The Printing Industry
> Author: Victor Strauss
> Publisher: Printing Industries of America, Arlington, VA, 1967

Status of Printing in the U.S.A. — 1969 - 1971 - 1973 - 1975 - 1977 - 1979 - 1981 - 1983 - 1984
> Editor/Publisher: Michael H. Bruno, 40 Northwood Dr., Nashua, NH 03063

Newsletters:

CTI — Communications Technology Impact
 Editor: Tony Powell
 Publisher: Elsevier International Bulletin, 52 Vanderbilt Ave.,
 New York, NY 10017

Digest of Information on Phototypesetting
 Editor: Michael L. Kleper
 Publisher: Graphic Dimensions, 8 Frederick Rd., Pittsford, NY
 14534

Dunn Report
 Editor: Dr. S. Thomas Dunn
 Publisher: Dunn Technology, 759 Vista Way, Vista, CA 92038-
 4197

ERA Newsletter
 Editor: A Bjurstedt
 Publisher: European Rotogravure Association, Streitfeldstrasse
 19, D-8000 Muenchen 80, W. Germany

Graphic Communications World
 Editor/Publisher: A.E. Gardner, Technical Information Inc,. Box
 9500, Tallahassee, FL 32315

GRI Newsletter
 Publisher: Gravure Research Institute, 22 Manhasset Ave., Port
 Washington, NY 11050

IFRA Newspaper Techniques
 Editor: George B. Smith
 Publisher: IFRA, Washington Platz 1, D-6100. Darmstadt, W.
 Germany

NAPL Special Reports
>Editor: James F. Burns
>Publisher: NAPL, Research and Educational Foundation, 780 Palisades Ave., Teaneck, NY 07666

Quality Control Scanner
>Editors: Professor Miles F. and Donna F. Southworth
>Publisher: Graphic Arts Publishing Co., 3100 Brown Hill Rd., Livonia, NY 14487

T&E Center Newsletter
>Editor: Ms. Pat Cost
>Publisher: RIT, 1 Lomb Memorial Drive, Rochester, NY 14623

Technology Watch
>Editors: Henry B. and Jean B. Freedman
>Publisher: Technology Watch Publications, P.O. Box 2206, Springfield, VA 22152

The Seybold Report
>Editor: Jonathan W. Seybold
>Publisher: John W. Seybold, P.O. Box 644, Media, PA 19063

What's New(s) in Graphic Communications
>Editor/Publisher: Michael H. Bruno, 40 Northwood Dr., Nashua, NH 03063

Magazines and Periodicals:

American Ink Maker
>Editor: John C. Vollmuth
>Publisher: MacNair-Dorland Company, 101 West 31st St., New York, NY 10001

American Paper Industry
> Editor: Peter W. Wuerl
> Publisher: Paper Industry Mgmt. Assn., 2400 East Oakton, Arlington Heights, IL 60005

American Printer & Lithographer
> Editor: Elizabeth Berglund
> Publisher: Maclean-Hunter Publishing Corp., 300 Adams St., Chicago, IL 60606

Book Production Industry
> Publisher/Editor: Bill Eisler, Innes Publishing Company, 425 Huehl Rd., Bldg. 11-B, Northbrook, IL 60062

Canadian Packaging
> Editor: Peter Cale
> Publisher: Maclean-Hunter Limited, 481 University Avenue, Toronto M5W 1A7, Ontario, Canada

Canadian Printer & Publisher
> Editor: Jack Homer
> Publisher: Maclean-Hunter Limited, 481 University Avenue, Toronto M5W 1A7, Ontario, Canada

Canadian Pulp & Paper Industry
> Editor: Larry Skory
> Publisher: Maclean-Hunter L imited, 481 University Avenue, Toronto M5W 1A7, Ontario, Canada

Chemical Abstracts Service
> Editor/Publisher: Julie A. Ackerman
> Publisher: American Chemical Society, P.O. Box 3012, Columbus, OH 43210

Communication News
>Managing Editor: Kenneth M. Bourne
>Publisher: Harcourt Brace Jovanovich Inc., 124 South First St.,
>Geneva, IL 60134

Dealer Communicator
>Publisher: O.M. Fichera, 2922 Northstate Rd., Margate, FL
>33063

Editor & Publisher
>Editor: Robert U. Brown
>Publisher: Editor & Publisher, 575 Lexington Ave., New York,
>NY 10022

El Arte Tipografico
>Editor: Walter Kubelius
>Publisher: North American Publishing Co., 401 North Broad St.,
>Philadelphia, PA 19108

Electronic Imaging
>Publisher/Editor: Dr. Leonard E. Ravich
>Publisher: Morgan-Grampian Publishing Co., 1050 Common-
>wealth Ave., Boston, MA 02215

Flexographic Technical Journal
>Editor: Joel J. Shulman
>Publisher: FTA, 95 West 19th St., Huntington Station, NY
>11746

Graphic Arts Monthly
>Editor Roger Ynostroza
>Publisher: M.R. Vinocur, Technical Publishing, 875 Third Ave.,
>New York NY 10022

Graphic News
>Editor: Pete May
>1314 North Commerce, Fort Worth TX 76106

Graphics

> Editor: Don Dunham
> P.O. Box 2028, Kissimee, FL 32741

Gravure Bulletin

> Editor: Sarita E. Gansler
> Publisher: Gravure Technical Association, 60 E. 42nd St. New York, NY 10165

GRI Newsletter

> Editor/Publisher: Harvey F. George, 22 Manhassett Avenue, Port Washington, NY 11050

HVP (High Volume Printing)

> Publisher: Virgil J. Busto
> P.O. Box 368, Northbrook, IL 60062

Impact: Information Technology

> Editor: Sam Dickey
> Publisher: Administrative Management Society, Maryland Road, Willow Grove PA 19090

Infosystems

> Editor: Arnold E. Keller
> Publisher: Hitchcock Publishing Company, Hitchcock Building, Wheaton, IL 60187

In-Plant Printer

> Editor: Robert Licker
> Publisher: Innes Publishing Company, 425 Huehl Rd., Bldg. 11-B, Northbrook IL 60062

Litho Tips

> Editor: P. Timothy Hartsfield
> Publisher: Coast Publishing, Inc., 3255 South U.S. 1, Fort Pierce, FL 33450

NAPL Management Bulletin
> Editor: James F. Burns
> Publisher: National Association of Printers and Lithographers, 780 Palisades Avenue, Teaneck, NJ 07666

New England Printer & Publisher
> Publisher/Editor: Norman G. Hansen
> P.O. Box 810, Newburyport, MA 01950

Pacific Printers Pilot
> Editor: Wynn Kessler
> 583 Monterey Pass Road, Monterey Park, CA 91754

Package Printing
> Editor: Hennie Marine
> Publisher: North American Publishing Co., 401 North Broad Street, Philadelphia, PA 19108

Paper Trade Journal
> Editor/Publisher: Jeremiah E. Flynn
> Publisher: Vance Publishing Corp., 133 East 58th St., New York, NY 10022

Photo Methods
> Editor: Fred Schmidt
> Publisher: Ziff-Davis Publishing Company, One Park Avenue, New York, NY 10016

Photoplatemakers Bulletin
> Editor: R.A. Harris
> Publisher: International Pre-Press Association 552 West 167th St., South Holland, IL 60473

PIA Communicator
> Editor: T. Randolph Shingler
> Publisher: Printing Industries of America, 1730 North Lynn St., Arlington, VA 22209

Presstime

    Editor: James E. Donahue

    Publisher: American Newspaper Publishers Association, News-
paper Center, Dulles Box 17407, Reston VA 20041

Print-Equip News

    Editor: Paul B. Kissel

    Publisher: P-EN Publications Inc., P.O. Box 10820, Glendale,
CA 91209

Printing Impressions

    Editor: Paul Gallanda

    Publisher: North American Publishing Co., 401 No. Broad St.,
Philadelphia, PA 19108

Printing News

    Publisher/Editor: Florence Joachim, 468 Park Ave. S., New York, NY
10016

Printing Views

    Editor: Len Berman

    Publisher: Midwest Publishing Company, 8328 North Lincoln
Ave., Skokie, IL 60077

Publishers Weekly

    Editor-In-Chief: Nat Brandt

    Publisher: R.R. Bowker Co., 1180 Ave. of Americas, New York,
NY 10036

Pulp & Paper

    Editor: Kenneth E. Lowe

    Publisher: Miller Freeman Publications, 500 Howard St., San
Francisco, CA 94105

Pulp & Paper Canada

    Editor: W. Schabas

    Publisher: Southam Communications Ltd., 310 Victoria Ave.,
Montreal, H3Z 2M9, Quebec, Canada

Register
>   Editor: F.J. Pieteski
>   Publisher: DuPont Photo Products, Chestnut Run, Wilmington, DE 19898

Review of the Graphic Arts
>   Editor: Aldus M. Cody
>   Publisher: International Association of Printing Craftsmen, 7599 Kenwood Road, Cincinnati, OH 45236

Screen Printing Magazine
>   Editor: Jonathan E. Schiff
>   Publisher: ST Publications, Inc., 407 Gilbert Ave., Cincinnati, OH 45202

The Seybold Report
>   Publisher/Editor: John Seybold, P.O. Box 644, Media, PA 19063

Southern Printer
>   Editor: Roy D. Conradi
>   Publisher: Ernest H. Abermethy Pub. Co., 75 Third St., NW, Atlanta, GA 30308

TAPPI — Technical Association of the Pulp and Paper Industry
>   Editorial Director: M. Kouris
>   One Dunwoody Park, Atlanta, GA 30338

Typeworld
>   Editor/Publisher: Sam Blum
>   Publisher: Blum Publications, 15 Oakridge Circle, Wilmington, MA 01887

The Typographer
>   Editor: Charles W. Mulliken
>   Publisher: International Typographic Composition Association, 2262 Hall Place, NW, Washington, DC 20007

INDEX

imposed by a U.S. patent owned by Milton Ruderman. This patent has expired so the process is free of restrictions.

Senefelder, A. — Credited with the invention of lithography in Germany about 1800 AD.

Shipley, Edd — Retired director of industry relations at Kingsport Press, now head of Southeastern Graphics Group, Kingsport, Tenn., which provides book design and production management and supervisory services and functions for publishers. He prepared the comprehensive layouts for the front matter, chapter openings, text pages and back matter and the cover design, and handled the production details of this book at Kingsport Press.

F. Sigg/RIT Study — Study of dot gain in 1970 to determine which dot area and dot shape was most sensitive to dot gain. Results showed that dot gain was a function of the perimeter of the dots. Square dots gained more than round dots.

Sigmagraph 2000 — Electronic color page makeup system made by Dainippon Screen Co., Japan and marketed in the U.S.A. by D.S. America Inc.

SPECTRA — Off-press color proofing process of the adhesive polymer-dry powder type made by Keuffel and Esser Co. and marketed by Heidelberg Eastern.

SPECTRUM — A series of annual conferences started in 1979 and sponsored by GCA in which the results of cooperative studies of magazine printing based on the SWOP specifications are reported. See pages 238-240 and 251-252.

SWOP — Specifications for Web Offset Publications — See pages 249-252.

Subtractive primaries — Yellow, Magenta and Cyan which when added together as pigments produce black. Each is the mixture of the two colors remaining when one primary color is subtracted from white light. **Yellow** is the combination of red and green when blue is subtracted from white light. **Magenta** is the combination of red and blue remaining when green is subtracted from white light. **Cyan** is the combination of green and blue remaining when red is subtracted from white light.

TAGA — See Research Institutes and Associations.

3M — Manufacturer of COLOR KEY, TRANSFER KEY and MATCHPRINT color proofing systems.

Tobias SCR — Off-line system for color measurement and control using a high speed densitometer to make as many as 54 readings across a 40 inch (1016 mm) wide sheet in 8 seconds. Other color functions are also displayed on a video display. The system is made and marketed by Tobias Associates. See page 235.

TOPPAN Color Proofing System CP525 — Digital System for making "soft" proofs from color separation films. It is made by TOPPAN in Japan and marketed in the U.S.A. by Phillips and Jacobs Co.

Transfer Key — First off-press color proofing process of the direct transfer type introduced in 1968, made and marketed by 3M.

Trapping — **Good Trapping** is achieved when the same amount of ink appears to transfer to a previously printed ink image as to the unprinted paper. When less ink appears to transfer it is **undertrapping**; when it appears as though more ink has transferred it is called **overtrapping**.

Trapping Equation-Brunner — Equation to calculate trapping conditions in printing.

Trapping Equation-Childers — Same definition as Trapping Equation-Brunner.

Trapping Equations-Preucil — Equations developed by Frank Preucil (GATF) to determine conditions for correct trapping, over- and under-trapping.

True Rolling — The concept of adjusting the packing of the plate, blanket and impression cylinders on an offset press to compensate for the distortion of the rubber blanket in printing is known as "True Rolling" and was invented in 1933 by Miehle Printing Press Co. (now Rockwell International, Miehle Div.). The principles are described in a paper presented at the 1953 TAGA Conference entitled "True Rolling and Cylinder Packing" by A.T. Kuehn and B.T. Sites and published in the 1953 TAGA Proceedings, pp. 72-77.

Van Dyke paper — Same as Brownprint paper.

Videojet — Ink-jet printer using a single jet to do variable printing, like addresses, computer letters, package coding, etc. It is made and marketed by A.B. Dick Co.

Watercote — The first commercial off-press color proofing process. It is a superposed sensitized ink color proofing process made and marketed by Direct Reproduction Corp.

Waterless Lithography — A process using planographic plates in which the image and non-image areas are essentially on the same plane. The image areas consist of ink and the non-image areas consist of silicone rubber. No water or dampening solution is needed in printing. 3M called their process **Driography** introduced in 1970 and withdrawn in 1977. TORAY (Japan) has introduced both positive and negative plates for waterless lithography which are running in limited markets in Japan, Europe and the U.S.A. See pages 97-98.

Wiley — John Wiley and Sons, publisher of "Principles of Color Proofing" by J.A.C. Yule.

Xerox 8700 & 9700 — High speed electrostatic copiers, sometimes called **intelligent copiers** used in electronic printing systems. A more sophisti-